KAREN HORNEY, M.D.

NEUROSIS

AND

HUMAN GROWTH

The Struggle Toward
Self-Realization

W · W · NORTON & COMPANY

New York · London

TO

my colleagues and the students of the
American Institute for Psychoanalysis

First published in the Norton Library 1970

ISBN 0-393-00135-0

W. W. Norton & Company, Inc. is also the publisher of the
works of Erik H. Erikson, Otto Fenichel, Karen Horney, Harry Stack
Sullivan, and The Standard Edition of the Complete Psychological
Works of Sigmund Freud.

W. W. Norton & Company, Inc., 500 Fifth Avenue,
New York, N.Y. 10110
W. W. Norton & Company Ltd., 37 Great Russell Street,
London WC1B 3NU

PRINTED IN THE UNITED STATES OF AMERICA
1 2 3 4 5 6 7 8 9 0

CONTENTS

INTRODUCTION: A MORALITY OF EVOLUTION   13

1. THE SEARCH FOR GLORY   17

2. NEUROTIC CLAIMS   40

3. THE TYRANNY OF THE SHOULD   64

4. NEUROTIC PRIDE   86

5. SELF-HATE AND SELF-CONTEMPT   110

6. ALIENATION FROM SELF   155

7. GENERAL MEASURES TO RELIEVE TENSION   176

8. THE EXPANSIVE SOLUTIONS: The Appeal of Mastery   187

9. THE SELF-EFFACING SOLUTION: The Appeal of Love   214

10. MORBID DEPENDENCY   239

11. RESIGNATION: The Appeal of Freedom   259

12. NEUROTIC DISTURBANCES IN HUMAN RELATION-
SHIPS   291

13. NEUROTIC DISTURBANCES IN WORK   309

14. THE ROAD OF PSYCHOANALYTIC THERAPY   333

15. THEORETICAL CONSIDERATIONS   366

REFERENCE READINGS   379

ACKNOWLEDGMENT

I feel sincere gratitude to Hiram Haydn for his thoughtful help in organizing the material of this book, his constructive criticism with regard to the clarification of certain
issues in it, and all his other active and time-consuming
efforts.

The writers to whom I feel indebted are referred to in the
text; but I also want to express my appreciation for some
stimulating discussions on the subject matter with Dr.
Harold Kelman and for helpful comments made by my
colleagues, Dr. Isidore Portnoy and Dr. Frederick A. Weiss;
and I should like to thank my secretary, Mrs. Gertrud
Lederer, for her intelligent interest and untiring efforts
regarding the manuscript and the Index.

K. H.

A MORALITY OF EVOLUTION

T HE NEUROTIC process is a special form of human development, and—because of the waste of constructive energies which it involves—is a particularly unfortunate one. It is not only different in quality from healthy human growth but, to a greater extent than we have realized, antithetical to it in many ways. Under favorable conditions man's energies are put into the realization of his own potentialities. Such a development is far from uniform. According to his particular temperament, faculties, propensities, and the conditions of his earlier and later life, he may become softer or harder, more cautious or more trusting, more or less self-reliant, more contemplative or more outgoing; and he may develop his special gifts. But wherever his course takes him, it will be *his* given potentialities which he develops.

Under inner stress, however, a person may become alienated from his real self. He will then shift the major part of his energies to the task of molding himself, by a rigid system of inner dictates, into a being of absolute perfection. For nothing short of godlike perfection can fulfill his idealized image of himself and satisfy his pride in the exalted attributes which (so he feels) he has, could have, or should have.

This trend in neurotic development (which is presented in detail in this book) engages our attention over and beyond the clinical or theoretical interest in pathological phenomena. For it involves a fundamental problem of morality—that of man's desire, drive, or religious obligation to attain perfection. No serious student concerned with man's development will doubt the undesirability of pride or arrogance, or that of the drive for perfection when pride is the motivating force. But there is a wide divergence of opinion about the desirability or necessity of a disciplinary inner control system for the sake of insuring moral conduct. Granted that these inner dictates have a cramping effect upon man's spontaneity, should we not, in accordance with the Christian injunction ("Be ye perfect . . ."), strive for perfection? Would it not be hazardous, indeed ruinous, to man's moral and social life to dispense with such dictates?

This is not the place to discuss the many ways in which this question has been raised and answered throughout human history, nor am I equipped to do so. I merely want to point out that one of the essential factors upon which the answer hinges is the quality of our belief about human nature.

Broadly speaking, there are three major concepts of the goal of morality which rest upon these different interpretations of essential human nature. Superimposed checks and controls cannot be relinquished by anyone who believes—in whatever terms—that man is by nature sinful or ridden by primitive instincts (Freud). The goal of morality must then be the taming or overcoming of the *status naturae* and not its development. The goal must be different for those who believe that there is inherent in human nature both something essentially "good" and something "bad," sinful, or destructive. It will center upon the insurance of the eventual victory of the inherent good, as refined, directed, or reinforced by such elements as faith, reason, will, or grace—in accordance with the particular dominating religious or ethical concept. Here the emphasis is not exclusively upon combating and suppressing evil, since there is also a positive program. Yet the positive program rests either upon supernatural aids of some sort or upon a strenuous ideal of reason or will, which in itself suggests the use of prohibitive and checking inner dictates.

Lastly, the problem of morality is again different when we believe that inherent in man are evolutionary constructive forces, which urge him to realize his given potentialities. This belief does not mean that man is essentially good—which would presuppose a given knowledge of what is good or bad. It means that man, by his very nature and of his own accord, strives toward self-realization, and that his set of values evolves from such striving. Apparently he cannot, for example, develop his full human potentialities unless he is truthful to himself; unless he is active and productive; unless he relates himself to others in the spirit of mutuality. Apparently he cannot grow if he indulges in a "dark idolatry of self" (Shelley) and consistently attributes all his own shortcomings to the deficiencies of others. He can grow, in the true sense, only if he assumes responsibility for himself.

We arrive thus at a *morality of evolution*, in which the criterion for what we cultivate or reject in ourselves lies in the question: is a particular attitude or drive inducive or obstructive to my human growth? As the frequency of neuroses shows, all kinds of pressure can easily divert our constructive energies into unconstructive or destructive channels. But, with such a belief in an autonomous striving toward self-realization, we do not need an inner strait jacket with which to shackle our spontaneity, nor the whip of inner dictates to drive us to perfection. There is no doubt that such disciplinary methods can succeed in suppressing undesirable factors, but there is also no doubt that they are injurious to our growth. We do not need them because we see a better possibility of dealing with destructive forces in ourselves: that of actually *outgrowing* them. The way toward this goal is an ever increasing awareness and understanding of ourselves. Self-knowledge, then, is not an aim in itself, but a means of liberating the forces of spontaneous growth.

In this sense, to work at ourselves becomes not only the prime moral obligation, but at the same time, in a very real sense, the prime moral *privilege*. To the extent that we take our growth seriously, it will be because of our own desire to do so. And as we lose the neurotic obsession with self, as we become free to grow ourselves, we also free ourselves to love and to feel concern for other people. We will then want to give them the opportunity for unhampered growth when they are young, and to help them in whatever way possible to find and realize themselves when they are blocked in their development. At any rate, whether for ourselves or for others, the ideal is the liberation and cultivation of the forces which lead to self-realization.

I hope that this book, by a clearer exposition of the obstructing factors, may, in its own way, help toward such liberation.

K. H.

CHAPTER 1

THE SEARCH FOR GLORY

WHATEVER the conditions under which a child grows up, he will, if not mentally defective, learn to cope with others in one way or another and he will probably acquire some skills. But there are also forces in him which he cannot acquire or even develop by learning. You need not, and in fact cannot, teach an acorn to grow into an oak tree, but when given a chance, its intrinsic potentialities will develop. Similarly, the human individual, given a chance, tends to develop his particular human potentialities. He will develop then the unique alive forces of his real self: the clarity and depth of his own feelings, thoughts, wishes, interests; the ability to tap his own resources, the strength of his will power; the special capacities or gifts he may have; the faculty to express himself, and to relate himself to others with his spontaneous feelings. All this will in time enable him to find his set of values and his aims in life. In short, he will grow, substantially undiverted, *toward self-realization.* And that is why I speak now and throughout this book of the *real self* as that central inner force, common to all human beings and yet unique in each, which is the deep source of growth.[1]

---

[1] When in the future a reference is made to growth, it is always meant in the sense presented here—that of free, healthy development in accordance with the potentials of one's generic and individual nature.

Only the individual himself can develop his given potentialities. But, like any other living organism, the human individuum needs favorable conditions for his growth "from acorn into oak tree"; he needs an atmosphere of warmth to give him both a feeling of inner security and the inner freedom enabling him to have his own feelings and thoughts and to express himself. He needs the good will of others, not only to help him in his many needs but to guide and encourage him to become a mature and fulfilled individual. He also needs healthy friction with the wishes and wills of others. If he can thus grow *with* others, in love and in friction, he will also grow in accordance with his real self.

But through a variety of adverse influences, a child may not be permitted to grow according to his individual needs and possibilities. Such unfavorable conditions are too manifold to list here. But, when summarized, they all boil down to the fact that the people in the environment are too wrapped up in their own neuroses to be able to love the child, or even to conceive of him as the particular individual he is; their attitudes toward him are determined by their own neurotic needs and responses.[2] In simple words, they may be dominating, overprotective, intimidating, irritable, overexacting, overindulgent, erratic, partial to other siblings, hypocritical, indifferent, etc. It is never a matter of just a single factor, but always the whole constellation that exerts the untoward influence on a child's growth.

As a result, the child does not develop a feeling of belonging, of "we," but instead a profound insecurity and vague apprehensiveness, for which I use the term *basic anxiety*. It is his feeling of being isolated and helpless in a world conceived as potentially hostile. The cramping pressure of his basic anxiety prevents the child from relating himself to others with the spontaneity of his real feelings, and forces him to find ways to cope with them. He must (unconsciously) deal with them in ways which do not arouse, or increase, but rather allay his basic anxiety. The particular attitudes resulting from such uncon-

---

[2] All the neurotic disturbances in human relations which are summarized in Chapter 12 of this book may operate.

Cf. also Karen Horney, *Our Inner Conflicts*, Chapter 2, The Basic Conflict and Chapter 6, The Idealized Image.

scious strategical necessities are determined both by the child's given temperament and by the contingencies of the environment. Briefly, he may try to cling to the most powerful person around him; he may try to rebel and fight; he may try to shut others out of his inner life and withdraw emotionally from them. In principle, this means that he can move toward, against, or away from others.

In a healthy human relationship the moves toward, against, or away from others are not mutually exclusive. The ability to want and to give affection, or to give in; the ability to fight, and the ability to keep to oneself—these are complementary capacities necessary for good human relations. But in the child who feels himself on precarious ground because of his basic anxiety, these moves become extreme and rigid. Affection, for instance, becomes clinging; compliance becomes appeasement. Similarly, he is driven to rebel or to keep aloof, without reference to his real feelings and regardless of the inappropriateness of his attitude in a particular situation. The degree of blindness and rigidity in his attitudes is in proportion to the intensity of the basic anxiety lurking within him.

Since under these conditions the child is driven not only in one of these directions, but in all of them, he develops fundamentally contradictory attitudes toward others. The three moves toward, against, and away from others therefore constitute a conflict, his basic conflict with others. In time, he tries to solve it by making one of these moves consistently predominant—tries to make his prevailing attitude one of compliance, or agressiveness, or aloofness.

This first attempt at solving neurotic conflicts is by no means superficial. On the contrary, it has a determining influence upon the further course his neurotic development takes. Nor does it exclusively concern attitudes toward others; inevitably, it entails certain changes in the whole personality. According to his main direction, the child also develops certain appropriate needs, sensitivities, inhibitions, and the beginnings of moral values. The predominantly complying child, for instance, tends not only to subordinate himself to others and to lean on them, but also tries to be unselfish and good. Similarly, the aggressive child starts to place value on strength and on the capacity to endure and to fight.

However, the integrating effect of this first solution is not as firm or comprehensive as in the neurotic solutions to be discussed later on. In one girl, for instance, compliant trends had become predominant. They showed in a blind adoration of certain authoritative figures, in tendencies to please and appease, in a timidity about expressing her own wishes, and in sporadic attempts to sacrifice. At the age of eight she placed some of her toys in the street for some poorer child to find, without telling anybody about it. At the age of eleven she tried in her childish way for a kind of mystic surrender in prayer. There were fantasies of being punished by teachers on whom she had a crush. But, up to the age of nineteen, she also could easily fall in with plans evolved by others to take revenge on some teacher; while mostly being like a little lamb, she did occasionally take the lead in rebellious activities at school. And, when disappointed in the minister of her church, she switched from a seeming religious devotion to a temporary cynicism.

The reasons for the looseness of integration achieved—of which this illustration is typical—lie partly in the immaturity of the growing individual and partly in the fact that the early solution aims chiefly at a unification of relations with others. There is therefore room, and indeed a need, for firmer integration.

The development described so far is by no means uniform. The particulars of the unfavorable environmental conditions are different in each case, as are those of the course the development takes, and its outcome. But it always impairs the inner strength and coherence of the individual, and thereby always generates certain vital needs for remedying the resulting deficiencies. Although these are closely interwoven, we can distinguish the following aspects:

Despite his early attempts at solving his conflicts with others, the individual is still divided and needs a firmer and more comprehensive *integration*.

For many reasons, he has not had the chance to develop real self-confidence: his inner strength has been sapped by his having to be on the defensive, by his being divided, by the way in which his early "solution" initiated a one-sided development, thereby making large areas of his personality unavailable for constructive uses. Hence, he desperately needs self-confidence, or a substitute for it.

He does not feel weakened in a vacuum, but feels specifically less substantial, less well equipped for life than others. If he had a sense of belonging, his feeling inferior to others would not be so serious a handicap. But living in a competitive society, and feeling at bottom—as he does—isolated and hostile, he can only develop an urgent need *to lift himself above others*.

Even more basic than these factors is his beginning alienation from self. Not only is his real self prevented from a straight growth, but in addition his need to evolve artificial, strategic ways to cope with others has forced him to override his genuine feelings, wishes, and thoughts. To the extent that safety has become paramount, his innermost feelings and thoughts have receded in importance—in fact, have had to be silenced and have become indistinct. (It does not matter what he feels, if only he is safe.) His feelings and wishes thus cease to be determining factors; he is no longer, so to speak, the driver, but is driven. Also the division in himself not only weakens him in general, but reinforces the alienation by adding an element of confusion; he no longer knows where he stands, or "who" he is.

This beginning alienation from self is more basic because it lends to the other impairments their injurious intensity. We can understand this more clearly if we imagine what would happen if it were possible for the other processes to occur without this alienation from the alive center of oneself. In that case the person would have conflicts, but would not be tossed around by them; his self-confidence (as the very word indicates, it requires a self upon which to place confidence) would be impaired, but not uprooted; and his relations to others would be disturbed without his having become inwardly unrelated to them. Hence, most of all, the individual alienated from himself needs—it would be absurd to say a "substitute" for his real self, because there is no such thing—something that will give him a hold, *a feeling of identity*. This could make him meaningful to himself and, despite all the weakness in his structure, give him a feeling of power and significance.

Provided his inner conditions do not change (through fortunate life circumstances), so that he can dispense with the needs I have listed, there is only one way in which he can seem to fulfill them, and seem to fulfill all of them at one stroke: through imagination. Gradually and unconsciously, the imagination sets to work and creates in his mind an *idealized image* of himself. In this process he endows himself with unlimited powers and with exalted faculties; he becomes a hero, a genius, a supreme lover, a saint, a god.

Self-idealization always entails a general self-glorification, and thereby gives the individual the much-needed feeling of significance and of superiority over others. But it is by no means a blind self-aggrandizement. Each person builds up his personal idealized image from the materials of his own special experiences, his earlier fantasies, his particular needs, and also his given faculties. If it were not for the personal character of the image, he would not attain a feeling of identity and unity. He idealizes, to begin with, his particular "solution" of his basic conflict: compliance becomes goodness; love, saintliness; aggressiveness becomes strength, leadership, heroism, omnipotence; aloofness becomes wisdom, self-sufficiency, independence. What—according to his particular solution—appear as shortcomings or flaws are always dimmed out or retouched.

He may deal with his contradictory trends in one of three different ways. They may be glorified, too, but remain in the background. It may, for instance, appear only in the course of analysis that an aggressive person, to whom love seems unpermissible softness, is in his idealized image not only a knight in shining armor but also a great lover.

Secondly, contradictory trends, besides being glorified, may be so isolated in the person's mind that they no longer constitute disturbing conflicts. One patient was, in his image, a benefactor of mankind, a wise man who had achieved a self-contained serenity, and a person who could without qualms kill his enemies. These aspects—all of them conscious—were to him not only uncontradictory but also even unconflicting. In literature this way of removing conflicts by isolating them has been presented by Stevenson in *Doctor Jekyll and Mr. Hyde*.

Lastly, the contradictory trends may be exalted as positive faculties or accomplishments so that they become compatible aspects of a rich personality. I have cited elsewhere [8] an example in which a gifted person turned his compliant trends into Christlike virtues, his aggressive trends into a unique faculty for political leadership, and his detachment into the wisdom of a philosopher. Thus the three aspects of his basic conflict were at once glorified and reconciled each with the others. He became, in his own mind, a sort of modern equivalent to *l'uomo universale* of the Renaissance.

Eventually the individual may come to identify himself with his idealized, integrated image. Then it does not remain a visionary image which he secretly cherishes; imperceptibly he becomes this image: the idealized image becomes an *idealized self*. And this idealized self becomes more real to him than his real self, not primarily because it is more appealing but because it answers all his stringent needs. This transfer of his center of gravity is an entirely inward process; there is no observable or conspicuous outward change in him. The change is in the core of his being, in his feeling about himself. It is a curious and exclusively human process. It would hardly occur to a cocker spaniel that he "really" is an Irish setter. And the transition can occur in a person only because his real self has previously become indistinct. While the healthy course at this phase of development—and at *any* phase—would be a move toward his real self, he now starts to abandon it definitely for the idealized self. The latter begins to represent to him what he "really" is, or potentially is—what he could be, and should be. It becomes the perspective from which he looks at himself, the measuring rod with which he measures himself.

Self-idealization, in its various aspects, is what I suggest calling a *comprehensive neurotic solution*—i.e., a solution not only for a particular conflict but one that implicitly promises to satisfy all the inner needs that have arisen in an individual at a given time. Moreover, it promises not only a riddance from his painful and unbearable feelings (feeling lost, anxious, inferior,

---

[8] *Our Inner Conflicts*

and divided), but in addition an ultimately mysterious fulfillment of himself and his life. No wonder, then, that when he
believes he has found such a solution he clings to it for dear life.
No wonder that, to use a good psychiatric term, it becomes
compulsive.[4] The regular occurrence of self-idealization in neurosis is the result of the regular occurrence of the compulsive
needs bred in a neurosis-prone environment.

We can look at self-idealization from two major vantage
points: it is the logical outcome of an early development and it
is also the beginning of a new one. It is bound to have far-reaching influence upon the further development because there simply is no more consequential step to be taken than the abandoning of the real self. But the main reason for its revolutionary
effect lies in another implication of this step. *The energies
driving toward self-realization are shifted to the aim of actualizing the idealized self.* This shift means no more and no less than
a change in the course of the individual's whole life and development.

We shall see throughout this book the manifold ways in
which this shift in direction exerts a molding influence upon
the whole personality. Its more immediate effect is to prevent
self-idealization from remaining a purely inward process, and to
force it into the total circuit of the individual's life. The individual wants to—or, rather, is driven to—express himself. And
this now means that he wants to express his idealized self, to
prove it in action. It infiltrates his aspirations, his goals, his
conduct of life, and his relations to others. For this reason, self-
idealization inevitably grows into a more comprehensive drive
which I suggest calling by a name appropriate to its nature and
its dimensions: *the search for glory.* Self-idealization remains its
nuclear part. The other elements in it, all of them always
present, though in varying degrees of strength and awareness
in each individual case, are the need for perfection, neurotic
ambition, and the need for a vindictive triumph.

Among the drives toward actualizing the idealized self *the
need for perfection* is the most radical one. It aims at nothing

---

[4] We shall discuss the exact meaning of *compulsiveness* when we have a more
complete view of some further steps involved in this solution.

less than molding the whole personality into the idealized self. Like Pygmalion in Bernard Shaw's version, the neurotic aims not only at retouching but at remodeling himself into his special kind of perfection prescribed by the specific features of his idealized image. He tries to achieve this goal by a complicated system of shoulds and taboos. Since this process is both crucial and complex, we shall leave its discussion for a separate chapter.[5]

The most obvious and the most extrovert among the elements of the search for glory is *neurotic ambition,* the drive toward external success. While this drive toward excelling in actuality is pervasive and tends toward excelling in everything, it is usually most strongly applied to those matters in which excelling is most feasible for the given individual at a given time. Hence the content of ambition may well change several times during a lifetime. At school a person may feel it an intolerable disgrace not to have the very best marks in class. Later on, he may be just as compulsively driven to have the most dates with the most desirable girls. And again, still later, he may be obsessed with making the most money, or being the most prominent in politics. Such changes easily give rise to certain self-deceptions. A person who has at one period been fanatically determined to be the greatest athletic hero, or war hero, may at another period become equally bent on being the greatest saint. He may believe, then, that he has "lost" his ambition. Or he may decide that excelling in athletics or in war was not what he "really" wanted. Thus he may fail to realize that he still sails on the boat of ambition but has merely changed the course. Of course, one must also analyze in detail what made him change his course at that particular time. I emphasize these changes because they point to the fact that people in the clutches of ambition are but little related to the *content* of what they are doing. What counts is the excelling itself. If one did not recognize this unrelatedness, many changes would be incomprehensible.

For the purposes of this discussion, the particular area of activity which the specific ambition covets is of little interest.

---

[5] *Cf.* Chapter 3, The Tyranny of the Should.

The characteristics remain the same whether it is a question of being a leader in the community, of being the most brilliant conversationalist, of having the greatest reputation as a musician or as an explorer, of playing a role in "society," of writing the best book, or of being the best-dressed person. The picture varies, however, in many ways, according to the nature of the desired success. Roughly, it may belong more in the category of power (direct power, power behind the throne, influence, manipulating), or more in the category of prestige (reputation, acclaim, popularity, admiration, special attention).

These ambitious drives are, comparatively speaking, the most realistic of the expansive drives. At least, this is true in the sense that the people involved put in actual efforts to the end of excelling. These drives also seem more realistic because, with sufficient luck, their possessors may actually acquire the coveted glamor, honors, influence. But, on the other hand, when they do attain more money, more distinction, more power, they also come to feel the whole impact of the futility of their chase. They do not secure any more peace of mind, inner security, or joy of living. The inner distress, to remedy which they started out on the chase for the phantom of glory, is still as great as ever. Since these are not accidental results, happening to this or that individual, but are inexorably bound to occur, one may rightly say that the whole pursuit of success is intrinsically unrealistic.

Since we live in a competitive culture, these remarks may sound strange or unworldly. It is so deeply ingrained in all of us that everybody wants to get ahead of the next fellow, and be better than he is, that we feel these tendencies to be "natural." But the fact that compulsive drives for success will arise only in a competitive culture does not make them any less neurotic. Even in a competitive culture there are many people for whom other values—such as, in particular, that of growth as a human being—are more important than competitive excelling over others.

The last element in the search for glory, more destructive than the others, is the drive *toward a vindictive triumph*. It may be closely linked up with the drive for actual achievement and success but, if so, its chief aim is to put others to shame or defeat them through one's very success; or to attain the power, by rising to prominence, to inflict suffering upon them—mostly of a humiliating kind. On the other hand, the drive for excelling may be relegated to fantasy, and the need for a vindictive triumph then manifests itself mainly in often irresistible, mostly unconscious impulses to frustrate, outwit, or defeat others in personal relations. I call this drive "vindictive" because the motivating force stems from impulses to take revenge for humiliations suffered in childhood—impulses which are reinforced during the later neurotic development. These later accretions probably are responsible for the way in which the need for a vindictive triumph eventually becomes a regular ingredient in the search for glory. Both the degree of its strength and the person's awareness of it vary to a remarkable extent. Most people are either entirely unaware of such a need or cognizant of it only in fleeting moments. Yet it is sometimes out in the open, and then it becomes the barely disguised mainspring of life. Among recent historical figures Hitler is a good illustration of a person who went through humiliating experiences and gave his whole life to a fanatic desire to triumph over an ever-increasing mass of people. In his case vicious circles, constantly increasing the need, are clearly discernible. One of these develops from the fact that he could think only in categories of triumph and defeat. Hence the fear of defeat made further triumphs always necessary. Moreover, the feeling of grandeur, increasing with every triumph, rendered it increasingly intolerable that anybody, or even any nation, should not recognize his grandeur.

Many case histories are similar on a smaller scale. To mention only one example from recent literature, there is *The Man Who Watched the Train Go By*.[6] Here we have a conscientious clerk, subdued in his home life and in his office, apparently never thinking of anything but doing his duty. Through the discovery of the fraudulent maneuvers of his boss, with the resultant bankruptcy of the firm, his scale of values crashes. The artificial distinction between superior beings, to whom every-

---

[6] By Georges Simenon, Reynal and Hitchcock, New York.

thing is allowed, and inferior ones like himself, to whom only the narrow path of correct behavior is permitted, crumbles. He too, he realizes, could be "great" and "free." He could have a mistress, even the very glamorous mistress of his boss. And his pride is by now so inflated that when he actually approaches her, and is rejected, he strangles her. Sought by the police, he is at times afraid, but his main incentive is to defeat the police triumphantly. Even in his attempted suicide this is the chief motivating force.

Much more frequently the drive toward a vindictive triumph is hidden. Indeed, because of its destructive nature, it is the most hidden element in the search for glory. It may be that only a rather frantic ambition will be apparent. In analysis alone are we able to see that the driving power behind it is the need to defeat and humiliate others by rising above them. The less harmful need for superiority can, as it were, absorb the more destructive compulsion. This allows a person to act out his need, and yet feel righteous about it.

It is of course important to recognize the specific features of the individual trends involved in the search for glory, because it is always the specific constellation that must be analyzed. But we can understand neither the nature nor the impact of these trends unless we see them as parts of a coherent entity. Alfred Adler was the first psychoanalyst to see it as a comprehensive phenomenon, and to point out its crucial significance in neurosis.[7]

There are various solid proofs that the search for glory is a comprehensive and coherent entity. In the first place, all the individual trends described above regularly occur together in one person. Of course one or another element may so predominate as to make us speak loosely of, say, an ambitious person, or of a dreamer. But that does not mean that the dominance of one element indicates the absence of the others. The ambitious person will have his grandiose image of himself too; the dreamer will want realistic supremacy, even though the

---

[7] See the comparisons with Adler's and with Freud's concepts in Chapter 15 of this book.

latter factor may be apparent only in the way in which his pride is offended by the success of others.[8]

Furthermore, all the individual trends involved are so closely related that the prevailing trend may change during the life-time of a given person. He may turn from glamorous daydreams to being the perfect father and employer, and again to being the greatest lover of all time.

Lastly, they all have in common *two general characteristics*, both understandable from the genesis and the functions of the whole phenomenon: their compulsive nature and their imaginative character. Both have been mentioned, but it is desirable to have a more complete and succinct picture of their meaning.

Their *compulsive nature* stems from the fact that the self-idealization (and the whole search for glory developing as its sequel) is a neurotic solution. When we call a drive compulsive we mean the opposite of spontaneous wishes or strivings. The latter are an expression of the real self; the former are determined by the inner necessities of the neurotic structure. The individual must abide by them regardless of his real wishes, feelings, or interests lest he incur anxiety, feel torn by conflicts, be overwhelmed by guilt feelings, feel rejected by others, etc. In other words, the difference between spontaneous and compulsive is one between "I want" and "I must in order to avoid some danger." Although the individual may consciously feel his ambition or his standards of perfection to be what he *wants* to attain, he is actually *driven* to attain it. The need for glory has him in its clutches. Since he himself is unaware of the difference between wanting and being driven, we must establish criteria for a distinction between the two. The most decisive one is the fact that he is driven on the road to glory with an utter *disregard for himself, for his best interests.* (I remember, for example, an ambitious girl, aged ten, who thought she would rather be blind than not become the first in her class.) We have reason to wonder whether more human lives—literally and

---

[8] Because personalities often look different in accordance with the trend which is prevailing, the temptation to regard these trends as separate entities is great. Freud regarded phenomena which are roughly similar to these as separate in-stinctual drives with separate origins and properties. When I made a first at-tempt to enumerate compulsive drives in neurosis they appeared to me too as separate "neurotic trends."

figuratively—are not sacrificed on the altar of glory than for any other reason. John Gabriel Borkman died when he started to doubt the validity and the possibility of realizing his grandiose mission. Here a truly tragic element enters into the picture. If we sacrifice ourselves for a cause which we, and most healthy people, can realistically find constructive in terms of its value to human beings, that is certainly tragic, but also meaningful. If we fritter away our lives enslaved to the phantom of glory for reasons unknown to ourselves, that assumes the unrelieved proportion of tragic waste—the more so, the more valuable these lives potentially are.

Another criterion of the compulsive nature of the drive for glory—as of any other compulsive drive—is its *indiscriminateness*. Since the person's real interest in a pursuit does not matter, he *must* be the center of attention, *must* be the most attractive, the most intelligent, the most original—whether or not the situation calls for it; whether or not, with his given attributes, he *can* be the first. He *must* come out victorious in any argument, regardless of where the truth lies. His thoughts in this matter are the exact opposite of those of Socrates: ". . . for surely we are not now simply contending in order that my view or that of yours may prevail, but I presume that we ought both of us to be fighting for the truth." [9] The compulsiveness of the neurotic person's need for indiscriminate supremacy makes him indifferent to truth, whether concerning himself, others, or facts.

Furthermore, like any other compulsive drive, the search for glory has the quality of *insatiability*. It must operate as long as the unknown (to himself) forces are driving him. There may be a glow of elation over the favorable reception of some work done, over a victory won, over any sign of recognition or admiration—but it does not last. A success may hardly be experienced as such in the first place, or, at the least, must make room for despondency or fear soon after. In any case, the relentless chase after more prestige, more money, more women, more victories and conquests keeps going, with hardly any satisfaction or respite.

---

[9] From Philebus, *The Dialogues of Plato*, translated into English by B. Jowett, M.A., Random House, New York.

Finally, the compulsive nature of a drive shows in the *reactions to its frustration*. The greater its subjective importance, the more impelling is the need to attain its goal, and hence the more intense the reactions to frustration. These constitute one of the ways in which we can measure the intensity of a drive. Although this is not always plainly visible, the search for glory is a most powerful drive. It can be like a demoniacal obsession, almost like a monster swallowing up the individual who has created it. And so the reactions to frustration must be severe. They are indicated by the terror of doom and disgrace that for many people is spelled in the idea of failure. Reactions of panic, depression, despair, rage at self and others to what is conceived as "failure" are frequent, and entirely out of proportion to the actual importance of the occasion. The phobia of falling from heights is a frequent expression of the dread of falling from the heights of illusory grandeur. Consider the dream of a patient who had a phobia about heights. It occurred at a time when he had begun to doubt his established belief of unquestioned superiority. In the dream he was at the top of a mountain, but in danger of falling, and was clinging desperately to the ridge of the peak. "I cannot get any higher than I am," he said, "so all I have to do in life is to hold on to it." Consciously, he referred to his social status, but in a deeper sense this "I cannot get any higher" also held true for his illusions about himself. He could not get higher than having (in his mind) a godlike omnipotence and cosmic significance!

The second characteristic inherent in all the elements of the search for glory is the great and peculiar role *imagination* plays in them. It is instrumental in the process of self-idealization. But this is so crucial a factor that the whole search for glory is bound to be pervaded by fantastic elements. No matter how much a person prides himself on being realistic, no matter how realistic indeed his march toward success, triumph, perfection, his imagination accompanies him and makes him mistake a mirage for the real thing. One simply cannot be unrealistic about oneself and remain entirely realistic in other respects. When the wanderer in the desert, under the duress of fatigue and thirst, sees a mirage, he may make actual efforts to reach it, but the mirage—the glory—which should end his distress is itself a product of imagination.

Actually imagination also permeates all psychic and mental functions in the healthy person. When we feel the sorrow or the joy of a friend, it is our imagination that enables us to do so. When we wish, hope, fear, believe, plan, it is our imagination showing us possibilities. But imagination may be productive or unproductive: it can bring us closer to the truth of ourselves—as it often does in dreams—or carry us far away from it. It can make our actual experience richer or poorer. And these differences roughly distinguish neurotic and healthy imagination.

When thinking of the grandiose plans so many neurotics evolve, or the fantastic nature of their self-glorification and their claims, we may be tempted to believe that they are more richly endowed than others with the royal gift of imagination—and that, for that very reason, it can more easily go astray in them. This notion is not borne out by my experience. The endowment varies among neurotic people, as it does among more healthy ones. But I find no evidence that the neurotic per se is by nature more imaginative than others.

Nevertheless the notion is a false conclusion based upon accurate observations. Imagination does in fact play a greater role in neurosis. However, what accounts for this are not constitutional but functional factors. Imagination operates as it does in the healthy person, but in addition it takes over functions which it does not normally have. It is put in the service of neurotic needs. This is particularly clear in the case of the search for glory, which, as we know, is prompted by the impact of powerful needs. In psychiatric literature imaginative distortions of reality are known as "wishful thinking." It is by now a well-established term, but it is nevertheless incorrect. It is too narrow: an accurate term would encompass not only thinking but also "wishful" observing, believing, and particularly feeling. Moreover, it is a thinking—or feeling—that is determined not by our *wishes* but by our *needs*. And it is the impact of these needs that lends imagination the tenacity and power it has in neurosis, that makes it prolific—and unconstructive.

The role imagination plays in the search for glory may show unmistakably and directly in daydreams. In the teen-ager they may have a frankly grandiose character. There is for instance the college boy who, although timid and withdrawn, has daydreams about being the greatest athlete, or genius, or Don Juan. There are also in later years people like Madame Bovary, who almost constantly indulge in dreams of romantic experiences, of a mystic perfection, or of a mysterious saintliness. Sometimes these take the form of imaginary conversations in which others are impressed or put to shame. Others, more complicated in their structure, deal with shameful or noble suffering through being exposed to cruelty and degradation. Frequently daydreams are not elaborate stories but, rather, play a fantastic accompaniment to the daily routine. When tending her children, playing the piano, or combing her hair, a woman may for instance simultaneously see herself in much the way a tender mother, a rapturous pianist, or an alluring beauty would be presented in the movies. In some cases such daydreams show clearly that a person may, like Walter Mitty, constantly live in two worlds. Again, in others equally engaged in the search for glory daydreams are so scarce and abortive that they may say in all subjective honesty that they have no fantasy life. Needless to say, they are mistaken. Even if they only worry about possible mishaps that might befall them, it is after all their imagination that conjures up such contingencies.

But daydreams, while important and revealing when they occur, are not the most injurious work of imagination. For a person is mostly aware of the fact that he is daydreaming, i.e., imagining things which have not occurred or are not likely to occur in the way he is experiencing them in fantasy. At least it is not too difficult for him to become aware of the existence and the unrealistic character of the daydreams. The more injurious work of imagination concerns the subtle and comprehensive distortions of reality which he is not aware of fabricating. The idealized self is not completed in a single act of creation: once produced, it needs continuing attention. For its actualization the person must put in an incessant labor by way of falsifying reality. He must turn his needs into virtues or into more than justified expectations. He must turn his intentions to be honest or considerate into the fact of being honest or considerate. The bright ideas he has for a paper make him a great scholar.

His potentialities turn into factual achievements. Knowing the "right" moral values makes him a virtuous person—often, indeed, a kind of moral genius. And of course his imagination must work overtime to discard all the disturbing evidence to the contrary.[10]

Imagination also operates in changing the neurotic's beliefs. He needs to believe that others are wonderful or vicious—and lo! there they are in a parade of benevolent or dangerous people. It also changes his feelings. He needs to feel invulnerable—and behold! his imagination has sufficient power to brush off pain and suffering. He needs to have deep feelings—confidence, sympathy, love, suffering: his feelings of sympathy, suffering, and the rest are magnified.

The perception of the distortions of inner and outer reality which imagination can bring about when put to the service of the search for glory leaves us with an uneasy question. Where does the flight of the neurotic's imagination end? He does not after all lose his sense of reality altogether; where then is the border line separating him from the psychotic? If there is any border line with respect to feats of imagination, it certainly is hazy. We can only say that the psychotic tends to regard the processes in his mind more exclusively as the only reality that counts, while the neurotic—for whatever reasons—retains a fair interest in the outside world and his place in it and has therefore a fair gross orientation in it.[11] Nevertheless, while he may stay sufficiently on the ground to function in a way not obviously disturbed, there is no limit to the heights to which his imagination can soar. It is in fact the most striking characteristic of the search for glory that it goes into the fantastic, into the realm of *unlimited possibilities*.

All the drives for glory have in common the reaching out for greater knowledge, wisdom, virtue, or powers than are given to human beings; they all aim at the *absolute*, the unlimited, the infinite. Nothing short of absolute fearlessness, mastery, or saint-

---

[10] Cf. the work of the Ministry of Truth in George Orwell's *Nineteen Eighty-Four*.

[11] The reasons for this difference are complicated. It would be worth examining whether crucial among them is a more radical abandoning of the real self (and a more radical shift to the idealized self) on the part of the psychotic.

liness has any appeal for the neurotic obsessed with the drive for glory. He is therefore the antithesis of the truly religious man. For the latter, only to God are all things possible; the neurotic's version is: nothing is impossible to *me*. His will power should have magic proportions, his reasoning be infallible, his foresight flawless, his knowledge all encompassing. The theme of the devil's pact which will run through this book begins to emerge. The neurotic is the Faust who is not satisfied with knowing a great deal, but has to know everything.

This soaring into the unlimited is determined by the power of the needs behind the drive for glory. The needs for the *absolute* and the *ultimate* are so stringent that they override the checks which usually prevent our imagination from detaching itself from actuality. For his well-functioning, man needs both the vision of possibilities, the perspective of infinitude, *and* the realization of limitations, of necessities, of the concrete. If a man's thinking and feeling are primarily focused upon the infinite and the vision of possibilities, he loses his sense for the concrete, for the here and now. He loses his capacity for living in the moment. He is no longer capable of submitting to the necessities in himself, "to what may be called one's limit." He loses sight of what is actually necessary for achieving something. "Every little possibility even would require some time to become actuality." His thinking may become too abstract. His knowledge may become "a kind of inhuman knowing for the production of which man's self is squandered, pretty much as men were squandered for the building of the Pyramids." His feelings for others may evaporate into an "abstract sentimentality for humanity." If, on the other hand, a man does not see beyond the narrow horizon of the concrete, the necessary, the finite, he becomes "narrow-minded and mean-spirited." It is not, then, a question of either-or, but of *both*, if there is to be growth. The recognition of limitations, laws, and necessities serves as a check against being carried away into the infinite, and against the mere "floundering in possibilities." [12]

The *checks on imagination are malfunctioning* in the search

---

[12] In this philosophical discussion I roughly follow Sören Kierkegaard, *Sickness unto Death*, Princeton University Press, 1941, written in 1844. The quotations in this paragraph are taken from this book.

for glory. This does not mean a general incapacity to see necessities and abide by them. A special direction in the further neurotic development may make many people feel safer to restrict their lives, and they may then tend to regard the possibility of being carried away into the fantastic as a danger to be avoided. They may close their minds to anything that to them looks fantastic, be averse to abstract thinking, and overanxiously cling to what is visible, tangible, concrete, or immediately useful. But while the conscious attitude toward these matters varies, every neurotic at bottom is loath to recognize limitations to what he expects of himself and believes it possible to attain. His need to actualize his idealized image is so imperative that he must shove aside the checks as irrelevant or nonexistent.

The more his irrational imagination has taken over, the more likely he is to be positively horrified at anything that is real, definite, concrete, or final. He tends to abhor time, because it is something definite; money, because it is concrete; death, because of its finality. But he may also abhor having a definite wish or opinion, and hence avoid making a definite commitment or a decision. To illustrate, there was the patient who cherished the idea of being a will-o'-the-wisp dancing in a ray of moonlight: she could become terrified when looking at a mirror—not because of seeing possible imperfections, but because it brought to bear on her the realization that she had definite contours, that she was substantial, that she "was pinned down to a concrete bodily shape." It made her feel like a bird whose wings were nailed to a board. And at a time when these feelings emerged to awareness, she had impulses to smash the mirror.

To be sure, the development is not always so extreme. But every neurotic, even though he may pass superficially for healthy, is averse to checking with evidence when it comes to his particular illusions about himself. And he must be so, because they would collapse if he did. The attitude toward external laws and regulations varies, but he always tends to deny laws operating within himself, refuses to see the inevitability of cause and effect in psychic matters, or of one factor following from the other or reinforcing the other.

There are endless ways in which he disregards evidence which he does not choose to see. He forgets; it does not count; it was accidental; it was on account of circumstances, or because others provoked him; he couldn't help it, because it was "natural." Like a fraudulent bookkeeper, he goes to any length to maintain the double account; but, unlike him, he credits himself only with the favorable one and professes ignorance of the other. I have not yet seen a patient in whom the frank rebellion against reality, as it is expressed in *Harvey* ("Twenty years I have fought with reality, and I have finally overcome it"), did not strike a familiar chord. Or, to quote again the classic expression of a patient: "If it were not for reality, I would be perfectly all right."

It remains to bring into clearer relief the difference between the search for glory and healthy human strivings. On the surface they may look deceptively similar, so much so that differences seem to be variations in degree only. It looks as though the neurotic were merely more ambitious, more concerned with power, prestige, and success than the healthy person; as though his moral standards were merely higher, or more rigid, than ordinary ones; as though he were simply more conceited, or considered himself more important than people usually do. And, indeed, who will venture to draw a sharp line and say: "This is where the healthy ends, and the neurotic begins"?

Similarities between healthy strivings and the neurotic drives exist because they have a common root in specific human potentialities. Through his mental capacities man has the faculty to reach beyond himself. In contrast to other animals, he can imagine and plan. In many ways he can gradually enlarge his faculties and, as history shows, has actually done so. The same is also true for the life of a single individual. There are no rigidly fixed limits to what he can make out of his life, to what qualities or faculties he can develop, to what he can create. Considering these facts, it seems inevitable that man is uncertain about his limitations and, hence, easily sets his goals either too low or too high. This existing uncertainty is the base without which the search for glory could not possibly develop.

The basic difference between healthy strivings and neurotic drives for glory lies in the forces prompting them. Healthy strivings stem from a propensity, inherent in human beings, to develop given potentialities. The belief in an inherent urge to grow has always been the basic tenet upon which our theoretical and therapeutic approach rests.[18] And this belief has grown ever since with ever-new experiences. The only change is in the direction of more precise formulation. I would say now (as indicated in the first pages of this book) that the live forces of the real self urge one toward self-realization.

The search for glory, on the other hand, springs from the need to actualize the idealized self. The difference is basic because all other dissimilarities follow from this one. Because self-idealization in itself is a neurotic solution, and as such compulsive in character, all the drives resulting from it are by necessity compulsive too. Because the neurotic, as long as he must adhere to his illusions about himself, cannot recognize limitations, the search for glory goes into the unlimited. Because the main goal is the attainment of glory, he becomes uninterested in the process of learning, of doing, or of gaining step by step—indeed, tends to scorn it. He does not want to climb a mountain; he wants to be on the peak. Hence he loses the sense of what evolution or growth means, even though he may talk about it. Because, finally, the creation of the idealized self is possible only at the expense of truth about himself, its actualization requires further distortions of truth, imagination being a willing servant to this end. Thereby, to a greater or lesser extent, he loses in the process his interest in truth, and the sense for what is true or not true—a loss that, among others, accounts for his difficulty in distinguishing between genuine feelings, beliefs, strivings, and their artificial equivalents (unconscious pretenses) in himself and in others. The emphasis shifts from being to appearing.

The difference, then, between healthy strivings and neurotic drives for glory is one between spontaneity and compulsion; between recognizing and denying limitations; between a focus upon the vision of a glorious end-product and a feeling for evo-

---

[18] By "our" I refer to the approach of the whole Association for the Advancement of Psychoanalysis.

In the introduction to *Our Inner Conflicts* I said: "My own belief is that man has the capacity as well as the desire to develop his potentialities. . . ." *Cf.* also Dr. Kurt Goldstein, *Human Nature*, Harvard University Press, 1940. Goldstein, however, does not make the distinction—which is crucial for human beings—between self-realization and the actualization of the idealized self.

lution; between seeming and being, fantasy and truth. The difference thus stated is not identical with that between a relatively healthy and a neurotic individual. The former may not be wholeheartedly engaged in realizing his real self nor is the latter wholly driven to actualize his idealized self. The tendency toward self-realization operates in the neurotic too; we could not in therapy give any help to the patient's growth if this striving were not in him to begin with. But, while the difference between the healthy and the neurotic person in this respect is simply one of degree, the difference between genuine striving and compulsive drives, despite surface similarities, is one of quality and not of quantity.[14]

The most pertinent symbol, to my mind, for the neurotic process initiated by the search for glory is the ideational content of the stories of the devil's pact. The devil, or some other personification of evil, tempts a person who is perplexed by spiritual or material trouble with the offer of unlimited powers. But he can obtain these powers only on the condition of selling his soul or going to hell. The temptation can come to anybody, rich or poor in spirit, because it speaks to two powerful desires: the longing for the infinite and the wish for an easy way out. According to religious tradition, the greatest spiritual leaders of mankind, Buddha and Christ, experienced such temptation. But, because they were firmly grounded in themselves, they recognized it as a temptation and could reject it. Moreover, the conditions stipulated in the pact are an appropriate representation of the price to be paid in the neurotic's development. Speaking in these symbolic terms, the easy way to infinite glory is inevitably also the way to an inner hell of self-contempt and self-torment. By taking this road, the individual is in fact losing his soul—his real self.

---

[14] When in this book I speak of "the neurotic" I mean a person in whom neurotic drives prevail over healthy strivings.

CHAPTER 2

NEUROTIC CLAIMS

THE NEUROTIC in his search for glory goes astray into the realm of the fantastic, of the infinite, of boundless possibilities. To all outward appearances, he may lead a "normal" life as a member of his family and of his community, attend to his work and participate in recreational activities. Without realizing it, or at least without realizing the extent of it, he lives in two worlds—that of his secret private life and that of his official life. And the two do not jibe; to repeat a patient's phrase quoted in a previous chapter: "Life is awful; it is so full of reality!"

No matter how averse the neurotic is to checking with evidence, reality inevitably obtrudes itself in two ways. He may be highly gifted, but he still is in all essentials like everybody else—with general human limitations and considerable individual difficulties to boot. His actual being does not jibe with his godlike image. Nor does the reality outside himself treat him as though it found him godlike. For him, too, an hour has but sixty minutes; he must wait in line, like everybody else; the taxidriver or the boss may act as though he were simply an ordinary mortal.

The indignities to which this individual feels exposed are nicely symbolized in a little incident a patient remembered from childhood. She was three years old, and daydreaming of being a

40

fairy queen when an uncle picked her up and said jokingly, "My, what a dirty face you have!" She never forgot her impotent and indignant rage. In this way, such a person is almost constantly faced with discrepancies, puzzling and painful. What does he do about it? How does he account for them, react to them, or try to do away with them? As long as his personal aggrandizement is too indispensable to be touched, he can but conclude that there is something wrong with the world. It ought to be different. And so, instead of tackling his illusions, he presents a claim to the outside world. He is entitled to be treated by others, or by fate, in accord with his grandiose notions about himself. Everyone ought to cater to his illusions. Everything short of this is unfair. He is entitled to a better deal.

The neurotic feels entitled to special attention, consideration, deference on the part of others. These claims for deference are understandable enough, and sometimes obvious enough. But they are merely part and parcel of a more comprehensive claim —that all his needs growing out of his inhibitions, his fears, his conflicts, and his solutions ought to be satisfied or duly respected. Moreover, whatever he feels, thinks, or does ought not to carry any adverse consequences. This means in fact a claim that psychic laws ought not to apply to him. Therefore he does not need to recognize—or at any rate to change—his difficulties. It is then no longer up to him to do something about his problems; it is up to others to see that they do not disturb him.

It was a German psychoanalyst, Harald Schultz-Hencke,[1] who was the first among modern analysts to see these claims which the neurotic harbors. He called them *Riessenansprueche* (gigantic claims), and ascribed to them a crucial role in neuroses. While I share his opinion of their importance, my own concept differs from his in many ways. I do not think that the term "gigantic claims" is fortunate. It is misleading because it suggests that the claims are excessive in content. True enough, in many instances they are not only excessive but plainly fantastic; others, however, appear quite reasonable. And to focus on the exorbitant content of claims makes it more difficult to discern in oneself and others those which appear to be rational.

---

[1] Harald Schultz-Hencke, *Einfuehrung zur Psychoanalyse.*

Take, for example, a businessman who is exasperated because a train does not leave at a time convenient for him. A friend, knowing that nothing important is at stake, might indicate to him that he really is too demanding. Our businessman would respond with another fit of indignation. The friend does not know what he is talking about. He is a busy man, and it is reasonable to expect a train to leave at a sensible time.

Surely his wish is reasonable. Who would not want a train to run on a schedule convenient to his arrangements? But—we are not *entitled* to it. This brings us to the essentials of the phenomenon: *a wish or need, in itself quite understandable, turns into a claim.* Its nonfulfillment, then, is felt as an unfair frustration, as an offense about which we have a right to feel indignant.

The difference between a need and a claim is a clear-cut one. Nevertheless, if the psychic undercurrents have changed the one into the other, the neurotic is not only unaware of the difference but is indeed averse to seeing it. He speaks of an understandable or natural wish when he really means a claim; and he feels entitled to many things which a bit of clear thinking could show him are not inevitably his. I am thinking, for instance, of some patients who are furiously indignant when they get a ticket for double parking. Once again, the wish to "get by" is completely understandable, but they are not entitled to exemption. It is not that they do not know the laws. But they argue (if they think about it at all) that others get by, and that it is therefore unfair that they should have been caught.

For these reasons it seems advisable to speak simply of irrational or neurotic claims. They are neurotic needs which individuals have unwittingly turned into claims. And they are irrational because they assume a right, a title, which in reality does not exist. In other words, they are excessive by the very fact of being made as claims instead of being recognized simply as neurotic needs. The special content of the claims that are harbored varies in detail, according to the particular neurotic structure. Generally speaking, however, the patient feels entitled to everything that is important to him—to the fulfillment of all his particular neurotic needs.

When speaking of a demanding person, we usually think of demands made upon other people. And human relationships do indeed constitute one important area in which neurotic claims are raised. But we underrate considerably the range of claims if we thus restrict them. They are directed just as much toward man-made institutions, and even, beyond that, toward life itself.

In terms of human relationships, an over-all claim was fairly well expressed by a patient who in his overt behavior was rather on the timid, withdrawn side. Without knowing it, he suffered from a pervasive inertia and was quite inhibited about tapping his own resources. "The world should be at my service," he said, "and I should not be bothered."

An equally comprehensive claim was harbored by a woman who at bottom was afraid of doubting herself. She felt entitled to have all her needs fulfilled. "It is unthinkable," she said, "that a man whom I want to fall in love with me should not do so." Her claims originally emerged in religious terms: "Everything that I pray for is given to me." In her case the claim had a reverse side. Since it would be an unthinkable defeat if a wish were not fulfilled, she put a check on most wants in order not to risk a "failure."

People whose need is to be always *right* feel entitled never to be criticized, doubted, or questioned. Those who are power ridden feel entitled to blind obedience. Others, for whom life has become a game in which other people are to be skillfully manipulated, feel entitled to fool everybody and, on the other hand, never to be fooled themselves. Those who are afraid to face their conflicts feel entitled to "get by," to "get around" their problems. The person who is aggressively exploiting and intimidates others into letting him put something over on them, will resent it as unfair if they insist on a square deal. The arrogant, vindictive person, who is driven to offend others but yet needs their recognition, feels entitled to "immunity." Whatever he perpetrates on others, he is entitled to having nobody mind anything he does. Another version of the same claim is the one for "understanding." No matter how morose or irritable one is, one is entitled to understanding. The individual for whom "love" is an over-all solution turns his need into a claim for exclusive and unconditional devotion. The detached person, seemingly quite undemanding, insists on one claim, however: not to be bothered. He feels that he does not want anything of others, and is therefore entitled to be left alone no matter what is at stake. "Not to be bothered" usually implies being exempt from criticism, expectations, or efforts—even if these latter are in his own behalf.

This may suffice as a fair sample of neurotic claims operating in personal relations. In more impersonal situations, or with reference to institutions, claims with a negative content prevail. Benefits accruing from laws or regulations, for example, are taken for granted, but it is felt as unfair when they turn out to be disadvantageous.

I am still grateful for an incident which occurred during the last war, because it opened my eyes to unconscious claims I harbored and, from these, to those of others. Coming back from a visit to Mexico, I was put off the flight in Corpus Christi because of priorities. Although I considered this regulation perfectly justified in principle, I noticed that I was furiously indignant when it applied to me. I was really exasperated at the prospect of a three-day train ride to New York, and became greatly fatigued. The whole upset culminated in the consoling thought that this might be a special provision by providence, because something might happen to the plane.

At that point I suddenly saw the ridiculousness of my reactions. And, starting to think about them, I saw the claims: first, to be the exception; second, to be taken special care of by providence. From then on my whole attitude toward the train ride changed. It was no less uncomfortable to sit day and night in overcrowded day coaches. But I was no longer tired, and even began to enjoy the trip.

I believe that anyone can easily duplicate and extend this experience with observations of himself or others. The difficulties many people have, for instance, in observing traffic regulations—as pedestrian or as driver—often result from an unconscious protest against them. *They* should not be subjected to such rules. Others resent the "insolence" of a bank in drawing their attention to the fact that they have overdrawn their account. Again, many fears of examinations, or the inability to prepare for them, stem from a claim to exemption. Similarly, indignation at seeing a bad performance may derive from feeling entitled to first-class entertainment.

This claim of being the exception pertains also in regard to natural laws, psychic or physical. It is amazing how obtuse otherwise intelligent patients can become when it is a matter of seeing the inevitability of cause and effect in psychic matters. I am thinking of rather self-evident connections such as these: if we want to achieve something, we must put in work; if we want to become independent, we must strive toward assuming responsibility for ourselves. Or: so long as we are arrogant, we will be vulnerable. Or: so long as we do not love ourselves, we cannot possibly believe that others love us, and must by necessity be suspicious toward any assertion of love. Patients presented with such sequences of cause and effect may start to argue, to become befogged or evasive.

Many factors are involved to produce this peculiar denseness.[2] We must realize in the first place that to grasp such cause-and-effect relations means confronting the patient with the necessity of inner changes. Of course it is always difficult to change any neurotic factor. But in addition, as we have already seen, many patients have an intense unconscious aversion to the realization that they should be subject to *any* necessity. The mere words "rules," "necessities," or "restrictions" may make them shudder if they let their meaning penetrate at all. In their private world everything is possible—to them. The recognition of any necessity applying to themselves, therefore, would actually pull them down from their lofty world into actuality, where they would be subject to the same natural laws as anybody else. And it is this need to eliminate necessity from their lives which turns into a claim. In analysis this shows in their feeling entitled to be above the necessity of changing. Thus they unconsciously refuse to see that they must change attitudes in themselves if they want to become independent or less vulnerable, or want to be able to believe in being loved.

---

[2] *Cf.* Chapter 7, The Process of Psychic Fragmentation and Chapter 11, The Aversion against any Change in the Resigned Person.

Most staggering are certain secret claims toward life in general. Any doubt about the irrational character of claims is bound to disappear in this area. Naturally it would shatter a person's feeling of godlikeness to face the fact that for him, too, life is limited and precarious; that fate can strike him at any time with an accident, bad fortune, illness, or death—and blast his feeling of omnipotence. For (to reiterate an ancient truth) there is very little we can do about it. We can avoid certain risks of dying and we can, nowadays, protect ourselves against financial losses connected with death; but we cannot avoid death. Unable to face the precariousness of his life as a human being, the neurotic individual develops claims of his inviolability, or claims of being the anointed, of luck always being on his side, of life being easy and without suffering.

In contrast to the claims operating in human relationships, those toward life in general cannot be asserted effectively. The neurotic with these claims can do but two things. He can deny, in his mind, that anything can happen to him. In that case he tends to be reckless—go out in cold weather when he has a fever, not take precautions against infections likely to occur, or have sexual intercourse without precautions. He will live as though he could never grow old, or die. Hence, of course, if some adversity does strike him, it is a crushing experience and may throw him into panic. Trivial though the experience may be, it shatters his lofty beliefs in his inviolability. He may turn to the other extreme, and become overcautious toward life. If he cannot rely on his claims for inviolability being respected, then anything can happen and he can rely on nothing. This does not mean that he has relinquished his claims. Rather, it means that he wants not to expose himself to another realization of their futility.

Other attitudes toward life and fate seem more sensible, as long as we do not recognize the claims behind them. Many patients directly or indirectly express a sentiment of its being unfair that they are afflicted with their particular difficulties. When talking about their friends, they will point out that despite their being neurotic, too, this one is more at ease in social situations; that one is more successful with women; another is more aggressive, or enjoys life more fully. Such meanderings, though futile, seem understandable. Each one, after all, suffers under his personal difficulties, and hence will feel it more desirable not to have the particular ones that harass him. But the patient's responses to being together with one of these "enviable" people point to a more serious process. He can suddenly develop a cold, or become despondent. Going after such responses, we discover the source of the trouble to be a rigid claim that he should not have any problems at all. He is entitled to be better endowed than anybody else. He is entitled, moreover, not only to a life devoid of personal problems but to the combined excellencies of those he knows in person, or, say, on the screen: to be as humble and intelligent as Charles Chaplin, as humane and courageous as Spencer Tracy, as victoriously virile as Clark Gable. The claim that I should not be I is too obviously irrational to be raised as such. It appears in the form of resentful envy toward anybody better endowed or more fortunate in his development; in imitation or adoration of them; in claims directed toward the analyst to supply him with all these desirable, often contradictory perfections.

This claim for being endowed with supreme attributes is rather crippling in its implications. It not only makes for a chronic smoldering envy and discontent, but constitutes a real drawback for analytic work. If it is unfair in the first place that the patient should have any neurotic difficulties, it certainly is doubly unfair to expect him to work at his problems. On the contrary, he feels entitled to be relieved of his difficulties without having to go through the laborious process of changing.

This survey of kinds of neurotic claims is not complete. Since every neurotic need can turn into a claim, we would have to discuss each single one in order to give an exhaustive picture of claims. But even a short survey gives us a feeling for their peculiar nature. We shall try now to bring their common characteristics into clearer relief.

To begin with, they are unrealistic in two regards. The person establishes a title which exists in his mind only, and he has little, if any, consideration for the possibility of the fulfillment of his claims. This is obvious in the frankly fantastic claims of being exempt from illness, old age, and death. But it is just as true for the others. The woman who feels entitled to having all her invitations accepted takes offense at anyone's declining, no matter how urgent are the reasons for not accepting. The scholar who insists that everything should come easily to him resents the work to be put into a paper or an experiment, regardless of how necessary such work is and often despite his realizing that it cannot be done without painstaking work. The alcoholic who feels entitled to having everybody help him in a financial calamity feels it is unfair if help is not immediately and gladly given, no matter whether others are in a position to do so or not.

These illustrations point implicitly to a second characteristic of neurotic claims: their *egocentricity*. It is often so blatant that it strikes the observer as "naïve," and reminds him of similar attitudes in spoiled children. These impressions lend weight to theoretical conclusions that all these claims are just "infantile" character traits in people who (at least, on this score) have failed to grow up. Actually this contention is fallacious. The small child also is egocentric, but only because it has not yet developed a feeling of relatedness to others. It simply does not know that others have their needs, and limitations too—such as the mother's needing sleep or not having the money to buy a toy. The neurotic's egocentricity is built on an entirely different and much more complicated base. He is consumed with himself because he is driven by his psychic needs, torn by his conflicts, and compelled to adhere to his peculiar solutions. Here are, then, two phenomena which look similar but are different. It follows that to tell a patient his claims are infantile is of utter therapeutic futility. It can merely mean to him that they are irrational (a fact which the analyst can show him in better ways), and this at best sets him thinking. Without much further work, it will not change anything.

So much for this distinction. The egocentricity of neurotic claims can be epitomized in terms of my own revealing experience: priorities in wartime are all right, but my own needs should have absolute priority. If the neurotic feels ill or wants something done, everybody should drop everything else and rush to his assistance. The analyst's polite assertion that he has no time available for a consultation often meets with a furious or insulting reply, or simply falls on deaf ears. If the patient needs it, there should be time. The less related the neurotic is to the world around him, the less is he aware of others and their feelings. As a patient who at the time showed a lofty disdain for reality once said: "I am an unattached comet, rushing in space. Which means that what I need is real—others with their needs are unreal."

A third characteristic of the neurotic's claims lies in his expectation that things are coming to him *without his making adequate efforts*. He does not admit that if he is lonely he might well call up somebody; somebody should call him up. The simple reasoning that he must eat less if he wants to take off weight often meets with so much inner opposition that he just keeps on eating, still considering it unfair that he does not look as slender as other people. Another may claim that he should be given an honorable job, a better position, an advance in salary without having done anything special to merit it and—what is more—without asking for it. He should not even have to be clear in his own mind what it is that he wants. He should be in the position *to refuse or to take anything*.

Frequently a person may express in most plausible and touching words how much he wants to be happy. But his family or his friends realize after a while that it is extremely difficult to make him happy. So they may tell him that there must be some discontent in him preventing him from attaining happiness. He may then go to an analyst.

The analyst will appreciate the patient's wish for happiness as a good motive for coming to analysis. But he will also ask himself why the patient, with all his desire for happiness, is not happy. He has many things which most people would enjoy: a pleasant home, a nice wife, financial security. But he does not do much of anything; he has no vigorous interest of any kind. There is a great deal of passivity and self-indulgence in the picture. It strikes the analyst in the very first interview that the patient does not talk about his difficulties, but rather, in a somewhat petulant way, presents a chart of wishes. The next hour confirms the first impressions. The patient's inertia in the analytic work proves to be the first hindrance. So the picture becomes clearer. Here is a person, tied hand and foot, unable to tap his own resources and filled to the brim with tenacious claims that all the good things in life, including contentment of soul, should come to him.

Another example illustrating the claim for help without effort throws further light on its nature. A patient who had to interrupt his analysis for a week was upset by some problem that had emerged in the previous analytical session. He expressed his wish to get over the difficulty before he left—a perfectly legitimate wish. So I tried hard to get at the root of the particular problem. After a while I noticed, however, that there was but little co-operative effort on his part. It was as if I had to drag him along. As the hour went on I sensed an increasing irritability on his side. Upon my direct question, he confirmed it by saying that of course he was irritated; he did not want to be left with his difficulty for a whole week and I had not yet said anything to alleviate it. I pointed out that his wish was certainly sensible, but that apparently it had turned into a claim, which did not make any sense. Whether or not we could come any closer to solving the particular problem would depend upon how accessible it was at this juncture, and how productive he and I could be. And, as far as he was concerned, there must be something that was preventing him from making efforts toward the desired end. After a good deal of back and forth which I omit here, he could not help seeing the truth of what I had said. His irritability disappeared; his irrational claims and his sense of urgency also disappeared. And he added one revealing factor: he had felt that I had caused the problem, so it was up to me to set it right. How was I responsible for it, in his mind? He did not mean that I had made a mistake; it was simply that in the previous hour he had realized that he had not yet overcome his vindictiveness—which he had barely started to perceive. Actually, at that time he did not even want to be rid of it, but only of certain upsets accompanying it. Since I had failed his claim to be freed from these immediately, he felt entitled to raise vindictive claims for retribution. With this explanation, he had pointed to the roots of his claims: his inner refusal to assume responsibility for himself and his lack of constructive self-interest. This paralyzed him, prevented him from doing anything for himself, and made for a need that somebody else—

here the analyst—should take all the responsibility and set things right for him. And this need, too, turned into a claim.

This example points to a fourth characteristic of neurotic claims: they can be *vindictive* in nature. The person may feel wronged, and insist on retribution. That this can occur is in itself old knowledge. It is obviously so in traumatic neuroses, in certain paranoid conditions. There are many descriptions of this characteristic in literature, among others Shylock's insisting on his pound of flesh and Hedda Gabler's laying claim to extravagant luxuries at the very moment when she has learned of the probability that her husband will not get the professorship they have hoped for.

The question I want to raise here is whether vindictive demands are a frequent, if not regular, element in neurotic claims. Naturally the individual's awareness of them will vary. In the case of Shylock, they were conscious; in the example of the patient's anger at me, they were on the threshold of awareness; in most instances they are unconscious. From my experience, I doubt their ubiquity. But I find them to be so frequent that I have made it a rule always to look out for them. As I mentioned in the context of the need for vindictive triumph, the amount of largely hidden vindictiveness we find in most neuroses is rather great. Vindictive elements are certainly operating when claims are made with reference to past frustration or suffering; when they are made in a militant manner; when the fulfillment of claims is felt as a triumph and their frustration as defeat.

How *aware* are people of their claims? The more a person's view of himself and the world around him is determined by his imagination, the more he and his life in general simply are as he needs to see them. There is no room then in his mind for seeing that he has any needs or any claims, and the mere mentioning of the possibility of his having claims may be offensive. People simply *do not* let him wait. He simply *does not* have any accidents, nor will he ever get older. The weather *is* fair when he goes on an excursion. Things *do* go his way and he *does* get by with everything.

Other neurotic individuals *seem* to be aware of their claims, for they obviously and openly demand special privileges for themselves. But what is obvious to the observer may not be obvious to the person himself. What the observer sees and what the observed one feels are two things, to be sharply distinguished. A person aggressively asserting his claims may, at most, be aware of certain expressions or implications of his claims, such as being impatient or not being able to stand disagreement. He may know that he does not like to ask for things or to say thank you. This awareness, however, is different from knowing that he feels entitled to have others do exactly what he wants. He may be aware of being reckless at times, but often he will embellish the recklessness as self-confidence or courage. He may, for instance, quit a fairly good job without any concrete prospect for another one, and may regard such a step as an expression of his self-confidence. This may actually be the case, but there may also be present a recklessness resulting from feeling entitled to having luck and fate on his side. He may know that in some hidden recess of his soul he secretly believes that he, for one, will not die. But even that is not yet an awareness of his feeling entitled to be above biological limitations.

In other instances the claims are concealed from both the person harboring them and the untrained observer. The latter then will accept whatever justifying reasons are proferred for the demands made. Usually he does so less because of psychological ignorance than because of neurotic reasons of his own. He may, for example, find it inconvenient at times that his wife or mistress makes absorbing demands on his time, but it also flatters his vanity to think that he is indispensable to her. Or, a woman may make consuming claims on the basis of helplessness and suffering. She herself will merely feel her needs. She may even be consciously overcareful not to impose upon others. These others, though, may either cherish the role of protector and helper or, because of secret codes of their own, feel "guilty" if they do not measure up to the woman's expectations.

However, even if a person is aware of having certain claims, he is never aware of his claims being unwarranted or irrational. Actually, any doubt of their validity would mean a first step toward undermining them. As long, therefore, as they are vitally important to him, the neurotic must build up in his mind an airtight case in order to make them entirely legitimate. He must feel thoroughly convinced of their being fair and just. The patient in analysis goes to a great length to prove that he expects only what is coming to him. Conversely, for the sake of therapy, it is important to recognize both the existence of a special claim and the nature of its justification. Since the claims stand and fall with the basis upon which they are put, this basis itself becomes a strategic position. If, for instance, a person feels entitled to all sorts of services on the grounds of merits, he must unwittingly so exaggerate these merits that he can feel righteously abused if the services are not forthcoming.

Claims often are justified on cultural grounds. Because I am a woman—because I am a man—because I am your mother—because I am your employer. . . . Since none of these reasons, serving plausibility or justification, actually entitles one to the demands made, their importance must be overemphasized. For instance, there is no rigid cultural code in this country that it offends masculine dignity to wash dishes. So, if there is a claim of being exempt from menial work, the dignity of being a man or a wage earner must be inflated.

The always present base is that of superiority. The common denominator on this score is: because I am something extra special, I am entitled to . . . In this blunt form, it is mostly unconscious. But the individual may lay stress upon the special significance of his time, his work, his plans, his always being right.

Those who believe that "love" solves everything, that "love" entitles one to everything, must then exaggerate the depth or the value of love—not by way of conscious pretense but by actually feeling more love than there is. The necessity to exaggerate often has repercussions which may contribute to building a vicious circle. This is particularly true for claims put on the grounds of helplessness and suffering. Many people, for instance, feel too timid to make inquiries by telephone. If the claim is made that somebody else make the inquiry for him, the person concerned feels his inhibitions greater than they actually are in order to validate them. If a woman feels too depressed or helpless to do her housekeeping, she will make herself feel more helpless or more depressed than she is—and then will in fact suffer more.

One should not, however, come to the hasty conclusion that it is desirable for others of the environment not to accede to neurotic claims. Both the acceding and the refusing can make the condition worse—that is, in both cases the claims may become more emphatic. Refusing usually helps only if the neurotic has begun or is beginning to assume responsibility for himself.

Perhaps the most interesting basis for claims is that of "justice." Because I believe in God, or because I have always worked, or because I have always been a good citizen—it is but a matter of justice that nothing adverse should happen to me and that things should go my way. Earthly benefits should follow from being good and pious. Evidence to the contrary (evidence that rewards do not *necessarily* follow virtue) is discarded. If this tendency is presented to a patient, he will usually point out that his feeling of justice also extends to others, that he is just as indignant if injustice is done to others. To some extent this is true, but it merely means that his own need to put his claims on the basis of justice is generalized into a "philosophy."

The emphasis on justice has a reverse side, moreover, which is to make other people responsible for any adversity which overtakes them. Whether a person applies this reverse aspect to himself depends upon the degree of his conscious rightness. If this is rigid, he will—at least consciously—experience every adversity of his as an injustice. But he will tend more easily to apply the law of "retributive justice" to others: perhaps a person who becomes unemployed did not "really" want to work; perhaps in some way the Jews are responsible for the persecutions.

In more personal matters such an individual feels entitled to receive value for value given. This might be proper if it were not for two factors which escape his attention. His own positive values assume exaggerated proportions in his mind (good intentions, for instance, are counted among them) while he ignores the difficulties he has brought into a relationship. And in addition the values put on the scale often are incongruous. An analysand, for instance, may put on his side of the scale his intention to be co-operative, his wish to get rid of disturbing symptoms, his coming and paying regularly. On the analyst's side of the scale is his obligation to make the patient well. Unfortunately, the two sides of the scale do not balance. The patient can get well only if he is willing and able to work at himself and to change. So if the patient's good intentions are not combined with effective efforts nothing much will happen. Disturbances keep recurring and the patient, with increasing irritation, will feel cheated; he will present his bill in the form of reproaches or complaints and will feel entirely justified in an increasing distrust of the analyst.

The overemphasis on justice may be, but is not necessarily, a camouflage for vindictiveness. When claims are raised primarily on the grounds of a "deal" with life, usually one's own merits are stressed. The more vindictive claims are, the more the injury done is stressed. Here, too, the injury done must be exaggerated, the feeling for it cultivated, until it looms so large that the "victim" feels entitled to exact any sacrifice or to inflict any punishment.

Since claims are crucial for the maintenance of a neurosis, it is of course important to *assert* them. This applies only toward those directed toward people, because, needless to say, fate and life have a way of deriding any assertion directed toward them. We shall come back to this question on several occasions. It suffices here to say that by and large the ways in which the neurotic tries to make others accede to his claims are intimately connected with the basis on which they are put. In short, he can try to impress others with his unique importance; he can please, charm, promise; he can put others under obligations and try to cash in by appealing to their sense of fairness or guilt; he can, by emphasizing his suffering, appeal to pity and guilt-feelings; he can, by stressing love for others, appeal to their yearning for love or to their vanity; he can intimidate with irritability and sullenness. The vindictive person, who may ruin others with insatiable claims, tries through hardhitting accusations to enforce their compliance.

Considering all the energies invested in justifying the claims, and in asserting them, we cannot but expect intense *reactions to their frustrations*. There are undercurrents of fear, but the prevailing response is anger or even rage. This anger is of a peculiar kind. Since the claims are subjectively felt as fair and just, the frustrations are experienced as unfair and unjust. The ensuing anger has therefore the character of a righteous indignation. The person feels, in other words, not only angry but the right to be angry—a feeling which is vigorously defended in analysis.

Before delving deeper into the various expressions of this indignation, I want to take a brief detour into theory—in particular the theory advanced by John Dollard and others that we react with hostility to any frustration; that, as a matter of fact, hostility essentially is a reaction to frustration.[3] Actually, fairly simple observations show that this contention is not valid. On the contrary, the amount of frustration human beings can bear without hostility is amazing. Hostility arises only if a frustration is unfair or if, on the basis of neurotic claims, it is felt to be unfair. And it has then the specific characteristic of indignation, or of feeling abused. The misfortune, or the injury, done then appears magnified to sometimes ludicrous proportions. If one feels abused by another person, that person suddenly becomes untrustworthy, nasty, cruel, contemptible—i.e., this indignation drastically influences our judgment of others. Here is one source for neurotic suspiciousness. Here is also a reason, and an important one, for many neurotic people being so insecure in their estimates of others and for their turning so easily from a positive friendly attitude to one of total condemnation.

If I may oversimplify, the acute reaction of anger, or even rage, may take one of three different courses. It may be suppressed, for whatever reason, and may then—like any suppressed hostility—appear in psychosomatic symptoms: fatigue, migraine, stomach upsets, etc. On the other hand, it may be freely expressed, or at least fully felt. In this case the less the anger is warranted in fact, the more one will have to exaggerate the wrong done; one will then inadvertently build up a case against the offender that looks logic tight. The more openly vindictive a person is, for whatever reason, the more prone will he be to take vengeance. The more openly arrogant he is, the surer will he be that such vengeance is the doling out of justice.

[3] The postulate is made on the basis of Freud's theory of instincts and entails the contention that every hostility is a reaction to frustrated instinctual urges or their derivatives. For those analysts who accept Freud's theory of a death-instinct, hostility in addition derives its energy from an instinctual need to destroy.

The third kind of reaction is to plunge into misery and self-pity. The individual then feels extremely hurt or abused, and may become despondent. "How can they do this to me!" he feels. Suffering in these cases becomes the medium to express reproaches.

It is easier to observe these reactions in others than in oneself, for the very reason that the conviction of righteousness inhibits self-examination. It is in our real interest, however, to examine our own reactions when we become preoccupied with a wrong done to us, or when we begin to ponder the hateful qualities of somebody, or when we feel the impulse to get back at others. We must then scrutinize the question of whether our reaction is in any reasonable proportion to the wrong done. And if with honest scrutiny we find a disproportion, we must search for hidden claims. Provided we are willing and able to relinquish some of our needs for special prerogatives, and provided we are familiar with the special forms our suppressed hostility may take, it is not too difficult to recognize an acute reaction to an individual frustration and to discover the particular claim behind it. Having seen the claims in one or two instances does not mean, however, that we are rid of all of them. We usually have overcome only those which were especially conspicuous and absurd. The process is reminiscent of a tapeworm cure in which parts of the worm are eliminated. But it will regenerate and keep sapping our strength until the head is removed. This means that we can relinquish our claims only to the extent to which we overcome the whole search for glory and all that it entails. However, unlike a tapeworm cure, in the process of coming back to ourselves every step counts.

The *effects* which pervasive claims have on a personality and his life are manifold. They may create in him a diffuse sense of frustration and a discontent so encompassing that it could loosely be called a character trait. There are other factors contributing to such chronic discontent. But among the sources generating it pervasive claims are outstanding. The discontent shows in the tendency in any life situation to focus on what is lacking, or on what is hard, and thus to become dissatisfied with the whole situation. For instance, a man is engaged in a most satisfactory work and has a family life which is largely constructive, but he has not enough time to play the piano, which means much to him; or perhaps one of his daughters has not turned out well; and these factors loom so large in his mind that he cannot appreciate the good he has. Or consider a person whose otherwise pleasant day can be spoiled by the failure of some ordered merchandise to arrive on time—or one who experiences in a beautiful excursion or trip only the inconvenience. These attitudes are so common that almost everyone must have encountered them. Persons having them sometimes wonder why they always look on the dark side of things. Or they dismiss the whole matter by calling themselves "pessimistic." This, aside from being no explanation at all, puts on a pseudophilosophical basis an entirely personal incapacity to tolerate adversities.

Through this attitude people make life harder for themselves in many ways. Any hardship becomes ten times harder if we consider it unfair. My own experience in the day coach is a good illustration of this. As long as I felt it to be an unfair imposition, it seemed almost more than I could endure. Then, after I had discovered the claim behind it—although the seats were just as hard, the time it took just as long—the very same situation became enjoyable. The point applies equally to work. Any work we do with the subversive feeling of its being unfair, or with a secret claim that it should be easy, is bound to become strenuous and fatiguing. In other words, through the neurotic claims we lose that part of the art of living which consists of taking things in our stride. Certainly there are experiences which are so severe as to be crushing. But these are rare. For the neurotic, minor happenings turn into catastrophes and life becomes a series of upsets. Conversely, the neurotic may focus on the bright aspects in the lives of others: this one has success, that one has children, another has more leisure or can do more with it, the houses of others are nicer, their pastures greener.

Although this is simple enough to describe, it is difficult to recognize, particularly in ourselves. It seems so real, so factual, this thing of paramount importance which we lack and which somebody else has. The bookkeeping is thus distorted both ways: in regard to self and to others. Most people have been told not to compare their own lives with the bright spots of others but rather with the totality. But even though they realize the validity of this advice, they cannot follow it because their distorted vision is not a matter of oversight or intellectual ignorance. It is, rather, an emotional blindness—i.e., a blindness which results from inner unconscious necessities.

The consequences are a mixture of envy and insensibility toward others. The envy has the quality of what Nietzsche called Lebensneid, an envy which does not pertain to this or that detail but to life in general. It goes with the feeling of being the only one to be excluded, the only one to worry, to be lonely, panicky, cramped. The insensibility, too, does not necessarily predicate an entirely callous person. It results from pervasive claims and then acquires a function of its own, that of justifying the person's egocentricity. Why should others, who are all better off than he, expect anything of him? Why should he, who is in greater need than anybody around—he, who is more neglected or ignored than others—not be entitled to look out for himself alone! Thus the claims become more firmly entrenched.

Another consequence is a general feeling of uncertainty about rights. This is a complex phenomenon and pervasive claims are but one of the determining factors. The private world, in which the neurotic feels entitled to everything, is so unrealistic that he becomes confused about his rights in the world of actuality. Being filled with presumptuous claims on the one hand, he may be too timid to feel or assert his rights when he actually could and should do so. The patient, for instance, who on the one hand felt that the whole world should be at his service was timid about asking me for a change of hours or for a pencil to jot down something. Another person, hypersensitive when neurotic claims for deference were not fulfilled, did put up with flagrant impositions on the part of some friends. The feeling of having no rights, then, may be the aspect under which the patient suffers, and it may become the focus of his complaints while he is unconcerned about the irrational claims which are the source of the trouble, or at least a relevant contributing source.[4]

Finally, the harboring of extensive claims is one of the rele-

---

[4] *Cf.* Chapter 8, The Self-Effacing Solution.

vant factors contributing to inertia, which in its open or hidden form is perhaps the most frequent neurotic disturbance. In contrast to idleness, which can be voluntary and enjoyable, inertia is a paralysis of psychic energies. It extends not only to doing things but to thinking and feeling as well. All claims, by definition, substitute for the neurotic's active work at his problems, and hence paralyze him with regard to his growth. In many instances they contribute toward a more comprehensive aversion to all efforts. The unconscious claim, then, is that the mere intention should be enough to bring about achievement, to get a job, to be happy, to overcome a difficulty. He is entitled to achieve all this without any output of energy. Sometimes this means that others should do the actual work—let George do it. If this does not happen, he has a reason for discontent. Thus it often occurs that he becomes tired at the mere prospect of doing some extra work, such as moving or shopping. Sometimes, in analysis, an individual fatigue can be removed quickly. One patient, for instance, had many things to do before going on a trip and felt fatigued even prior to starting in on his work. I suggested that he might take the problem of how to get everything done as a challenge to his ingenuity. This appealed to him, the fatigue disappeared, and he was able to accomplish everything without feeling rushed or tired. But although he had thus experienced his ability to be active and joy in being so, his impulse to make efforts of his own soon receded, for his unconscious claims were still too deeply entrenched.

The more vindictive the claims involved, the stronger the degree of inertia seems to be. The unconscious argument, then, runs as follows: Others are responsible for the trouble I am in— so I am entitled to repair. And what kind of repair would it be, if I made all the effort! Naturally, only a person who has lost constructive interest in his life can argue that way. It is no longer up to him to do something about his life; it is up to "them," or to fate.

The *tenacity* with which the patient adheres to his claims and defends them in analysis points to the considerable subjective value they must have for him. He has not one but several lines of defense and shifts them repeatedly. First, he has no claims at all, he does not know what the analyst is talking about; then they are all rational; then he proceeds to defend their subjective foundations which serve as justification. When at last he realizes that he does have claims and that they are unwarranted in reality, he seems to lose interest in them: they are unimportant or at any rate harmless. He cannot help, though, seeing in time that the ensuing consequences to himself are manifold and serious: that, for instance, they make him irritable and discontented; that it would be much better for him if he himself were more active instead of always expecting things to come to him; that, indeed, his claims paralyze his psychic energies. He also cannot close his mind to the fact that the practical gains he derives from his claims are minimal. True, by exerting pressure on others he can sometimes rush to make them cater to his demands, expressed or unexpressed. But, even so, who is made happier by it? As far as his general claims on life are concerned, they are futile anyhow. Whether or not he feels entitled to be the exception, psychic or biological laws apply to him. His claim for the combined excellencies of others does not change him an iota.

The realization of both the adverse consequences of the claims and of their intrinsic futility does not make a real dent; it does not carry conviction. The analyst's hope that these insights will uproot the claims frequently remains unfulfilled. Usually, through analytic work their intensity is diminished; but instead of being uprooted they are driven underground. Pressing farther, we get an insight into the depth of the patient's unconscious irrational imagination. While intellectually realizing the futility of his claims, unconsciously he holds on to the belief that to the magic of his will power nothing is impossible. If he wishes hard enough, what he wishes will come true. If he insists hard enough that things go his way, they will. If it has not yet come true, the reason does not lie in his reaching out for the impossible—as the analyst wants to make him believe—but in his not having willed them vigorously enough.

This belief puts a somewhat different complexion on the whole phenomenon. We have seen already that the patient's claims are unrealistic in the sense of his arrogating to himself a nonexistent title to all kinds of prerogatives. Also, we have seen that certain claims are frankly fantastic. Now we recognize that all of them are pervaded by expectations of magic. And only now do we grasp the whole extent to which the claims are an indispensable means of actualizing his idealized self. They do not represent an actualization in the sense of proving his excellence by achievement or success, but they provide him with necessary proofs and alibis. He must prove that he is above psychic and natural laws. And if time and again he sees that others do not accede to his claims, that laws do apply to him, that he is not above common troubles and failures—all of this is no evidence against his unlimited possibilities. It merely proves that, *as yet*, he has had an unfair deal. But if only he upholds his claims, some day they will come true. *The claims are his guaranty for future glory.*

We understand now why the patient responds with only lukewarm interest to seeing the damaging effects which his claims have upon his actual life. He does not dispute the damage, but the present is negligible in view of the prospect of the glorious future. He is like a person who believes he has a warranted claim to an inheritance; instead of making constructive efforts in living, he puts all his energies into a more effective assertion of his claims. In the meantime his actual life loses interest for him; he becomes impoverished; he neglects all that could make life worth living. And so the hope for future possibilities becomes more and more the only thing he lives for.

The neurotic actually is worse off than the hypothetical person claiming an inheritance. For he has the underlying feeling that he would lose his title for future fulfillment if he became interested in himself and his growth. This is logical on the basis of his premises—for, in that case, the actualization of his idealized self would indeed become meaningless. As long as he is possessed by the lure of that goal, the alternative way is positively deterring. It would mean seeing himself as a mortal like everybody else, harassed by difficulties; it would mean assuming responsibility for himself and recognizing that it is up to him to outgrow his difficulties and to develop whatever potentialities he has. It is deterring because it would make him feel as though he were losing everything. He can consider this alternative road—which is the way to health—only to the extent that he becomes strong enough to dispense with the solution he found in self-idealization.

We do not fully understand the tenacity of the claims so long as we regard them merely as a "naïve" expression of what the neurotic, with his glorified image of himself, feels is coming to him; or as an understandable desire to have his many compulsive needs fulfilled by others. The tenacity with which the neurotic adheres to any attitude is a sure indication that the attitude fulfills functions which seem indispensable in the framework of his neurosis. We have seen that claims seem to solve many problems for him. Their over-all function is to perpetuate his illusions about himself, and to shift responsibility to factors outside himself. By raising his needs to the dignity of claims, he denies his own troubles and places the responsibility for himself on other people, on circumstances, or on fate. It is unfair that he had any difficulties in the first place, and he is entitled to life's being so arranged that they should not trouble him. For example, he is asked for a loan or for a contribution. He becomes upset and, in his mind, heaps abuse on the person asking him. Actually he is indignant because of his claim not to be bothered. What makes his claim so necessary? The request actually confronts him with a conflict within himself, which is roughly that between his need to comply and his need to frustrate others. But so long as he is too scared or too unwilling to face this conflict—for whatever reason—he must hold on to his claim. He puts it in terms of not wanting to be bothered, but more precisely it is the claim that the world should behave in such a way as not to mobilize (and make him aware of) his conflicts. We shall understand later on why the shedding of responsibility is so vital to him. But we can see already that, in effect, claims prevent him from squaring himself with his difficulties, and that thereby they perpetuate his neurosis.

CHAPTER 3

THE TYRANNY OF THE SHOULD

We HAVE discussed so far chiefly how the neurotic tries to actualize his idealized self with regard to the *outside world:* in achievements, in the glory of success or power or triumph. Neurotic claims, too, are concerned with the world outside himself: he tries to assert the exceptional rights to which his uniqueness entitles him whenever, and in whatever ways, he can. His feeling entitled to be above necessities and laws allows him to live in a world of fiction as if he were indeed above them. And whenever he falls palpably short of being his idealized self, his claims enable him to make factors outside himself responsible for such "failures."

We shall now discuss that aspect of self-actualization, briefly mentioned in the first chapter, in which the focus is *within himself.* Unlike Pygmalion, who tried to make another person into a creature fulfilling his concept of beauty, the neurotic sets to work to mold himself into a supreme being of his own making. He holds before his soul his image of perfection and unconsciously tells himself: "Forget about the disgraceful creature you actually *are;* this is how you *should* be; and to be this idealized self is all that matters. You should be able to endure everything, to understand everything, to like everybody, to be always productive"—to mention only a few of these inner dictates. Since they are inexorable, I call them "the tyranny of the should."

The inner dictates comprise all that the neurotic should be able to do, to be, to feel, to know—and taboos on how and what he should not be. I shall begin by enumerating some of them out of context, for the sake of a brief survey. (More detailed examples will follow as we discuss the characteristics of the shoulds.)

He should be the utmost of honesty, generosity, considerateness, justice, dignity, courage, unselfishness. He should be the perfect lover, husband, teacher. He should be able to endure everything, should like everybody, should love his parents, his wife, his country; or, he should not be attached to anything or anybody, nothing should matter to him, he should never feel hurt, and he should always be serene and unruffled. He should always enjoy life; or, he should be above pleasure and enjoyment. He should be spontaneous; he should always control his feelings. He should know, understand, and foresee everything. He should be able to solve every problem of his own, or of others, in no time. He should be able to overcome every difficulty of his as soon as he sees it. He should never be tired or fall ill. He should always be able to find a job. He should be able to do things in one hour which can only be done in two to three hours.

This survey, roughly indicating the scope of inner dictates, leaves us with the impression of demands on self which, though understandable, are altogether too difficult and too rigid. If we tell a patient that he expects too much of himself, he will often recognize it without hesitation; he may even have been aware of it already. He will usually add, explicitly or implicitly, that it is better to expect too much of himself than too little. But to speak of too high demands on self does not reveal the peculiar *characteristics of inner dictates*. These come into clear relief under closer examination. They are overlapping, because they all result from the necessity a person feels to turn into his idealized self, and from his conviction that he can do so.

What strikes us first is the same *disregard for feasibility* which pervades the entire drive for actualization. Many of these demands are of a kind which no human being could fulfill. They are plainly fantastic, although the person himself is not aware of it. He cannot help recognizing it, however, as soon as his expectations are exposed to the clear light of critical thinking. Such an intellectual realization, however, usually does not change much, if anything. Let us say that a physician may have clearly realized that he cannot do intensive scientific work in addition to a nine-hour practice and an extensive social life; yet, after abortive attempts to cut down one or another activity, he keeps going at the same pace. His demands that limitations in time and energies should not exist for him are stronger than reason. Or take a more subtle illustration. At an analytic session a patient was dejected. She had talked with a friend about the latter's marital problems, which were complicated. My patient knew the husband only from social situations. Yet, although she had been in analysis for several years and had enough understanding of the psychological intricacies involved in any relationship between two people to know better, she felt that she should have been able to tell her friend whether or not the marriage was tenable.

I told her that she expected something of herself which was impossible for anybody, and pointed out the multitude of questions to be clarified before one could even begin to have a more than dim impression of the factors operating in the situation. It turned out then that she had been aware of most of the difficulties I had pointed out. But she had still felt that she *should* have a kind of sixth sense penetrating all of them.

Other demands on self may not be fantastic in themselves yet show a complete *disregard for the conditions* under which they could be fulfilled. Thus many patients expect to finish their analysis in no time because they are so intelligent. But the progress in analysis has little to do with intelligence. The reasoning power which these people have may, in fact, be used to obstruct progress. What counts are the emotional forces operating in the patients, their capacity to be straight and to assume responsibility for themselves.

This expectation of easy success operates not only in reference to the length of the whole analysis, but equally so in regard to an individual insight gained. For instance, recognizing some of their neurotic claims seems to them the equivalent of having outgrown them altogether. That it requires patient work; that the claims will persist as long as the emotional necessities for having them are not changed—all of this they ignore. They believe that their intelligence should be a supreme moving power. Naturally, then, subsequent disappointment and discouragement are unavoidable. In a similar way, a teacher may expect that, with her long experience in teaching, it should be easy for her to write a paper on a pedagogical subject. If the words do not flow from her pen, she feels utterly disgusted with herself. She has ignored or discarded such relevant questions as: Has she something to say? Have her experiences crystallized to some useful formulations? And even if the answers are affirmative, a paper still means plain work in formulating and expressing thoughts.

The inner dictates, exactly like political tyranny in a police state, operate with a supreme *disregard for the person's own psychic condition*—for what he can feel or do as he is at present. One of the frequent shoulds, for instance, is that one should never feel hurt. As an absolute (which is implied in the "never") anyone would find this extremely hard to achieve. How many people have been, or are, so secure in themselves, so serene, as never to feel hurt? This could at best be an ideal toward which we might strive. To take such a project seriously must mean intense and patient work at our unconscious claims for defense, at our false pride—or, in short, at every factor in our personality that makes us vulnerable. But the person who feels that he should never feel hurt does not have so concrete a program in mind. He simply issues an absolute order to himself, denying or overriding the fact of his existing vulnerability.

Let us consider another demand: I should always be understanding, sympathetic, and helpful. I should be able to melt the heart of a criminal. Again, this is not entirely fantastic. Rare people, such as the priest in Victor Hugo's *Les Miserables,* have achieved this spiritual power. I had a patient to whom the figure of the priest was an important symbol. She felt she should be like him. But she did not, at this juncture, have any of the attitudes or qualities which enabled the priest to act as he did toward the criminal. She could act charitably at times because she felt that she *should* be charitable, but she did not *feel* charitable. As a matter of fact, she did not feel much of anything for anybody. She was constantly afraid lest somebody take advantage of her. Whenever she could not find an article, she thought it had been stolen. Without being aware of it, her neurosis had made her egocentric and bent on her own advantage—all of which was covered up by a layer of compulsive humility and goodness. Was she at that time willing to see these difficulties in herself, and to work at them? Of course not. Here, too, it was a question of a blind issuing of orders which could lead only to self-deception or unfair self-criticism.

In trying to account for the amazing blindness of the shoulds, we again have to leave many loose ends. This much, however, is understandable from their origin in the search for glory and their function to make oneself over into one's idealized self: *the premise on which they operate is that nothing should be, or is, impossible for oneself.* If that is so, then, logically, existing conditions need not be examined.

This trend is most apparent in the application of demands directed toward the past. Concerning the neurotic's childhood, it is not only important to elucidate the influences which set his neurosis going, but also to recognize his present attitudes toward the adversities of the past. These are determined less by the good or the bad done to him than by his present needs. If he has developed, for instance, a general need to be all sweetness and light, he will spread a golden haze over his childhood. If he has forced his feelings into a strait jacket, he may feel that he does love his parents because he should love them. If he generally refuses to assume responsibility for his life, he may put all the blame for all his difficulties on his parents. The vindictiveness accompanying this latter attitude, in turn, may be out in the open or repressed.

He may finally go to the opposite extreme, and seemingly assume an absurd amount of responsibility for himself. In this case he may have become aware of the full impact of intimidating and cramping early influences. His conscious attitude is quite objective and plausible. He may point out, for instance, that his parents could not help behaving the way they did. The patient sometimes wonders himself why he does not feel any resentment. One of the reasons for the absence of conscious resentment is a retrospective *should* that interests us here. Though he is aware that what has been perpetrated on him was quite sufficient to crush anybody else, *he* should have come out of it unscathed. He should have had the inner strength and fortitude not to let these factors affect him. So, since they did, it proved that he was no good from the beginning. In other words, he is realistic up to a point; he would say: "Sure, that was a cesspool of hypocrisy and cruelty." But then his vision becomes blurred: "Although I was helplessly exposed to this atmosphere, I should have come out of it like a lily out of a swamp."

If he could assume a matter-of-fact responsibility for his life instead of such a spurious one, he would think differently. He would admit that the early influences could not fail to mold him in an unfavorable way. And he would see that, no matter what the origin of his difficulties, they do disturb his present and future life. For this reason he had better muster his energies to outgrow them. Instead, he leaves the whole matter at the completely fantastic and futile level of his demand that he should not have been affected. It is a sign of progress when the same patient at a later period reverses his position and rather gives himself credit for not having been entirely crushed by the early circumstances.

The attitude toward childhood is not the only area in which the retrospective shoulds operate with this deceptive counterfeit of responsibility, and the same resultant futility. One person will maintain that he should have helped his friend by voicing a frank criticism; another that he should have brought up his children without their becoming neurotic. Naturally we all regret having failed in this or that regard. But we can examine why we failed, and learn from it. We must also recognize that in view of the neurotic difficulties existing at the time of the "failures," we may actually have done the best we could at that time. But, for the neurotic, to have done his best is not good enough. In some miraculous way he should have done better.

Similarly, the realization of any present shortcoming is unbearable for anybody harassed by dictatorial shoulds. Whatever the difficulty, it must be removed quickly. How this removal is effected varies. The more a person lives in imagination, the more likely it is that he will simply spirit away the difficulty. Thus a patient who discovered in herself a colossal drive for being the power behind the throne, and who saw how this drive had operated in her life, was convinced by the next day that this drive was now entirely a matter of the past. She should not be power ridden; so she was not. After such "improvements" occurred frequently, we realized that the drive for actual control and influence was but one expression of the magic power she possessed in her imagination.

Others try to remove by dint of sheer will power the difficulty of which they have become aware. People can go to an extraordinary length in this regard. I am thinking, for instance, of two young girls who felt that they should never be afraid of anything. One of them was scared of burglars and forced herself to sleep in an empty house until her fear was gone. The other was afraid of swimming when the water was not transparent because she felt she might be bitten by a snake or a fish. She forced herself to swim across a shark-infested bay. Both girls managed in this way to crush their fears. Thus the incidents seem to be grist for the mills of those who regard psychoanalysis as newfangled nonsense. Do they not show that all that is necessary is to pull oneself together? But actually the fears of burglars or snakes were but the most obvious, manifest expression of a general, more hidden apprehensiveness. And this pervasive undercurrent of anxiety remained untouched by the acceptance of the particular "challenge." It was merely covered up, driven deeper by disposing of a symptom without touching the real disorder.

In analysis we can observe how the will-power machinery is switched on in certain types as soon as they become aware of foibles. They resolve, and try, to keep a budget, to mix with people, to be more assertive or more lenient. This would be fine if they showed an equal interest in understanding the implications and sources of their troubles. Unfortunately, this interest is sadly lacking. The very first step, which is to see the whole extent of the particular disturbance, would go against their grain. It would indeed be the exact opposite to their frantic drive to make the disturbance *disappear*. Also, since they feel they should be strong enough to conquer it by conscious control, the process of careful disentangling would be an admission of weakness and defeat. These artificial efforts are bound, of course, to abate sooner or later; then, at best, the difficulty is a little more under control. All that is sure is that it has been driven underground and that it continues to operate in a more disguised form. The analyst, naturally, should not encourage such efforts but should analyze them.

Most neurotic disturbances resist even the most strenuous efforts at control. Conscious efforts simply do not avail against a depression, against a deeply ingrained inhibition to work, or against consuming daydreams. One would think that this would be clear to any person who has gained some psychological understanding during analysis. But again the clarity of thinking does not penetrate to the "I should be able to master it." The result is that he suffers more intensely under depressions, etc., because, in addition to its being painful anyhow, it becomes a visible sign of his lack of omnipotence. Sometimes the analyst can catch this process at the beginning and nip it in the bud. Thus a patient who had revealed the extent of her daydreaming, while exposing in detail how subtly it pervaded most of her activities, came to realize its harmfulness—at least to the extent of understanding how it sapped her energies. The next time she was somewhat guilty and apologetic because the daydreams persisted. Knowing her demands on herself, I injected my belief that it would be neither possible nor even wise to stop them artificially, because we could be sure that they fulfilled as yet important functions in her life—which we would have to come to understand gradually. She felt very much relieved and now told me that she had decided to stop the daydreams. But since she hadn't been able to she felt I would be disgusted with her. Her own expectation of herself had been projected to me.

Many reactions of despondence, irritability, or fear occurring during analysis are less a response to the patient's having discovered a disturbing problem in himself (as the analyst tends to assume) than to his feeling impotent to remove it right away.

Thus the inner dictates, while somewhat more radical than other ways to maintain the idealized image, like the others do not aim at real change but at immediate and absolute perfection. They aim at making the imperfection disappear, or at making it appear *as if* the particular perfection were attained. This becomes especially clear if, as in the last example, the inner demands are externalized. Then what a person actually is, and even what he suffers, becomes irrelevant. Only what is visible to others creates intense worries: a shaking of the hand, a blush, an awkwardness in social situations.

The shoulds, therefore, *lack the moral seriousness of genuine ideals.* People in their grip are not striving, for instance, toward approximating a greater degree of honesty but are driven to attain the absolute in honesty—which is always just around the corner, or is attained in imagination.

They can achieve at best a behavioristic perfection, such as Pearl Buck has described in the character of Madame Wu in the *Pavilion of Women.* Here is the portrait of a woman who always seems to do, feel, think the right thing. The superficial appearance of such people is, needless to say, most deceptive. They themselves are bewildered when, seemingly out of a blue sky, they develop a street phobia or functional heart trouble. How is that possible, they ask. They have always managed life perfectly, have been the leaders in their class, the organizers, the model marriage partners or parents. Eventually a situation which they cannot manage in their usual way is bound to occur. And, having no other way to deal with it, their equilibrium is disturbed. The analyst, when getting acquainted with them and the enormous tension under which they operate, rather marvels that they have kept going as long as they have without gross disturbances.

The more we get a feeling for the nature of the shoulds, the more clearly do we see that the difference between them and real moral standards or ideals is not a quantitative but a qualitative one. It was one of Freud's gravest errors to regard the inner dictates (some of the features of which he had seen and described as superego), as constituting morality in general. To begin with, their connection with moral questions is not too close. True enough, the commands for moral perfection do assume a prominent place among the shoulds, for the simple reason that moral questions are important in all our lives. But we cannot separate these particular shoulds from others, just as insistent, which are plainly determined by unconscious arrogance, such as "I should be able to get out of a Sunday-afternoon traffic jam" or "I should be able to paint without laborious training and working." We must also remember that many demands conspicuously lack even a moral pretense, among them "I should be able to get away with anything," "I should always get the better of others," and "I should always be able to get back at others." Only by focusing on the totality of the picture are we able to get the proper perspective on the demands for moral perfection. Like the other shoulds, they are permeated by the spirit of arrogance and aim at enhancing the neurotic's glory and at making him godlike. They are, in this sense, the neurotic counterfeit of normal moral strivings. When one adds to all this the unconscious dishonesty necessarily involved in making blemishes disappear, one recognizes them as an immoral rather than a moral phenomenon. It is necessary to be clear about these differences for the sake of the patient's eventual reorientation from a make-believe world into the development of genuine ideals.

There is one further quality of the shoulds that distinguishes them from genuine standards. It is implied in the previous comments but carries too much weight of its own not to be stated separately and explicitly. That is their *coercive character*. Ideals, too, have an obligating power over our lives. For instance, if among them is the belief in fulfilling responsibilities which we ourselves recognize as such, we try our best to do so even though it may be difficult. To fulfill them is what we ourselves ultimately want, or what we deem right. The wish, the judgment, the decision is ours. And because we are thus at one with ourselves, efforts of this kind give us freedom and strength. In obeying the shoulds, on the other hand, there is just about as much freedom as there is in a "voluntary" contribution or ovation within a dictatorship. In both instances there are quick retributions if we do not measure up to expectations. In the case of the inner dictates, this means violent emotional reactions to nonfulfillment—reactions which traverse the whole range of anxiety, despair, self-condemnation, and self-destructive impulses. To the outsider they appear entirely out of proportion to the provocation. But they are entirely in proportion to what it means to the individual.

Let me cite still another illustration of the coercive character of the inner dictates. Among the inexorable shoulds of one woman was that of having to foresee all contingencies. She was very proud of what she considered her gift of foresight and of preserving her family from dangers through her prescience and prudence. Once she had made elaborate plans to persuade her son to be analyzed. She had failed, however, to consider the influence of a friend of her son's who was antagonistic toward analysis. When she realized that she had left this friend out of her calculations she had a physical shock-reaction, and felt as if the ground had been pulled away from under her. Actually it was more than dubitable whether the friend was as influential as she thought, and also whether she could have engaged his help in any case. The reaction of shock and collapse was entirely due to her sudden realization that she *should* have thought of him. Similarly a woman who was an excellent driver lightly bumped a car ahead of her and was called out of the car by a police officer. She had a sudden feeling of unreality, although the accident was minimal and she was not afraid of policemen whenever she felt in the right.

Reactions of anxiety often escape attention because the customary defenses against anxiety are set going instantaneously. Thus a man who felt he should be a saintlike friend realized that he had been harsh toward a friend when he might have been helpful, and went on a heavy drinking spree. Again a woman who felt that she should always be pleasant and likable was mildly criticized by a friend for not having invited another friend to a party. She felt a fleeting anxiety, was for a moment physically close to fainting, and reacted to that with an increased need for affection—which was her way of checking anxiety. A man, under the duress of unfulfilled shoulds, evolved an acute urge to sleep with some woman. Sexuality for him was a means to feel wanted and to re-establish his sunken self-respect.

No wonder then, in view of such retributions, that the shoulds have a coercive power. A person may function fairly well as long as he lives in accordance with his inner dictates. But he may be thrown out of gear if he is caught between two contradictory shoulds. For instance, one man felt that he should be the ideal physician and give all his time to his patients. But he should also be the ideal husband and give his wife as much time as she needed to be happy. When realizing he could not do both to the full, mild anxiety ensued. It remained mild because he immediately tried to solve the Gordian knot by cutting it with a sword: by determining to settle down in the country. This implied giving up his hopes for further training and thus jeopardizing his whole professional future.

The dilemma was finally solved satisfactorily by analyzing it. But it shows the amount of despair that can be generated by conflicting inner dictates. One woman almost went to pieces because she could not combine being an ideal mother with being an ideal wife, the latter meaning to her being all enduring toward an alcoholic husband.

Naturally such contradictory shoulds render it difficult, if not indeed impossible, to make a rational decision between them because the opposing demands are equally coercive. One patient had sleepless nights because he could not decide whether he should go with his wife on a short vacation or stay in his office and work. Should he measure up to his wife's expectations or to the alleged expectations of his employer? The question as to what *he* wanted most did not enter his mind at all. And, on the basis of the shoulds, the matter simply could not be decided.

A person is never aware either of the full impact of the inner tyranny or of its nature. But there are *great individual differences* in the *attitudes toward this tyranny and the ways of experiencing it*. They range between the opposite poles of compliance and rebellion. While elements of such different attitudes operate in each individual, usually one or the other prevails. To anticipate later distinctions, the attitudes toward and ways of experiencing inner dictates are primarily determined by the greatest appeal life holds for the individual: mastery, love, or freedom. Since such differences will be discussed later,[1] I shall here indicate only briefly how they operate with regard to the shoulds and taboos.

The expansive type, for whom mastery of life is crucial, tends to identify himself with his inner dictates and, whether consciously or unconsciously, to be proud of his standards. He does not question their validity and tries to actualize them in one way or other. He may try to measure up to them in his actual behavior. He should be all things to all people; he should know everything better than anybody else; he should never err; he should never fail in anything he attempts to do—in short, fulfill whatever his particular shoulds are. And, in his mind, he does measure up to his supreme standards. His arrogance may be so great that he does not even consider the possibility of failure, and discards it if it occurs. His arbitrary rightness is so rigid that in his own mind he simply never errs.

The more he is engulfed in his imagination, the less necessary it is for him to make actual efforts. It is sufficient, then, that in his mind he is supremely fearless or honest, no matter how beset he is by fears or how dishonest he actually is. The border line between these two ways of "I should" and "I am" is vague for him—for that matter, probably not too sharp for any of us. The German poet Christian Morgenstern has expressed this concisely in one of his poems. A man was lying in a hospital with a broken leg after having been run over by a truck. He read that in the particular street in which the accident happened trucks were not allowed to drive. And so he arrived at the conclusion that the whole experience was only a dream. For, "sharp as a knife," he concluded that nothing can happen that should not happen. The more a person's imagination prevails over his reasoning, the more the border line disappears and he *is* the model husband, father, citizen, or whatever he should be.

The self-effacing type, for whom love seems to solve all problems, likewise feels that his shoulds constitute a law not to be

---

[1] *Cf.* Chapters 8, 9, 10, 11.

questioned. But when trying—anxiously—to measure up to them, he feels most of the time that he falls pitiably short of fulfilling them. The foremost element in his conscious experience is therefore self-criticism, a feeling of guilt for *not* being the supreme being.

When carried to the extreme, both these attitudes toward the inner dictates render it difficult for a person to analyze himself. Tending toward the extreme of self-righteousness may prevent him from seeing any flaws in himself. And tending toward the other extreme—that of too readily feeling guilty—entails the danger of insights into shortcomings having a crushing rather than a liberating effect.

The resigned type, finally, to whom the idea of "freedom" appeals more than anything else, is, of the three, most prone to rebel against his inner tyranny. Because of the very importance which freedom—or his version of it—has for him, he is hypersensitive to any coercion. He may rebel in a somewhat passive way. Then everything that he feels he should do, whether it concerns a piece of work or reading a book or having sexual relations with his wife, turns—in his mind—into a coercion, arouses conscious or unconscious resentment, and in consequence makes him listless. If what is to be done is done at all, it is done under the strain produced by the inner resistance.

He may rebel against his shoulds in a more active way. He may try to throw them all overboard, and sometimes go to the opposite extreme by insisting upon doing only what he pleases when he pleases. The rebellion may take violent forms, and then often is a rebellion of despair. If he can't be the ultimate of piety, chastity, sincerity, then he will be thoroughly "bad," be promiscuous, tell lies, affront others.

Sometimes a person who usually complies with the shoulds may go through a phase of rebellion. It is usually then directed against external restrictions. J. P. Marquand has described such temporary rebellions in a masterly way. He has shown us how easily they can be put down, for the very reason that the restricting external standards have a mighty ally in the internal dictates. And then afterward the individual is left dull and listless.

Finally, others may go through alternating phases of self-castigating "goodness" and a wild protest against any standards. To the observant friend such people may present an insoluble puzzle. At times they are offensively irresponsible in sexual or financial matters, and at others they show highly developed moral sensibilities. So the friend who has just been despairing of their having any sense of decency is reassured about their being fine persons after all, only to be thrown into severe doubts again shortly thereafter. In others there may be a constant shuttling between an "I should" and "no, I won't." "I should pay a debt. No, why should I?" "I should keep to a diet. No, I won't." Often these people give the impression of spontaneity and mistake their contradictory attitudes toward their shoulds for "freedom."

Whatever the prevailing attitude, a great deal of the process is always externalized; it is experienced as going on between self and others. Variations in this regard concern the particular aspect that is externalized, and the way in which it is done. Roughly, a person may primarily impose his standards upon others and make relentless demands as to *their* perfection. The more he feels himself to be the measure of all things, the more he insists—not upon general perfection but upon his particular norms being measured up to. The failure of others to do so arouses his contempt or anger. Still more irrational is the fact that his own irritation with himself for not being, at any moment and under all conditions, what he should be may be turned outward. Thus, for instance, when he is not the perfect lover, or is caught in a lie, he may turn angrily against those he failed and build up a case against them.

Again he may primarily experience his expectations of himself as coming from others. And, whether these others actually do expect something or whether he merely thinks they do, their expectations then turn into demands to be fulfilled. In analysis he feels that the analyst expects the impossible from him. He attributes to the analyst his own feelings that he should always be productive, should always have a dream to report, should always talk about what he thinks the analyst wants him to discuss, should always be appreciative of help and show it by getting better.

If he believes in this way that others are expecting or demanding things of him, he may, again, respond in two different ways. He may try to anticipate or guess at their expectations and be eager to live up to them. In that case he usually also anticipates that they would condemn him or drop him at a moment's notice if he fails. Or, if he is hypersensitive to coercion, he feels that they are imposing upon him, meddling in his affairs, pushing him or coercing him. He then minds it bitterly, or even openly rebels against them. He may object to giving Christmas presents, because they are expected. He will be at his office or at any appointment just a little later than expected. He will forget anniversaries, letters, or any favor for which he has been asked. He may forget a visit to relatives just because his mother had asked him to make it, although he liked them and meant to see them. He will overreact to any request made. He will then be less afraid of the criticism of others than resentful of it. His vivid and unfair self-criticism also becomes tenaciously externalized. He then feels that others are unfair in their judgment of him or that they always suspect ulterior motives. Or, if his rebellion is more aggressive, he will flaunt his defiance and believe that he does not in the least care what they think of him.

The overreaction to requests made is a good lead to recognizing the inner demands. Reactions which strike us ourselves as being out of proportion may be particularly helpful in self-analysis. The following illustration, in part self-analysis, may be useful in showing also certain faulty conclusions we may draw from self-observations. It concerns a busy executive whom I saw occasionally. He was asked by phone whether he could go to the pier and meet a refugee writer coming from Europe. He had always admired this writer and had met him socially on a visit to Europe. Since his time was jammed with conferences and other work, it would actually have been unfeasible to comply with this request, particularly since it might have involved waiting on the pier for hours. As he realized later on, he could have reacted in two ways, both of them sensible. He could either have said that he would think it over and see whether he could make it, or he could have declined with regret and asked whether there was anything else he could do for the writer. Instead he reacted with immediate irritation and said abruptly that he was too busy and never would call for anybody at the pier.

Soon after this he regretted his response, and later went to some length to find out where the writer was located so that he could help him if necessary. He not only regretted the incident; he also felt puzzled. Did he not think as highly of the writer as he had thought he did? He felt sure that he did. Was he not as friendly and helpful as he believed himself to be? If so, was he irritated because he was put on the spot in being asked to prove his friendliness and helpfulness?

Here he was on a good track. The mere fact of his being able to question the genuineness of his generosity was for him quite a step to take—for, in his idealized image, he was the bene-factor of mankind. It was, however, more than he could digest at this juncture. He rejected this possibility by remembering that afterward he was eager to offer and give help. But while closing one avenue in his thought he suddenly hit upon another clue. When he *offered* help the initiative was his, but the first time he had been *asked* to do something. He then realized that he had felt the request as an unfair imposition. Provided he had known about the writer's arrival, he would certainly have con-sidered on his own the possibility of meeting him at the boat. He now thought of many similar incidents in which he had reacted irritably to a favor asked and realized that apparently he felt as imposition or coercion many things which in actual fact were mere requests or suggestions. He also thought of his irritability over disagreements or criticism. The conclusion he arrived at was that he was a bully and wanted to dominate. I mention this here because reactions of this kind are easily mis-taken for tendencies to dominate. What he had seen on his own was his hypersensitivity to coercion and to criticism. He could not stand coercion because he felt in a strait jacket anyhow. And he could not stand criticism because he was his own worst critic. In this context we also could pick up the track he had abandoned when questioning his friendliness. To a large ex-tent he was helpful because he *should* be helpful and not because of his rather abstract love for humanity. His attitude toward concrete individuals was much more divided than he realized. Thus any request plunged him into an inner conflict: he should accede to it and be very generous and also he should not allow anybody to coerce him. The irritability was an expression of feeling caught in a dilemma which at that time was insoluble.

The *effects* the shoulds have on a person's personality and life vary to some extent with his way of responding to them or experiencing them. But certain effects show inevitably and regularly, though to a greater or lesser degree. The shoulds always produce a feeling of *strain*, which is all the greater the more a person tries to actualize his shoulds in his behavior. He may feel that he stands on tiptoe all the time, and may suffer from a chronic exhaustion. Or he may feel vaguely cramped, tense, or hemmed in. Or, if his shoulds coincide with attitudes culturally expected of him, he may feel merely an almost imperceptible strain. It may be strong enough, however, to contribute to a desire in an otherwise active person to retire from activities or obligations.

Furthermore, because of externalizations, the shoulds always contribute to *disturbances in human relations* in one way or another. The most general disturbance on this score is hypersensitivity to criticism. Being merciless toward himself, he cannot help experiencing any criticism on the part of others— whether actual or merely anticipated, whether friendly or unfriendly—as being just as condemnatory as his own. We shall understand the intensity of this sensitivity better when we realize how much he hates himself for any lagging behind his self-imposed standards.[2] Otherwise the kinds of disturbance in human relations depend upon the kind of prevailing externalization. They may render him too critical and harsh of others or too apprehensive, too defiant, or too compliant.

Most important of all, the shoulds further *impair the spontaneity* of feelings, wishes, thoughts, and beliefs—i.e., the ability

---

[2] *Cf.* Chapter 5, Self-Hate and Self-Contempt.

to feel his own feelings, etc., and to express them. The person, then, can at best be "spontaneously compulsive" (to quote a patient) and express "freely" what he *should* feel, wish, think, or believe. We are accustomed to think that we cannot control feelings but only behavior. In dealing with others we can enforce labor but we cannot force anybody to love his work. Just so, we are accustomed to think that we can force ourselves to act as if we were not suspicious but we cannot enforce a feeling of confidence. This remains essentially true. And, if we needed a new proof, analysis could supply it. But if the shoulds issue an order as to feelings, imagination waves its magic wand and the border line between what we *should* feel and what we *do* feel evaporates. We consciously believe or feel then as we should believe or feel.

This appears in analysis when the spurious certainty of pseudofeelings is shaken, and the patient then goes through a period of bewildering uncertainty which is painful but constructive. A person for instance who believed she liked everybody because she should do so may then ask: Do I really like my husband, my pupils, my patients? Or anybody at that? And at that point the questions are unanswerable because only now can all the fears, suspicions, and resentments that have always prevented a free flow of positive feelings, and yet were covered up by the shoulds, be tackled. I call this period constructive because it represents a beginning search for the genuine.

The extent to which spontaneous wishes can be crushed by the inner dictates is amazing. To quote from a patient's letter written after she discovered the tyranny of her shoulds:

I saw that I was quite simply unable to *want* anything, not even death! And certainly not "life." Until now I had thought my trouble was just that I was unable to *do* things; unable to give up my dream, unable to gather up my own things, unable to accept or control my irritability, unable to make myself more human, whether by sheer will power, patience, or grief.

Now for the first time I saw it—I was literally unable to *feel* anything. (Yes, for all my famous supersensitivity!) How well I knew pain—every pore of me clogged with inward rage, self-pity, self-contempt, and despair for the last six years and over and over again and again! Yet I saw it now—all was negative, reactive, compulsive, *all imposed from without;* inside there was absolutely nothing of mine.[3]

The creation of make-believe feelings is most striking in those whose idealized image lies in the direction of goodness, love, and saintliness. They should be considerate, grateful, sympathetic, generous, loving, and so in their minds they *have* all these qualities. They talk and go through the motions *as if* they simply were that good and loving. And, since they are convinced of it, they even can be temporarily convincing to others. But of course these make-believe feelings have no depth and no sustaining power. Under favorable circumstances they may be fairly consistent and then, naturally, are not questioned. Madame Wu, in *Pavilion of Women,* started to question the genuineness of her feelings only when difficulties arose in the family situation and when she met a man who was straight and honest in his emotional life.

More often the shallowness of the made-to-order feelings shows in other ways. They may disappear easily. Love readily makes way for indifference, or for resentment and contempt, when pride or vanity is hurt. In these instances people usually do not ask themselves: "How does it happen that my feelings or opinions change so easily?" They simply feel that here is another person who has disappointed their faith in humanity, or that they never "really" trusted him. All of this does not mean that they may not have slumbering capacities for strong and alive feelings, but what appears on more conscious levels often is a massive pretense with very little that is genuine in it. In the long run they give the impression of something unsubstantial, elusive, or—to use a good slang word—of being phonies. An irruptive anger often is the only feeling that is really fair.

At the other extreme, feelings of callousness and ruthlessness can also be exaggerated. The taboos on feelings of tenderness, sympathy, and confidence can be just as great in some neurotics as the taboos on hostility and vindictiveness are in others. These people feel that they should be able to live without any close personal relations, so they believe that they do not need them.

---

[3] From "Finding the Real Self," *American Journal of Psychoanalysis,* 1949. *A Letter,* with Foreword by Karen Horney.

They should not enjoy anything; so they believe they do not care. Their emotional life then is less distorted than plainly impoverished.

Naturally the emotional pictures engendered by the inner commands are not always as streamlined as in these two extreme groups. The orders issued can be contradictory. You should be so sympathetic that you shun no sacrifices whatever, but you should also be so coldblooded that you can carry out any act of vengeance. As a result, a person is convinced at times that he is callous and at others that he is extremely kindhearted. In other people so many feelings and wishes are checked that a general emotional deadness ensues. There may be, for instance, a taboo on wanting anything for themselves, which puts the lid on all alive wishes and creates pervasive inhibitions about doing anything for themselves. Then, partly because of these inhibitions, they develop just as pervasive claims on the grounds of which they feel entitled to have everything in life presented on a silver platter. And then the resentment over the frustration of such claims may be choked off by a dictate that they should put up with life.

We are less aware of the harm done our feelings by these pervasive shoulds than of other damage inflicted by them. Yet it is actually the heaviest price we pay for trying to mold ourselves into perfection. Feelings are the most alive part of ourselves; if they are put under a dictatorial regime, a profound uncertainty is created in our essential being which must affect adversely our relations to everything inside and outside ourselves.

We can hardly overrate the *intensity* of the impact of the inner dictates. The more the drive to actualize his idealized self prevails in a person, the more the shoulds become the sole motor force moving him, driving him, whipping him into action. When a patient who is still far removed from his real self discovers some of the cramping effects of his shoulds, he may nevertheless be entirely unable to consider relinquishing them because without them—so he feels—he would or could not do anything. He may sometimes express this concern in terms of the belief that one cannot make other people do the "right" thing except by force, which is an externalized expression of his inner experience. The shoulds then acquire a subjective value for the patient with which he can dispense only when he experiences the existence of other spontaneous forces in himself.

When we realize the enormous coercive power of the shoulds we must raise one question, the answer to which we shall discuss in the fifth chapter: what does it do to a person when he recognizes that he cannot measure up to his inner dictates? To anticipate the answer briefly: then he starts to hate and despise himself. We cannot in fact understand the full impact of the shoulds unless we see the extent to which they are interwoven with self-hate. It is the threat of a punitive self-hate that lurks behind them, that truly makes them a regime of terror.

CHAPTER 4

NEUROTIC PRIDE

WITH ALL his strenuous efforts toward perfection and with all his belief in perfection attained, the neurotic does not gain what he most desperately needs: self-confidence and self-respect. Even though godlike in his imagination, he still lacks the earthy self-confidence of a simple shepherd. The great positions to which he may rise, the fame he may acquire, will render him arrogant but will not bring him inner security. He still feels at bottom unwanted, is easily hurt, and needs incessant confirmation of his value. He may feel strong and significant as long as he wields power and influence and is supported by praise and deference. But all of these feelings of elation collapse easily when, in a strange environment, this support is lacking; when he incurs failure; or when he is by himself. The kingdom of heaven does not come through external gestures.

Let us survey what happens to self-confidence in the course of a neurotic development. Apparently, for self-confidence to grow, the child needs help from the outside. He needs warmth, feeling welcome, care, protection, an atmosphere of confidence, encouragement in his activities, constructive discipline. These factors given, he will develop "basic confidence," to use a well-chosen term of Marie Rasey's [1] which includes both confidence in others and in self.

Instead, a combination of injurious influences prevents a child's healthy growth. We have discussed these factors and their general influence in the first chapter. Here I want to add a few more reasons which render it specifically difficult for him to arrive at a proper self-evaluation. A blind adoration may inflate his feeling of significance. He may feel wanted, liked, and appreciated not for what he is but merely for satisfying his parents' needs for adoration, prestige, or power. A rigid regime of perfectionist standards may evoke in him a feeling of inferiority for not measuring up to such demands. Misdemeanors or bad marks at school may be severely reprimanded, while good behavior or good marks are taken for granted. Moves toward autonomy or independence may be ridiculed. All these factors, in addition to a general lack of genuine warmth and interest, give him the feeling of being unloved and unworthy—or at any rate of not being worth anything unless he is something he is not.

Moreover the neurotic development, initiated by the early unfavorable constellation, weakens him at the core of his being. He becomes alienated from himself and divided. His self-idealization is an attempt to remedy the damage done by lifting himself in his mind above the crude reality of himself and others. And, as in the stories of the devil's pact, he gets all the glory in imagination and sometimes in reality. But instead of solid self-confidence he gets a glittering gift of most questionable value: neurotic pride. The two feel and look so much alike that an understandable confusion is created in most minds about their differences. A definition in an old edition of Webster, for instance, says that pride is self-esteem, based either on real or imagined merits. The distinction is made between real and imagined merits, but they are both called "self-esteem," as if this difference did not greatly matter.

The confusion also develops through the fact that most patients regard self-confidence as a mysterious quality arising from nowhere but most desirable to have. It is but logical then that

---

[1] Marie I. Rasey, "Psychoanalysis and Education," paper read before the Association for Advancement of Psychoanalysis, 1946.

they expect the analyst to instill it into them in some way or other. Which always reminds me of a cartoon in which a rabbit and a mouse got an injection of courage; they then grew to five times their ordinary size, were bold and full of indomitable fighting spirit. What the patients do not know—and are anxious indeed not to realize—is the strict cause-and-effect relation between existing personal assets and the feeling of self-confidence. This relation is not any less definite than the way in which the financial status of a person depends upon his properties, his savings, or his earning capacity. If these factors are satisfactory, a person will have a feeling of economic security. Or, to take another example, the fisherman's confidence rests on such concrete factors as his boat being in good shape, his nets being mended, his knowledge of weather and water conditions, and his muscular strength.

What are regarded as personal assets vary to some degree with the culture in which we live. For Western civilization they include such qualities or attributes as having autonomous convictions and acting upon them, having the self-reliance that stems from tapping our own resources, assuming responsibility for ourselves, taking a realistic appraisal of our assets, liabilities and limitations, having strength and directness of feelings, and having the capacity for establishing and cultivating good human relations. The well-functioning of these factors shows subjectively in a feeling of self-confidence. To the extent that they are impaired, self-confidence will be shaky.

Healthy pride likewise is based on substantial attributes. It may be a warranted high regard for special achievements, such as feeling proud of a deed of moral courage or of a job well done. Or it may be a more comprehensive feeling of our own value, a quiet feeling of dignity.

Considering the extreme sensitivity of a neurotic pride to hurt, we are inclined to consider it as a rank growth of healthy pride. The essential difference, however, as we have so often before found true, is not one of quantity but of quality. Neurotic pride is by comparison unsubstantial, and it is based on entirely different factors, all of which belong to or support the glorified version of oneself. They may be extraneous assets—prestige values—or they may consist of attributes and faculties which one arrogates to oneself.

Of the varieties of neurotic pride that in prestige value seems the most normal. In our civilization it is an average reaction to be proud of having an attractive girl, of coming from a respectable family, of being native born, a Southerner, or New Englander, belonging to a political or professional group enjoying prestige, meeting important people, being popular, having a good car or address.

This kind of pride is the least typical for neurosis. To many people with considerable neurotic difficulties these things mean no more than they do to the comparatively healthy person; to many others they mean distinctly less, if indeed anything. But there are some who have such a heavy investment of neurotic pride in these prestige values, and for whom they are so crucial, that their lives revolve around them and they often fritter away their best energies in their service. For these people it is an absolute must to be associated with groups that carry prestige, to be affiliated with prominent institutions. Of course all their hectic activities are rationalized in terms of genuine interest or the legitimate wish to get ahead. Anything that accrues to this prestige then may evoke real elation; any failure of the group to enhance such a person's prestige, or any diminution of the prestige of the group itself, provokes all the hurt-pride reactions which we shall discuss presently. For example, a member of someone's family not "making good," or being mentally ill, may be a heavy blow to his pride, mostly hidden behind superficial concern for the relative. Again there are many women who prefer to abstain from going to a restaurant or a theater than to go without a male escort.

All of this looks similar to what anthropologists tell us about certain so-called primitive people among whom the individual primarily is and feels as a part of the group. Pride then is invested not in personal matters but in institutions and group activities. But while these processes seem to be similar, they are essentially different. The main difference is that the neurotic is at bottom unrelated to the group. He does not feel part of it, does not have a feeling of belonging, but rather uses it for his personal prestige.

Although a person may be consumed by thinking of and chasing after prestige, and although in his mind he rises and falls with his prestige, this often is not clearly seen as a neurotic problem to be analyzed—either because it is such a common occurrence, or because it looks like a cultural pattern, or because the analyst himself is not free from this disease. A disease it is, and a devastating one at that, because it makes people opportunistic and in this way mars their integrity. Far from being close to normal, it is on the contrary indicative of a severe disturbance. Indeed it occurs only in those who are so profoundly alienated from themselves that even their pride is largely invested outside of themselves.

Neurotic pride furthermore rests on the attributes which a person arrogates to himself in his imagination, on all those belonging to his particular idealized image. Here the peculiar nature of neurotic pride comes into clear relief. The neurotic is not proud of the human being he actually is. Knowing his wrong perspective on himself, we are not surprised that his pride blots out difficulties and limitations. But it goes further than this. Mostly he is not even proud of his existing assets. He may be but hazily aware of them; he may actually deny them. But even if he is cognizant of them they carry no weight for him. For instance, if the analyst calls to his attention his great capacity for work or the tenacity he has actually demonstrated in making his way in life, or points out that—his difficulties notwithstanding—he did write a good book, the patient may literally or figuratively shrug his shoulders and pass over the praise lightly, with noticeable indifference. He especially has no appreciation for all that is "merely" striving and not accomplishment. He rather discards, for instance, the honest striving to get to the roots of his trouble, which he has shown in making one serious attempt after another to take up analysis or to analyze himself.

Peer Gynt may serve as a famous illustration from literature. He does not make much of his existing assets, his great intelligence, spirit of adventure, vitality. But he is proud of the one thing he is not, of "being himself." Actually he is—in his mind —not himself but his idealized self, with unlimited "freedom" and unlimited powers. (He has lifted his boundless egocentricity to the dignity of a life philosophy with his maxim "To thyself be true," which—as Ibsen points out—is a glorification of "To thyself be enough.")

There are many Peer Gynts among our patients, anxious to preserve their illusions of being a saint, a mastermind, of having absolute poise, etc.; and they feel as if they would lose their "individuality" if they budged an inch from these estimates of themselves. Imagination itself may become of supreme value, regardless of the use to which it is put, since it allows its bearer to look down with contempt on the drab and pedestrian people who are concerned with truth. The patient of course would not say "truth" but would speak in vague terms of "reality." One patient for instance, whose claims were so grandiose as to expect the world to be at his service, at first took a clear stand toward this claim, calling it absurd and even degrading. But the next day he had retrieved his pride: the claims were now a "magnificent mental creation." The true meaning of irrational claims had submerged and pride in imagination was triumphant.

More frequently, pride is not specifically attached to imagination but to all mental processes: intellect, reason, and will power as well. The infinite powers the neurotic ascribes to himself are, after all, powers of the mind. No wonder, then, that he is fascinated by it and proud of it. The idealized image is a product of his imagination. But this is not something which is created overnight. Incessant work of intellect and imagination, most of it unconscious, goes into maintaining the private fictitious world through rationalizations, justifications, externalizations, reconciling irreconcilables—in short, through finding ways to make things appear different from what they are. The more a person is alienated from himself, the more his mind becomes supreme reality. ("A person has no existence apart from my thought; I have no existence apart from my thought.") Like the Lady of Shalott, he cannot see the reality directly but only through a mirror. More accurately: he sees in the mirror only *his thoughts* about the world and himself. This is why the pride in intellect, or rather in the supremacy of the mind, is not restricted to those engaged in intellectual pursuits but is a regular occurrence in all neurosis.

Pride also is invested in faculties and prerogatives to which the neurotic feels entitled. Thus he may be proud of an illusive invulnerability which, on the physical plane, means never to incur illness or any physical damage and, on the psychic side, never to feel hurt. Another may be proud of good luck, of being "the darling of the gods." It is a matter of pride then not to fall ill in a malaria district, to win in gambling, or to have fair weather for an excursion.

It is indeed a matter of pride in all neuroses to assert one's claims effectively. Those who feel entitled to get something for nothing feel proud if they can manipulate others into lending them money, running their errands, giving them medical treatment without charge. Others, feeling entitled to manage other people's lives, experience it as a blow to their pride if a protégé of theirs does not follow a piece of advice immediately, or if he does something on his own initiative without having asked their advice first. Still others feel entitled to exoneration as soon as they indicate that they are in some distress. They are proud then if they are able to elicit sympathy and forgiveness and they feel offended if the other person remains critical.

The neurotic's pride in measuring up to his inner dictates may on the surface look more substantial, but it is in fact just as rickety as other kinds of pride since it is inevitably interwoven with pretenses. The mother who is proud of being the perfect mother usually is so in her imagination only. The person who is proud of his unique honesty may not tell obvious lies but is usually pervaded by unconscious and semiconscious dishonesties. Those who are proud of their unselfishness may not be openly demanding but will impose upon others through their helplessness and suffering, besides mistaking their taboos on healthy self-assertion for the virtue of humility. In addition the shoulds themselves may have a merely subjective merit in that they serve neurotic purposes but no objective value. Thus, for instance, the neurotic may be proud of not asking and not accepting any help even though it would be more sensible to do so—a problem well known in social work. Some may be proud of driving a hard bargain, others of never bargaining at all—depending on whether they must always be on the winning side or should never be out for their own advantage.

Lastly, it may be merely the very loftiness and severity of the compulsive standards which are invested with pride. The fact of knowing "the good" and "the evil" makes them godlike, just as the serpent promised it would to Adam and Eve. A neurotic person's very high standards make him feel that he is a moral wonder to be proud of, regardless of how he actually is and behaves. He may have recognized in analysis his ravaging hunger for prestige, his poor sense of truth, his vindictiveness; but all of that does not make him any more humble or make him feel any less a superior moral being. To him these actual flaws do not count. His pride is not in being moral, but in knowing how he should be. Even though temporarily he may have recognized the futility of his self-reproaches, or even at times have been terrified at their viciousness, he still may not relent in his demands on self. What does it matter, after all, if he suffers? Is not his suffering another proof of his superior moral sensibilities? Hence to sustain this pride seems worth the price.

When we proceed from these general viewpoints to the particulars of individual neuroses, the picture at first sight is confusing. There is simply nothing that may not be invested with pride. What is a shining asset to one person is a disgraceful liability to the next. One person is proud of being rude to people; another is ashamed of anything that could be construed as rudeness and is proud of his sensitiveness to others. One is proud of his ability to bluff his way through life; still another is ashamed of any trace of bluffing. Here is one who is proud of trusting people and there is one equally proud of distrusting them—and so forth and so on.

But this diversity is bewildering only as long as we regard the special kinds of pride out of the context of the whole personality. As soon as we see each of them from the perspective of the individual's total character structure, an ordering principle emerges: his need to be proud of himself is so imperative that he cannot tolerate the idea of being in the clutches of blind needs; so he uses his imagination to turn these needs into virtues, to transform them into assets of which he can be proud. But only those compulsive needs which serve his drive to actualize his idealized self undergo this transformation. Conversely, he tends to suppress, deny, despise those which obstruct this drive.

His capacity for this unconscious reversal of values is perfectly amazing. The best medium through which to present it would be cartoons. There it could be shown most vividly how people afflicted with some undesirable trait take a brush, paint over the trait with beautiful colors, and present with blustering pride the picture of their assets. Thus inconsistency turns into unlimited freedom, blind rebellion against an existing code of morals into being above common prejudice, a taboo on doing anything for oneself into saintly unselfishness, a need to appease into sheer goodness, dependency into love, exploiting others into astuteness. A capacity to assert egocentric claims appears as strength, vindictiveness as justice, frustrating techniques as a most intelligent weapon, aversion to work as "successfully resisting the deadly habit of work," and so on.

These unconscious processes often remind me of the Trolls in Ibsen's *Peer Gynt,* for whom "black looks white, and ugly fair, big looks little, and filthy clean." Most interestingly, Ibsen accounts for this reversal of values in a way similar to our own. As long as you live in a self-sufficient dream world like Peer Gynt, Ibsen says, you cannot be true to yourself. Between the two there is no bridge. They are too different in principle to allow for any compromise solution. And if you are not true to yourself, but live an egocentric life of imagined grandeur, then you will play ducks and drakes with your values too. Your scale of values will be just as topsy-turvy as is that of the Trolls. And this indeed is the tenor of everything we have discussed in this chapter. As soon as we go off on the search for glory we stop being concerned about the truth of ourselves. *Neurotic pride, in all its forms, is false pride.*

Once having grasped the principle that only those trends are invested with pride that serve to actualize the idealized self, the analyst will be alert to detect hidden pride in any position which is tenaciously adhered to. The connection between the subjective value of a trait and neurotic pride in it seems to be a regular one. Recognizing either one of these factors, the analyst can safely conclude that in all probability the other one will be there too. Sometimes the one, sometimes the other will come into focus first. Thus a patient at the beginning of analytical work may express pride in his cynicism or in his power to frustrate others. And although at this juncture the analyst does not understand the meaning that the given factor has for the patient, he can be reasonably certain of its playing a significant part of the particular neurosis.

It is necessary for therapy that the analyst gradually gain a clear picture of the particular kinds of pride operating in each individual patient. Naturally a patient cannot regard a drive, an attitude, or a reaction as a problem to be tackled as long as he is unconsciously or consciously proud of it. A patient may, for instance, have become aware of his need to outwit others. The analyst may feel it self-evident that this is a problematic trend to be tackled, and to be overcome eventually, because he considers the interest of the patient's real self. He realizes the trend's compulsive character, the disturbance it creates in human relations, the waste of energies which could be employed for constructive purposes. The patient on the other hand, without being aware of it, may feel that just this very capacity to outwit others makes him a superior person; and he is secretly proud of it. He is interested therefore not in analyzing the tendency to outwit but in the factors in himself which interfere with his doing it to perfection. As long as this difference in evaluation is under cover, analyst and patient will move on different planes and analyze at cross-purposes.

Neurotic pride resting on such shaky foundations is as insubstantial as a card house and, like the latter, collapses at the slightest draft. In terms of subjective experience it makes a person *vulnerable*, and does so exactly to the extent that he is obsessed by pride. It can be hurt as easily from within as from without. The two typical reactions to hurt pride are shame and humiliation. We will feel ashamed if we do, think, or feel something that violates our pride. And we will feel humiliated if others do something that hurts our pride, or fail to do what our pride requires of them. In any reaction of shame or humiliation that seems out of place or out of proportion we must answer these two questions: What in the particular situation has aroused this response? And what special underlying pride has been hurt by it? They are closely interrelated, and neither can be given a quick answer. The analyst may know, for instance, that masturbation provokes excessive shame in a person who in general has a rational, sensible attitude to the problem and would not disapprove of it in others. There, at least, the shame-provoking factor seems to be clear. But is it? Masturbation may mean different things to different people, and the analyst cannot know offhand which of the many factors that may be involved in masturbation is relevant to arousing the shame. Does it mean for the particular patient a sexual activity that is degraded because it is separate from love? Is the satisfaction attained greater than in sexual intercourse, and thereby disturbing to the image of being geared only to love? Is it a question of the concomitant fantasies? Does it mean the admission of having any needs? Is it too much self-indulgence for a stoical person? Does it mean loss of self-control? Only to the extent that the analyst grasps the relevance of these factors for the patient can he then raise the second question as to the kind of pride that has been hurt by masturbation.

I have yet another illustration to show the necessity for accuracy with regard to the factors arousing shame or humiliation. Many unmarried women are deeply ashamed of having a lover, although in their conscious thinking they are quite unconventional. In the case of such a woman it is of importance to ascertain first whether her pride is hurt by the particular lover. If so, has the shame to do with his not being sufficiently glamorous or devoted? With her allowing him to treat her badly? With her being dependent on him? Or does the shame pertain to the fact of having a lover at all, regardless of his status and personality? If so, is it for her a matter of prestige to be married? Is the situation of having a lover, but remaining single, a proof of being unworthy and unattractive? Or should she be above sexual desires, like a vestal virgin?

Often the very same incident may elicit either reaction—that of shame or that of humiliation—the one or the other prevailing. A man is rejected by a girl; he can either feel humiliated by her and react with a "Who does she think she is?" or he can feel ashamed that his charm or his virility seems not to be absolutely compelling. A comment made in a discussion falls flat; he can either feel humiliated by "these darned fools who do not understand me" or he can feel ashamed of his own awkwardness. Somebody takes advantage of him; he can either feel humiliated by the exploiter or ashamed of himself for not having asserted his own interests. His children are not brilliant or popular; he can feel humiliated by this fact, and take it out on them, or he can feel with shame that in some way or other he has failed them.

These observations point to the necessity of reorienting our thinking. We are inclined to put too great an emphasis on the actual situation, and to think that it determines our reactions. We are inclined, for instance, to regard it as "natural" for a person to react with *shame* if he is caught in a lie. But then the next fellow does not feel that way at all; instead he feels *humiliated* by the one who found him out and turns against him. Our reactions are thus determined not merely by the situation but even more by our own neurotic needs.

More specifically, the same principle operates in the reaction of shame or humiliation as in the transformation of values. In aggressive expansive types, reactions of shame can be strikingly absent. Even the minute scrutiny of the analytical searchlight may not detect any traces at the beginning. These are people who either live so much in the imagination that in their own mind they are without blemish, or they have so covered themselves with a protective layer of militant rightness that everything they do, *eo ipso, is* right. Injuries to their pride can come only from the outside. Any questioning of their motivations, any uncovering of a handicap is felt as an insult. They can but suspect malicious intent in any person who does this to them.

In self-effacing types, reactions of humiliation are by far overshadowed by feelings of shame. On the surface they are subdued and preoccupied with an anxious concern to measure up to their shoulds. But for reasons to be discussed later, they focus rather on their failure to be the ultimate of perfection and hence feel easily ashamed. The analyst can therefore, from the prevalence of one or the other reaction, draw tentative conclusions as to relevant trends in the underlying structure.

Thus far the connections between pride and the reactions to its hurt are simple and direct. And, since they are typical, it would seem easy for the analyst or for the person analyzing himself to draw inferences from one to the other. Recognizing a special brand of neurotic pride, he can be alert to the kind of provocation liable to produce shame or humiliation. And, vice versa, the occurrence of these reactions would stimulate him to discover the underlying pride and to examine its specific nature. What complicates matters is the fact that these reactions may be blurred by several factors. A person's pride may be extremely vulnerable, but he does not consciously express any feeling of hurt. Self-righteousness, as we have already mentioned, can prohibit the feelings of shame. Moreover a pride in invulnerability may forbid him to admit to himself that he feels hurt. A god may show wrath at the imperfection of mortals, but he *just is not hurt* by a boss or a taxi driver; he should be big enough to overlook it and strong enough to take everything in his stride. "Insults" therefore hurt him in a twofold way: feeling humiliated by others and feeling ashamed of the very fact of his being hurt. Such a person is in an almost permanent dilemma: he is vulnerable to an absurd degree, but his pride does not allow him to be vulnerable at all. This inner condition greatly contributes to a diffuse irritability.

The issue may also be blurred because the direct reactions to hurt pride can be automatically transformed into feelings other than shame or humiliation. It may essentially hurt our pride if a husband or a lover is interested in another woman, does not remember our wishes, or is preoccupied with his work or hobbies. But all we may consciously feel is grief over unrequited love. A slight may be felt merely as disappointment. Feelings of shame may appear in our awareness as vague uneasiness, as embarrassment, or, more specifically, as feelings of guilt. This last transformation is of particular importance because it allows for a rather quick understanding of certain guilt-feelings. If, for instance, a person full of pervasive unconscious pretenses is guiltily perturbed by a comparatively harmless and inconsequential lie, we may safely assume that he is more concerned with appearing than with being honest; and that his pride is hurt by not having been able to maintain the fiction of ultimate and absolute veracity. Or if an egocentric person feels guilty about some inconsiderateness, we have to ask whether this guilt feeling is not shame about having besmirched the halo of goodness rather than an honest regret for not having been as sensitive to others as he would like to be.

Furthermore, it may be that none of these reactions, whether direct or transformed, is consciously felt; we may merely be aware of our reactions to these reactions. Prominent among such "secondary" reactions are rage and fear. That any hurt to our pride may provoke vindictive hostility is well known. It goes all the way from dislike to hate, from irritability to anger to a blind murderous rage. Sometimes the connection between rage and pride is easily enough established—for the observer. For instance, a person is enraged against his boss who he feels has treated him cavalierly, or against a taxi driver who has cheated him—incidents which, at most, would account for annoyance. The person himself would only be aware of a justified anger at the bad behavior of others. The observer, let us say the analyst, would see that his pride was hurt by the incidents, that he felt humiliated and then reacted with rage. The patient may accept this interpretation as most likely accounting for the excessive reaction, or he may insist that his reaction was not excessive at all and that his anger was a warranted reaction to the wickedness or stupidity of others.

While of course not all irrational hostility is due to hurt pride, it does play a greater part than is generally assumed. The analyst always should be alert to this possibility, particularly concerning the patient's reaction to him, to interpretations, and to the whole analytic situation. The connection with hurt pride is more easily discernible if the hostility has ingredients of derogation, contempt, or intent to humiliate. What operates here is the straight law of retaliation. The patient, without knowing it, has felt humiliated and returns in kind. After such incidents it is sheer waste of time to talk about the patient's hostility. The analyst must go straight to the point by raising a question as to what has registered in the patient's mind as humiliation. Sometimes impulses to humiliate the analyst, or thoughts about it unaccompanied by any effect, appear right at the beginning of the analysis, before the analyst has touched any sore spot. In this case it is likely that the patient feels unconsciously humiliated by the very fact of being analyzed, and it is the analyst's job to bring this connection into clear focus.

Naturally, what happens in analysis also happens outside. And if we thought more often of the possibility that offensive behavior may stem from hurt pride, we would save ourselves many painful or even heartbreaking troubles. Thus, when a friend or relative behaves in an obnoxious fashion after we have liberally helped him, we should not be upset over his ingratitude but consider how badly his pride may have been hurt by accepting help. And, according to circumstances, we might either talk to him about it or try ourselves to help him in a way that saves his face. Likewise, in the case of a generally contemptuous attitude toward people, it is not enough to resent a person's arrogance; we must also regard him as someone who goes through life with a raw skin because of being pervasively vulnerable through his pride.

What is less well known is that the same hostility, hate, or contempt may be directed against ourselves if we feel we have offended our own pride. Violent self-reproaches are not the only form this rage at self may assume. Vindictive self-hatred has so many far-reaching implications, indeed, that we would lose the thread if we discussed it now among the reactions to hurt pride. We shall therefore wait to discuss it in the following chapter.

Fear, anxiety, panic may occur as reactions both to anticipated humiliations or to ones that have taken place. Anticipatory fears may concern examinations, public performances, social gatherings, or a date; in such instances they are usually described as "stage fright." It is a good enough descriptive term if we use it metaphorically for any irrational fear preceding public or private performance. It covers situations in which we want either to make a good impression—as, for instance, on new relatives, or some important personage, or perhaps a headwaiter in a restaurant—or in which we start new activities, such as beginning a new job, starting to paint, going to a public-speaking class. People who are afflicted with such fears often refer to them as fears of failure, disgrace, ridicule. This seems to be exactly what they are afraid of. Nevertheless, it is mis-leading to put it this way because it suggests a rational fear of a realistic failure. It leaves out the fact that what constitutes failure for a given person is subjective. It may encompass all that falls short of glory and perfection, and the anticipation of this possibility is precisely the essence of the milder forms of stage fright. A person is afraid of not performing as superbly as his exacting shoulds demand, and therefore fears that his pride will be hurt. There is a more pernicious form of stage fright which we will understand later on; in it unconscious forces operate in a person, obstructing his capacities in the very act of performing. The stage fright then is a fear that through his own self-destructive tendencies he will be ridiculously awkward, forget his lines, "choke up," and thus disgrace himself instead of being glorious and victorious.

Another category of anticipatory fears does not concern the quality of a person's performance but the prospect of having to do something that will hurt his special pride—such as asking for a raise or a favor, making an application, or approaching a woman—because it entails the possibility of being rejected. It may occur before sexual intercourse if the latter means for him being humiliated.

Reactions of fear also may follow "insults." Many people react with trembling, shaking, perspiration, or some other ex-pression of fear to a lack of deference or to arrogant behavior on the part of others. These reactions are a mixture of rage and fear, the fear being in part a fear of one's own violence. Similar reactions of fear may follow a feeling of shame without the latter being experienced as such. A person may suddenly feel overwhelmed by a feeling of uncertainty, or even panic, if he has been awkward, timid, or offensive. For instance, there is the case of a woman who drove up a mountain road, from the end of which a small path led up to the top. Though fairly steep, the path would have been easy to walk had it not been muddy and slippery. Moreover she was not properly dressed: she wore a new suit, high-heeled shoes, and had no stick. She tried nevertheless; but, after having slipped several times, she gave it up. While resting, she saw farther down a big dog barking furiously at passers-by and she became frightened of the dog. This fear startled her, because she was usually not afraid of dogs and because she also realized that there was no sound reason to be afraid since there were people around to whom the dog obviously belonged. So she started to think about this, and there occurred to her an incident from her adolescence which had caused her to be terribly ashamed. She recognized then that she was actually just as ashamed in the present situation on account of her "failure" to get to the mountain top. "But," she said to herself, "it really would not have been sensible to force the issue." Next she thought, "But I *should* have been able to make it." This gave her the clue: she recognized that it was a "stupid pride," as she put it, that was injured and made her feel helpless toward a possible attack. As we shall understand later on, she was helplessly delivered to her own attacks on herself and had externalized the danger. Though not quite complete, the piece of self-analysis was effective: her fear disappeared.

We have a more immediate understanding of the reactions of rage than of those of fear. But in the last analysis they are interlinked and we do not understand one without the other. Both occur because a hurt to our pride constitutes a terrifying danger. The reason for it lies in part in pride substituting for self-confidence, which we have discussed before. This, however, is not the whole answer. As we shall see later on, the neurotic lives between the two alternatives of pride and self-contempt, so that hurt pride rushes him into the abyss of self-contempt. This is a most important connection to keep in mind for the understanding of many spells of anxiety.

Though both the reaction of rage and that of fear may in our own mind have nothing to do with pride, they may nevertheless serve as road signs pointing in that direction. The whole issue is far more beclouded if even these secondary reactions do not appear as such, for they in their turn may be repressed—for whatever reason. In this case they may lead or contribute to certain symptomatic pictures, such as psychotic episodes, depressions, drinking, psychosomatic disorders. Or the need to sit tight on the emotions of anger and fear may become one of the factors conducive to a general flattening out of emotion. Not only anger and fear but all feelings then tend to become less full and less sharp.

The pernicious character of neurotic pride lies in the combination of its being vitally important to the individual and at the same time rendering him extremely vulnerable. This situation creates tensions, which because of their frequency and intensity are so unbearable that they call for remedies: *automatic endeavors to restore pride when it is hurt and to avoid injuries when it is endangered.*

The need to save face is urgent, and there is more than one way of effecting it. As a matter of fact, there are so many different ways, gross and subtle, that I must restrict my presentation to the more frequent and important ones. The most effective and, it seems, almost ubiquitous one is interlinked with the impulse to take revenge for what is felt as humiliation. We discussed it as a reaction of hostility to the pain and the danger involved in a hurt pride. But vindictiveness may in addition be a means toward self-vindication. It involves the belief that by getting back at the offender one's own pride will be restored. This belief is based on the feeling that the offender, by his very power to hurt our pride, has put himself above us and has defeated us. By our taking revenge and hurting him more than he did us, the situation will be reversed. We will be triumphant and will have defeated him. The aim of the neurotic vindictive revenge is not "getting even" but triumphing by hitting back harder. Nothing short of triumph *can* restore the imaginary grandeur in which pride is invested. It is this very capacity to restore pride that gives neurotic vindictiveness its incredible tenacity and accounts for its compulsive character.

Since vindictiveness will be discussed later on in some detail,[2] I shall at this time merely present in barest outline some essential factors. Because the power to retaliate is so valuable for the restoration of pride, this power can itself be invested with pride. In the minds of certain neurotic types it is equal to strength,

---

[2] In Chapter 7, The Expansive Solutions.

and often is the only strength they know. Conversely, the incapacity to hit back usually registers as weakness, no matter whether external or internal factors prohibited a vindictive move. Thus when such a person feels humiliated, and either the situation or something within him does not allow him to retaliate, he suffers a double injury: the original "insult" and the "defeat," as opposed to a vindictive triumph.

The need for a vindictive triumph, as stated before, is a regular ingredient in the search for glory. If it is the dominant motivating force in life, it sets going a vicious circle that is most difficult to disentangle. The determination then to rise above others in every possible way is so gigantic that it reinforces the whole need for glory, and with that the neurotic pride. The inflated pride in turn enhances the vindictiveness, and thereby makes for a still greater need for triumph.

Among ways to restore pride the next in importance is losing interest in all situations or people who in some way hurt this pride. Many people relinquish their interest in sports, politics, intellectual pursuits, etc. because their impatient need to excel, or to do a perfect job, is not satisfied. The situation then may become so unbearable for them that they give up. They do not know what has happened; they merely become uninterested, and may instead turn to an activity which is actually beneath their potentialities. A person may have been a good teacher but, assigned to a task he cannot master right away or which he feels degrading, his interest in teaching wanes. Such changes in attitudes also are relevant to the learning process. A gifted person may start dramatics or painting with enthusiasm. His teachers or friends find him promising, and encourage him. But with all his gifts he is not a Barrymore or a Renoir overnight. He realizes that he is not the only gifted one in his class. He is naturally awkward in his initial efforts. All of this hurts his pride, and he may suddenly "realize" that painting or dramatics is not in his line, that he never was "really" interested in this pursuit. He loses his zest, skips classes, and soon gives up altogether. He starts something else, only to repeat the same cycle. Often for economic reasons, or because of his own inertia, he may stay with the particular activity but does it so listlessly that he does not make out of it what would otherwise have been possible.

The same process may occur in relations with other people. Of course we may stop liking a person for good reasons: we may have overrated him in the first place or our developments may go in divergent directions. But it is in any case worth examining why our liking turns into indifference, instead of simply putting it down to lack of time or deciding that it was an error in the first place. What may actually have happened is that something in this relationship has hurt our pride. It may be a comparison with the other fellow in his favor. Perhaps he had paid us less deference than before. We realize that we have failed him and, hence, feel ashamed with regard to him. All of this may play an incisive role in a marriage or love relationship and we are inclined then to let it stay at "I don't love him any more."

All these withdrawals entail a considerable waste of energy and often much misery. But the most ruinous aspect of them is that we lose interest in our real self because we are not proud of it—a subject which we will leave to a later discussion.

There are further diverse ways to restore pride, which are well known but seldom understood in this context. We may, for example, have said something which later on appears silly to us —off the point, inconsiderate, too arrogant or too apologetic— and we may forget about it, deny that we said it, or contend that it meant something quite different. Akin to such denials are distortions of an incident—minimizing our share, omitting certain factors, emphasizing others, interpreting them in our favor —so that in the end we are whitewashed and our pride is unscathed. The embarrassing incident may also stay in our mind unchanged but be whisked away by excuses and alibis. Somebody admits having made a nasty scene, but it was because he had not slept for three nights or because others provoked him. He has hurt somebody's feelings, was indiscreet or inconsiderate, but his intentions were good. He has failed a friend who needs him, but it was because of lack of time. All these excuses may be partly or wholly true, but in the person's mind they do not serve as extenuating circumstances for a failing but erase it altogether. Similarly, many people feel that to say they are very sorry about something sets everything right.

All these devices have in common the tendency to refuse responsibility for self. Whether we forget something we are not proud of, or embellish it, or blame somebody else, we want to save face by not owning up to shortcomings. The declining of responsibility for self can also be hidden behind a pseudo-objectivity. A patient may make astute observations about himself and give a fairly accurate report of what he dislikes in himself. On the surface it seems as though he is perceptive and honest about himself. But "he" may be merely the intelligent observer of a fellow who is inhibited, fearful, or arrogantly demanding. Hence, since he is not responsible for the fellow he observes, the hurt to his pride is cushioned—all the more so because the flashlight of his pride is focused on his faculty for keen objective observations.

Others do not care for being objective, or even truthful, about themselves. But when—despite the diffuse evasiveness this attitude entails—such a patient does become aware of some neurotic trend, he may make a neat distinction between "him" and his "neurosis" or his "unconscious." His "neurosis" is something mysterious that has nothing whatever to do with "him." This sounds startling. Actually it is for him not only a face-saving but a life-saving, or at any rate a sanity-saving, measure. The vulnerability of his pride has assumed such extreme proportions that he would be split wide open by owning up to his disturbances.

A last face-saving device to be mentioned here is the use of humor. It is naturally a sign of inner liberation when a patient can squarely recognize his difficulties and take them with a grain of humor. But some patients at the beginning of analysis make incessant jokes about themselves, or exaggerate their difficulties in so dramatic a way that they will appear funny, while they are at the same time absurdly sensitive to any criticism. In these instances humor is used to take the sting out of an otherwise unbearable shame.

So much for the devices employed to restore pride when it has been hurt. But the pride is both so vulnerable and so precious that it also must be protected *in the future*. The neurotic may build an elaborate *system of avoidances* in the hope of circumventing future hurts. This too is a process that goes on automatically. He is not aware of wanting to avoid an activity because it might hurt his pride. He just avoids it, often without even being aware that he is. The process pertains to activities, to associations with people, and it may put a check on realistic strivings and efforts. If it is widespread it can actually cripple a person's life. He does not embark on any serious pursuits commensurate with his gifts lest he fail to be a brilliant success. He would like to write or to paint and does not dare to start. He does not dare to approach girls lest they reject him. He may not even dare to travel lest he be awkward with hotel managers or porters. Or he may go only to places where he is well known since he would feel like a nonentity with strangers. He withdraws from social contacts lest he be self-conscious. So, according to his economic status, he either does nothing worth while or sticks to a mediocre job and restricts his expenses rigidly. In more than one way he lives beneath his means. In the long run this makes it necessary for him to withdraw farther from others, because he cannot face the fact of lagging behind his age group and therefore shuns comparisons or questions from anybody about his work. In order to endure life he must now entrench himself more firmly in his private fantasy-world. But, since all these measures are more a camouflage than a remedy for his pride, he may start to cultivate his neuroses because the neurosis with a capital N then becomes a precious alibi for the lack of accomplishment.

These are extreme developments and, needless to say, pride is not the only factor operating in them, although it is one of the essential ones. More often, avoidances are restricted to certain areas. A person may be quite active and effective in those pursuits in which he is least inhibited and which are in the service of glory. He may, for instance, work hard and successfully in his field but shun social life. Conversely, he may feel safe in social activities, or in a Don Juan role, but would not dare to venture into any serious work which would put to a test his potential capacities. He may feel safe in his role as an organizer but avoid any personal relations because he would feel vulnerable in them. Among the many fears of getting emotionally involved with others (neurotic detachment) the fear of injuries to pride often plays a prominent part. Also, for many reasons, a person may be particularly afraid of not being glamorously successful with the opposite sex. He unconsciously anticipates—in the case of a man—that when approaching women, or having sexual relations with them, his pride will be hurt. Women then present to him a potential threat (to his pride). This fear can be powerful enough to dampen, or even crush, his feelings of attraction to them and thereby cause him to avoid heterosexual contacts. The inhibition thus generated does not alone account for his turning homosexual, but it is indeed one of the contributing factors to a preference for one's own sex. Pride in many diverse ways is the enemy of love.

The avoidance may concern many different specific matters. Thus a person may avoid speaking in public, participating in sports, telephoning. If somebody else is around to do the telephoning, to make a decision, or to deal with the landlord, he will leave it to him. In these specific activities he is most likely to be aware of shirking something, while in the larger areas the issue is often more befogged by an attitude of "I can't" or "I don't care."

Examining these avoidances, we see in operation two principles which determine their character. One is, briefly, safety through restricting one's life. It is safer to renounce, to withdraw, or to resign than to take the risk of exposing one's pride to injury. Perhaps nothing demonstrates so impressively the overwhelming importance of pride in many instances as the willingness, for its benefit, to restrict one's life to an often cramping degree. The other principle is: It is safer not to try than to try and fail. This latter maxim gives the avoidance the stamp of finality because it deprives the person of the chance of gradually overcoming whatever difficulties he has. It is even unrealistic on the basis of the neurotic's premises, for he has not only to pay the price of unduly restricting his life but in the long run his very recoiling damages his pride more deeply. But of course he does not think in long-range terms. He is concerned with the immediate danger of trial and error. If he does not try at all it does not reflect on him. He can find an alibi of some sort. At least in his own mind he can have the comforting thought that he could have passed the examination, secured a better job, won a woman, if he had tried. Often it is more fantastic: "If I applied myself to composing or writing, I would be greater than Chopin or Balzac."

In many instances the avoidances extend to reaching out in our feelings for anything desirable: in short, they may encompass our wishes. I mentioned people who feel it a disgraceful defeat not to attain something they wish to have. The mere wishing then entails too great a risk. Such a check on wishes, however, means putting a lid on our aliveness. Sometimes people also have to avoid any thought that would hurt their pride. The most significant avoidance on this score is shunning thoughts about death, because the idea of having to get older and having to die like any other mortal is unbearable. Oscar Wilde's *Dorian Gray* is an artistic presentation of the pride in eternal youth.

The development of pride is the logical outcome, the climax and consolidation of the process initiated with the search for glory. The individual may first have relatively harmless fantasies in which he pictures himself in some glamorous role. He proceeds by creating in his mind an idealized image of what he "really" is, could be, should be. Then comes the most decisive step: his real self fades out and the energies available for self-realization are shifted to the actualization of the idealized self. The claims are his attempt to assert his place in the world, a place that is adequate to the significance of the idealized self and one that supports it. With his shoulds, he drives himself to actualize the perfection of this self. And, lastly, he must develop a system of private values which, like "the Ministry of Truth" in *Nineteen Eighty-Four* (by George Orwell), determines what to like and accept in himself, what to glorify, what to be proud of. But this system of values must by necessity also determine what to reject, to abhor, to be ashamed of, to despise, to hate. It cannot do the one without the other. Pride and self-hate belong inseparably together; they are two expressions of one process.

CHAPTER 5

SELF-HATE AND
SELF-CONTEMPT

WE HAVE now traced a neurotic development that begins with self-idealization and evolves step by step with inexorable logic to a transformation of values into the phenomenon of neurotic pride. This development in actual fact is more involved than I have presented it hitherto. It is both intensified and complicated by another process operating simultaneously—a process which is seemingly opposite, though it is likewise initiated by self-idealization.

Briefly, when an individual shifts his center of gravity to his idealized self, he not only exalts himself but also is bound to look at his actual self—all that he is at a given time, body, mind, healthy and neurotic—from a wrong perspective. The glorified self becomes not only a *phantom* to be pursued; it also becomes a measuring rod with which to measure his actual being. And this actual being is such an embarrassing sight when viewed from the perspective of a godlike perfection that he cannot but despise it. Moreover, what is dynamically more important, the human being which he actually is keeps interfering—significantly—with his flight to glory, and therefore he is bound to hate it, to hate himself. And since pride and self-hate are actually one entity, I suggest calling the sum total of the factors involved by a common name: *the pride system*. Yet with self-hate we are considering a completely new aspect of the process, one which considerably alters our view of it. We have advisedly set the question of self-hate aside until now in order to obtain first a clear picture of the straight drive toward actualization of the idealized self. But we must now complete the picture.

No matter how frantically our Pygmalion tries to mold himself into a being of splendid dimensions, his drive is doomed to failure. He may at best be able to eliminate from awareness some disturbing discrepancies, but they continue to exist. The fact remains that he has to live with himself; whether he eats, sleeps, goes to the bathroom, whether he works or makes love, he is always there. He sometimes thinks that everything would be better if he could only divorce his wife, take another job, move to another apartment, or go on a trip; but in fact he must always take himself along. Even if he functions like a well-oiled machine, there are still limitations of energy, of time, of power, of endurance—the limitations of a human being.

The best way to describe the situation is in terms of two people. There is the unique, ideal person; and there is an omnipresent stranger (the actual self), always interfering, disturbing, embarrassing. Describing the conflict in terms of "he and the stranger" seems pertinent because it comes close to what the individual feels. Moreover, even though he may discard factual disturbances as irrelevant or unrelated to himself, he can never escape so far from himself as not to "register" [1] them. Although he may be successful, may function fairly well, or even be carried away by grandiose fantasies of unique achievement, he will nevertheless feel inferior or insecure. He may have a gnawing feeling of being a bluff, a fraud, a freak—feelings for which he cannot account. His inside knowledge of himself shows unmistakably in his dreams, when he is close to the reality of himself.

Usually the reality of himself intrudes painfully and unmistakably. Godlike in his imagination, he is awkward in social situations. Wanting to make an indelible impression on some-

---

[1] *Cf. The Neurotic Personality of Our Time* where I used the term "register" to denote the fact that, as it were, we feel in our guts and bones what is going on in ourselves without its reaching awareness.

body, his hands shake or he stammers or blushes. Feeling himself a unique lover, he may suddenly be impotent. Speaking in his imagination to his boss like a man, he merely musters a silly smile. The brilliant remark which would settle a discussion for good and all occurs to him only the next day. The desired sylph-like slenderness is never attained because, compulsively, he eats too much. The actual, empirical self becomes the offensive stranger to whom the idealized self happens to be tied, and the latter turns against this stranger with hate and contempt. The actual self becomes the victim of the proud idealized self.

Self-hate makes visible a rift in the personality that started with the creation of an idealized self. It signifies that there is a war on. And this indeed is the essential characteristic of every neurotic: he is at war with himself. Actually the foundation has been laid for two different kinds of conflicts. One of them is within the pride system itself. As we shall elaborate later on, it is the potential conflict between expansive drives and self-effacing ones. The other, deeper conflict is between the whole pride system and the real self. The latter, though shoved into the background and suppressed as pride ascended to supremacy, still is potentially powerful and may, under favorable circumstances, gain its full effectiveness. We shall discuss the characteristics and the phases of its development in the next chapter.

This second, deeper conflict is not apparent at the beginning of analysis. But as the pride system totters and the person becomes closer to himself; as he starts to feel his own feelings, to know his wishes, to win his freedom of choice, to make his own decisions and assume responsibility for them, the opposing forces get lined up. With increasing clarity the battle is now drawn between the pride system and the real self. Self-hate now is not so much directed against the limitations and shortcomings of the actual self as against the emerging constructive forces of the real self. It is a conflict of greater dimensions than any neurotic conflict I have discussed hitherto. I suggest calling it the *central inner conflict.*[2]

---

[2] Following a suggestion by Dr. Muriel Ivimey.

I should like to interpolate here a theoretical remark because it will help to bring this conflict into clearer focus. When previously, in my other books, I have used the term "neurotic conflict," I have meant one operating between two incompatible compulsive drives. The central inner conflict, however, is one between healthy and neurotic, constructive and destructive forces. We will therefore have to enlarge our definition and say that a neurotic conflict can operate either between two neurotic forces or between healthy and neurotic ones. This difference is important, over and beyond terminological clarification. There are two reasons for the conflict between the pride system and the real self having a much greater power to split us apart than other conflicts. The first lies in the difference between partial and total involvement. By analogy with a State, it is the difference between clashing interests of individual groups and the whole country's being involved in a civil war. The other reason lies in the fact that the very core of our being, our real self with its capacity for growth, is fighting for its life.

Hate for the real self is more remote from awareness than that for the limitations of the actual self, but it forms the never absent background of self-hate—or the undercurrent that always supplies the main energies, even though hate for the limitations of the actual self may be in the foreground. Hence, hate for the real self can appear in almost pure form while hate for the actual self is always a mixed phenomenon. If for instance our self-hate takes the form of a ruthless self-condemnation for being "selfish"—i.e., for doing anything in our own behalf—this may be, and most likely is, both a hate for not measuring up to the *absolute* of saintliness *and* a way of crushing our real self.

A German poet, Christian Morgenstern, concisely expressed the nature of self-hate in his poem *Entwicklungsschmerzen* [8] ("Growing Pains"):

> I shall succumb, destroyed by myself
> I who am two, what I could be and what I am.

[8] Collection of poems *Auf vielen Wegen*, R. Piper and Co., Munich, 1921. Translation of this poem by Caroline Newton.

> And in the end one will annihilate the other.
> The *Would-be* is like a prancing steed
> (*I am* is fettered to his tail),
> Is like a wheel to which *I am* is bound,
> Is like a fury whose fingers twine
> Into his victim's hair, is like a vampire
> That sits upon his heart and sucks and sucks.

A poet has thus expressed the process in a few lines. He says that we may hate ourselves with an enervating and tormenting hatred—a hatred so destructive that we are helpless against it and may psychically destroy ourselves. And he says that we do not hate ourselves because we are worthless but because we are driven to reach beyond ourselves. The hatred, he says, results from the discrepancy between what I would be and what I am. There is not only a split, but a cruel and murderous battle.

The *power and tenacity of self-hate* is astounding, even for the analyst who is familiar with the way it operates. When trying to account for its depth, we must realize the rage of the proud self for feeling humiliated and held down at every step by the actual self. We must also consider the ultimate impotence of this rage. For, much as the neurotic may try to regard himself as a disembodied spirit, he is *dependent* on the actual self for being and hence for attaining glory. If he would kill the hated self he must at the same time kill the glorious self, as Dorian Gray did when slashing to pieces the picture expressing his degradation. On the one hand, this dependency as a rule prevents suicide. If it were not for this dependency, suicide would be the logical outcome of self-hate. Actually suicide is a comparatively rare occurrence, and it results from a combination of factors among which self-hate is but one. On the other hand, the very dependency makes self-hate all the more cruel and merciless, as is the case in any powerless rage.

Furthermore, self-hate is not only a result of self-glorification but also serves to maintain it. More precisely, it serves the drive to actualize the idealized self and to find a full integration on that exalted level by eliminating conflicting elements. The very condemnation of imperfection confirms the godlike standards with which the person identifies himself. We can observe this function of self-hate in analysis. When we uncover the patient's self-hate we may naïvely expect that he will be eager to get rid of it. Sometimes such a healthy response actually does occur. More often his response is divided. He cannot help recognizing the formidable burden and danger of self-hate, but he may feel it even more dangerous to rebel against the yoke. He may plead in most plausible terms the validity of high standards and the danger of becoming lax through greater tolerance toward self. Or he may gradually reveal his conviction that he fully deserves the contempt with which he treats himself, which indicates that he is not yet able to accept himself on any lesser terms than those of his arrogant standards.

The third factor that renders self-hate such a cruel and merciless force we have already implied. It is the alienation from self. In simpler terms: the neurotic has no feeling for himself. There must first be some sympathy for the suffering self, some experiencing of this suffering, before the recognition of beating himself down can set going a constructive move. Or, to take another aspect, there must first be some owning up to the existence of his own wishes before the realization of self-frustration can start to disquiet or even to interest him.

What about the *awareness of self-hate?* What is expressed in *Hamlet, Richard III,* or in the poems cited here is not restricted to the poet's clear-sighted knowledge of the agonies of human souls. During longer or shorter intervals many people *experience* self-hate or self-contempt as such. They may have flashing feelings of "I hate myself" or "I despise myself"; they may be furious at themselves. But such alive experiencing of self-hate occurs only in periods of distress and is forgotten as the distress subsides. As a rule the question does not arise whether such feelings—or thoughts—are more than a temporary response to a "failure," a "stupidity," a feeling of wrong done, or a realization of some psychic handicap. Hence there is no awareness of the subversive and lasting operation of self-hate.

With regard to that form of self-hate which is expressed in self-accusations, the range of differences in awareness is too wide to allow for any general statement. Those neurotics who have entrenched themselves in a shell of self-righteousness have so silenced all self-accusations that nothing reaches awareness. Opposed to these are the self-effacing types who frankly express self-reproaches and guilt-feelings, or betray the existence of such feelings by their flagrantly apologetic or defensive behavior. Such individual differences in awareness are significant indeed. We shall discuss later on what they mean and how they come about. But they do not justify the conclusion that the self-effacing types are aware of self-hate; because even those neurotics who are aware of self-recriminations are aware neither of their intensity nor of their destructive nature. They are also unaware of their intrinsic futility, and tend to regard them as testimony to their high moral sensitivity. They do not question their validity, and as a matter of fact cannot do so as long as they judge themselves from the perspective of a godlike perfection.

However, almost all neurotics are aware of the *results* of self-hate: feeling guilty, inferior, cramped, tormented. Yet they do not in the least realize that they themselves have brought about these painful feelings and self-evaluations. And even the bit of awareness they may have, can be blurred by neurotic pride. Instead of suffering from feeling cramped, they are proud of being "unselfish . . . ascetic . . . self-sacrificing . . . a slave to duty"—terms which may hide a multitude of sins against the self.

The conclusion we arrive at from these observations is that self-hate in all essentials is an unconscious process. In the last analysis there is a survival interest in *not* being aware of its impact. This is the ultimate reason that the bulk of the process is usually externalized, i.e., experienced as operating not within the individual himself but between him and the outside world. We can roughly distinguish between active and passive externalization of self-hate. The former is an attempt to direct self-hate outward, against life, fate, institutions, or people. In the latter the hate remains directed against the self but is perceived or experienced as coming from the outside. In both ways the tension of the inner conflict is released by being turned into an interpersonal one. We shall discuss the special forms this process may assume, and its influence upon human relations, in later contexts. I introduce it here only because many varieties of self-hate can best be observed and described in their externalized forms.

The expressions of self-hate are identically the same as those of hate in interpersonal relations. To illustrate the latter by an historical example that is still fresh in our memory, Hitler's hatred for the Jews, we see that he intimidated and accused them viciously, he humiliated them, he disgraced them in public, he deprived and frustrated them in every form, shape and manner, he destroyed their hopes for the future, and in the end tortured and killed them systematically. In more civilized and concealed forms we can observe most of these expressions of hate in everyday life, in families or between competitors.

We shall now survey the *main expressions of self-hate* and their direct effects on the individual. All of them have been observed by great writers. Most of the individual data presented have also been described in psychiatric literature since Freud as self-accusations, self-minimizing, inferiority-feelings, the incapacity to enjoy things, direct self-destructive actions, masochistic trends. But, apart from Freud's concept of the death-instinct and its elaboration by Franz Alexander and Karl Menninger,[4] no comprehensive theory has been offered that would account for all the phenomena. Freud's theory, however, though dealing with similar clinical material, is based upon such different theoretical premises that the understanding of the problems involved and the therapeutic approach to them are entirely changed. We shall discuss these differences in a later chapter.

In order not to get lost in detail, let us distinguish six *modes of operation* in, or expressions of, self-hate, while keeping in mind the fact that they are overlapping. Roughly they are: relentless demands on self, merciless self-accusation, self-contempt, self-frustrations, self-tormenting, and self-destruction.

When in a previous chapter we discussed *demands on self* we regarded them as a means of the neurotic individual to make himself over into his idealized self. We have also stated, how-

---

[4] Franz Alexander, *The Psychoanalysis of the Total Personality*. Nervous and Mental Disease Publishing Co., 1930.

Karl A. Menninger, *Man Against Himself*, Harcourt, Brace and Co., 1938.

ever, that the inner dictates constitute a coercive system, a tyranny, and that people may respond with shock and panic when failing to fulfill them. We are in the position now to understand more fully what accounts for the coerciveness, what renders the attempts to comply with the dictates so frantic, and why the responses to "failure" are so profound. The shoulds are as much determined by self-hate as by pride, and the furies of self-hate are unleashed when they are not fulfilled. They can be compared to a holdup in which a gunman points a revolver at a person, saying: "Either you give me all you have, *or else* I'll shoot you." The gunman's holdup is likely to be the more humane of the two. It is possible for the threatened person to save himself by complying, while the shoulds cannot be appeased. And also, being shot, for all the finality of death, seems less cruel than a lifelong suffering under self-hate. To quote from the letter of a patient: [5] "His real self is stifled by the neurosis, the Frankenstein monster originally designed for his protection. And it makes little difference whether you live in a totalitarian country or a private neurosis, either way you are apt to end up in a concentration camp where the whole point is to destroy the self as painfully as possible."

The shoulds are in fact self-destructive in their very nature. But as yet we have seen only one aspect of their destructiveness: that they put a person into a strait jacket and deprive him of inner freedom. Even if he manages to mold himself into a behavioristic perfection, he can do so only at the expense of his spontaneity and the authenticity of his feelings and beliefs. The shoulds aim in fact, like any political tyranny, at the extinction of individuality. They create an atmosphere similar to that in the seminary described by Stendhal in *The Red and the Black* (or George Orwell in *Nineteen Eighty-Four*), in which any individual thinking and feeling are suspect. They require an unquestioning obedience, which is not even felt as obedience.

Besides, many shoulds show their self-destructive character in their very contents. As an illustration I should like to refer to three shoulds, all of which operate in the condition of morbid

---

[5] Published in the *American Journal of Psychoanalysis*, vol. IX, 1949.

dependency and which will be elaborated in that context: I should be big enough to mind absolutely nothing that is done to me; I should be able to make her love me; and I should sacrifice absolutely everything for "love"! The combination of these three shoulds is indeed bound to perpetuate the tortures of a morbid dependency. Another frequent should demands of a person that he assume full responsibility for his relatives, friends, pupils, employees, etc. He should be able to solve everyone's problem to everyone's instant satisfaction. This implies that *anything* that goes wrong is his fault. If a friend or relative is upset for any reason, complains, criticizes, is discontented, or wants something, such a person is forced to be the helpless victim who must feel guilty and set everything right. He is, to quote a patient, like the harassed manager of a summer hotel: the guests are always right. Whether or not any of the mishaps are actually his fault does not matter.

This process is well described in a recent French book *The Witness*.[6] The main character and his brother are out boating; the boat leaks, a storm comes up, and they are capsized. Since the brother has a badly injured leg, he is not able to swim in the violent water. He is doomed to drown. The hero tries to swim ashore, supporting his brother, but soon realizes that he cannot do it. The alternatives are that both drown or that the hero save himself alone. Clearly realizing this, he decides to save himself. But he feels as if he were a murderer, and this is so real to him that he is convinced everybody else will regard him as a murderer. His reason is of no avail, and cannot be effective, as long as he operates on the premise that he *should* be responsible in *any* case. To be sure, this is an extreme situation. But the hero's emotional response illustrates exactly what people do feel when driven by this particular should.

An individual can also impose tasks upon himself which are detrimental to his whole being. A classic example of this kind of should is to be found in Dostoevski's *Crime and Punishment*. Raskolnikov, in order to prove to his satisfaction his Napoleonic qualities, felt that he *should* be able to kill a human being. As Dostoevski shows us in unmistakable terms, despite Raskolni-

---

[6] Jean Bloch-Michel, *The Witness*, Pantheon Press, 1949.

kov's manifold resentments against the world, nothing was more distasteful to his sensitive soul than to kill. He had to beat himself into doing it. What he actually felt is expressed in a dream in which he sees a scrawny, underfed little mare forced by drunken peasants to try to pull an impossibly heavy cartload. It is brutally and mercilessly whipped and finally beaten to death. Raskolnikov himself rushes to the mare in an upsurge of deep compassion.

This dream appeared at a time when Raskolnikov was engaged in a violent inner struggle. He felt both that he *should* be able to kill and that it was so utterly distasteful that he simply could not do it. In the dream he realized the senseless cruelty with which he was beating himself into doing something that was as impossible for him as it was for the mare to pull the heavy cartload. And from the depth of his being emerged a profound compassion for himself over what he was doing to himself. Having thus experienced his true feelings, he felt more at one with himself after the dream and decided against the killing. But his Napoleonic self soon afterward again got the upper hand, because at that time his real self was as helpless against it as the underfed mare was against the brutal peasants.

The third factor which renders the shoulds self-destructive and which, more than others, accounts for their coerciveness, is the self-hate with which we may turn against ourselves when we violate them. Sometimes this connection is fairly clear, or can be established easily. A person has not been as all knowing or all helpful as he feels he should be and, as in the story *The Witness,* is filled with unreasoning self-reproaches. More often he is not aware of such a violation but, seemingly out of the blue, feels low, uneasy, fatigued, anxious, or irritable. Let us recall the example of the woman who was suddenly scared of a dog after not having climbed to the mountain top. The sequence here was as follows: first, she experienced as a failure her sensible decision to give up the climbing—a failure in the light of a dictate telling her that she should manage everything (and which remained unconscious). Next followed her self-contempt, which likewise remained unconscious. Then came the response to her self-berating, in the form of feeling helpless and scared, the first of the emotional processes that reached awareness. If she had not analyzed herself, the scare of the dog would have remained a puzzling incident, puzzling because it was disconnected from all that preceded it. In other instances a person experiences in conscious awareness only the special ways in which he automatically protects himself from his self-hate, such as his special ways to allay anxiety (eating sprees, drinking or shopping sprees, etc.), his feeling victimized by others (passive externalization), or irritable at others (active externalization. We shall have ample opportunity to see from various viewpoints how these attempts at self-protection operate. In this context I want to discuss still another similar one, because it easily escapes attention and can lead to an impasse in therapy.

This attempt is made when a person is on the verge of realizing, unconsciously, that he cannot possibly measure up to his particular shoulds. It can happen then that a patient who is otherwise reasonable and co-operative may become agitated and go, as it were, on a wild spree of feeling abused by everybody and everything: his relatives exploit him, his boss is unfair, his dentist has messed up his teeth, analysis does him no good, etc. He may be quite abusive toward the analyst and may have violent fits of temper at home.

In trying to understand his upset, the first factor that strikes us is his making insistent claims for special consideration. According to the particular situation, he may insist on getting more help in his office, on his wife or his mother leaving him alone, on his analyst giving him more time, or on his school making exceptions in his favor. Our first impression then is that of frenzied claims and a feeling of abuse at their frustration. But when these claims are brought to his attention the patient's frenzy increases. He may become still more openly hostile. If we listen carefully, we find a theme running through his abusive comments. It is as if he said: "Don't you realize, you darned fool, that I really am in need of something?" If we now recall our knowledge that claims stem from neurotic needs, we can see that a sudden increase of claims points to a sudden increase of rather urgent needs. Following this lead, we have a chance to understand the patient's distress. It may turn out then that, without his knowing it, he has realized that he cannot fulfill certain of his imperative shoulds. He may have felt, for instance, that he simply cannot make a go of some important love relation; or that he has so overloaded himself with work that even with the utmost straining he cannot swing it; or he may have recognized that certain problems which have come up in analysis did get him down and are beyond even his endurance, or that they deride his efforts to dispel them by sheer exertion of will power. These realizations, mostly unconscious, make him panicky because he feels he *should* be able to overcome all these odds. In this condition then there are but two alternatives. One is to realize that his demands on himself are fantastic. The other is to claim frantically that his life situation be so changed that he will not have to face his "failure." In his agitation he had taken the second road, and it is the task of therapy to show him the first one.

It is of great importance for therapy to recognize the possibility that the patient's realization of shoulds being unfulfillable can give rise to hectic claims. It is important because these claims can create a condition of agitation that is most difficult to handle. But it also is important in terms of theory. It helps us toward a better understanding of the urgency many claims have. And it forcefully demonstrates the urgency the individual feels to measure up to his shoulds.

Finally, if even a dim realization of a failure—or impending failure—to measure up to the shoulds can create a frantic despair, then there is a stringent inner necessity to prevent such realizations. We have seen that one of the ways in which the neurotic avoids them is by fulfilling the shoulds in his imagination. ("I *should* be able to be, or act, in a certain way—so, I *am* able to be so, or to do so.") We understand better now that this seemingly slick and glib way of avoiding truth is actually determined by the lurking terror of coming face to face with the fact that he does not and cannot measure up to his inner dictates. It is therefore an illustration of the contention propounded in the first chapter that imagination is put to the service of neurotic needs.

Among the many unconscious self-deceptive measures thus made necessary I comment here on only two, because of their basic significance. One of them is to lower the threshold of awareness of self. Sometimes an astute observer of others, the neurotic may maintain a tenacious unawareness of his own feelings, thoughts, or actions. Even in analysis, when some problem is called to his attention, he will shut off further discussion with an "I am not aware of that" or "I do not feel it." The other unconscious device to be mentioned here is a peculiarity of most neurotics—that of experiencing themselves only as reacting beings. This goes deeper than putting the blame on others. It amounts to an unconscious denial of their own shoulds. Life is experienced then as a sequence of pushes and pulls, coming from the outside. In other words, the shoulds themselves are externalized.

To summarize in more general terms: any person subjected to a tyrannical regime will resort to means of circumventing its dictates. He is forced into a duplicity which, in the case of an external tyranny, may be entirely conscious. In the case of the inner tyranny, which in itself is unconscious, the subsequent duplicity can have only the character of unconscious self-deceptive pretenses.

All these devices prevent the upsurge of self-hate which otherwise would follow a realization of "failure"; therefore they have a great subjective value. But they also make for a diffuse impairment of the sense of truth; thereby they factually contribute both to an alienation from self [7] and to the great autonomy of the pride system.

The demands on self thus assume a crucial position in the structure of a neurosis. They constitute the individual's attempt to actualize his idealized image. They are in a twofold way instrumental in increasing his alienation from himself: by forcing him into a falsification of his spontaneous feelings and beliefs and by engendering a diffuse unconscious dishonesty. They are also determined by his self-hate; and, finally, the realization of his inability to comply with them unleashes his self-hate. In a way all forms of self-hate are sanctions for unfulfilled shoulds—which is merely another way of saying that he would feel no self-hate if he actually could be a superhuman being.

Condemnatory *self-accusations* are another expression of self-hate. Most of them follow with merciless logic from our central

---

[7] *Cf.* Chapter 6, Alienation from Self.

premise. If the individual fails to reach the *absolutes* of fearlessness, generosity, poise, will power, etc., his pride speaks the verdict of "guilty."

Some self-accusations are directed against existing inner difficulties. They may therefore look deceptively rational. At any rate the person himself feels them to be entirely warranted. After all, is not such severity commendatory since it is commensurate with high standards? Actually, he takes the difficulties out of context and hurls at them the full fury of moral condemnation. They are lodged regardless of the person's responsibility for them. Whether he could, in any way, have felt, thought, acted differently, whether he was even aware of them does not matter in the least. A neurotic problem to be examined and worked at thus turns into a hideous blemish branding the person as being beyond redemption. He may for instance be unable to defend his interests or his opinions. He notices that he was rather appeasing when he should have voiced his dissenting opinion or defended himself against exploitation. To have observed this squarely is not only actually all to his credit but could be a first step toward a gradual recognition of the forces compelling him to appease rather than to assert himself. Instead, in the grip of destructive self-reproaches, he will beat himself down for having "no guts" or being a disgusting coward, or he will feel that the people around him despise him for being a weakling. Thus the whole effect of his self-observation is to make him feel "guilty" or inferior, with the result that his lowered self-esteem makes it still harder for him to speak up the next time.

Similarly, somebody who is overtly afraid of snakes or of driving a car may be well informed about the facts that such fears stem from unconscious forces over which he has no control. His reason tells him that the moral condemnation of "cowardice" makes no sense. He may even argue with himself about being "guilty" or "not guilty," back and forth. But he cannot possibly arrive at any conclusion because it is an argument involving different levels of being. As a human being he can allow himself to be subject to fears. But as a godlike being he should have the attribute of absolute fearlessness, and he can only hate and despise himself for having any fears. Again, a writer is inhibited in doing creative work because of several factors within himself which make writing an ordeal. His work therefore proceeds slowly; he fiddles around or does irrelevant things. Instead of being sympathetic with himself for this affliction, and examining it, he calls himself a lazy good-for-nothing or a fraud who is not really interested in his work.

Self-accusations as to being a bluff or a fraud are most common. They are not always directly thrust at self for some concrete matter. More often a neurotic person feels a resulting vague uneasiness on this score—doubts which are not attached to anything and are dormant at times and at others consciously tormenting. Sometimes he becomes aware only of the fear with which he reacts to his self-accusation, the fear of being found out: if people knew him better they would see that he was no good. At the next performance his incompetence will show. People will realize that he merely managed to show off, with no solid knowledge behind his "front." Again what exactly might be "found out" at closer contact, or in any test situation, remains vague. This self-reproach too, however, is not plucked from thin air. It refers to the sum total of existing unconscious pretenses—pretenses of love, of fairness, of interest, of knowledge, of modesty. And the frequency of this particular self-accusation corresponds to the frequency of pretense in each neurosis. Its destructive nature shows here too in the fact of its merely producing feelings of guilt and fear rather than contributing to a constructive search for existing unconscious pretenses.

Other self-accusations hit less at existing difficulties than at the motivations for doing something. These may seem the very image of conscientious self-scrutiny. And only the whole context can show whether a person really wants to find out about himself, whether he is merely faultfinding, or whether both drives operate. This procedure is all the more deceptive since actually our motivations rarely are pure gold; they are usually alloyed with one of several metals less noble than what is visible. Yet, if the major part is gold, we still may call it gold. If in giving advice to a friend the major motivation is a friendly intention of constructive help, we may well be satisfied. Not so the person in the clutches of faultfinding. He will say: "Yes, I gave him advice, maybe even good advice. But I did not do it gladly. Part of me hated to be bothered." Or: "Maybe I did it only to enjoy feeling superior to him, or giving him a dig for not handling the particular situation better." This is deceptive just because there are grains of truth in such reasoning. An outsider with a little wisdom may sometimes be able to dispel the spook. He, the wiser person, might reply: "Assuming all the elements you mentioned, is it not all the more to your credit that in actual fact you gave your friend sufficient time and interest to be of real help to him?" To look at the incident in this way would never occur to the victim of self-hate. In his blinkered staring at his faults he does not see the forest for the trees. Moreover, even if a minister, a friend, or an analyst presents things to him in the right perspective he may not be convinced. He may politely acknowledge the obvious truth but make the mental reservation that it was said for the sake of encouragement or reassurance.

Responses like these are noteworthy because they show how hard it is to shake the neurotic loose from his self-hate. His error in judging the entirety of a situation is clearly shown. He may see that he overfocuses on certain aspects and ignores others. Nevertheless he sticks to his verdict. The reason is that his logic operates on different premises from those of a healthy person. Since the advice he gave was not the *absolute* of helpfulness, the whole action was morally objectionable, and so he starts to beat himself down and refuses to let himself be dissuaded from his self-accusations. These observations refute the assumption sometimes made by psychiatrists that self-blame is merely a clever device to elicit reassurance or to escape blame and punishment. That of course does occur. On the part of children, or of grownups, toward intimidating authorities it may actually be nothing but a strategy. Even so, we have to be careful with our judgment and should examine the need for so much reassurance. To generalize about these instances and to regard self-accusations as such as only serving strategic ends means a total failure to appreciate their destructive power.

Self-accusations furthermore may focus on adversities which are outside the individual's control. These are most conspicuous in psychotics, who may accuse themselves for instance of a murder they read about, of responsibility for a flood in the Middle West six hundred miles away. Seemingly absurd self-accusations often are the outstanding symptom in melancholic conditions. But the self-accusations in neurosis, while less grotesque, may be no less unrealistic. As an illustration, I cite an intelligent mother whose child fell from a neighbor's porch while playing with the children who lived there. The child had a slight concussion; otherwise, the accident was harmless. The mother severely accused herself of carelessness for years thereafter. It was all her fault. If she had been present, the child would not have climbed up the railing and would not have fallen. This mother subscribed to the inadvisability of overprotecting children. She knew of course that even an overprotective mother cannot be present all the time. Yet she stuck to her verdict.

Similarly a young actor reproached himself bitterly for temporary failures in his career. He was fully aware that he was up against odds beyond his control. In talking the situation over with friends he would point out these adverse factors, but he did it in a defensive manner, as if to assuage a feeling of guilt and to protest his innocence. If friends asked him what exactly he could have done differently, he could not pin it down to anything concrete. No scrutiny, no reassurance, no encouragement availed against his self-recrimination.

This kind of self-accusations may well arouse our curiosity, because the opposite happens much more frequently. Usually the neurotic seizes avidly upon situational difficulties or misfortunes for the purpose of exonerating himself: he did all he could; he was, to make a long story short, simply wonderful. But the others, the whole situation, or accidental mishaps spoiled it all. While these two attitudes superficially look like opposites, the similarities are strangely enough greater than the differences. In both ways the attention is diverted from subjective factors and focused on the externals. To them is ascribed the decisive influence for happiness and success. The function in both is to ward off the onslaughts of self-condemnation for not being one's idealized self. In the instances mentioned other neurotic factors also interfered with being the ideal mother or with having a brilliant career as an actor. The woman at that time was too consumed with her own problems to be a consistently good mother; the actor had certain inhibitions against making necessary contacts and competing for a job. Both were to some extent aware of these difficulties, but they mentioned them casually, forgot about them, or subtly embellished them. In a person who is happy go lucky this would not strike us as peculiar. But in our two instances—which are typical in this regard—there is a simply stunning discrepancy between a gingerly dealing with their shortcomings on the one hand and merciless, unreasoning self-accusations for occurrences outside their control on the other. Such discrepancies may easily escape observation as long as we are not aware of their significance. Actually they contain an important clue for understanding the dynamics of self-condemnation. They point to a self-recrimination for personal flaws so severe that the person must resort to self-protective measures. And they use two such measures: to treat themselves in a gingerly way and to shift responsibility to circumstances. The question remains why, with this latter move, they do not succeed better in getting rid of self-accusations, at least in their conscious minds? The answer is simply that they do not feel that these outside factors are outside their control. Or, more accurately: they *should* not be out of control. Consequently everything that goes wrong reflects on themselves and shows them up in their disgraceful limitations.

While the self-accusations mentioned thus far focus on something concrete—on existing inner difficulties, on motivations, on externals—others remain vague and intangible. A person may feel haunted by guilt-feelings without being able to attach them to anything definite. In his desperate search for a reason he may finally resort to the idea that perhaps they concern a guilt incurred in some previous incarnation. Sometimes, though, a more concrete self-accusation will emerge and he will believe that now he has found the reason that he hates himself. Let us assume for instance that he has realized that he is not interested in other people and does not do enough for them. He tries hard to change this attitude and hopes, by doing so, to get rid of his self-hate. But if he has really turned against himself, such efforts —though all to his credit—will not rid him of the enemy because he has put the cart before the horse. *He does not hate him-*

self because his self-reproach is in part valid, but rather accuses himself because he hates himself. And one self-accusation will follow another. He does not take revenge; therefore he is a weakling. He is vindictive; therefore he is a brute. He is helpful; therefore he is a sucker. He is not helpful; therefore he is a selfish pig; and so on and so forth.

If he externalizes the self-accusations he may feel that everybody is imputing ulterior motives to everything he does. This, as we mentioned before, may be so real to him that he resents others as unfair. In defense he may wear a rigid mask so that nobody will guess from his facial expressions, his tone of voice, or his gestures what is going on within him. Or he may even be unaware of such externalizations. In his conscious mind then everybody is very nice. And only during the analytic process will he realize that he actually feels under constant suspicion. Like Damocles, he may live in terror lest the sword of some severe accusation fall on him at any moment.

I do not think that any psychiatric book could give a more penetrating presentation of these intangible self-accusations than Kafka did in *The Trial.*[8] Just like Mr. K, the neurotic may spend his best energies in a futile and defensive battle against unknown and unfair judges, and become more and more hopeless in the process. Here too the accusations have a foundation in a real failure of Mr. K's. As Erich Fromm has so ably demonstrated in his analysis of *The Trial,*[9] it rests on the whole dullness of Mr. K's life, in his drifting, in his lack of autonomy and growth—all of which Fromm calls, in a good phrase, "his unproductive living." Any person living that way, Fromm points out, is bound to feel guilty, and does so for good reasons: because he *is* guilty. He is always on the lookout for somebody else to solve his problems instead of turning to himself and his own resources. There is profound wisdom in this analysis, and I certainly agree with the concept applied in it. But I think it is incomplete. It does not consider the futility of the self-accusations, their merely condemnatory character. In other words it leaves out the point that Mr. K's very attitude toward his guilt

[8] Franz Kafka, *The Trial,* Alfred A. Knopf, 1937.
[9] Erich Fromm, *Man For Himself,* Rinehart, 1947.

is in its turn unconstructive, and it is so because he deals with it in the spirit of self-hate. This too is unconscious; he does not feel that he accuses himself mercilessly. The whole process is externalized.

Finally, a person may accuse himself for actions or attitudes which, viewed objectively, seem harmless, legitimate, or even desirable. He may brand taking sensible care of himself as pampering; enjoying food as gluttony; considering his own wishes instead of blindly complying as hard-boiled selfishness; considering analytic treatment—which he needs and can afford—as self-indulgence; asserting an opinion as presumptuous. Here too we have to ask which inner dictate or which pride is offended by a pursuit. Only a person taking pride in asceticism would accuse himself of "gluttony"; only a person proud of self-effacement would brand an assertive move as egotistical. But the most important thing about this kind of self-accusations is that they often concern the fight against the emerging real self. They mostly occur—or, more precisely, come into the foreground—in later phases of analysis, and are an attempt to discredit and discourage moves toward healthy growth.

The viciousness of self-accusations (as in any form of self-hate) calls for self-protective measures. And we can observe these clearly in the analytic situation. As soon as the patient is faced with one of his difficulties he may go on the defensive. He may respond with righteous indignation, with feeling misunderstood, or with becoming argumentative. He points out that it was true in the past but is already much better; that the difficulty would not exist if his wife didn't behave the way she does; that it would not have developed in the first place if his parents had been different. He may also develop counterattacks and find fault with the analyst, often in a threatening manner—or, on the contrary, become appeasing and ingratiating. In other words he reacts as if we had hurled at him a severe accusation too frightening for him to be able to test it out quietly. He can fight it blindly, according to the means at his disposal: by wriggling out of it, by putting the blame on somebody else, by pleading guilty, by going on the offensive. We have here one of the major retarding factors in psychoanalytic therapy. But also, apart from analysis, it is one of the main causes preventing people from being objective toward their problems. The necessity to ward off any self-accusation stunts the capacity for constructive self-criticism and thereby mars the possibility of learning from mistakes.

I want to summarize these comments on neurotic self-accusations by contrasting them with the healthy conscience. The latter vigilantly guards the very best interests of our true self. It represents, to use Erich Fromm's excellent term, "man's recall to himself." It is the reaction of our true self to the proper functioning or the malfunctioning of our total personality. Self-accusations, on the other hand, stem from neurotic pride and express the discontent of the proud self with the individual's not measuring up to its requirements. They are not *for* his true self but directed *against* it, and are meant to crush it.

The uneasiness, or the remorse coming from our conscience, can be eminently constructive because it can set in motion a constructive examination of what is wrong with a particular action or reaction, or even with our whole way of living. What happens when our conscience is disquieted differs from the neurotic process from the beginning. We try to face squarely the wrong done or the faulty attitude which has come to our attention, without magnifying or minimizing it. We try to find out what is responsible for it in ourselves and work toward overcoming it eventually, in whatever accessible ways. Self-accusations, by contrast, issue a condemnatory verdict by declaring the whole personality to be no good. And with this verdict they stop. This stopping at a point when a positive move could set in constitutes their intrinsic futility. To put it in most general terms, our conscience is a moral agency serving our growth, while self-accusations are amoral in origin and immoral in effect because they keep the individual from soberly examining his existing difficulties and thereby interfere with his human growth.

Fromm contrasts the healthy conscience with the "authoritarian" conscience, which he defines as the "internalized fear of authority." Actually, in its common use, the word "conscience" connotes three entirely different things: the unwitting inner submission to external authorities with the concomitant fear of discovery and punishment; the condemnatory self-accusations; and the constructive discontent with self. In my opinion the name "conscience" should be reserved for the last one only, and I will use it in this sense alone.

Self-hate expresses itself, thirdly, in *self-contempt*. I use this expression as an over-all term for the manifold ways of undermining self-confidence: self-belittling, self-disparaging, self-doubting, self-discrediting, self-ridiculing. The distinction from self-accusation is a fine one. Certainly it is not always possible to say whether a person feels guilty as a result of self-recrimination or inferior, worthless, or contemptible as a result of disparaging himself. In such cases we can with certainty say only that these are different ways of beating ourselves down. Yet there are discernible distinctions between the ways in which these two forms of self-hate operate. Self-contempt is mainly directed against any striving for improvement or achievement. There are enormous differences in the degree of awareness to it, the reasons for which we shall understand later on. It may be hidden behind an imperturbable front of righteous arrogance. However, it may be felt and expressed directly. For instance, an attractive girl wanting to powder her nose in public found herself saying: "How ridiculous! Ugly duckling, trying to look pretty!" Again, an intelligent man whose interest was captivated by a psychological subject, and who considered writing about it, remarked to himself: "You conceited ass, what makes you think you could write a paper on anything!" Even so, it would be erroneous to assume that people who are so open in their sarcastic comments about themselves are usually aware of their full significance. Other apparently frank comments may be less openly vicious—may indeed be witty and humorous. As I said before, these are more difficult to evaluate. They may be the expression of a greater freedom from a stultifying pride, but they may instead be simply an unconscious face-saving device. To be more explicit: they may protect the pride and save the individual from succumbing to his self-contempt.

Self-discrediting attitudes can easily be observed, although they may be praised as "modesty" by others and felt to be such by the person himself. Thus a person, after having taken good care of a sick relative, may think or say: "That's the least I could do." Another may discount praise for being a good storyteller by thinking: "I do that merely to impress people." A physician may ascribe a cure to good luck or to the patient's vitality. But, conversely, he would consider it *his* failure if the patient did not improve. Moreover, although self-contempt may not be recognized, certain resultant fears are often fairly transparent—to others. Thus many well-informed people do not speak up in discussions because they are afraid of appearing ridiculous. Naturally such disavowing or discrediting of assets and achievements is pernicious to the development or recovery of self-confidence.

Lastly, in subtle and gross ways self-contempt shows in the whole behavior. People may place insufficient value upon their time, their work done or to be done, their wishes, opinions, convictions. Of the same sort are those who have seemingly lost the capacity to take seriously anything that they do, say, or feel and who are astonished if others do. They develop a cynical attitude toward themselves which may in turn extend to the world in general. More conspicuously, self-contempt is apparent in an abject, obsequious, or apologetic behavior.

Just as in other forms of self-hate, the self-berating may appear in dreams. And it may show at times when it is still remote from the dreamer's conscious mind. He may present himself through the symbol of a cesspool, some loathsome creature (a cockroach, say, or a gorilla), a gangster, a ridiculous clown. He may dream of houses with a pompous façade but inside as messy as a pigsty, of houses dilapidated beyond repair, of his having sexual relations with some low, despicable partner, of somebody making a fool of himself in public, etc.

To gain a more comprehensive grasp on the poignancy of the problem we shall consider here four consequences of self-contempt. The first is the compulsive need of certain neurotic types *to compare themselves* with everybody with whom they come in contact, and to their own disadvantage. The other fellow is more impressive, better informed, more interesting, more attractive, better dressed; he has the advantage of age or youth, of a better position, of greater importance. But even though the comparisons may strike the neurotic himself as lop-sided, he does not think them through clearly; or, if he does, the feeling of comparative inferiority still remains. The compari-sons made are not only unfair to himself; they often do not make any sense. Why should an older man who could be proud of his own accomplishments compare himself with a youngster who is a better dancer? Or why should somebody who has never been interested in music feel inferior to musicians?

This practice makes sense, however, when we remember the unconscious claims to be superior to others in *every* regard. We must add here that the neurotic's pride also demands that he *should* be superior to everybody and everything. Then of course any "superior" skill or quality of others must be disturbing, and must call forth a self-destructive berating. Sometimes the con-nection operates in reverse: the neurotic, already in a self-be-rating frame of mind, utilizes the "shining" qualities of others, as he encounters them, to reinforce and buttress his castigating self-criticism. To express it in terms of two people: it is as if an ambitious and sadistic mother used the better marks or cleaner fingernails of Jimmy's friend to put Jimmy to shame. It is insufficient to describe these processes simply as a recoiling from competition. The recoiling from competition in these instances is rather the result of self-disparagement.

A second consequence of self-contempt is *vulnerability* in hu-man relations. Self-contempt makes the neurotic hypersensitive to criticism and rejection. On little or no provocation he feels that others look down on him, do not take him seriously, do not care for his company, and in fact slight him. His self-contempt adds considerably to the profound uncertainty he has about himself, and hence cannot but make him as profoundly uncer-tain about the attitudes of others toward him. Being unable to accept himself as he is, he cannot possibly believe that others, knowing him with all his shortcomings, can accept him in a friendly or appreciative spirit.

What he feels in deeper layers is much more drastic, and may amount to an unshakable conviction that others plainly despise him. And such a conviction may live in him although he is not consciously aware of even a trace of self-contempt. Both of these factors—the blind assumption that others despise him and a relative or total awareness of his own self-contempt—point to the fact that the bulk of self-contempt is externalized. This may lead to a subtle poisoning of all his human relations. He may become unable to take any positive feelings of others at their face values. A compliment may, in his mind, register as a sarcastic comment; an expression of sympathy as condescending pity. Somebody wants to see him—it is because he wants something of him. Others express a liking for him—it can only be because they do not know him well, because they themselves are worthless or "neurotic," or because he has been or could be useful to them. Similarly, incidents which in fact have no hostile meaning are interpreted as evidence of an existing contempt. Somebody has not greeted him on the street or in the theater, has not accepted his invitation, or has not replied right away—it can only be a slight. Somebody makes a good-natured joke about him—it is a clear intent to humiliate him. An objection to, or a criticism of, some suggestion or activity of his does not constitute an honest criticism of the particular activity, etc., but becomes evidence of the other's despising him.

The person himself, as we see in analysis, is either unaware of his experiencing his relations with others in this way or he is unaware of the distortions involved. In the latter case he may take it for granted that others' attitudes toward him are really of this sort, and even pride himself on being "realistic." In the analytic relationship we can observe to what extent a patient can take it for granted that others look down on him. After much analytic work is done, and the patient is apparently on good friendly terms with his analyst, he may mention casually and without affectation that it was always so self-evident to him that the analyst was looking down on him that he did not feel it necessary to mention it or to give it any extended thought.

All these distorted perceptions in human relations are understandable because the attitudes of others are indeed open to several interpretations, particularly when torn out of context, while the externalized self-contempt feels unmistakably real. Also the self-protective character of such a shift in responsibility is evident. It is probably intolerable, if possible at all, to live with a constantly awake, sharp self-contempt. Seen from this viewpoint, the neurotic has an unconscious interest in regarding others as the offenders. Although it is painful for him, as it would be for anybody, to feel slighted and rejected, it is less painful than coming face to face with his own self-contempt. It is a long and hard lesson for anybody to learn that others can neither hurt nor establish self-esteem.

The vulnerability in human relations caused by self-contempt combines with that brought about by neurotic pride. It is often difficult to say whether a person feels humiliated because something has hurt his pride or because he has externalized his self-contempt. They are so inseparably interwoven that we have to tackle such reactions from both angles. Of course, at a given time, one or the other aspect will be the more easily observable and the more accessible. If a person reacts to a seeming disregard with vindictive arrogance, hurt pride is uppermost in the picture. If, as a result of the same provocation, he turns abject and tries to ingratiate himself, self-contempt sticks out most clearly. But in either case the reverse aspect is also operating and should be kept in mind.

Thirdly, a person in the clutches of self-contempt often *takes too much abuse* from others. He may not even recognize a flagrant abuse, whether it be humiliation or exploitation. Even if indignant friends call it to his attention he tends to minimize or justify the offender's behavior. This occurs only under certain conditions, such as in a morbid dependency, and is the outcome of a complicated inner constellation. But essential among the factors producing it is the defenselessness produced by the person's conviction that he does not deserve any better treatment. For instance, a woman whose husband is flaunting his affairs with other women may be unable to complain or even to feel conscious resentment because she feels unlovable and regards most other women as more attractive.

A last consequence to be mentioned is the need to *alleviate or balance self-contempt with the attention, regard, appreciation, admiration, or love of others.* The pursuit of such attention is compulsive, because of the compelling need not to be at the mercy of self-contempt. It is also determined by a need to triumph, and may amount to an all-consuming life goal. The result is a total dependence on others for self-evaluation: it rises or falls with the attitudes of others toward him.

Thinking along broader theoretical lines, observations like these help us to understand better why the neurotic clings so tenaciously to the glorified version of himself. He must maintain it because he feels only one alternative: to succumb to the terror of self-contempt. There is thus a vicious circle operating between pride and self-contempt, one always reinforcing the other. This can change only to the extent that he gets interested in the truth about himself. But again self-contempt renders it difficult to find himself. As long as his degraded image of himself is real to him his self appears despicable.

What exactly does the neurotic despise in himself? Sometimes everything: his human limitations; his body, its appearance and functioning; the faculties of his mind—reasoning, memory, critical thinking, planning, special skills or gifts—any activity, from simple private actions to public performances. While the tendency to disparage may be more or less pervasive, it is usually focused on some areas more sharply than on others, depending on the importance which certain attitudes, faculties, or qualities have for the main neurotic solution. The aggressive vindictive type, for instance, will despise in himself most deeply anything he conceives as "weakness." This may comprise positive feelings he has for others, any failure to get back at others, any compliance (including a reasonable giving in), any lack of control over himself or others. In the framework of this book it is not possible to give a complete survey of all the possibilities. It is not necessary either, since the principles at work are always the same. For illustrations I shall discuss merely two of the more frequent expressions of self-contempt—those concerning attractiveness and intelligence.

With regard to looks and appearance, we find the whole range from a person's feeling unattractive to feeling repulsive. At first glance it is astonishing to find this tendency in women who are attractive beyond average. But we must not forget that what counts are not objective facts or opinions of others but the discrepancy a woman feels between her idealized image and her actual self. Thus, even though by common acclaim she may be a beauty, she still is not the *absolute* beauty—such as never was and never will be. And so she may focus on her imperfections—a scar, a wrist not slender enough, or hair not naturally wavy—and run herself down on this score, sometimes to the extent of hating to look at a mirror. Or the fear of being repulsive to others may be aroused easily, for instance by the mere fact of having somebody who has been sitting beside her in the movies change his seat.

Dependent on other factors in the personality, the contemptuous attitude toward appearance may lead either to excessive efforts to counteract violent self-berating or to a "don't care" attitude. In the first case an inordinate amount of time, money, and thought is spent on hair, complexion, dresses, hats, etc. If the disparaging is focused on special aspects, like the nose or the breasts or an overweight condition, it may lead to drastic "cures," like operations or enforced reducing. In the second, pride interferes with taking even reasonable care of skin, posture, or dresses. A woman may then be so deeply convinced of being ugly or repulsive that any attempt to improve her looks seems ridiculous to her.

The self-berating on the score of looks becomes more poignant when one realizes that it is also fed from a deeper source. The question "Am I attractive?" is inseparable from another one: "Am I lovable?" Here we touch upon a crucial problem in human psychology, and will again have to leave a loose end because the problem of lovableness is better discussed in another context. The two questions are interlinked in more than one way but they are not identical. The one means: Is my appearance sufficiently beautiful to attract love? The other: Have I qualities which make me lovable? Although the first one is important, particularly in younger years, the second goes into the core of our being and is the one relevant to attaining happiness in love life. But lovable qualities have to do with personality, and as long as the neurotic is remote from himself his personality is too nebulous to interest him. Also, while imperfections in terms of attractiveness often are negligible for all practical purposes, lovableness is factually impaired in all neuroses for many reasons. Yet, strangely enough, the analyst hears plenty of concern about the first and very little, if any, about the second. Is not this one of the many shifts taking place in neurosis from the essentials to the periphery? From what really matters for our self-fulfillment to the shining surface? Is not this process also in line with the search for glamor? There is no glamor in having and developing lovable qualities, but there may be glamor in having just the right figure or just the right dress. In this context it is inevitable that all questions of appearance are overloaded with significance. And it is understandable that the self-disparaging will focus on them.

The self-disparaging concerning intelligence, with the resultant feeling of stupidity, corresponds to pride in the omnipotence of reason. And it depends upon the whole structure as to whether pride or self-contempt on this score is in the foreground. Actually in most neuroses there are disturbances which constitute valid reasons for discontent with the functioning of the mind. A fear of being aggressive may hamper critical thinking; a general reluctance to commit oneself may render it difficult to arrive at an opinion. The compelling need to appear omniscient may interfere with the capacity to learn. General tendencies to becloud personal issues may also befog the clarity of thinking; just as people blind themselves to their inner conflicts, they may be oblivious to other sorts of contradictions. They may be too fascinated in the glory to be achieved to be sufficiently interested in the work they are doing.

I remember a time when I thought that such actual difficulties accounted fully for the feeling of stupidity; when I hoped to be helpful in saying something like: "Your intelligence is perfectly in order—but what about your interest, your courage; what about all that has to go into your capacity to work?" Of course, to work at all these factors are necessary. But the patient is not interested in freeing himself to use his intelligence in his life; what he is interested in is the *absolute* intelligence of the "master mind." What I did not recognize at that time was the power of the self-devaluating process, which sometimes reaches gigantic proportions. Even people who have attained genuine intellectual achievements may prefer to insist on considering themselves stupid than to avow their aspirations, since at any cost they must avoid the danger of ridicule. And in quiet despair they accept this verdict, rejecting all evidence or assurance to the contrary.

The self-belittling processes disturb the active pursuit of any interest to a varying degree. The effect may show before, during, or after activities. A neurotic succumbing to self-contempt may feel so discouraged that it does not occur to him that he could change a tire, speak a foreign language, or talk in public. Or he may start some activity but give it up at the first difficulty that arises. Or he may become frightened before or at public performances (stage fright). Again, as in regard to vulnerability, both pride and self-contempt operate to engender these inhibitions and fears. To summarize, they result from a dilemma caused by needs for a sweeping acclaim on the one hand and active self-disgracing or self-defeating forces on the other.

When, despite all these difficulties, a piece of work is finished, well done, and well received, the self-disparaging does not end. "Anybody could have achieved the same thing with so much work put in"; the one passage that did not come out to perfection in a piano recital looms large; "this time I got by, but the next will be a debacle." A failure, on the other hand, calls forth the full force of self-contempt, and this is discouraging far beyond its actual significance.

Before we discuss a fourth aspect of self-hate, *self-frustration*, we must first narrow down the subject to its proper proportions by distinguishing it from phenomena which either look similar or have a similar effect. We must distinguish it in the first place from *healthy self-discipline*. A well-organized person will forgo certain activities or satisfactions. But he does so because other goals are of greater importance to him, and hence require precedence in his hierarchy of values. Thus a young married couple may deprive themselves of pleasures because they would rather save for a home of their own. A scholar or an artist devoted to his work will restrict his social life because quietness and concentration are for him the greater values. Such discipline presupposes the recognition of limitations (in neuroses, sadly lacking) in time, energy, and money. It presupposes also knowing one's real wishes and having the capacity to renounce a less important for a more important one. This is difficult for the neurotic because his "wishes" are mostly compulsive needs. And it is in their nature that they rank equal in importance; hence none can be renounced. In analytic therapy then healthy self-discipline is more a goal to be approximated than an actuality. I would not mention this here at all if I did not know from experience that neurotic patients do not know the difference between voluntary renunciation and frustration.

We must also consider that, to the extent a person is neurotic, he actually is a frustrated being, although he may not be aware of it. His compulsive drives, his conflicts, his pseudosolutions of these conflicts, and his alienation from self prevent him from realizing his given potentialities. In addition he often feels frustrated because his claims for unlimited powers remain unfulfilled.

These frustrations, however—real or imagined—do not result from an *intent at self-frustration*. The need for affection and approval, for instance, in fact entails a frustration of the real self, of its spontaneous feelings. The neurotic develops such a need because, despite his basic anxiety, he must cope with others. The self-deprivation, though crucial, is in this case an unfortunate by-product of the process. What interests us here, in the context of self-hate, are rather the active self-frustrations perpetrated from the expressions of self-hate discussed hitherto. The tyranny of the should actually is a frustration of the freedom of choice. Self-accusations and self-contempt are frustrations of self-respect. There are, moreover, other aspects in which the active frustrating character of self-hate stands out even more clearly. These are the taboos on enjoyment and the crushing of hopes and aspirations.

The taboos on enjoyment destroy the innocence of wishing for, or doing, anything that is in our true self-interest and thereby life enriching. The more aware of himself a patient becomes in general, the more distinctly does he experience these inner taboos. He wants to go on a trip, and the inner voice says: "You don't deserve it." Or, in other situations: "You have no right to rest, or to go to a movie, or to buy a dress." Or, in an

even more general sense: "Good things are not for you." He
wants to analyze in himself an irritability which he suspects to
be irrational, and feels "as if an iron hand closes a heavy door."
So he gets tired and desists from doing the analytic work which
he knows might benefit him. Sometimes he has inner dialogues
about the subject. After having done a good day's work he is
tired and wants to rest. The voice says: "You are just lazy." "No,
I am really tired." "Oh, no, that is sheer self-indulgence; this
way you will never get anywhere." And after such a back and
forth he either takes a rest with a guilty conscience or forces
himself to continue working—without deriving any benefit
either way.

How a person may literally beat himself down when reaching
out for enjoyment often appears in dreams. Thus a woman
dreamed she was in a garden full of luscious fruit. As soon as
she wanted to pick one, or succeeded in picking one, somebody
whipped it out of her hands. Or the dreamer in desperation
tries to open a heavy door, but he cannot do it. Or he runs to
reach a train, but it has just left. He wants to kiss a girl, but the
girl vanishes and he hears a mocking laughter.

The taboos on enjoyment may be hidden behind a front of
social consciousness: "As long as other people live in slums I
should not have a nice apartment. . . . As long as some people
are starving I should not spend anything on food. . . ." Of
course one has to examine in these instances whether such objections stem from a genuinely deep feeling of social responsibility or whether they are only a screen for a taboo on enjoyment. Often a simple question clarifies the issue and reveals a
false halo: would the person actually send the packages to
Europe with the money he does not spend on himself?

We can also infer the existence of such taboos from resulting
inhibitions. Certain types for instance can enjoy things only
when sharing them with others. True enough, for many people,
shared enjoyment is double enjoyment. But they may insist
compulsively that others listen with them to a record whether
they care for it or not, and they may be quite incapable of enjoying anything when alone. Others may be so stingy about
expenditures for themselves that even they themselves cannot
rationalize about it any more. This is particularly striking

when, at the same time, they spend lavishly on things that add to their prestige, such as giving to charity in a conspicuous way, giving a party, or buying antiques which do not mean anything to them. They act as if governed by a law allowing them to slave for glory but forbidding anything that would "merely" add to their own comfort, happiness, or growth.

As in any other taboos, the penalty of breaking them is anxiety or its equivalents. A patient who instead of gulping down her coffee fixed a nice breakfast for herself was entirely taken aback when I vociferously approved of it as a good sign. She had expected me to blame her for such "selfishness." Moving to a better apartment, though it may be sensible in every way, may arouse a host of fears. Enjoying a party may be followed by panic. An inner voice may say at such occasions: "You are going to pay for this." A patient buying some new furniture found herself saying: "You will not live to enjoy this," which in her particular case meant that a fear of cancer which she had now and then surged up at this very moment.

The *crushing of hopes* can be clearly observed in the analytic situation. The word "never," with all its formidable finality, may keep recurring. In spite of actual improvements, the voice will say: "You will never get over your dependency or over your panic; you will never be free." The patient may respond with fear and frantically ask for reassurance that he can be cured, that others have been helped, etc. Even though a patient sometimes cannot help admitting improvement, he may say: "Yes, analysis has helped me that far, but it cannot help me any further; so what is the good of it?" When the crushing of hopes is pervasive a feeling of doom results. One sometimes feels reminded of Dante's *Inferno*, with the inscription at its entrance: "Abandon hope, all ye who enter here." The repercussions to undeniable improvement often occur so regularly as to be predictable. A patient feels better, has been able to forget about a phobia, has seen an important connection that shows him a way out—and then comes back, profoundly discouraged and depressed. Another patient who for all essentials has resigned from living develops severe panic and comes to the verge of suicide each time he realizes an existing asset in himself. If the unconscious determination to keep himself down is deeply entrenched, the patient may reject any reassurance with sarcastic remarks. In some instances we can trace the process leading up to a relapse. Having seen that a certain attitude would be desirable—such as giving up irrational claims—the patient feels that he has changed, and in his imagination he surges to the heights of *absolute* freedom. Then, hating himself for not being able to do so, he tells himself: "You are no good, and will never get anywhere."

A last and most insidious self-frustration is the *taboo on any aspiration*—not simply on any grandiose fantasy, but on any striving that means using one's own resources or becoming a better and stronger person. Here the border line between self-frustration and self-disparaging is particularly vague. "Who are you to want to act, to sing, to marry? You will never amount to anything."

Some of these factors show in the history of a man who later on became remarkably productive and achieved something in his field. About a year before his work took a turn for the better —without a change in any of the external factors—he had a talk with an older woman in which she asked him what he wanted to do with his life, what he wished or expected to achieve. It turned out that despite his intelligence, thoughtfulness, and diligence he had never thought about the future. All he answered was: "Oh, I guess I shall always make a living." Though he had always been regarded as promising, the idea of doing anything of some importance had simply been blotted out. With the help of outside stimulation and some self-analysis he then became increasingly productive. But his findings in research occurred without his being aware of their significance. He even did not experience having achieved anything. Hence it did not accrue to his self-confidence. He might forget about his findings, and rediscover them accidentally. When finally he came to analysis, mainly on account of remaining inhibitions in his work, his taboos on wanting anything for himself and aspiring for something, or realizing his particular gifts, were still formidable. Apparently his existing gifts and a hidden ambition driving him toward achievement were too strong to be altogether stunted. So he got things done—even though under torture—but he had to keep this fact from awareness and was unable to own it and enjoy it. In others the result is still less favorable. They resign, do not dare to venture into something new, expect nothing from life, put their goals too low, and hence live beneath their abilities and psychic means.

As in other aspects of self-hate, self-frustration may show in externalization. A person complains that if it were not for his wife, boss, lack of money, the weather, or the political situation he would be the happiest person in the world. Needless to say, we should not go to the other extreme and regard all these factors as necessarily irrelevant. Certainly they may affect our well-being. But in our evaluation of them we should scrutinize how great their actual influence is, and how much is shifted to them from inner sources. Very often a person will feel serene and content because he is on better terms with himself, despite the fact that no external difficulties have changed.

Self-torture is in part an inevitable by-product of self-hate. Whether the neurotic tries to whip himself into a perfection impossible to attain, hurls accusations against himself, or disparages or frustrates himself, he is actually torturing himself. Making self-torture a separate category among the expressions of self-hate involves the contention that there is, or may be, an *intent* at self-tormenting. We must of course, in any case of neurotic anguish, consider all possibilities. Consider for instance self-doubts. They may result from inner conflicts and may show in endless and inconclusive inner dialogues, in which a person tries to defend himself against his own self-accusations; they may be an expression of self-hate, aimed at undermining the ground on which a person stands. Actually they can be most tormenting. Like Hamlet—or even worse than he—people can be eaten up by self-doubts. Certainly we have to analyze all the reasons for their operating, but do they also constitute an unconscious *intent* at self-torture?

A further example of this same caliber: procrastination. As we know, many factors may be responsible for delaying decision or action, such as general inertia or a pervasive incapacity to take a stand. The procrastinator himself knows that things postponed often will loom larger and larger, and that in actual fact he may inflict considerable suffering upon himself. And here we sometimes get a first glimpse that goes beyond inconclusive questions. When, on account of his postponing, he does get into an unpleasant or threatening situation he may say to himself with unmistakable glee: "It serves you right." That still does not mean that he procrastinates because he is driven to torture himself, but it does suggest a kind of *Schadenfreude*, a vindictive satisfaction at the self-inflicted distress. No evidence so far, then, for an active tormenting—but rather the gleeful attitude of a bystander watching the victim squirm and writhe.

All of this would remain inconclusive if it were not for a crescendo of other observations, showing the existence of active self-tormenting drives. In certain forms of stinginess with self, for instance, the patient observes that his petty economizing is not simply an "inhibition" but is peculiarly satisfying, sometimes almost amounting to a passion. Then there are certain patients with hypochondriac propensities who not only have their honest-to-God fears but also seem to frighten themselves in a rather cruel way. A touch of a sore throat turns into tuberculosis, a stomach upset into cancer, an aching muscle into poliomyelitis, a headache into a brain tumor, a spell of anxiety into insanity. One such patient went through what she called the "poisonous process." At slight initial signs of restlessness or sleeplessness she would tell herself that now she was in for a new cycle of panic. Each night thereafter it would become worse and worse until it reached unbearable proportions. Comparing the initial fears to a little snowball, it was as if she rolled it on and on until it grew into an avalanche which in the end would bury her. In a poem she wrote at that time she speaks of "the sweet self-torture which is my whole delight." In these hypochondriac cases one factor which sets the self-torture going can be isolated. They feel that they should have *absolute* health, poise, and fearlessness. Any little sign to the contrary makes them turn mercilessly against themselves.

Furthermore, when analyzing a patient's sadistic fantasies and impulses, we recognize that these may originate in sadistic impulses directed against himself. Certain patients have at times compulsive urges or fantasies to torture others. These seem to focus mostly on children or helpless people. In one instance they concerned a hunchbacked servant, Anne, in a boardinghouse where the patient lived. The patient was disquieted partly by the intensity of the impulses and partly because he felt bewildered by them. Anne was pleasant enough and had never hurt his feelings. Before the sadistic fantasies started he had alternatingly felt loathing and sympathy for her physical deformity. Both of these feelings he had recognized as stemming from his identifying himself with the girl. He was physically strong and healthy, but when he felt hopeless and contemptuous in regard to his psychic entanglements he would refer to himself as a cripple. The sadistic impulses and fantasies started when he first noticed in Anne a certain overeagerness to serve and a tendency to make a doormat out of herself. Most likely Anne had long been this way. However, his observation struck at the very point when his own self-effacing trends had come closer to awareness and rumblings of self-hate on these grounds had become audible. The compulsive urge to torture her was hence interpreted as an active externalization of impulses to torture himself which, in addition, gave him a thrilling feeling of power over a weaker creature. The active urge then dwindled to sadistic fantasies, and these disappeared as his self-effacing trends and his loathing of them came into clearer focus.

I do not believe that all sadistic impulses—or actions—toward others have their sole origin in self-hate. But I think it likely that the externalization of self-tormenting drives is always a contributing factor. At any rate the connection is sufficiently frequent to cause us to be alert to its possibilities.

In other patients fears of torture appear without any external provocation. They also arise at times of increased self-hate, and express a reaction of fear to a passive externalization of self-tormenting drives.

Finally, there are masochistic and sexual activities and fantasies. I am thinking of masturbation fantasies which extend from being degraded to being cruelly tortured; masturbatory activities that accompany scratching or slapping oneself, pulling out hair, walking in too tight shoes, assuming painfully twisted positions; sexual acts in which the person must be scolded, beaten, tied, or forced to perform menial or disgusting tasks before he can reach sexual satisfaction. The structure of these practices is rather complicated. I believe that we must distinguish at least two different kinds. In one of them the person experiences a vindictive pleasure from torturing himself; in the other he is identified with the degraded self and can, for reasons to be discussed later, gain sexual satisfaction this way only. There is, however, reason to believe that this distinction is valid only for the conscious experience—that in fact he is always both the torturer and the tortured, that he derives satisfaction from being degraded as well as from degrading himself.

One of the implications for analytical therapy is to look out in all instances of factual self-torture for a secret *intent* at self-torment. Another one is to be alert to the possibility of externalizations of self-tormenting tendencies. Whenever an intent at self-torture seems reasonably clear, we must examine carefully the intrapsychic situation and ask ourselves whether (and for what reasons) self-hate was increased at that time.

Self-hate finally culminates in pure and direct *self-destructive impulses and actions*. These may be acute or chronic, openly violent or insidious and slow grinding, conscious or unconscious, carried out in action or performed in imagination only. They may concern minor or major issues. They aim ultimately at physical, psychic, and spiritual self-destruction. When one considers all these possibilities, suicide ceases to be an isolated enigma. There are many ways in which we can kill something which is essential to our life; actual physical suicide is simply the most extreme and the final expression of self-destructiveness.

Self-destruction drives directed against the body are the most easily accessible to observation. Actual physical violence against self is more or less restricted to psychoses. In neuroses we find minor self-destructive activities, which mostly pass as "bad habits"—such as nailbiting, scratching, picking at rashes, pulling out hair. But there are also sudden impulses of stark violence which, in contrast to the psychotic, stay in imagination. They seem to occur only in those who live in imagination to such a degree that they scorn reality, including of course the reality of themselves. They emerge often after flashes of insight, and the whole process goes on with such lightning speed that we can catch the sequence only in the analytic situation: a sudden penetrating vision of some imperfection, flaring up and passing quickly, is followed just as abruptly by a violent impulse to tear out one's eyes, to slash one's throat, or to stab a knife into one's stomach and cut one's guts to pieces. This type may also have at times suicidal impulses, such as jumping from a balcony or a precipice, impulses which arise under similar conditions and seem to come out of the clear sky. They may vanish so quickly that there is hardly a chance of carrying them out. On the other hand, the urge to jump from a height may suddenly be so strong that the person has to hold on to something in order not to give in and do it. Or it may lead to an actual suicide attempt. Even so, this type has no realistic notion of the finality of death. He rather feels like jumping from the twentieth floor and then picking himself up and going home. It often depends on accidental factors whether or not such attempts succeed. If I may be allowed the anomaly, nobody would be more astonished to find him actually dead than he himself.

The far-gone alienation from self must be kept in mind for many more serious attempts at suicide. However, as a rule an unrealistic attitude toward death is more characteristic for suicidal impulses or abortive attempts than for those which are planned and seriously tried. Of course there are always many reasons leading to such steps, the self-destructive tendency being simply the most regular element in them.

Self-destructive impulses may remain unconscious as such and yet be actualized in reckless driving, swimming, climbing, or in a rash disregard for physical disabilities. We have seen that these activities may not appear reckless to the person himself because he harbors a claim for being inviolable ("nothing can happen to me"). In many instances this is the main factor involved. But we should always be aware of the possibility of self-destructive drives operating in addition, particularly when the disregard for actual dangers assumes drastic proportions.

Finally there are those who unconsciously but systematically ruin their health by drinking or by using drugs, though here too other factors—such as the constant need for a narcotic—

operate. We can see in Stefan Zweig's picture of Balzac the tragedy of a genius who, driven by a pathetic craving for glamor, actually ruined his health by excessive work, neglect of sleep, and abuse of coffee. To be sure, Balzac's need for glamor rushed him into debt so that his overwork in part was a consequence of a wrong way of living. But certainly the question is justified—here as in similar instances—whether self-destructive drives were not also at work, leading in the end to a premature death.

In other cases bodily damage is incurred, as it were, accidentally. We all know that in a "bad mood" we are more likely to cut ourselves, to take a wrong step and fall, to pinch our fingers. But it can be fatal if we do not pay attention to traffic when crossing the street, or to traffic regulations when driving.

There is, finally, the still open question about the silent operating of self-destructive drives in organic illness. While by now more is known about psychosomatic relations, it would be difficult to isolate with sufficient accuracy the specific role of self-destructive trends. Of course every good physician knows that in severe illness the patient's "wish" to recover and live, or to die, is crucial. But again the availability of psychic energies in one or the other direction can be determined by many factors. All that we can say now is that, considering the unity of body and soul, the possibility of a silent operating of self-destructiveness, not only in the phase of recovery but in producing or aggravating an illness, must be seriously considered.

Self-destructiveness directed against other values in life may appear as an inopportune accident. There is the example of Eilert Lovborg in *Hedda Gabler* losing his precious manuscript. Ibsen shows us in Lovborg a crescendo of self-ruining reactions and actions. First, following a flimsy suspicion of his faithful friend Mrs. Elvstedt, he tries to ruin that relationship by going on a binge. While drunk, he loses the manuscript, then shoots himself—and in the house of a prostitute at that. On a minor scale there are the cases of a person forgetting things in an examination or being late or drunk for an important interview.

Most frequently the ruining of psychic values strikes us

through its repetitiousness. A person gives up one pursuit just when he appears to be getting somewhere. We may grant him his claim that it was not what he "really" wanted. But when a similar process occurs three, four, or five times we begin to look for deeper determinants. Self-destructiveness is often prominent among them, though more deeply buried than other factors. Without in the least being aware of it, he simply has to spoil his every chance. This also applies when he loses or quits one job after another, or if one relationship after another goes on the rocks. In both these latter cases it frequently seems to him as though he were always the victim of iniquities and crass in- gratitude on the part of others. Actually what he does is to in- vite, through his persistent fussing at and over the relationship, the very consummation he has so dreaded. In short, he often drives the employer or friend to the point where he or she really can no longer put up with him.

We may understand such repetitious occurrences when we see him operating in the analytic relationship. He may co-operate in formalities; he may often try to do the analyst all sorts of favors (which the latter does not want); nevertheless, in all es- sentials he is so provocative in his offensive behavior that the analyst too may feel a stirring sympathy with those who have turned against the patient previously. In short, the patient lit- erally has tried, and keeps on trying, to make others the execu- tioners of his self-ruining intents.

To what extent do active self-destructive trends operate in gradually destroying a person's depth and integrity? To a greater or lesser extent, in gross and subtle ways, the integrity of a person is impaired as a consequence of the neurotic develop- ment. The alienation from self, the unavoidable unconscious pretenses, the also unavoidable unconscious compromises due to unsolved conflicts, the self-contempt—all these factors lead to a weakening of the moral fiber in the nucleus of which is a diminished capacity for being sincere with oneself.[10] The ques- tion is whether, in addition, a person may silently but actively collaborate toward his own moral deterioration. Certain obser- vations force us to answer this question in the affirmative.

[10] *Cf.* Karen Horney, *Our Inner Conflicts*, W. W. Norton, 1945, Chapter 10, The Impoverishment of Personality.

We can observe conditions, chronic or acute, which can best be described as an impairment of morale. A person neglects his appearance, he lets himself become untidy, sloppy, and fat; he drinks too much, sleeps too little; he does not take care of his health—does not, for instance, go to the dentist. He eats too much or too little, does not take walks; he neglects his work, or whatever serious interest he has, and becomes slothful. He may become promiscuous or at least prefer the company of shallow or deteriorated people. He may become unreliable in money matters, beat his wife and children, start to lie or to steal. This process is most obvious in advanced alcoholics, as is well described in *The Lost Weekend*. But it can operate in very hidden and subtle ways as well. In conspicuous instances even an untrained observer can see that these people "let themselves go to pieces." In analysis we recognize that this description is not adequate. These conditions occur when people are so flooded with self-contempt and hopelessness that their constructive forces can no longer counteract the impact of self-destructive drives. The latter then have free sway and express themselves in a mostly unconscious determination to demoralize themselves actively. In an externalized form the active, planned intent at demoralization is described by George Orwell in his *Nineteen Eighty-Four;* every experienced analyst will recognize in his presentation a true picture of what a neurotic may do to himself. Dreams also indicate that he may actively throw himself into the gutter.

The neurotic's response to this inner process varies. It may be glee; it may be self-pity; it may be fright. These reactions are usually disconnected in his conscious mind from the self-demoralizing process.

The reaction of self-pity was particularly strong in one patient after the following dream. The patient who dreamed it had in periods past wasted much of her life by drifting; she had turned her back on ideals by becoming cynical. Though at the time of her dream she was working hard on herself, she was not yet able to take herself seriously and do anything constructive with her life. She dreamed that a woman who stood for everything that was fine and likable, about to enter a religious order, was accused of some offense against it. She was condemned and exposed to public disgrace in a parade. Although the dreamer was convinced of her essential innocence, she too was participating in the parade. On the other hand, she tried to plead in her favor with a priest. The priest, although sympathetic, could do nothing for the accused. Later the accused was on a farm, not only utterly destitute but dull and half witted. The dreamer, still in her dream, felt a heart-rending pity for the victim and wept for hours after waking. Barring details, the dreamer here says to herself: There is something fine and likable in me; through my self-condemnation and self-destructiveness I may actually ruin my personality; my steps against such drives are ineffectual; though I want to save myself, I also avoid a real fight and, in some way, collaborate with my destructive drives.

In dreams we are closer to the reality of ourselves. And this dream in particular seemed to emerge from a great depth, and to present a profound and square insight into the danger of the dreamer's particular self-destructiveness. The reaction of pity for self, in this instance as in many others, was at that time not constructive: it did not move her to do anything in her own behalf. Only when the hopelessness and the intensity of self-contempt abates, can the unconstructive self-pity turn into a constructive sympathy with self. And this indeed is a forward move of great significance for anybody in the clutches of self-hate. It goes with a beginning feeling for his real self and a beginning wish for inner salvation.

The reaction to the deteriorating process can also be stark terror. And, considering the formidable danger of self-destructiveness, this reaction is completely adequate as long as one continues to feel a helpless prey to these merciless forces. In dreams and associations they may appear in many succinct symbols, such as a homicidal maniac, Dracula, monsters, a white whale, or ghosts. This terror is the nucleus of many fears otherwise inexplicable, such as the fear of the unknown and of the dangerous depth of the sea; the fear of ghosts; of anything mysterious; of any destructive process within the body, such as poison, worms, cancer. It is a part of the terror many patients feel toward anything that is unconscious, and therefore mysterious. It may be the center of panic without apparent reason. It would be impossible for anybody to live with such a terror if it were always present and alive. He must and does find ways to assuage it. Some of these have been mentioned; others we shall discuss in subsequent chapters.

Surveying self-hate and its ravaging force, we cannot help but see in it a great tragedy, perhaps the greatest tragedy of the human mind. Man in reaching out for the Infinite and Absolute also starts destroying himself. When he makes a pact with the devil, who promises him glory, he has to go to hell—to the hell within himself.

CHAPTER 6

ALIENATION FROM SELF

THIS BOOK began with a vigorous emphasis on the importance of the real self. The real self, we said, is the alive, unique, personal center of ourselves; the only part that can, and wants to, grow. We saw that unfortunate conditions prevent its unimpeded growth from the very beginning. Since then our interest has been centered on those forces in the individual which usurp its energies and lead to the formation of a pride system which becomes autonomous and exerts a tyrannical and destructive power.

This shift of interest in the book from the real self to the idealized self and its development is an exact replica of the neurotic's shift of interest from the one to the other. But, unlike the neurotic, we still have a clear vision of the importance of the real self. We shall therefore bring it back into the focus of our attention and consider in a more systematic way than before the reasons for its being abandoned and the loss this means for the personality.

In terms of the devil's pact, the abandoning of self corresponds to the selling of one's soul. In psychiatric terms we call it the "alienation from self." This latter term is applied chiefly to those extreme conditions in which people lose their feeling of identity, as in amnesias and depersonalizations, etc. These conditions have always aroused general curiosity. It is strange and even startling that a person who is not asleep and has no organic brain disease does not know who he is, where he is, or what he does or has been doing.

These are, however, less bewildering if we do not regard them as isolated occurrences but see their relation to less conspicuous forms of alienation from self. In these forms there is no gross loss of identity and orientation, but the general capacity for conscious experience is impaired. There are for instance many neurotics who live as if they were in a fog. Nothing is clear to them. Not only their own thoughts and feelings but also other people, and the implications of a situation, are hazy. Also related, in still less drastic terms, are conditions in which the dimming out is restricted to intrapsychic processes. I am thinking of people who can be rather astute observers of others, who can lucidly size up a situation or a trend of thought; yet experiences of all kinds (in relation to others, nature, etc.) do not penetrate to their feelings, and their inner experiences do not penetrate to awareness. And these states of mind in turn are not unrelated to those of apparently healthy people who suffer from occasional partial blackouts or from blind spots concerning certain areas of inner or outer experience.

All these forms of alienation from self can concern as well the "material self" [1]—the body and the possessions. A neurotic may have but little feeling of or for his body. Even his bodily sensations may be numbed. When asked for instance whether his feet are cold, he may have to arrive at an awareness of feeling cold through a process of thinking. He may not recognize himself when seeing himself unexpectedly in a full-length mirror. Similarly, he may have no feeling of his home being his home— it is for him as impersonal as a hotel room. Others have no feeling that the money they possess is their money, even though it may have been earned through hard work.

These are only a few variations of what we could properly call an alienation from the actual self. All of what a person actually is or has, including even his connection of his present

---

[1] Here, as in many other comments, I roughly follow William James, *The Principles of Psychology*, Henry Holt and Co., New York, the chapter on "The Consciousness of Self." The quotes in the paragraph are quotations from this chapter.

life with his past, the feeling for this continuity of his life, may be blotted out or dimmed out. Some of this process is intrinsic in every neurosis. Sometimes patients may be aware of disturbances on this score, as in the case of one patient who described himself as a lamppost with a brain on top. More often they are unaware of it, although it may be fairly extensive; and it may gradually unfold only in analysis.

At the core of this alienation from the actual self is a phenomenon that is less tangible although more crucial. It is the remoteness of the neurotic from his own feelings, wishes, beliefs, and energies. It is the loss of the feeling of being an active determining force in his own life. It is the loss of feeling himself as an organic whole. These in turn indicate an alienation from that most alive center of ourselves which I have suggested calling the *real self*. To present more fully its propensities in the terms of William James: it provides the "palpitating inward life"; it engenders the spontaneity of feelings, whether these be joy, yearning, love, anger, fear, despair. It also is the source of spontaneous interest and energies, "the source of effort and attention from which emanate the fiats of will"; the capacity to wish and to will; it is the part of ourselves that wants to expand and grow and to fulfill itself. It produces the "reactions of spontaneity" to our feelings or thoughts, "welcoming or opposing, appropriating or disowning, striving with or against, saying yes or no." All this indicates that our real self, when strong and active, enables us to make decisions and assume responsibility for them. It therefore leads to genuine integration and a sound sense of wholeness, oneness. Not merely are body and mind, deed and thought or feeling, consonant and harmonious, but they function without serious inner conflict. In contrast to those artificial means of holding ourselves together, which gain in importance as the real self is weakened, there is little or no attendant strain.

The history of philosophy shows that we can deal with the problems of self from many vantage points. Yet it seems as though everyone treating this subject has found it difficult to go beyond describing his special experiences and interests. From the viewpoint of clinical usefulness, I would distinguish the actual or empirical [2] self from the idealized self on the one hand, and the real self on the other. The actual self is an all-inclusive term for everything that a person is at a given time: body and soul, healthy and neurotic. We have it in mind when we say that we want to know ourselves; i.e., we want to know ourselves as we are. The idealized self is what we are in our irrational imagination, or what we should be according to the dictates of neurotic pride. The real self, which I have defined several times, is the "original" force toward individual growth and fulfillment, with which we may again achieve full identification when freed of the crippling shackles of neurosis. Hence it is what we refer to when we say that we want to find ourselves. In this sense it is also (to all neurotics) the *possible* self —in contrast to the idealized self, which is *impossible* of attainment. Seen from this angle, it seems the most speculative of all. Who, seeing a neurotic patient, can separate the wheat from the chaff and say: this is his possible self. But while the real or possible self of a neurotic person is in a way an abstraction, it is nevertheless *felt* and we can say that every glimpse we get of it feels more real, more certain, more definite than anything else. We can observe this quality in ourselves or in our patients when, after some incisive insight, there is a release from the grip of some compulsive need.

Although one cannot always distinguish neatly between alienation from the actual self and that from the real self, the latter will be in the following discussion the focus of our interest. The loss of self, says Kierkegaard, is "sickness unto death"; [3] it is despair—despair at not being conscious of having a self, or despair at not being willing to be ourselves. But it is a despair (still following Kierkegaard) which does not clamor or scream. People go on living as if they were still in immediate contact with this alive center. Any other loss—that of a job, say, or a leg—arouses far more concern. This statement of Kierkegaard's coincides with clinical observation. Apart from the pronounced pathologic conditions mentioned before, its loss does not strike the eye directly and forcefully. Patients coming for consultation complain about headaches, sexual dis-

---

[2] The term "empirical self" is used by William James.
[3] Sören Kierkegaard, *Sickness unto Death*, Princeton University Press, 1941.

turbances, inhibitions in work, or other symptoms; as a rule, they do not complain about having lost touch with the core of their psychic existence.

Let us now, without going into detail, obtain a comprehensive picture of the forces responsible for the alienation from self. It is in part the consequences of the whole neurotic development, especially of *all that is compulsive in neurosis*. Of all that implies "I am driven instead of being the driver." It does not matter in this context what the particular compulsive factors are—whether they operate in relation to others (compliance, vindictiveness, detachment, etc.) or in the relation to self, as in self-idealization. The very compulsive character of these drives inevitably deprives the person of his full autonomy and spontaneity. As soon as, for instance, his need to be liked by everybody becomes compulsive, the genuineness of his feelings diminishes; so does his power to discriminate. As soon as he is driven to do a piece of work for the sake of glory, his spontaneous interest in the work itself decreases. Conflicting compulsive drives, in addition, impair his integration, his faculty to decide and give direction. Last but not least, the neurotic pseudo-solutions,[4] though representing attempts at integration, also deprive him of autonomy because they become a compulsive way of living.

Secondly, the alienation is furthered through processes, likewise compulsive, which can be described as *active moves away from* the real self. The whole drive for glory is such a move, particularly through the neurotic's determination to mold himself into something he is not. He feels what he *should* feel, wishes what he *should* wish, likes what he *should* like. In other words, the tyranny of the should drives him frantically to be something different from what he is or could be. And in his imagination he *is* different—so different, indeed, that his real self fades and pales still more. Neurotic claims, in terms of self, mean the abandoning of the reservoir of spontaneous energies. Instead of making his own efforts, for instance, with regard to human relations, the neurotic insists that others should adjust to him. Instead of putting himself into his work, he feels en-

---

[4] *Cf. Our Inner Conflicts* and the following chapters of this book.

titled to having it done for him. Instead of making his own decisions, he insists that others should be responsible for him. Therefore his constructive energies lie fallow, and he actually *is* less and less a determining factor in his own life.

Neurotic pride removes him a step further from himself. Since he now becomes ashamed of what he actually is—of his feelings, resources, activities—he actively withdraws his interest from himself. The whole process of externalization is another active moving away from his self, actual and real. It is astonishing, by the way, how closely this process coincides with Kierkegaard's "despair of not wanting to be oneself."

Finally, there are *active moves against* the real self, as expressed in self-hates. With the real self in exile, so to speak, one becomes a condemned convict, despised and threatened with destruction. The idea of being oneself even becomes loathsome and terrifying. The terror sometimes appears undisguised, as one patient felt it when thinking: "This is me." This appeared at a time when the neat distinction she had made between "me" and "my neurosis" started to crumble. As a protection against this terror the neurotic "makes himself disappear." He has an unconscious interest in not having a clear perception of himself —in making himself, as it were, deaf, dumb, and blind. Not only does he blur the truth about himself but he has a vested interest in doing to—a process which blunts his sensitiveness to what is true and what is false not only inside but also outside himself. He has an interest in maintaining his haziness, although he may consciously suffer under it. One patient, for instance, in his associations often used the monsters of the Beowulf legend, who emerged at night from the lake, to symbolize his self-hate. And once he said: "If there is a fog, the monsters can't see me."

The result of all these moves is an alienation from self. When we use this term we must be aware that it focuses on only one aspect of the phenomenon. What it expresses accurately is the subjective feeling of the neurotic of being removed from himself. He may realize in analysis that all the intelligent things he has said about himself were in reality disconnected from him and his life, that they concerned some fellow with whom he had little if anything to do and the findings about whom were interesting but did not apply to his life.

In fact, this analytic experience leads us straight into the core of the problem. For we must keep in mind that the patient does not talk about weather or television: he talks about his most intimate personal life experiences. Yet they have lost their personal meaning. And, just as he may talk about himself without "being in it," so he may work, be with friends, take a walk, or sleep with a woman without being in it. His *relation to himself has become impersonal;* so has his relation to his whole life. If the word "depersonalization" did not already have a specific psychiatric meaning, it would be a good term for what alienation from self essentially is: it is a depersonalizing, and therefore a devitalizing, process.

I have already said that the alienation from self does not show as directly and blatantly as its significance would suggest, except (speaking of neuroses only) in the state of depersonalization, feelings of unreality, or amnesia. While these conditions are temporary, they can occur only in people who are estranged from themselves anyhow. The factors precipitating the feelings of unreality are usually severe injuries to pride together with an acute increase of self-contempt, exceeding what is tolerable for the particular person. Conversely, when—with or without therapy—these acute conditions subside, his alienation from self is not thereby essentially changed. It is merely again restrained within such limits that he can function without conspicuous disorientation. Otherwise the trained observer would be able to perceive certain general symptoms pointing to an existing alienation from self, such as deadness of the eyes, an aura of impersonality, an automatonlike behavior. Writers like Camus, Marquand, and Sartre have described such symptoms excellently. For the analyst it is a source of never-ending astonishment how comparatively well a person can function with the core of himself not participating.

What, then, are the *effects* that alienation from self has on an individual's personality and on his life? In order to obtain a clear and comprehensive picture we shall discuss successively the bearing it has on his emotional life, his energies, his faculty for giving direction to his life, to assume responsibility for himself, and his integrating powers.

Offhand, it would seem difficult to say anything about the *capacity to feel* or the *awareness of feelings* that is valid for all neuroses. Some are overemotional in their joy, enthusiasm, or suffering; others appear to be cold, or at any rate hide behind a façade of impassivity; again, in others feelings seem to have lost their intensity and are dulled and flattened out. Despite endless variations, however, one characteristic seems to be pertinent for all neuroses of any severity. Awareness, strength, and kind of feelings are determined mainly by the pride system. Genuine feelings for self are dampened or diminished, sometimes to a vanishing point. In short, *pride governs feelings*.

The neurotic is liable to play down those feelings which run counter to his particular pride and to overemphasize those which add to it. If in his arrogance he feels vastly superior to others, he cannot allow himself to feel envy. His pride in asceticism may put a lid on feelings of enjoyment. If he is proud of his vindictiveness, vindictive rage may be keenly felt. However, if his vindictiveness is glorified and rationalized in terms of dealing out "justice," he does not experience vindictive rage as such, although it is so freely expressed that nobody else has any doubt about it. Pride in *absolute* endurance may prohibit any feeling of suffering. But if suffering plays an important part within the pride system—as a vehicle for expressing resentment and as a basis for neurotic claims—it is not only emphasized in front of others but actually felt more deeply. A feeling of compassion may be choked off if it is regarded as weakness, but may be fully experienced if registered as a godlike attribute. If pride is mainly focused on self-sufficiency, in the sense of not needing anything or anybody, then to own to any feelings or needs is like an "unbearable bowing down to go through a narrow gate. . . . If I like somebody, he could have a hold on me. . . . If I like anything, I might get dependent on it."

Sometimes in analysis we can observe directly how pride interferes with genuine feelings. X may respond in a spontaneously friendly way to a friendly approach of Z, although he usually resents Z, mainly on the ground of injured pride. Then a minute later something in him says, "You are a fool to be taken in by friendliness." So the friendly feeling goes by the board. Or a picture may awaken a warm, glowing enthusiasm in him. But his pride mars it when he thinks to himself, "Nobody else can appreciate pictures as you do."

Up to this point pride acts as a kind of censorship, encouraging or forbidding feelings to come to awareness. But it may govern feelings in a still more basic way. The more pride has taken over, the more a person can respond emotionally to life only with his pride. It is as if he had shut away his real self in a soundproof room and could hear the voice of pride alone. His feeling satisfied or dissatisfied, dejected or elated, his likes or dislikes of people, then, are mainly pride responses. Likewise the suffering he consciously feels is mainly a suffering of his pride. This is not apparent on the surface. It feels convincingly real to him that he suffers from failures, from feelings of guilt, loneliness, unrequited love. And he does indeed. But the question is: who suffers? In analysis it turns out that it is mainly his proud self. He suffers because he feels that he has failed to achieve supreme success, to do things to ultimate perfection, to be so irresistibly attractive as to be sought out always, to make everybody love him. Or he suffers because he feels entitled to success, popularity, etc., which is not forthcoming.

Only when the pride system is considerably undermined does he begin to feel true suffering. Only then can he feel sympathy for this suffering self of his, a sympathy that can move him to do something constructive for himself. The self-pity he felt before was rather a maudlin writhing of the proud self for feeling abused. He who has not experienced the difference may shrug his shoulders and think that it is irrelevant—that suffering is suffering. But it is true suffering alone that has the power to broaden and deepen our range of feelings and to open our hearts for the suffering of others. In *De Profundis* Oscar Wilde has described the liberation he felt when, instead of suffering from injured vanity, he started to experience true suffering.

Sometimes the neurotic can experience even his pride responses only through others. He may not *feel* humiliated by the arrogance or the neglect of a friend, but he feels ashamed at the thought that his brother or his colleagues would regard it as a humiliation.

There are of course variations in the degree to which pride governs feelings. Even a neurotic who is severely crippled emotionally may have certain feelings which are strong and sincere, such as feelings for nature or for music. These, then, are not touched by his neurosis. One might say that his real self is allowed this much freedom. Or, even though his likes and dislikes are mainly determined by his pride, genuine elements also may be present. Nevertheless, as a result of these trends, there is in neurosis a general impoverishment of the emotional life showing in a diminished sincerity, spontaneity, and depth of feelings, or at least in a restricted range of possible feelings.

A person's conscious attitude toward this disturbance varies. He may not regard his emotional dearth as a disturbance at all, but be rather proud of it. He may be seriously concerned about an increasing emotional deadness. He may realize for instance that his feelings increasingly have a merely reactive character. When not reacting to friendliness or hostility his feelings remain inactive, silent. His heart does not go out actively toward the beauty of a tree or a picture and so they remain meaningless to him. He may respond to a friend complaining about a predicament but he does not actively visualize the other's life situation. Or he may become aware with dismay that even such reactive feelings are dulled. "If at least he had been able to discover in himself a trifling emotion that was veritably, though modestly, alive . . ." writes Jean-Paul Sartre of one of his characters in *The Age of Reason*. Finally, he may not be aware of any impoverishment. Only in his dreams will he then present himself as a dummy, a marble statue, a two-dimensional cardboard figure, or a corpse whose lips he has pulled up so that he seems to smile. The self-deception in these latter instances is understandable, because on the surface the existing impoverishment may be camouflaged in either of the three following ways.

Some neurotics may display a scintillating vivacity and a false spontaneity. They may be easily enthused or discouraged, easily incited to love or to anger. But these feelings do not come out of any depth; they are not in them. They live in a world of their own imagination and respond superficially to whatever captures their fancy or hurts their pride. Often the need to impress people is in the foreground. And their alienation from self makes it possible for them to change their personality according to the requirements of the situation. Chameleonlike, they always play some role in life without knowing that they do it and, like good actors, produce the feelings that go with the roles. Hence they may seem to be genuine, whether they impersonate a frivolous man of the world, a man seriously interested in music or politics, or a helping friend. It is deceptive to the analyst too, because in analysis such persons play, appropriately, the role of patients eager to learn about themselves and to change their ways. The problem to be tackled here is the ease with which they slip into a role and change it for another—just as easily as one may slip into a dress and then change it.

Others mistake for emotional strength their pursuit of, and excited participation in, say, reckless driving, an intrigue, or a sexual escape. But, on the contrary, the need for thrill and excitement is a trustworthy indication of painful inner emptiness. Only the sharp stimuli of the unusual can elicit any response from such a person's inert emotions.

Others, finally, seem to have quite a sureness of feeling. They seem to know what they feel, and their feelings are adequate to the situation. But again, not only is the range of feelings restricted but they are on a low key, as if they were generally toned down. More intimate knowledge shows that these people automatically feel what, according to their inner dictates, they *should* feel. Or they may merely react with the feelings which others expect of them. Observations of this kind are more deceptive when personal shoulds coincide with cultural ones; in any case we can keep from erroneous conclusions by considering the totality of the emotional pictures. Feelings which come from the core of our being have spontaneity, depth, and sincerity; if one of these qualities is lacking, we had better examine the underlying dynamics.

The *availability of energies* in neurosis varies in all gradations from a pervasive inertia through sporadic unsustained efforts to consistent, even exaggerated, outputs of energy. We cannot say that neurosis per se makes a neurotic person more or less energetic than a healthy one. But this inclusiveness obtains only as long as we think of energies in a merely quantitative way, separate from motivations and aims. One of the main characteristics of neurosis, as we have stated in general and elucidated in particular, is the shift of energies from developing the given potentials of the real self to developing the fictitious potentials of the idealized self. The fuller the grasp we have of the meaning of this process, the less are we puzzled by seeing incongruities in the output of energies. I shall mention here but two implications.

The more energies absorbed in the service of the pride system, the fewer are those available for the constructive drive toward self-realization. To illustrate this with a common example: the ambition-ridden person can display an astounding energy in order to attain eminence, power, and glamor, yet on the other hand have no time, interest, or energy for his personal life and his development as a human being. Actually it is not only a question of "having no energies left" for his personal life and its growth. Even if he had energies left he would unconsciously refuse to use them in behalf of his real self. To do so would run contrary to the intent of his self-hate, which is to keep his real self down.

The other implication is the fact that the neurotic does not *own* his energies (feel his energies as his own). He has the feeling of not being a moving force in his own life. In different kinds of neurotic personalities different factors may contribute to this deficiency. When a person for instance feels that he must do everything that is expected of him, he is actually set in motion by the pushes and pulls of others, or what he interprets as such—and he may stand still like a car with a run-down battery when left to his own resources. Or, if somebody has become scared of his own pride and has set a taboo on ambition, he must deny—to himself—his active share in his doings. Even if he has made a place for himself in the world, he does not feel that he has done it. What prevails is the feeling of "it happened." But, quite apart from such contributing factors, the feeling of not being the moving force in his own life is in a deeper sense true to facts. For he is indeed not moved primarily by his own wishes and aspirations but by the needs evolving from his pride system.

Naturally the course of our life is in part determined by factors outside our influence. But we can have a sense of direction. We can know what we want to make out of our life. We can have ideals, toward the approximation of which we strive and on the basis of which we make moral decisions. This sense of direction is conspicuously absent in many neurotics, whose *directive powers* are weakened in direct proportion to the degree of alienation from self. These people shift without plan or purpose, wherever their fancy takes them. Futile daydreaming may take the place of directed activities; sheer opportunism, the place of honest strivings; cynicism may choke off ideals. Indecision may reach such an extent as to prohibit any purposeful functioning.

Even more widespread and more difficult to recognize are the *hidden* disturbances of this sort. A person may appear well organized, in fact streamlined, because he is driven toward such neurotic goals as perfection or triumph. The directive control is in such cases taken over by compulsive standards. The artificiality of the directives which then develop may show only when he finds himself caught between contradictory shoulds. The anxiety which will arise in such situations is great because he has no other directives to follow. His real self is, as it were, confined in an oubliette; he cannot consult with it, and for this very reason he is a helpless prey to contradictory pulls. This is true for other neurotic conflicts as well. The degree of helplessness toward them and the fear of facing them not only point to the magnitude of the conflicts but even more to his alienation from self.

Lack of inner direction also may not appear as such because a person's life has moved in traditional channels and has made it possible to evade personal plans and decisions. Procrastination may veil indecision. And people may become aware of their indecision only if a decision which they alone can make has to be made. Such a situation may then be an ordeal of the worst order. But, even so, they usually do not recognize the general nature of the disturbance and ascribe it to the difficulty of the particular decision to be made.

Finally, an insufficient sense of direction may be hidden behind an attitude of compliance. People then do what they think others expect them to do; they are what they think others desire them to be. And they may develop considerable astuteness about what others need or expect. Usually they will, in a secondary way, glorify this skill as sensitivity or considerateness. When they become aware of the compulsive character of such "compliance," and try to analyze it, they will focus usually on factors pertaining to personal relations, such as a need to please or to ward off the hostility of others. However, they "comply" also in situations in which these factors do not apply, as for instance in the analytic situation. They leave the initiative to the analyst and want to know or to guess what he expects them to tackle. They do so contrary to explicit encouragements on the part of the analyst to follow their own interests. Here the background of the "compliance" becomes clear. Without being in the least aware of it, they are compelled to leave the direction of their lives to others instead of taking it in their own hands. They will feel lost when left to their own resources. In dreams such symbols will appear as being in a boat without a rudder, having lost a compass, being without a guide in a strange and dangerous territory. That the lack of inner directive powers is the essential element in their "compliance" also becomes apparent at a later time, when the struggle for inner autonomy begins. The anxiety occurring during this process has to do with abandoning accustomed aids without as yet daring to trust themselves.

While the impairment or loss of the directive powers may be hidden, there is another insufficiency that is always clearly discernible, at least to the trained observer: the *faculty of assuming responsibility for self.* The term "responsibility" may connote three different things. I do not, in this context, refer to dependability in the sense of fulfilling obligations or keeping promises, or to the assumption of responsibility for others. Attitudes on these scores vary too much to single out constant characteristics for all neuroses. The neurotic may be utterly reliable, or he may assume too much or too little responsibility in regard to others.

Nor do we mean to embark here upon the philosophical intricacies of moral responsibility. The compulsive factors in neuroses are so prevailing that freedom of choice is negligible. For all practical purposes we take it for granted that in general the patient could not develop otherwise than he did; that in particular he could not help doing, feeling, thinking what he did do, feel, think. This viewpoint, however, is not shared by the patient. His lofty disregard for all that means laws and necessities extends to himself too. The fact that, everything considered, his development could go only in certain directions is beneath his consideration. Whether some drive or attitude was conscious or unconscious does not matter. However insuperable the odds against which he had to struggle he *should* have met them with unfailing strength, courage, and equanimity. If he did not do so, it proves that he is no good. Conversely, in self-protection he may rigidly reject any guilt, declare himself infallible, and put the blame for any difficulties, past or present, on others.

Here again, as in other functions, pride has taken over responsibility and hounds him with condemnatory accusations when he fails to do the impossible. This then makes it close to impossible to assume the only responsibility that matters. This is, at bottom, no more but also no less than *plain, simple honesty about himself and his life*. It operates in three ways: a square recognition of his being as he is, without minimizing or exaggerating; a willingness to bear the consequences of his actions, decisions, etc., without trying to "get by" or to put the blame on others; the realization that it is up to him to do something about his difficulties without insisting that others, or fate, or time will solve them for him. This does not preclude accepting help but, on the contrary, implies getting all the help he possibly can. But even the best help from outside does not avail if he himself does not make efforts toward a constructive change.

To illustrate with an example which is actually a composite of many similar cases: a young married man constantly spends more money than he can afford, despite regular financial help from his father. He offers to himself and to others plenty of explanations: it is the fault of his parents, who never trained him to deal with money; it is the fault of his father, who gives him too small an allowance. This, in turn, continues because he is too intimidated to ask for more; he needs money because his wife is not economical or because his child needs a toy; then there are taxes and doctors' bills—and isn't everybody entitled to a little fun now and then?

All these reasons are relevant data for the analyst. They show the patient's claims and his tendency to feel abused. To the patient they not only account completely and satisfactorily for his dilemma but, to come directly to the point, he uses them as a magic wand to dispel the simple fact that, for whatever reason, he did spend too much money. This statement of facts, this calling a spade a spade, is often close to impossible for the neurotic caught in the push and pull of pride and self-condemnation. Of course the consequences do not fail to appear: his bank account is overdrawn; he runs into debt. He is furious at the banker who politely notifies him of the state of his account, and furious at his friends who do not want to lend him money. When the predicament is drastic enough he presents his father or a friend with the accomplished fact and more or less forces them to come to his rescue. He does not face the simple connection that the difficulties are the consequences of his own undisciplined spending. He makes resolutions concerning the future which cannot possibly carry weight because he is too busy justifying himself and blaming others to mean what he plans. What has not penetrated is the sober realization that the lack of discipline is *his* problem, that it actually makes *his* life difficult, and that consequently it is up to *him* to do something about it.

Another illustration of how tenaciously a neurotic can blind himself to the consequences of his problems or his actions: a person harboring an unconscious conviction of his immunity to ordinary cause and effect may have recognized his arrogance and his vindictiveness. But he simply does not see the consequence of others resenting it. If they turn against him it is an unexpected blow; he feels abused, and may often be quite astute in pointing out the neurotic factors (in others!) which make them resent his behavior. He discards lightly all the evidence presented. He considers it an attempt by the others involved to try to rationalize away their own guilt or responsibility.

These illustrations, though typical, do not begin to cover all the ways of avoiding responsibility for self. We have discussed most of them in speaking earlier of face-saving devices and protective measures against the onslaught of self-hate. We have seen how the neurotic puts responsibility on everybody and everything except himself; how he makes himself a detached observer of himself; how neatly he distinguishes between himself and his neurosis. As a result his real self becomes increasingly weaker or more remote. If for instance he denies that unconscious forces are part of his total personality, they may become a mysterious power which scares him out of his wits. And the weaker his contact with his real self becomes through such unconscious evasions, the more does he become a helpless prey to his unconscious forces and the more and more reason he has in fact to dread them. On the other hand, every step he takes toward assuming responsibility for all of this complex which is himself makes him visibly stronger.

Moreover, the shirking of responsibility for self makes it harder for any patient to face and to overcome his problems. If we could tackle this subject at the very beginning of an analysis, it would reduce considerably the time and hardship of the work. However, as long as the patient *is* his idealized image he cannot even start to doubt his straightness. And if the pressure of self-condemnation is in the foreground, he may respond to the idea of responsibility for self with stark terror and without gaining anything from it. Also we must keep in mind that the inability to assume any responsibility for self is but one expression of the whole alienation from self. It is therefore futile to tackle this problem before the patient has gained some feeling of and for himself.

Finally, when the real self is "locked out" or exiled, one's *integrating power* too will be at a low ebb. A healthy integration is a result of being oneself, and can be attained only on this basis. If we are sufficiently ourselves to have spontaneous feelings, to make our own decisions, and to assume responsibility for them, then we have a feeling of unity on a solid basis. In the words of a poet who speaks in jubilant tones of finding herself:

> All fuses now, falls into place
> From wish to action, word to silence.
> My work, my loves, my time, my face
> Gathered into one intense
> Gesture of growing like a plant.[5]

The lack of spontaneous integration we usually regard as a direct consequence of neurotic conflicts. This remains true, but we do not quite understand the power of disintegrating forces unless we consider the vicious circles which are operating. If as the result of many factors we lose ourselves, we have then no firm ground to stand on from which we can try to disentangle our inner conflicts. We are at their mercy, a helpless prey to their disintegrating force, and must seize upon any means available to solve them. This is what we call neurotic attempts at solution—and neurosis, from this vantage point, is a series of such attempts. But in these attempts we lose ourselves more and more, and the disintegrating impact of the conflicts grows. So we need artificial means to hold ourselves together. The shoulds, an instrument of pride and an instrument of self-hate, acquire a new function: that of protecting us from chaos. They rule a person with an iron fist but, like a political tyranny, they do create and maintain a certain superficial order. Rigid control through will power and reasoning is another strenuous means of attempting to bind together all the disconnected parts of the personality. We shall discuss it, together with other measures to relieve inner tensions, in the next chapter.

The general significance of these disturbances for the patient's life is fairly obvious. His not being an active determining factor in his own life creates a deep feeling of uncertainty, no matter how much overlaid by compulsive rigidities. His not feeling his own feelings makes him unalive, no matter how great his surface vivacity. His not assuming responsibility for

---

[5] From "Now I Become Myself," by May Sarton, in *The Atlantic Monthly*, 1948.

himself robs him of true inner independence. In addition, the inactivity of his real self has a significant influence upon the course of the neurosis. It is in this fact that the "vicious-circle" aspect of alienation from self becomes clearest. Itself the result of neurotic processes, it is a cause of their further development. For the greater the alienation from self, the more helpless a victim to the machinations of the pride system the neurotic is. He has less and less alive strength with which to resist it.

Serious doubts may arise in some cases whether this most alive source of energy is not altogether dried up or permanently immobilized. In my experience it is the better part of wisdom to suspend judgment. More often than not, with sufficient patience and skill on the part of the analyst, the real self does return from exile or "come to life." It is a hopeful sign for instance if energies, though unavailable for his personal life, are put into constructive efforts for others. Needless to say, such efforts can be and are made by well-integrated people. But those who interest us here show a striking discrepancy between seemingly limitless energies spent in the service of others and a lack of constructive interest or concern for their own personal lives. Even when they are in analysis their relatives, friends, or pupils often benefit more from their analytic work than they do themselves. Nevertheless, as therapists, we hold on to the fact that their interest in growth is alive even though it is rigidly externalized. However, it may not be easy to bring home their interest to themselves. Not only are there formidable forces militating against constructive change in themselves, but they are also not too eager to consider such changes because the outward direction of their endeavors creates a kind of equilibrium and gives them a feeling of worth.

The role of the real self comes into clearer relief when we compare it with Freud's concept of the "ego." Though starting from entirely different premises and going along entirely different roads, I seemingly arrive at the same result as Freud, with his postulate of the weakness of the "ego." True enough, there are obvious differences in theory. For Freud the "ego" is like an employee who has functions but no initiative and no executive powers. For me the real self is the spring of emotional forces, of constructive energies, of directive and judiciary powers. But, granted that the real self has all these potentials and that they actually operate in the healthy person, what great difference is there between my position and Freud's as far as neuroses are concerned? Is it not the same for all practical purposes whether on the one hand the self is weakened, or paralyzed, or "driven from sight" by the neurotic process or on the other hand *inherently* is not a constructive force?

When looking at the beginning phases of most analyses we would have to answer this question in the affirmative. At that time very little of the real self is visibly operating. We see the possibility of certain feelings or beliefs being authentic. We can surmise that the patient's drive to develop himself contains genuine elements besides the more obvious grandiose ones; that, over and beyond his need for intellectual mastery, he is also interested in the truth about himself; and so on and so forth—but this is still surmise.

During the analytic process, however, this picture changes radically. As the pride system is undermined, the patient, instead of automatically being on the defensive, does become interested in the truth about himself. He does start to assume responsibility for himself in the sense described: to make decisions, to feel his feelings, and to develop his own beliefs. All the functions which, as we have seen, have been taken over by the pride system gradually regain spontaneity with the return to power of the real self. A redistribution of factors takes place. And in this process the real self, with its constructive forces, proves to be the stronger party.

We shall discuss later the individual steps necessary for this therapeutic process. I have merely indicated here the fact of its occurrence; otherwise, this discussion of alienation from self would leave us with too negative an impression of the real self, an impression of its being a phantom, desirable to regain but forever elusive. Only when acquainted with the later phases of analysis can we recognize that the contention of its potential strength is not a speculative one. Under favorable conditions, such as constructive analytic work, it can again become an alive force.

Only because this is a realistic possibility can our therapeutic

work go beyond symptomatic relief and hope to help the individual in his human growth. And only with the vision of this
realistic possibility can we understand that the relation between
pseudoself and real self is that of a conflict between two rival
forces, as suggested in the previous chapter. This conflict can
turn into an open battle only at a point when the real self has
again become active enough for one to risk it. Until such a time
the individual can do one thing only: protect himself from the
disruptive power of the conflicts by finding pseudosolutions.
These we will discuss in the following chapters.

CHAPTER 7

GENERAL MEASURES TO RELIEVE TENSION

ALL THE processes described so far bring about an inner situation that is replete with disruptive conflicts, unbearable tensions, and potential terrors. Nobody can function, or even live, under such conditions. The individual must make, and does make, automatic attempts at solving these problems, attempts at removing conflicts, allaying tensions, and preventing terrors. The same integrating forces start working as in the process of self-idealization, which is itself the boldest and most radical neurotic attempt at solution: to do away with all conflicts and resulting difficulties by putting oneself above them. But there is a difference between that endeavor and the ones to be described presently. We cannot define this distinction accurately, for it is not a difference of quality but of "more of" or "less of." The search for glory, while likewise born from compelling inner necessities, is more of a creative process. Although destructive in its consequences, it nevertheless stems from man's best desires—to expand beyond his narrow confines. It is, in the last analysis, its colossal egocentricity that distinguishes it from healthy strivings. As for the difference between this solution and the others to follow, it is not caused by the ex-

GENERAL MEASURES TO RELIEVE TENSION

haustion of the power of imagination. That keeps working—but to the impairment of the inner condition. This condition was already precarious when the individual took his original flight toward the sun: by now (under the rending impact of the conflicts and tensions mentioned) the danger of psychic destruction is imminent.

Before presenting the new attempts at solution we must become familiar with certain measures aiming at relieving tension which operate all of the time.[1] It suffices to enumerate them briefly because they have already been discussed in this book and in previous publications, and they will be resumed in subsequent chapters.

Alienation from self, seen from this aspect, is one of these measures and probably ranks first in importance. We have discussed the reasons which bring about and reinforce the alienation from self. It is, to repeat in part, a mere consequence of the neurotic's being driven by compulsive forces; in part, it results from active moves away from the real self and against it. We have to add in this context that he also has a definite interest in disavowing it in order to avoid an inner battle and to keep the inner tension at a minimum.[2] The principle involved is the same as that operating in all attempts to solve inner conflicts. Any conflict within or without can vanish from sight and actually be (artificially) diminished if one aspect of it is suppressed and the other made predominant.[3] Speaking in terms of two people or two groups with conflicting needs and interests, the open conflict disappears when one individual or group is subdued. Between a bullying father and subdued child there is no visible conflict. The same holds true for inner conflicts. We may have a sharp conflict between our hostility toward people and our need to be liked. But if we suppress the hostility—or the need to be liked—our relations tend to become streamlined.

---

[1] They correspond in principle, if not in content, to what I called "auxiliary approaches to artificial harmony" in *Our Inner Conflicts*.

[2] This interest constitutes another factor which is reinforcing the alienation from self; it belongs in the category of moves away from the real self.

[3] *Cf.* Karen Horney, *Our Inner Conflicts*, Chapter 2, The Basic Conflict.

Similarly, if we exile our real self the conflict between it and the pseudoself not only disappears from awareness but the distribution of forces is so changed that it actually abates. Naturally this release of tension can be achieved only at the cost of an increased autonomy of the pride system.

The fact that the disavowing of the real self is dictated by self-protective interest becomes particularly clear in the last phase of analysis. As I have already indicated, we can actually observe the raging of an inner battle when the real self becomes stronger. Anybody who has experienced the fierceness of this battle, in self or others, can understand that the earlier withdrawing of the real self from the field of action has been dictated by the need for survival, by the desire not to be torn apart.

This self-protective process manifests itself mainly in the patient's interest in beclouding issues. No matter how co-ordinated he seems on the surface, he is at bottom a confused person. He has not only an astounding capacity to befog issues but is not easily dissuaded from doing so. This interest must operate, and in fact does operate, the same way as it functions on the conscious level in any fraudulent person: the spy who must hide his identity, the hypocrite who must present a front of honesty, the criminal who must create false alibis. The neurotic who, without knowing it, does lead a double life must similarly, *unconsciously*, blur the truth of what he is, wants, feels, believes. And all his self-deception follows from this basic one. To bring the dynamics into clear focus: he is not merely intellectually confused about the meaning of freedom, independence, love, goodness, strength; as long as he is not ready to come to grips with himself he has a stringent subjective interest in maintaining a confusion—which, in turn, he may cover up by false pride in his all-penetrating intellect.

Next in importance is the *externalization of inner experiences*. This means (to repeat) that the intrapsychic processes are not experienced as such but are perceived or felt as occurring between the self and the outside world. It is a rather radical means of relieving the inner system from tension and is always made at the expense of inward impoverishment and at that of increased disturbances in human relations. I first described externalization [4] as a means of maintaining the idealized image by laying on other people's doorsteps all the blame for the short-comings or ailments that he cannot fit into his particular image. I next saw it as an attempt to deny the existence of, or to smooth over the inner battle between, self-destructive forces; and I distinguished between active and passive externalization: "I am not doing anything to myself but to others—and rightly so"—versus "I am not hostile to others; they are doing things to me." And now, finally, I have taken a further step in the understanding of externalization. There is hardly one of the inner processes I have described which may not be externalized. A neurotic may for instance feel compassion for others when it would be utterly impossible to feel it for himself. His longing for his own inner salvation may be vigorously denied but express itself in an astute spotting of others being stuck in their growth, and in a sometimes astounding capacity to help them. His rebellion against the coercion of inner dictates may appear as defiance of conventions, laws, influences. Unaware of his own overbearing pride, he may hate it—or be fascinated by it—in others. He may despise in others his own cowering before the dictatorship of his pride system. Not knowing that he is smoothing over the ruthless cruelty of his self-hate, he may develop a Pollyannalike attitude toward life in general, removing from it all harshness, cruelty, or even death.

Another general measure is the neurotic's tendency to experience himself in a piecemeal way, as if we were the sum total of disconnected parts. This is known in psychiatric literature as *compartmentalization*,[5] or *psychic fragmentation*, and seems to be merely a reiteration of the fact that he has no feeling for himself as a whole organism, one in which every part is related to the whole and interacts with every other part. Certainly only an individual who is alienated and divided *can* lack such a feeling of wholeness. What I want to stress here, however, is the neurotic's active interest in disconnecting. He can grasp a connection intellectually when it is presented to him. But it comes

---

[4] *Cf.* Karen Horney, *Our Inner Conflicts*, Chapter 7, Externalization.

[5] *Cf.* Edward A. Strecker and Kenneth Appel, *Discovering Ourselves*, Macmillan, 1943.

to him as a surprise; penetration is only skin deep and lost soon after.

He has an unconscious interest, for example, in not seeing cause and effect: that one psychic factor follows from another, or reinforces another; that one attitude must by necessity be maintained because it protects some important illusion; that any compulsive trend has an effect on his human relations or on his life in general. He may not see even the simplest cause-and-effect connections. It may remain strange to him that his discontent has anything to do with his claims, or that his too great need of people—for whatever neurotic reasons—makes him dependent upon others. It may come to him as a startling discovery that his sleeping late has anything to do with his going to bed late.

He may have an equally strong interest in not perceiving *contradictory values* coexisting in him. Quite literally, he may utterly fail to see that he tolerates and even cherishes in himself two sets of values, both conscious, which are mutually contradictory. He may not for instance be disturbed by the fact that his placing value on saintliness is contradictory to his also placing value on making others subservient to himself, or by the fact that his honesty does not jibe with his passion to "get by." Even when he tries to examine himself he merely arrives at a static picture, as if he saw disconnected parts of a jigsaw puzzle: of timidity, contempt for others, ambition, masochistic fantasies, the need to be liked, and so on. The individual pieces may be seen correctly, but nothing can change because they are seen out of context without any feeling for interconnection, for process, or for dynamics.

Although psychic fragmentation is essentially a disintegrating process, its function is to preserve the *status quo*, to protect the neurotic equilibrium from collapsing. By his refusal to be puzzled by inner contradictions the neurotic keeps himself from facing the underlying conflicts, and thereby keeps the inner tension at a low ebb. He does not have even a rudimentary interest in them, and so they remain remote from his awareness.

The same result is attained of course by disconnecting cause and effect. Clipping the link between the two prevents him from becoming aware of the intensity and the relevance of certain inner forces. An important and common illustrative example is that of a person who may experience at times the full impact of a spell of vindictiveness. But he may have the greatest difficulties in grasping, even intellectually, the fact that his hurt pride and the need to restore it are the motivating forces; and, even when clearly seen, the connection remains meaningless. Again he may have gained a fairly clear impression of his practice of scathing self-berating. He may have seen in dozens of detailed instances that such expressions of crushing self-contempt follow his failure to measure up to the fantastic dictates of his pride. But again his mind imperceptibly disrupts the connection. Hence both the intensity of his pride and its bearing on self-contempt remain, at best, vague theoretical considerations—which relieve him of the necessity to tackle his pride. It remains in power, and the tensions are kept in a low key because no conflict emerges and he can maintain a deceptive feeling of unity.

The three attempts at preserving a semblance of inner peace described so far have in common the character of doing away with elements which carry the potentials to disrupt the neurotic structure: eliminating the real self, removing all kinds of inner experiences, doing away with connections which (if realized) would disrupt the equilibrium. Another measure, *automatic control*, follows in part the same trend. Its main function is to put a check on feelings. In a structure that is on the verge of disintegration, feelings are a source of danger because they are, as it were, the untamed elementary forces within us. I am not speaking here of conscious self-control by dint of which we can check, if we choose, impulsive actions or an outburst of anger or enthusiasm. The automatic control system checks not only the acting on impulses or the expression of feelings but the impulses and feelings themselves. It operates like an automatic burglar or fire alarm, giving an alarm signal (of fear) when unwanted feelings arise.

But, in contrast to the other attempts, this one is also, as the name implies, a control system. If through alienation from self and psychic fragmentation a feeling of organic unity is lacking, some artificial control system is necessary to hold together the discrepant parts of ourselves.

Such automatic control can encompass all impulses and feelings of fear, hurt, anger, joy, affection, enthusiasm. The corresponding physical expressions of a widespread control system are muscular tightness, showing in constipation, gait, posture, facial rigidity, difficulties in breathing, etc. The conscious attitude toward the control itself varies. Some people are still sufficiently alive to chafe under it and, at least at times, wish desperately they could let go, could laugh heartily, could fall in love, or could be carried away by some enthusiasm. Others have cemented the control by a more or less open pride which they may express in various ways. They may call it dignity, poise, stoicism, wearing a mask, showing a poker face, being "realistic," "unsentimental," "undemonstrative."

In other types of neurosis the control operates in a more selective way. Certain feelings then go scot-free or are even encouraged. Thus, for instance, people with strong self-effacing trends tend to exaggerate feelings of love or of misery. The check here is primarily on the whole range of hostile feelings: suspicion, anger, contempt, vindictiveness.

Of course feelings may be flattened out or suppressed as a result of many other factors, among them alienation from self, forbidding pride, self-frustration. But that a vigilant control system is operating over and beyond these factors shows in many instances by fright responses at the mere prospect of lessened control—such as fears of falling asleep, of being under anesthesia or under the influence of alcohol, of lying on the couch and associating freely, of letting go in skiing downhill. Feelings—whether of compassion, fear, or violence—that do penetrate the control system may arouse panic. Such panic may be caused by the person's fearing and rejecting these feelings because they jeopardize something specific in the neurotic structure. But he also may become panicky simply because he realizes that his control system is not functioning. If this is analyzed the panic subsides, and only then do the particular feelings and the patient's attitude toward them become accessible to work.

The last general measure to be discussed here is the neurotic's belief in the *supremacy of the mind*. While feelings—because unruly—are suspects to be controlled, the mind—imagination and reason—expands like a genie from a bottle. Thus, factually, another dualism is created. It is no longer mind *and* feelings but mind *versus* feelings; no longer mind *and* body but mind *versus* body; no longer mind *and* self but mind *versus* self. But, like the other fragmentations, this one too serves to release tensions, to cover up conflicts, and to establish a semblance of unity. It can do so in three ways.

The mind can become a spectator of self. As Zuzuki says: "The intellect is after all the spectator, and when it does some work, it is as a hireling, for better or for worse." [6] In the case of the neurotic the mind is never a friendly, concerned spectator; it may be more or less interested, more or less sadistic, but it is always detached—as if looking at a stranger with whom it has been accidentally thrown together. Sometimes self-observations of this sort may be quite mechanical and superficial. A patient will then give a more or less accurate report of events, activities, symptoms that increase or decrease without touching upon the meaning these events had for him or his personal responses to them. He can also be, or become during analysis, keenly interested in his psychic processes. But his interest in them is rather a delight in the astuteness of his observations or in the mechanics with which they operate, much in the manner that an entomologist may be fascinated by the functioning of an insect. The analyst likewise may be delighted, mistaking all this eagerness of the patient for real interest in himself. And only after a while will he discover that the patient is quite uninterested in the meaning his findings have for his life.

This detached interest may also be openly faultfinding, gleeful, sadistic. In these instances it is often externalized, both in an active and in a passive way. He may, as it were, turn his back on himself and be most astute in observing others and their problems—in the same detached, unrelated way. Or he may feel that he is under the hateful and gleeful observation of others—a feeling pronounced in paranoid conditions but by no means restricted to them.

Whatever the quality of being an onlooker at himself, he is no longer a participant in the inner struggle and has removed

---

[6] D. T. Zuzuki, *Essays on Zen Buddhism*, Luzac and Co., London, 1927.

himself from his inner problems. "He" is his observing mind, and as such has a feeling of unity; his brain then is the only part of him that feels alive.

The mind also works as a *co-ordinator*. With this function we are already familiar. We have seen the imagination at work in the very creation of an idealized image, in the ceaseless labor of the pride to blot out this, spotlight that, turn needs into virtues, potentialities into realities. Similarly, reason can be subservient to pride in the process of rationalizing: anything then may appear or feel reasonable, plausible, rational—as indeed it is from the perspective of the unconscious premises upon which the neurotic operates.

The co-ordinating functions also operate in eliminating any self-doubts, all the more necessary the more shaky the whole structure. There is then, to quote a patient, a "fanatic logic," a logic which usually goes with an unshakable belief in infallibility. "My logic prevails, because it is the only logic. . . . If the others do not consent, they are idiots." In relation to others such an attitude shows as an arrogant righteousness. With regard to inner problems it closes the door to constructive investigation but at the same time diminishes tensions by establishing a certainty of sterility. As is so often true in other neurotic contexts, the opposite extreme—a pervasive self-doubting—leads to the same end of quieting tensions. If nothing is as it seems, why bother? In many patients such all-encompassing skepticism can be quite hidden. On the surface they graciously accept everything but make silent reservations, as a result of which their own findings, as well as the analyst's suggestions, are lost in the quicksand.

The mind, finally, is the magic *ruler* for which, as for God, everything is possible. Knowledge of inner problems no longer is a step toward changing, but knowing *is* changing. Patients operating on this premise without being aware of it often feel puzzled that this or that disturbance does not vanish since they know so much about its dynamics. The analyst may point out that there must still be essential factors they do not know—which is usually true. But even when other relevant factors do come into sight nothing changes. And again the patient is bewildered and discouraged. So there may be an endless search for more knowledge, valuable in itself but nevertheless doomed to futility as long as the patient insists that the rays of knowledge should dispel every cloud in his life without his doing the actual changing.

The more he tries to manage all his life with pure intellect, the less tolerable it is for him to acknowledge the existence of unconscious factors in him. If they unavoidably intrude they may arouse disproportionate fear or, in others, be disavowed and reasoned away. This is particularly important in the case of a patient seeing a neurotic conflict in himself for the first time with even a little clarity. He realizes in a flash that, even with his power of reason or imagination, he cannot make incompatibles compatible. He feels trapped and may respond with fright. Then he may muster all his mental energies to escape facing the conflict. How can he get around it? [7] How can he get by? Where is the hole in the trap through which he can escape? Simplicity and trickiness don't go together—well, could he not be simple in some situations and tricky in others? Or if he is driven to be vindictive and proud of it while the idea of serenity also has a great hold on him, he becomes captivated by the notion of attaining a serene vindictiveness, of walking through life unruffled, and of annihilating offenders against his pride as he might brush aside bushes. Such a need to get by can amount to a veritable passion. All the good work put in to bring a conflict into clear relief then becomes ineffectual, but the inner "peace" is re-established.

All these measures in different ways relieve inner tension. In a way we could call them attempts at solution because in all of them integrating forces are at work. By compartmentalizing, for instance, the person disconnects conflicting currents and thereby no longer experiences conflicts as conflicts. If a person experiences himself as a spectator of himself, he establishes thereby a feeling of unity. But we could not possibly describe a person satisfactorily by saying that he is an onlooker at himself. It would all depend on what he observes while looking at himself, and upon the spirit in which he does it. Similarly the process of

---

[7] *Cf.* Ibsen's *Peer Gynt*, the scene with the great Bogy.

externalization concerns but one aspect of his neurotic structure, even if we know what he externalizes and how he does it. In other words all these measures are only partial solutions. I would prefer to speak of neurotic solutions only if these have the encompassing character I have described in the first chapter. They give form and direction to the whole personality. They determine the kinds of satisfactions which are attainable, the factors to be avoided, the hierarchy of values, the relation to others. They also determine the kind of general integrating measures employed. In short they are a *modus vivendi*, a way of life.

CHAPTER 8

THE EXPANSIVE SOLUTIONS: THE APPEAL OF MASTERY

IN ALL neurotic developments the alienation from self is the nuclear problem; in all of them we find the search for glory, the shoulds, the claims, the self-hate and the various measures to relieve tension. But we do not yet have a picture of how these factors operate in a *particular* neurotic structure. Such a picture depends upon the kind of solution the individual finds for his intrapsychic conflicts. Before we can adequately describe these solutions, however, we must clarify the inner constellation generated by the pride system and the conflicts involved in it. We understand that there is a conflict between the pride system and the real self. But, as I have already indicated, a major conflict also arises within the pride system itself. Self-glorification and self-contempt do not constitute a conflict. In fact, as long as we think only in terms of these two diametrically opposed images of ourselves, we recognize contradictory and yet complementary self-evaluations—but we are not aware of the conflicting drives. This picture changes when we look at it from a different perspective and focus on the question: how do we experience ourselves?

The inner constellation produces a fundamental uncertainty about the feeling of identity. Who am I? Am I the proud super-human being—or am I the subdued, guilty and rather despicable creature? Unless he is a poet or a philosopher, the individual usually does not raise such questions consciously. But the existing bewilderment does appear in dreams. In many ways the loss of identity can there be expressed directly and succinctly. The dreamer may have lost his passport or when asked to identify himself be unable to do so. Or perhaps an old friend of his will appear in his dream looking quite different from the way he remembers him. Or he may look at a portrait but the picture frame encloses an empty canvas.

Much more frequently the dreamer is not explicitly puzzled by the question of his identity but presents himself in terms of divergent symbols: different people, animals, plants, or inanimate objects. He may appear in one and the same dream as himself, as Sir Galahad, and as a threatening monster. He may be the kidnapped victim and the gangster, the prisoner and the jailer, the judge and the culprit, the torturer and the tortured, the frightened child and the rattlesnake. This self-dramatization shows the divergent forces operating within a person, and the interpretation can be of great assistance in recognizing them. The dreamer's tendency toward resignation, for instance, may be expressed by a resigned person playing a role in the dream; his self-contempt, by cockroaches on the kitchen floor. But this is not the entire significance of self-dramatization. The very fact of its occurrence (the reason for mentioning it here) also indicates our capacity to experience ourselves as different selves. The same capacity also shows in the often blatant discrepancy between the way a person experiences himself in daily life on the one hand and in his dreams on the other. In his conscious mind he may be the master mind, the savior of mankind, the one for whom no achievement is impossible; while at the same time in his dreams he may be a freak, a sputtering idiot, or a derelict lying in the gutter. Finally, even in his conscious way of experiencing himself, a neurotic may shuttle between a feeling of arrogant omnipotence and of being the scum of the earth. This is particularly obvious in (but by no means restricted to) alcoholics, who at one moment may be up in the clouds, making great gestures and grandiose promises, and at the next be abject and cringing.

These multiple ways of experiencing self correspond to the existing inner configuration. Leaving out more complex possibilities, the neurotic can feel himself as his glorified self, as his despised self, and at times (although this is mostly blocked out) as his true self. He thus in fact must feel uncertain about his identity. And as long as the inner constellation obtains, the question "who am I?" is unanswerable indeed. What interests us more at this juncture is the fact that these different experiences of self are by necessity conflicting. To be more exact, a conflict is bound to arise because the neurotic identifies himself *in toto* with his superior proud self and with his despised self. If he experiences himself as a superior being, he tends to be expansive in his strivings and his belief about what he can achieve; he tends to be more or less openly arrogant, ambitious, aggressive and demanding; he feels self-sufficient; he is disdainful of others; he requires admiration or blind obedience. Conversely, if in his mind he is his subdued self he tends to feel helpless, is compliant and appeasing, depends upon others and craves their affection. In other words the identification *in toto* with one or the other self entails not only opposite kinds of self-evaluation but also opposite attitudes toward others, opposite kinds of behavior, opposite sets of values, opposite drives, and opposite kinds of satisfaction.

If these two ways of experiencing himself operate at the same time he must feel like two people pulling in opposite directions. And this indeed is the significance of the identification *in toto* with the two existing selves. There is not only a conflict, but a conflict of sufficient impact to tear him apart. If he does not succeed in diminishing the resulting tension, anxiety is bound to arise. He may then, if so disposed for other reasons, take to drinking to allay his anxiety.

But usually, as in any conflict of great intensity, attempts at solution set in automatically. There are three main ways of solving such a solution. One of them is presented in literature as the story of Doctor Jekyll and Mr. Hyde. Dr. Jekyll recognizes that there are two sides of him (roughly presented as the

sinner and the saint, with neither of them being himself) at perennial war with each other. "If each, I told myself, could be
housed in separate identities, life would be relieved of all that
was unbearable." And he compounds a medicine by dint of
which he can dissociate these two selves. If the story is divested
of its fantastic garb, it represents the attempt to solve the
conflict by *compartmentalizing*. Many patients veer in this direction. They experience themselves successively as extremely
self-effacing and as grandiose and expansive without feeling
disquieted by this contradiction, because in their minds the two
selves are disconnected.

But, as Stevenson's story indicates, this attempt cannot be
successful. As we put it in the last chapter, it is too partial a solution. A more radical one follows the pattern of *streamlining*,
which is typical of so many neurotic patients. This is the attempt
to suppress permanently and rigidly one self and be exclusively
the other. A third way of solving the conflict is by withdrawing
interest from the inner battle and *resigning* from active psychic
living.

There are then, to recapitulate, two major intrapsychic conflicts brought about by the pride system: the central inner conflict and the one between the proud and the despised self. In the
analyzed person, or in the patient at the beginning of analysis,
these do not, however, appear as two separate conflicts. This is
partly because the real self is a potential force but not yet an
actual one. Also, however, the patient tends to despise sum-
marily in himself all that is not invested with pride—which
would include his real self. For these reasons the two conflicts
seem to merge into one, that between being expansive and being
self-effacing. Only after much analytic work does the central
inner conflict appear as a separate conflict.

At the present state of knowledge the major neurotic solutions for intrapsychic conflicts seem to be the most appropriate
basis for establishing types of neuroses. We must keep in mind,
though, that our desire for neat classification better satisfies our
need for order and guidance than it does justice to the
multifariousness of human life. To speak of human types—or,
as we do here, of neurotic types—is after all merely a means of

looking at personalities from certain vantage points. And what we use as criteria will be those factors which appear crucial in the framework of the particular psychological system. In this restricted sense every attempt to establish types has certain merits and also definite limitations. In the framework of my psychological theories the neurotic character structure is central. And so my criteria for "types" cannot be this or that symptomatic picture, or this or that individual trend. It can be only the peculiarities of a whole neurotic structure. These in turn are largely determined by the major solutions a person has found for his inner conflicts.

While this criterion is more comprehensive than many others used in typologies, its usefulness is nevertheless also limited—because of the many reservations and qualifications we must make. To begin with, although people tending toward the same main solution have characteristic similarities they may differ widely with regard to the level of human qualities, gifts, or achievements involved. Moreover, what we regard as "types" are actually cross sections of personalities in which the neurotic process has led to rather extreme developments with pronounced characteristics. But there is always an indeterminate range of intermediate structures deriding any precise classification. These complexities are further enhanced by the fact that, owing to the process of psychic fragmentation, even in extreme instances there is often more than one main solution. "Most cases are mixed cases," [1] says William James, "and we should not treat our classifications with too much respect." Perhaps it would be more nearly correct to speak of directions of development than of types.

With these qualifications in mind, we can distinguish three major solutions from the aspect of the problems presented in this book: the expansive solution, the self-effacing solution, and resignation. In the *expansive solutions* the individual prevailingly identifies himself with his glorified self. When speaking of "himself" he means, with Peer Gynt, his very grandiose self. Or, as one patient put it, "I exist only as a superior being." The

[1] *Cf.* William James, *The Varieties of Religious Experience*, p. 148, Longmans, Green and Co., 1902.

feeling of superiority that goes with this solution is not necessarily conscious but—whether conscious or not—largely determines behavior, strivings, and attitudes toward life in general. The appeal of life lies in its mastery. It chiefly entails his determination, conscious or unconscious, to overcome every obstacle—in or outside himself—and the belief that he should be able, and in fact *is* able, to do so. He should be able to master the adversities of fate, the difficulties of a situation, the intricacies of intellectual problems, the resistances of other people, conflicts in himself. The reverse side of the necessity for mastery is his dread of anything connoting helplessness; this is the most poignant dread he has.

When looking superficially at the expansive types we get a picture of people who, in a streamlined way, are bent on self-glorification, on ambitious pursuits, on vindictive triumph, with the mastery of life through intelligence and will power as the means to actualize their idealized self. And, barring all differences in premises, individual concepts and terminology, this is the way Freud and Adler have seen these people (as driven by the need for narcissistic self-aggrandizement or for being on top). However, when we go far enough in the analysis of such patients, we discover self-effacing trends in all of them—trends which they have not only suppressed but which they hate and loathe. The first picture we get is the one-sided aspect of themselves which they pretend is their whole being in order to create a subjective feeling of unity. The rigidity with which they hang on to the expansive trends is not only owing to the compulsive character of these trends [2] but also to the necessity to eliminate from awareness all traces of self-effacing trends and all traces of self-accusations, self-doubts, self-contempt. Only in this way can they maintain the subjective conviction of superiority and mastery.

The point of danger on this score is the realization of unfulfilled shoulds, because this would elicit feelings of guilt and unworthiness. Since nobody can in actual fact measure up to shoulds he has, it is indispensable for such a person to use all available means to deny his "failures" to himself. By dint of

---

[2] As described in the first chapter.

imagination, highlighting "good" qualities, blotting out others, behavioristic perfection, externalizations, he must try to maintain in his mind a picture of himself of which he can be proud. He must, as it were, put up an unconscious bluff and live with the pretense of being all knowing, all generous, all fair, etc. He must never, and under any conditions, be aware that by comparison with his glorified self he has feet of clay. In relation to others one of two feelings may prevail. He may be extremely proud, consciously or unconsciously, of his faculty of fooling everybody—and in his arrogance and contempt for others believes that he actually succeeds in this. Conversely, he is most afraid of being fooled himself and may feel it as a profound humiliation if he is. Or he may have a constant lurking fear of being just a bluff, more intensely so than other neurotic types. Even though, for instance, he may have gained success or honors through honest work he will still feel that he has achieved them by putting something over on others. This makes him excessively sensitive to criticism and failure, or to the mere possibility of failure or of his "bluff" being called by criticism.

This group in turn includes many heterogeneous types, as demonstrated by a brief survey anyone can make of patients, friends, or literary characters. Among the individual differences the most crucial one concerns the capacity to enjoy life and to have positive feelings for others. Both Peer Gynt and Hedda Gabler, for instance, *are* their aggrandized versions of themselves—but what a difference in emotional climate! Other relevant differences depend upon the ways in which the type eliminates from awareness the realization of "Imperfections." There are also variations in the nature of the claims made, their justifications, and the means of their assertion. We must consider at least three subdivisions of the "expansive type": the narcissistic, the perfectionistic and the arrogant-vindictive type. I shall be brief about the first two, because they have been well described in psychiatric literature, but go into greater detail with the last one.

I use the term *narcissism* with some hesitation, because in the classic Freudian literature it includes rather indiscriminately every kind of self-inflation, egocentricity, anxious concern with one's welfare, and withdrawal from others.[3] I take it here in its original descriptive sense of being "in love with one's idealized image.[4] More precisely: the person is his idealized self and seems to adore it. This basic attitude gives him the buoyancy or the resiliency entirely lacking in the other groups. It gives him a seeming abundance of self-confidence which appears enviable to all those chafing under self-doubts. He has (consciously) no doubts; he *is* the anointed, the man of destiny, the prophet, the great giver, the benefactor of mankind. All of this contains a grain of truth. He often is gifted beyond average, early and easily won distinctions, and sometimes was the favored and admired child.

This unquestioned belief in his greatness and uniqueness is the key to understanding him. His buoyancy and perennial youthfulness stem from this source. So does his often-fascinating charm. Yet clearly, his gifts notwithstanding, he stands on precarious ground. He may speak incessantly of his exploits or of his wonderful qualities and needs endless confirmation of his estimate of himself in the form of admiration and devotion. His feeling of mastery lies in his conviction that there is nothing he cannot do and no one he cannot win. He is often charming indeed, particularly when new people come into his orbit. Regardless of their factual importance for him, he *must* impress them. He gives the impression to himself and others that he "loves" people. And he can be generous, with a scintillating display of feeling, with flattery, with favors and help—in anticipation of admiration or in return for devotion received. He endows his family and his friends, as well as his work and plans, with glowing attributes. He can be quite tolerant, does not

---

[3] *Cf.* the discussion of this concept in *New Ways in Psychoanalysis*. The difference between the present concept and that propounded in *New Ways* is as follows: In *New Ways* I put the emphasis on self-inflation and I derived this from the alienation from others, the loss of self, and the impairment of self-confidence. All of this remains true, but the process leading up to narcissism as I see it now is more complex. I would be inclined to differentiate now between self-idealization and narcissism, using the latter in the sense of feeling identified with one's idealized self. Self-idealization occurs in all neuroses and represents an attempt to solve early inner conflicts. Narcissism on the other hand is one of the several solutions of the conflict between expansive and self-effacing drives.

[4] Sigmund Freud, *On Narcissism: An Introduction*, Coll. Papers IV.

Cf. also Bernard Glueck, "The God Man or Jehovah Complex," *Medical Journal*, New York, 1915.

expect others to be perfect; he can even stand jokes about himself, so long as these merely highlight an amiable peculiarity of his; but he must never be questioned seriously.

His shoulds are no less inexorable than in other forms of neurosis, as appears during analytic work. But it is characteristic for him to deal with them by the use of a magic wand. His capacity to overlook flaws, or to turn them into virtues, seems unlimited. A sober onlooker would often call him unscrupulous, or at least unreliable. He does not seem to mind breaking promises, being unfaithful, incurring debts, defrauding. (Consider John Gabriel Borkman.) He is not, however, a scheming exploiter. He feels rather that his needs or his tasks are so important that they entitle him to every privilege. He does not question his rights and expects others to "love" him "unconditionally," no matter how much he actually trespasses on their rights.

His difficulties appear both in his relations to people and in his work. His being at bottom unrelated to others is bound to show in close relations. The simple fact that others have wishes or opinions of their own, that they may look at him critically or take exception to his shortcomings, that they expect something of him—all these are felt as a poisonous humiliation and arouse a smoldering resentment. He may then explode in a burst of rage and go to others who "understand" him better. And, since this process occurs in most of his relations, he is often lonely.

His difficulties in work life are manifold. His plans are often too expansive. He does not reckon with limitations. He overrates his capacities. His pursuits may be too diversified, and therefore failures occur easily. Up to a point his resilience gives him a capacity to bounce, but on the other hand repeated failures in enterprises or in human relations—rejections—may also crush him altogether. The self-hate and self-contempt, successfully held in abeyance otherwise, may then operate in full force. He may go into depressions, psychotic episodes, or even kill himself or (more often), through self-destructive urges, incur an accident or succumb to an illness.[5]

A final word about his feeling toward life in general. On the

[5] James M. Barrie has described such an outcome in his *Tommy and Grizel*, published by Charles Scribner's Sons, 1900.

Cf. also Arthur Miller, *The Death of a Salesman*, Random House, 1949.

surface he is rather optimistic, turns outward toward life, and wants joy and happiness. But there are undercurrents of despondency and pessimism. Measuring by the yardstick of infinitude, of the attainment of fantastic happiness, he cannot help sensing a painful discrepancy in his life. As long as he is on the crest of a wave, he cannot possibly admit that he has failed in anything, especially in mastering life. The discrepancy is not in him but in life as such. Thus he may see a tragic quality in life, not the one that does exist but the one which he brings to it.

The type of the second subgroup, moving in the direction of *perfectionism,* identifies himself with his standards. This type feels superior because of his high standards, moral and intellectual, and on this basis looks down on others. His arrogant contempt for others, though, is hidden—from himself as well—behind polished friendliness, because his very standards prohibit such "irregular" feelings.

His ways of beclouding the issue of unfulfilled shoulds are twofold. In contrast to the narcissistic type, he does make strenuous efforts to measure up to his shoulds by fulfilling duties and obligations, by polite and orderly manners, by not telling obvious lies, etc. When speaking of perfectionistic people, we often think merely of those who keep meticulous order, are overly punctilious and punctual, have to find just the right word, or must wear just the right necktie or hat. But these are only the superficial aspects of their need to attain the highest degree of excellence. What really matters is not those petty details but the flawless excellence of the whole conduct of life. But, since all he can achieve is behavioristic perfection, another device is necessary. This is to equate in his mind standards and actualities—*knowing* about moral values and *being* a good person. The self-deception involved is all the more hidden from him since, in reference to others, he may insist upon their actually living up to his standards of perfection and despise them for failing to do so. His own self-condemnation is thus externalized.

As confirmation of his opinion of himself, he needs respect from others rather than glowing admiration (which he tends to scorn). Accordingly his claims are based less on a "naïve" belief in his greatness than (as we have described it in Chapter 2 on neurotic claims) on a "deal" he had secretly made with life. Because he is fair, just, dutiful, he is entitled to fair treatment by others and by life in general. This conviction of an infallible justice operating in life gives him a feeling of mastery. His own perfection therefore is not only a means to superiority but also one to control life. The idea of undeserved fortune, whether good or bad, is alien to him. His own success, prosperity, or good health is therefore less something to be enjoyed than a proof of his virtue. Conversely, any misfortune befalling him—such as the loss of a child, an accident, the infidelity of his wife, the loss of a job—may bring this seemingly well-balanced person to the verge of collapse. He not only resents ill fortune as unfair but, over and beyond this, is shaken by it to the foundations of his psychic existence. It invalidates his whole accounting system and conjures up the ghastly prospect of helplessness.

His other breaking points we mentioned when discussing the tyranny of the should: his recognition of an error or failure of his own making, and his finding himself caught between contradictory shoulds. Just as a misfortune pulls the ground away from under him, so does a realization of his own fallibility. Self-effacing trends and undiluted self-hate, kept in check successfully hitherto, then may come to the fore.

The third type, moving in the direction of *arrogant vindictiveness*, is identified with his pride. His main motivating force in life is his need for vindictive triumph. As Harold Kelman [6] said with reference to traumatic neuroses, vindictiveness here becomes a way of life.

The need for vindictive triumph is a regular ingredient in any search for glory. Our interest therefore is not so much concerned with the existence of this need but with its overwhelming intensity. How can the idea of triumph get such a hold on an individual that he spends all his life chasing after it? Surely it must be fed by a multitude of powerful sources. But the

[6] Harold Kelman, "The Traumatic Syndrome," *American Journal of Psychoanalysis*, vol. VI, 1946.

knowledge of these sources alone does not sufficiently elucidate its formidable power. In order to arrive at a fuller understanding we must approach the problem from still another vantage point. Even though in others the impact of the need for vengeance and triumph can be poignant, it usually is kept within limits by three factors: love, fear, and self-preservation. Only if these checks are temporarily or permanently malfunctioning can the vindictiveness involve the total personality—thereby becoming a kind of integrating force, as in Medea—and sway it altogether in the one direction of vengeance and triumph. And in the type to be discussed it is the combination of these two processes—powerful impulse and insufficient checks—that accounts for the magnitude of vindictiveness. Great writers have intuitively grasped this combination and have presented it in more impressive forms than a psychiatrist can hope to do. I am thinking for instance of Captain Ahab in *Moby Dick,* of Heathcliff in *Wuthering Heights,* and of Julien in *The Red and the Black.*

We shall start by describing how vindictiveness shows in human relations. An impelling need for triumph makes this type extremely competitive. As a matter of fact he cannot tolerate anybody who knows or achieves more than he does, wields more power, or in any way questions his superiority. Compulsively he has to drag his rival down or defeat him. Even if he subordinates himself for the sake of his career, he is scheming for ultimate triumph. Not being tied by feelings of loyalty, he easily can become treacherous. What he actually achieves with his often indefatigable work depends on his gifts. But with all his planning and scheming he will often achieve nothing worth while, not only because he is unproductive but because he is too self-destructive, as we shall see presently.

The most conspicuous manifestations of his vindictiveness are violent rages. These spells of vindictive fury can be so formidable that he himself may become frightened lest he do something irreparable when out of control. Patients may, for instance, actually be scared of killing somebody when under the influence of alcohol—i.e., when their usual controls do not operate. The impulse for revengeful actions can be strong enough to override the cautious prudence which usually governs their behavior. When seized by vindictive wrath, they may indeed jeopardize their lives, their security, their jobs, their social positions. An example from literature is Stendhal's *The Red and the Black*, where Julien shoots Madame de Rênal after having read the letter slandering him. We shall understand the recklessness involved later on.

Even more important than these, after all, rare eruptions of vindictive passion is the permanent vindictiveness which pervades the attitude of this type toward people. He is convinced that everybody at bottom is malevolent and crooked, that friendly gestures are hypocritical, that it is only wisdom to regard everyone with distrust unless he has been proved honest. But even such proof will readily make room for suspicion at the slightest provocation. In his behavior toward others he is openly arrogant, often rude and offensive, although sometimes this is covered up by a thin veneer of civil politeness. In subtle and gross ways, with or without realizing it, he humiliates others and exploits them. He may use women for the satisfaction of his sexual needs with utter disregard for their feelings. With a seemingly "naïve" egocentricity, he will use people as a means to an end. He frequently makes and maintains contacts exclusively on the basis of their serving his need for triumph: people he can use as steppingstones in his career, influential women he can conquer and subdue, followers who give him blind recognition and augment his power.

He is a past master in frustrating others—frustrating their small and big hopes, their needs for attention, reassurance, time, company, enjoyment.[7] When others remonstrate against such treatment, it is their neurotic sensitivity that makes them react this way.

---

[7] Most expressions of vindictiveness have been described by others, and by myself, as sadistic trends. The term "sadistic" focuses on the satisfaction to be gained from the power to subject others to pain or indignity. Satisfaction—excitement, thrill, glee—undoubtedly can be present in sexual and nonsexual situations, and for these the term "sadistic" seems to be sufficiently meaningful. My suggestion to replace the term "sadistic" in its general use by "vindictive" is based on the contention that for all so-called sadistic trends vindictive needs are the crucial motivating force.

Cf. Karen Horney, *Our Inner Conflicts,* Chapter 12, Sadistic Trends.

When these trends come into clear relief during analysis he may regard them as legitimate weapons in the struggle of all against all. He would be a fool not to be on guard, not to muster his energies for a defensive warfare. He must always be prepared to strike back. He must always and under all conditions be the invincible master of the situation.

The most important expression of his vindictiveness toward others is in the kind of claims he makes and the way he asserts them. He may not be openly demanding and not at all aware of having or making any claims, but in fact he feels entitled both to having his neurotic needs implicitly respected and to being permitted his utter disregard of others' needs or wishes. He feels entitled for instance to the unabridged expression of his unfavorable observations and criticisms but feels equally entitled never to be criticized himself. He is entitled to decide how often or how seldom to see a friend and what to do with the time spent together. Conversely he also is entitled not to have others express any expectations or objections on this score.

Whatever accounts for the inner necessity of such claims, they certainly express a contemptuous disregard for others. When they are not fulfilled there ensues a punitive vindictiveness which may run the whole gamut from irritability to sulking, to making others feel guilty, to open rages. In part these are his responses of indignation to feeling frustrated. But the undiluted expression of these feelings also serves as a measure to assert his claims by intimidating others into a subdued appeasement. Conversely, when not insisting upon his "rights" or when not being punitive, he becomes furious at himself and scolds himself for "getting soft." When in analysis he complains about his inhibitions or "compliance," in part he means to convey, without knowing it, his dissatisfaction with the imperfection of these techniques. And their improvement is one of the things he secretly expects from analysis. In other words he does not want to overcome his hostility but rather to become less inhibited or more skillful in expressing it. Then he would be so awe inspiring that everybody would rush to fulfill his claims. Both of these factors put a kind of premium on being discontented. And he is indeed the chronically discontented person. He has, in his mind, reasons to be so, and he certainly has an interest in letting it be known—all of which, including the fact of his dis-content, may be unconscious.

Partly he justifies his claims by his superior qualities, which in his mind are his better knowledge, "wisdom," and foresight. More specifically, his claims are demands for retribution for injury done. In order to solidify this basis for claims he must, as it were, treasure and keep alive injuries received, whether ancient or recent. He may compare himself to the elephant who never forgets. What he does not realize is his vital interest in not forgetting slights, since in his imagination they are the bill to present to the world. Both the need to justify his claims and his responses to their frustration work like vicious circles, sup-plying a constant fuel to his vindictiveness.

So pervasive a vindictiveness naturally enters into the analytic relationship, too, and shows itself in many ways. It is one part of the so-called negative therapeutic reaction,[8] by which we mean an acute impairment of condition after a constructive move ahead. Any move toward people, or toward life in general, would in fact jeopardize his claims and all that is entailed in his vindictiveness. As long as it is subjectively indispensable he must defend it in analysis. Only the smallest part of this defense is explicit and direct. When it is, the patient may de-clare frankly that he is determined not to relinquish his vindic-tiveness. "You won't take that away from me; you want to make me a goody-goody; it gives me a thrill; it makes me feel alive; it is strength," etc. Most of his defense is disguised in subtleties and indirections. And it is of the greatest clinical importance for the analyst to know the forms it may assume, because it may not merely delay the analytic process but may wreck it alto-gether.

It can do so in two main ways. It can greatly influence, if not govern, the analytic relationship. To defeat the analyst then may seem more important than progress. And (which is less well known) it can determine which problems he is interested in

[8] Sigmund Freud, *The Ego and the Id,* Institute of Psychoanalysis and Hogarth Press, London, 1927. Karen Horney, "The Problem of the Negative Therapeutic Reaction," *Psychoanalytic Quarterly,* 1936. Muriel Ivimey, "The Negative Thera-peutic Reaction," *American Journal of Psychoanalysis,* vol. VIII, 1948.

tackling. Speaking again in terms of extreme instances, the patient is interested in everything that might in the end make for a bigger and better vindictiveness—for a vindictiveness that would at once be more effective and be carried out without cost to himself, with superior poise and serenity. This selective process is not done by conscious reasoning, but by dint of an intuitive sense of direction which operates with unfailing certainty. He is for instance keenly interested in getting over compliant trends or over his feeling of having no rights. He is interested in getting over his self-hate, because it weakens him in the battle against the world. On the other hand he is uninterested in diminishing his arrogant claims or his feelings of being abused by others. He may hold on to his externalizations with curious tenacity. Indeed he may be altogether unwilling to analyze his human relationships, emphasizing the fact that all he wants in this respect is not to be bothered. The whole analysis then may easily confuse the analyst until he grasps the formidable logic of the selective process.

What are the sources of such vindictiveness, and whence its intensity? Like every other neurotic development, this one started in childhood—with particularly bad human experiences and few, if any, redeeming factors. Sheer brutality, humiliations, derision, neglect, and flagrant hypocrisy, all these assailed a child of especially great sensitivity. People who have endured years in concentration camps tell us that they could survive only by stifling their softer feelings, including particularly that of compassion for self and others. It seems to me that a child under the conditions I have described also goes through such a hardening process in order to survive. He may make some pathetic and unsuccessful attempts to win sympathy, interest, or affection but finally chokes off all tender needs. He gradually "decides" that genuine affection is not only unattainable for him but that it does not exist at all. He ends by no longer wanting it and even rather scorning it. This, however, is a step of grave consequence, because the need for affection, for human warmth and closeness is a powerful incentive for developing qualities that make us likable. The feeling of being loved and—even more—of being lovable is perhaps one of the greatest values in life. Conversely, as we shall discuss in the following chapters, the feeling of not being lovable can be a source of profound distress. The vindictive type tries to do away with such distress in a simple and radical way; he convinces himself that he just is not lovable and does not care. So he no longer is anxious to please but can give free range, at least in his mind, to his ample supply of bitter resentment.

Here is the beginning of what we see later in the fully developed picture: the expressions of vindictiveness may be checked by considerations of prudence or expediency, but they are counteracted very little by feelings of sympathy, fondness, or gratitude. In order to understand why this process of crushing positive feelings persists later on, when people may want his friendship or love, we have to take a look at his second means of survival: his imagination and his vision of the future. He is and will be infinitely better than "they" are. He will become great and put them to shame. He will show them how they have misjudged and wronged him. He will become the great hero (in Julien's case, Napoleon), the persecutor, the leader, the scientist attaining immortal fame. Driven by an understandable need for vindication, revenge, and triumph, these are not idle fantasies. They determine the course of his life. Driving himself from victory to victory, in large and small matters, he lives for the "day of reckoning."

The need for triumph and the need to deny positive feelings, both stemming from an unfortunate childhood situation, are thus, from the beginning, intimately interrelated. And they remain so because they reinforce each other. The hardening of feelings, originally a necessity for survival, allows for an unhampered growth of the drive for a triumphant mastery of life. But eventually this drive, with the insatiable pride that accompanies it, becomes a monster, more and more swallowing all feelings. Love, compassion, considerateness—all human ties —are felt as restraints on the path to a sinister glory. This type should remain aloof and detached.

In the character of Simon Fennimore [9] Maugham has described such a deliberate crushing of human desires as a conscious process. Simon forces himself to reject and destroy love, friendship, and everything that could make life enjoyable for the purpose of becoming the dictatorial head of "justice" in a totalitarian state. No human stirring in himself or others shall touch him. He sacrifices his real self for the sake of a vindictive triumph. This is an artist's accurate vision of what goes on, gradually and unconsciously, in the arrogant-vindictive type. To admit any human need becomes a sign of despicable weakness. When after much analytic work feelings do emerge, they sicken and frighten him. He feels he is "getting soft," and either redoubles his sulky sadistic attitudes or turns against himself with acute suicidal impulses.

We have so far mainly followed the development of his human relationships. And much of his vindictiveness and coldness becomes understandable this way. But we are still left with many open questions—questions about the subjective value and intensity of the vindictiveness, about the ruthlessness of his claims, etc. We shall arrive at a fuller understanding if we now focus on the intrapsychic factors, and consider their influence upon the interpersonal peculiarities.

The main motivating force on this score is his need for vindication. Feeling like a pariah, he must prove his own worth to himself. And he can prove it to his satisfaction only by arrogating to himself extraordinary attributes, the special qualities of which are determined by his particular needs. For a person as isolated and as hostile as he, it is of course important not to need others. Hence he develops a pronounced pride in a godlike self-sufficiency. He becomes too proud to ask for anything, and cannot receive anything graciously. To be on the receiving end is so humiliating to him that it chokes off any feelings of gratitude. Having smothered positive feelings, he can rely upon only his intellect for the mastery of life. Hence his pride in his intellectual powers reaches unusual dimensions: pride in vigilance, in outwitting everybody, in foresight, in planning. Furthermore, from the very beginning life has been to him a merciless struggle of all against all. Hence, to have invincible strength and to be inviolable must appear to him not only desirable but indispensable. Actually, as his pride becomes all consuming, his vulnerability also assumes unbearable dimensions. But he never allows himself to *feel* any hurt because his pride prohibits it. Thus the hardening process, which originally was necessary to protect real feelings, now must gather momentum for the sake of protecting his pride. His pride then lies in being above hurts and suffering. Nothing and nobody, from mosquitoes to accidents to people, can hurt him. This measure, however, is double edged. His not consciously feeling the hurts allows him to live without constant sharp pain. Besides it is questionable whether the diminished awareness of hurts does not actually dampen the vindictive impulses too; whether, in other words, he would not be more violent, more destructive without this lessened awareness. Certainly there is a diminished awareness of vindictiveness as such. In his mind it turns into a warranted wrath at a wrong done and into the right to punish the wrongdoer. If, however, a hurt does penetrate through the protective layer of invulnerability, then the pain becomes intolerable. In addition to his pride being hurt—for instance, by a lack of recognition—he also suffers the humiliating blow of having "allowed" something or somebody to hurt him. Such a situation can provoke an emotional crisis in an otherwise stoical person.

Closely akin to his belief and pride in inviolability or invulnerability, and indeed complementing it, is that in immunity and impunity. This belief, entirely unconscious, results from a claim which entitles him to the freedom to do to others whatever he pleases, and to having nobody mind it or try to get back at him. In other words, nobody can hurt me with impunity but I can hurt everybody with impunity. In order to understand the necessity for this claim we must reconsider his attitudes toward people. We have seen that he offends people easily through his militant rightness, arrogant punitiveness, and his rather openly using them as a means to his ends. But he does not nearly express all the hostility he feels; in fact, he tones it down considerably. As Stendhal has described it in *The Red and the Black*, Julien, unless carried away by an uncontrollable vindictive rage, is rather overcontrolled, guarded, and vigilant. We get therefore the curious impression of this type being both reckless and guarded in his dealings with people. And this impression is an accurate reflection of the forces operating in him. He must indeed keep an even balance between letting others feel his righteous anger and between holding it back. What drives him to express it is not only the magnitude of his vindictive urges but even more his need to intimidate others and to keep them in awe of an armed fist. This in turn is so necessary because he sees no possibility of coming to friendly terms with others, because it is a means to assert his claims, and—more generally—because in a warfare of all against all taking the offensive is the best defense.

His need to tone down his aggressive impulses, on the other hand, is determined by fears. Though he is much too arrogant to admit to himself that anybody could intimidate him or even affect him in any way, he is in actual fact afraid of people. Many reasons combine to engender this fear. He is afraid that others may retaliate for the offenses he perpetrates on them. He is afraid that they may interfere with whatever plans he has with regard to them, if he "goes too far." He is afraid of them because they do have the power to hurt his pride. And he is afraid of them because in order to justify his own hostility he must in his mind exaggerate that of others. To deny these fears to himself, however, is not sufficient to eliminate them; he needs some more powerful assurance. He cannot cope with this fear by not expressing his vindictive hostility—and he must express it without awareness of fear. The claim for immunity, turning into an illusory conviction of immunity, seems to solve this dilemma.

A last kind of pride to be mentioned is pride in his honesty, his fairness, and his justice. Needless to say, he is neither honest, fair, nor just and cannot possibly be so. On the contrary, if anybody is determined—unconsciously—to bluff his way through life with a disregard for truth, it is he. But we can understand his belief that he possesses these attributes to a high degree if we consider his premises. To hit back or—preferably —to hit first appears to him (logically!) as an indispensable weapon against the crooked and hostile world around him. It is nothing but intelligent, legitimate self-interest. Also, not questioning the validity of his claims, his anger, and the expression of it must appear to him as entirely warranted and "frank."

There is still another factor which greatly contributes to his conviction that he is a particularly honest person and which is important to mention for other reasons. He sees around him many compliant people who pretend to be more loving, more sympathetic, more generous than they actually are. And in this regard he is indeed more honest. He does not pretend to be a friendly person; in fact he disdains doing so. If he could leave it at an "At least I do not pretend . . ." level he would be on safe ground. But his need to justify his own coldness forces him to take a further step. He tends to deny that a wish to be helpful, or a friendly act, is ever genuine. He does not dispute the occurrence of friendliness in the abstract, but when it comes to concrete people he tends to regard it indiscriminately as hypocrisy. This move then again puts him on top of the heap. It makes him appear to himself as the one person who is above common hypocrisy.

This intolerance of the pretense of love has a still much deeper root than his need for self-justification. Only after considerable analytic work there appear here too, as in every expansive type, self-effacing trends. With his having made of himself an instrument for the attainment of an eventual triumph, the necessity to bury such trends is even more stringent than in the other expansive types. A period ensues when he feels altogether contemptible and helpless and tends to prostrate himself for the sake of being loved. We understand now that in others he despised not only the pretense of love but their compliance, their self-degrading, their helpless hankering for love. In short he despised in them the very self-effacing trends he hates and despises in himself.

The self-hate and self-contempt that now appear are appalling in their dimensions. Self-hate is always cruel and merciless. But its intensity or its effectiveness depends on two sets of factors. One is the degree to which an individual is under the sway of his pride. The other is the degree to which constructive forces counteract the self-hate—forces such as faith in positive values in life, the existence of constructive goals in life, the existence of some warm or appreciative feelings toward oneself. Since all these factors are unfavorable in the aggressive-vindictive type, his self-hate has a more pernicious quality than is usually the case. Even outside the analytic situation one can observe the extent to which he is a ruthless slavedriver of himself, and frustrates himself—glorifying the frustration as asceticism.

Such self-hate calls for rigorous self-protective measures. Its externalization seems a matter of sheer self-preservation. As in all expansive solutions, it is primarily an active one. He hates and despises in others all he suppresses and hates in himself: their spontaneity, their joy of living, their appeasing trends, their compliance, their hypocrisy, their "stupidity." He imposes his standards upon others, and is punitive when they do not measure up to them. His frustration of others is in part an externalization of self-frustrating impulses. Hence his punitive attitude toward others, which looks altogether vindictive, is instead a mixed phenomenon. It is partly an expression of vindictiveness; it is also the externalization of his condemnatory punitive trends toward himself; and, finally, it serves as a means of intimidating others for the purpose of asserting his claims. All three of these sources must be tackled successively in analysis.

The salient point in protecting himself against his self-hate is here, as everywhere, the necessity to ward off any realization of not being what, according to the dictates of his pride, he should be. Aside from his externalizations, his main defense on this score is an armor of self-righteousness so thick and so impenetrable that it often makes him inaccessible to reason. In arguments that may arise he seems to be unconcerned about the truth of any statement he interprets as hostile attack, but automatically responds with counterattacks—like a porcupine when it is touched. He simply cannot afford to consider even remotely anything that might engender a doubt in his rightness.

A third way in which he protects himself from the realization of any shortcoming is in his claims on others. In discussing these we have stressed the vindictive elements involved in his arrogating all rights to himself and denying any to others. But, with all his vindictiveness, he could be more reasonable in what he demands of others if it were not for the cogent necessity of protecting himself against the onslaughts of his own self-hate. Seen from this viewpoint, his claims are that others should behave in such a way as not to arouse in him any guilt feelings or any self-doubts. If he can convince himself that he is entitled to exploit or frustrate them without their complaining, criticizing, or resenting it, then he can keep from becoming aware of his tendencies to exploit or to frustrate. If he is entitled to having them *not* expect tenderness, gratitude, or consideration, then their disappointment is their hard luck and does not reflect on his not giving them a fair deal. Any doubt he might allow to emerge about his failings in human relations, about others having reason to resent his attitudes, would be like a hole in a dike, through which the flood of self-condemnation would break and sweep away his whole artificial self-assurance.

When we recognize the role of pride and self-hate in this type, we not only have a more accurate understanding of the forces operating within him but may also change our whole outlook on him. As long as we primarily focus on how he operates in his human relations we can describe him as arrogant, callous, egocentric, sadistic—or by any other epithet indicating hostile aggression which may occur to us. And any of them would be accurate. But when we realize how deeply he is caught within the machinery of his pride system, when we realize the efforts he must make not to be crushed by his self-hate, we see him as a harassed human being struggling for survival. And this picture is no less accurate than the first one.

Of these two different aspects, seen from two different perspectives, is one more essential, more important than the other? It is a question difficult to answer, and perhaps unanswerable, but it is in his inner struggle that analysis can reach him at a time when he is averse to examining his difficulties in regard to others, and when these difficulties are indeed quite remote. In part he is more accessible on this score because his human relations are so infinitely precarious that he rather anxiously avoids touching them. But there is also an objective reason for tackling the intrapsychic factors first in therapy. We have seen that they contribute in many ways to his outstanding trend, the arrogant vindictiveness. We cannot, in fact, understand the height of his arrogance without considering his pride and its vulnerability —or the intensity of his vindictiveness without seeing his need for protecting himself against his self-hate, etc. But to take a further step: these are not only reinforcing factors; they are the ones which make his hostile-aggressive trends *compulsive*. And this is the decisive reason that it is and must be ineffective and indeed futile to tackle the hostility directly. The patient cannot possibly evolve any interest in seeing it, and still less in examining it, as long as the factors which render it compulsive persist (in simple terms: as long as he cannot do anything about it anyhow).

His need for a vindictive triumph, for instance, certainly is a hostile-aggressive trend. But what makes it compulsive is the need to vindicate himself in his own eyes. This desire originally is not even neurotic. He starts so low on the ladder of human values that he simply must justify his existence, prove his values. But then the need to restore his pride and to protect himself from lurking self-contempt makes this desire imperative. Similarly, his need to be right and the resulting arrogant claims, while militant and aggressive, become compulsive through the necessity to prevent any self-doubt and self-blame from emerging. And, finally, the bulk of his faultfinding, his punitive and condemnatory attitudes toward others—or, at any rate, what renders these attitudes compulsive—stem from the dire need to externalize his self-hate.

Moreover, as we pointed out at the beginning, a rank growth of vindictiveness can occur if the forces usually counteracting it are malfunctioning. And again the intrapsychic factors constitute the main reason for these checks not operating. The choking off of tender feelings, starting in childhood and described as the hardening process, is necessitated by the actions and attitudes of other people and is meant to protect him against others. The need to make himself insensitive to suffering is greatly reinforced by the vulnerability of his pride and climaxed by his pride in invulnerability. His wish for human warmth and affection (both giving and receiving it), originally thwarted by the environment and then sacrificed to the need for triumph, is finally frozen by the verdict of his self-hate branding him as unlovable. Thus in turning against others he has nothing precious to lose. He unconsciously adopts the maxim of the Roman emperor: *oderint dum metuant*. In other words: "It is out of the question that they should love me; they hate me anyhow, so they should at least be afraid of me." Moreover healthy self-interest, which otherwise would check vindictive impulses, is kept at a minimum through his utter disregard for his personal welfare. And even the fear of others, though operating to some extent, is held down by his pride in invulnerability and immunity.

In this context of missing checks one factor deserves special mention. He has very little, if any, sympathy for others. This absence of sympathy has many causes, lying in his hostility toward others and in his lacking sympathy for himself. But what perhaps contributes most to his callousness toward others is his envy of them. It is a bitter envy—not for this or that particular asset, but pervasive—and stems from his feeling excluded from life in general.[10] And it is true that, with his entanglements, he actually *is* excluded from all that makes life worth living—from joy, happiness, love, creativeness, growth. If tempted to think along too neat lines, we would say here: has not he himself turned his back on life? Is he not proud of his ascetic not-wanting and not-needing anything? Does he not keep on warding off positive feelings of all sorts? So why should he envy others? But the fact is, he does. Naturally, without analysis his arrogance would not permit him to admit it in plain words. But as his analysis proceeds he may say something to the effect that of course everybody else is better off than he is. Or he may realize that he is infuriated at somebody for no other reason than that the latter is always cheerful or intensely interested in something. He himself indirectly offers an explanation. He feels that such a person wants to humiliate him viciously by flaunting his happiness in his face. Experiencing things this way not only gives rise to such vindictive impulses as wanting to kill joy but produces a curious kind of callousness by stifling his sympathy for others' suffering. (Ibsen's Hedda Gabler provides a good illustration of such vindictive callousness.) Thus far his envy reminds us of the dog-in-the-manger attitude. It hurts his pride that anybody could have something which, whether he wants it or not, is out of his reach.

But this explanation does not go deep enough. In analysis it

---

[10] *Cf.* Friedrich Nietzsche's expression *Lebensneid* and Max Scheler, *Das Resentiment im Aufbau der Moralen, der Neue Geist Verlag,* Leipzig, 1919.

gradually appears that the grapes of life, though he has declared them sour, are still desirable. We must not forget that his turning against life was not a voluntary move, and that the surrogate for which he exchanged living is a poor one. In other words his zest for living is stifled but not extinguished. In the beginning of analysis this is only a hopeful belief, but it proves justified in many more instances than is usually assumed. Upon its validity hinge the auspices for therapy. How could we help him if there were not something in him that does want to live more fully?

This realization is also relevant for the analyst's attitude toward such a patient. Most people respond to this type either by being intimidated into submissiveness or by rejecting him altogether. Neither attitude will do for the analyst. Naturally, when accepting him as a patient, the analyst wants to help him. But if the analyst is intimidated, he will not dare to tackle his problems effectively. If the analyst inwardly rejects him, he cannot be productive in his analytic work. The analyst will, however, have the necessary sympathetic and respectful understanding when he realizes that this patient too, despite his protestations to the contrary, is a suffering and struggling human being.

Looking back at the three kinds of expansive solutions, we see that they all aim at mastering life. This is their way of conquering fears and anxieties; this gives meaning to their lives and gives them a certain zest for living. They try to achieve such mastery in different ways: by self-admiration and the exercise of charm; by compelling fate through the height of their standards; by being invincible and conquering life in the spirit of a vindictive triumph.

Correspondingly, there are striking differences in the emotional atmosphere—from an occasional glowing warmth and joy of living to coolness and, finally, chilliness. The particular atmosphere is determined mainly by their attitudes toward their positive feelings. The narcissistic type can be friendly and generous under certain conditions, out of a feeling of abundance, even though this arises on a partly spurious basis. The perfectionistic type can show friendliness because he *should* be friendly. The arrogant-vindictive type tends to crush friendly feelings and to scorn them. There is much hostility in all of them, but in the narcissistic it can be overruled by generosity; in the perfectionistic it is subdued because he *should* not be hostile; in the arrogant-vindictive person it is more out in the open and, for reasons discussed, potentially more destructive. Expectations from others range from a need for devotion and admiration to one for respect to one for obedience. The unconscious foundations for their claims on life go from a "naïve" belief in greatness to a meticulous "deal" with life to feeling entitled to retribution for injuries done.

We might expect that the chances for therapy diminish in accordance with this scale. But here again we must keep in mind that these classifications merely indicate directions of neurotic development. The chances actually depend on many factors. The most relevant question in this regard is: how deeply entrenched are the trends, and how great is the incentive or potential incentive to outgrow them?

THE SELF-EFFACING SOLUTION: THE APPEAL OF LOVE

T HE SECOND major solution of inner conflicts, which we shall now discuss, is the self-effacing solution. It represents a move in a direction which is in all essentials opposite to that of the expansive solution. In fact the salient features of the self-effacing solution immediately come into clear relief when we see them in the light of this contrast. Therefore we shall briefly review some outstanding characteristics of the expansive type, focusing upon the questions: What does he glorify in himself—and what does he hate and despise? What does he cultivate in himself—and what does he suppress?

He glorifies and cultivates in himself everything that means mastery. Mastery with regard to others entails the need to excel and to be superior in some way. He tends to manipulate or dominate others and to make them dependent upon him. This trend is also reflected in what he expects their attitude toward him to be. Whether he is out for adoration, respect, or recognition, he is concerned with their subordinating themselves to him and looking up to him. He abhors the idea of his being compliant, appeasing, or dependent.

Furthermore he is proud of his ability to cope with any contingency and is convinced that he can do so. There is, or should be, nothing that he cannot accomplish. Somehow he must be—and feels that he is—the master of his fate. Helplessness may make him feel panicky and he hates any trace of it in himself.

Mastery with regard to himself means that he *is* his idealized proud self. Through will power and reason he is the captain of his soul. Only with great reluctance does he recognize any forces in himself which are unconscious, i.e., not subject to his conscious control. It disturbs him inordinately to recognize a conflict within himself, or any problem that he cannot solve (master) right away. Suffering is felt as a disgrace to be concealed. It is typical for him that in analysis he has no particular difficulty in recognizing his pride, but he is loath to see his shoulds, or at any rate that aspect of them which implies that he is shoved around by them. Nothing should push him around. As long as possible he maintains the fiction that he can lay down laws to himself and fulfill them. He abhors being helpless toward anything in himself as much as or more than being helpless toward any external factor.

In the type veering in the direction of the self-effacing solution we find a reverse emphasis. He must *not* feel consciously superior to others or display any such feelings in his behavior. On the contrary he tends to subordinate himself to others, to be dependent upon them, to appease them. Most characteristic is the diametrically opposite attitude from that of the expansive type toward helplessness and suffering. Far from abhoring these conditions, he rather cultivates and unwittingly exaggerates them; accordingly anything in the attitude of others, like admiration or recognition, that puts him in a superior position makes him uneasy. What he longs for is help, protection, and surrendering love.

These characteristics also prevail in his attitude toward himself. In sharp contrast to the expansive types, he lives with a diffuse sense of failure (to measure up to his shoulds) and hence tends to feel guilty, inferior, or contemptible. The self-hate and self-contempt elicited by such a sense of failure are externalized in a passive way: others are accusing or despising him. Conversely he tends to deny and eliminate expansive feelings about himself such as self-glorification, pride, and arrogance. Pride, no matter what it concerns, is put under a strict and extensive taboo. As a result it is not consciously felt; it is denied or disowned. He is *his subdued self*; he is the stowaway without any rights. In accordance with this attitude he also tends to suppress in himself anything that connotes ambition, vindictiveness, triumph, seeking his own advantage. In short he has solved his inner conflict by suppressing all expansive attitudes and drives and making self-abnegating trends predominant. Only in the course of analysis do these conflicting drives come to the fore.

The anxious shunning of pride, triumph, or superiority shows in many ways. Characteristic and easy to observe is the fear of winning in games. A patient, for instance, who had all the earmarks of morbid dependency could at times play an excellent game of tennis or chess. As long as she was oblivious of her good position all went well. But as soon as she became aware of being ahead of her opponent she suddenly missed the ball or (in playing chess) overlooked the most obvious moves that would ensure victory. Even prior to analysis she was quite aware that her reason was not her not caring to win but her not daring to do so. But, although she was angry at herself for defeating herself, the process operated so automatically that she was helpless to stop it.

Exactly the same attitude obtains in other situations. It is characteristic for this type not to be aware of being in a stronger position and not to be able to make use of it. Privileges, in his mind, turn into liabilities. He is often not aware of his superior knowledge, and at the crucial moment not able to show it. He is at sea in any situation in which his rights are not clearly defined—as for instance in relation to domestic or secretarial help. Even when making perfectly legitimate requests he feels as though he were taking undue advantage of the other person. And he either refrains from asking or does it apologetically, with a "guilty" conscience. He may even be helpless toward people who are actually dependent upon him, and cannot defend himself when they treat him in an insulting fashion. No wonder then that he is an easy prey for people who are out to take advantage of him. He is defenseless, often becomes aware of it only much later, and may then react with intense anger at himself and the exploiter.

His fear of triumph in more serious matters than games applies to success, acclaim, limelight. Not only is he afraid of any public performance, but when he is successful in some pursuit cannot give himself credit for it. He either gets frightened, minimizes it, or ascribes it to good luck. In the latter case, instead of feeling "I have done it" he merely feels that "it happened." There is often an inverse ratio between success and inner security. Repeated achievements in his field do not make him more secure, but more anxious. And this may reach such proportions of panic that a musician or an actor, for example, will sometimes decline promising offers.

Moreover he must shun any thought, feeling, or gesture that is "presumptuous." In an unconscious but systematic process of self-minimizing he leans over backward to avoid anything which he feels to be arrogant, conceited, or presumptuous. He forgets what he knows, what he has accomplished, what good he has done. It is conceit to think that he could manage his own affairs, that people would like to come when he invites them, that an attractive girl could like him. "Anything I want to do is arrogant." If he does achieve something, it was through good luck or a bluff. He may already feel it presumptuous to have an opinion or conviction of his own and hence he yields easily, without even consulting his own beliefs, to any suggestion vigorously propounded. Therefore, like a weather vane, he may yield to the opposite influence as well. Most legitimate self-assertion also appears presumptuous to him, such as speaking up when unjustly reprimanded, ordering a meal, asking for a raise, seeing to his rights when making a contract, or making advances toward a desirable person of the other sex.

Existing assets or achievements may be recognized indirectly, but they are not emotionally experienced. "My patients seem to think I am a good doctor." "My friends say I am a good storyteller." "Men have told me that I am attractive." Sometimes even an honest positive appraisal coming from others will be disowned: "My teachers think I am very intelligent, but they are mistaken." The same attitude prevails toward financial assets. Such a person may not have the feeling of owning the money he has earned through his own work. If he is financially well off, he nevertheless experiences himself as poor. Any ordinary observation or self-observation lays bare the fears behind all this overmodesty. They emerge as soon as he raises his head. Whatever sets the self-minimizing process to work, it is maintained by powerful taboos on trespassing the narrow confines he has set for himself. He should be content with little. He should not wish or strive for more. Any wish, any striving, any reaching out for more feels to him like a dangerous or reckless challenging of fate. He should not want to improve his figure by dieting or gymnastics, or to improve his appearance by dressing better. Last but not least, he should not improve himself by analyzing himself. He may be able to do so when under duress. But otherwise he simply will not find the time for it. I am not referring here to individual fears of tackling special problems. There is over and beyond these usual difficulties something that holds him back from doing it at all. Often, in sharp contrast to his conscious conviction about the value of self-analysis, it appears to him as "selfish" to "waste that much time" on himself.

What he scorns as "selfishness" is almost as comprehensive as what is to him "presumptuous." To him selfishness includes doing anything that is just for himself. He is often capable of enjoying many things but it would be "selfish" to enjoy them alone. He is often unaware of operating under such taboos and merely deems it "natural" to want to share a joy. Actually the sharing of pleasures is an absolute must. Whether it is food, music, or nature, it loses flavor and meaning if not shared with somebody else. He cannot spend money for himself. His stinginess with personal expenses may reach absurd degrees, which is particularly striking when contrasted with his often lavish spending for others. When he trespasses this taboo and does spend money on himself, even though it may be objectively reasonable, he will become panicky. The same holds true with regard to the use of time and energies. He often cannot read a book in his free time unless it is useful for his work. He may not grant himself the time for writing a personal letter, but furtively squeezes it in between two appointments. He often cannot make or keep order in his personal belongings—unless it is for somebody who would appreciate it. Similarly, he may neglect his appearance unless he has a date, a professional or social engagement—i.e., again unless it is for others. Conversely he may display considerable energy and skill in attaining something for others, such as helping them to make desirable contacts or to get a job; but he is tied hand and foot when it comes to doing the same thing for himself.

Although much hostility is generated in him, he cannot express it except when emotionally upset. Otherwise he is afraid of fighting and even friction for several reasons. Partly this is because a person who has thus clipped his wings is not and cannot possibly be a good fighter. In part he is terrified lest anybody be hostile toward him, and prefers to give in, to "understand" and forgive. We shall understand this fear better when we discuss his human relationships. But also, consistent with the other taboos and actually implied in them, is one on being "aggressive." He cannot stand up for his dislike of a person, an idea, a cause—and fight them if necessary. He cannot keep a sustained hostility nor can he carry a grudge, consciously. Hence vindictive drives remain unconscious and can only be expressed indirectly and in a disguised form. He cannot be openly demanding nor can he reprimand. It is most difficult for him to criticize, to reproach, or to accuse,—even when it seems warranted. He cannot even in joking make a sharp, witty, sarcastic remark.

Summarizing all this, we could say that there are taboos on all that is presumptuous, selfish, and aggressive. If we realize in detail the scope covered by the taboos, they constitute a crippling check on the person's expansion, his capacity for fighting and for defending himself, his self-interest—on anything that might accrue to his growth or his self-esteem. The taboos and self-minimizing constitute a *shrinking process* that artificially reduces his stature and leaves him feeling like one patient's dream in which, as a result of some merciless punishment, a person had shrunk to half his bodily size and was reduced to utter destitution and a moronic condition.

The self-effacing type, then, cannot make any assertive, aggressive, expansive move without trespassing against his taboos.

Their violation arouses both his self-condemnation and his self-contempt. He responds either with a general panicky feeling, without special content, or with feeling guilty. If self-contempt is in the foreground, he may respond with a fear of ridicule. Being in his self-feeling so small and so insignificant, any reaching out beyond his narrow confines may easily arouse the fear of ridicule. If this fear is conscious at all, it is usually externalized. Others would think it ridiculous if he spoke up in a discussion, ran for an office, or had the ambition to write something. Most of this fear, however, remains unconscious. At any rate he never seems to be aware of its formidable impact. It is, however, a relevant factor in keeping him down. The fear of ridicule is specifically indicative of self-effacing trends. It is alien to the expansive type. He can be blusteringly presumptuous without even realizing that he might be ridiculous or that others might so regard him.

While curtailed in any pursuit on his own behalf, he is not only free to do things for others but, according to his inner dictates, should be the ultimate of helpfulness, generosity, considerateness, understanding, sympathy, love, and sacrifice. In fact love and sacrifice in his mind are closely intertwined: he should sacrifice everything for love—love *is* sacrifice.

Thus far the taboos and shoulds have a remarkable consistency. But sooner or later contradictory trends appear. We might naïvely expect that this type would rather abhor aggressive, arrogant or vindictive traits in others. But actually his attitude is divided. He does abhor them but also secretly or openly adores them, and does so indiscriminately—without distinguishing between genuine self-confidence and hollow arrogance, between real strength and egocentric brutality. We easily understand that, chafing under his enforced humility, he adores in others aggressive qualities which he lacks or which are unavailable to him. But gradually we realize that this is not the complete explanation. We see that a more deeply hidden set of values, entirely opposite to the one just described, is also operating in him and that he admires in an aggressive type the expansive drives which for the sake of his integration he must so deeply suppress in himself. This disavowing of his own pride and aggressiveness, but admiring them in others, plays a great part in his morbid dependency, a possibility which we shall discuss in the next chapter.

As the patient becomes strong enough to face his conflict, his expansive drives come into sharper focus. He should also have the *absolute* of fearlessness; he should also go all out for his advantage; he should be able to hit back at anybody who offends him. Accordingly he despises himself at bottom for any trace of "cowardice," of ineffectualness and compliance. He is thus under a constant cross fire. He is damned if he does do something, and he is damned if he does not. If he refuses the request for a loan or for any favor, he feels that he is a repulsive and horrible creature; if he grants such requests, he feels that he is a "sucker." If he puts the insulter in his place, he gets frightened and feels utterly unlikable.

As long as he cannot face this conflict and work at it the need to keep a check on the aggressive undercurrents makes it all the more necessary to adhere tenaciously to the self-effacing pattern, and thereby enhances its rigidity.

The main picture that emerges so far is that of a person who holds himself down to the extent of shriveling in stature in order to avoid expansive moves. Moreover, as indicated before and elaborated later on, he feels subdued by an ever-alive readiness to accuse and despise himself; he also feels easily frightened and, as we shall see, spends a good deal of his energies in assuaging all these painful feelings. Before discussing further details and implications of his basic condition, let us get some understanding of its development by considering the factors which drive him in this direction.

People who later on tend toward the self-effacing solution usually have solved their early conflicts with people by "moving toward" them.[1] The early environment in typical instances is characteristically different from that of the expansive types, who either got early admiration, grew up under the pressure of rigid standards, or were harshly treated—exploited and humiliated. The self-effacing type, on the other hand, grew up *under the*

---

[1] *Cf.* Karen Horney, *The Neurotic Personality of Our Time,* Chapters 6–8 on The Neurotic Need for Affection. Karen Horney, *Our Inner Conflicts,* Chapter 3, Moving Toward People.

shadow of somebody: of a preferred sibling, of a parent who was generally adored (by outsiders), of a beautiful mother or of a benevolently despotic father. It was a precarious situation, liable to arouse fears. But affection of a kind was attainable—at a price: that of a self-subordinating devotion. There may have been, for instance, a long-suffering mother who made the child feel guilty at any failure to give her exclusive care and attention. Perhaps there was a mother or a father who could be friendly or generous when blindly admired, or a dominating sibling whose fondness and protection could be gained by pleasing and appeasing.[2] And so after some years, in which the wish to rebel struggled in the child's heart with his need for affection, he suppressed his hostility, relinquished the fighting spirit, and the need for affection won out. Temper tantrums stopped and he became compliant, learned to like everybody and to lean with a helpless admiration on those whom he feared most. He became hypersensitive to hostile tension, had to appease and smooth things over. Because the winning over of others became paramount in importance, he tried to cultivate in himself qualities that would make him acceptable and lovable. Sometimes, during adolescence, there was another period of rebellion, combined with a hectic and compulsive ambition. But he again relinquished these expansive drives for the benefit of love and protection, sometimes with his first falling in love. The further development largely depended upon the degree to which rebellion and ambition were suppressed or how complete the swing toward subordination, affection, or love became.

Like every other neurotic, the self-effacing type solves the needs evolving from his early development by self-idealization. But he can do it in one way only. His idealized image of himself primarily is a composite of "lovable" qualities, such as unselfishness, goodness, generosity, humility, saintliness, nobility, sympathy. Helplessness, suffering, and martyrdom are also secondarily glorified. In contrast to the arrogant-vindictive type, a premium is also placed on feelings—feelings of joy or suffering, feelings not only for individual people but for humanity, art, nature, values of all sorts. To have deep feelings is part of

---

[2] *Cf.* Karen Horney, *Self-Analysis*, Chapter 8, Systematic Self-analysis of a Morbid Dependency. (Claire's childhood is typical in this regard.)

his image. He can fulfill the resulting inner dictates only if he reinforces the self-abnegating trends which have grown out of his solution of his basic conflict with people. He must therefore develop an ambivalent attitude toward his own pride. Since the saintly and lovable qualities of his pseudoself are all the values he has, he cannot help being proud of them. One patient, when recovering, said about herself: "I took my moral superiority humbly for granted." Although he disavows his pride, and although it does not show in his behavior, it appears in the many indirect forms in which neurotic pride usually manifests itself —in vulnerability, face-saving devices, avoidances, etc. On the other hand his very image of saintliness and lovableness prohibits any *conscious* feeling of pride. He must lean over backward to eradicate any trace of it. Thus begins the shrinking process which leaves him small and helpless. It would be impossible for him to identify himself with his proud glorious self. He can only experience himself as his subdued victimized self. He feels not only small and helpless but also guilty, unwanted, unlovable, stupid, incompetent. He is the underdog and identifies himself readily with others who are downtrodden. Hence the exclusion of pride from awareness belongs to his way of solving the inner conflict.

The weakness of this solution, as far as we have traced it, lies in two factors. One of them is the shrinking process, which in biblical terms entails the "sin" (against oneself) of hiding one's talent in the earth. The other concerns the way in which the taboo on expansiveness renders him a helpless prey to self-hate. We can observe this in many self-effacing patients at the beginning of analysis, when they respond with stark terror to any self-reproach. This type, often unaware of the connection between self-accusation and terror, merely experiences the fact of being frightened or panicky. He is usually aware of being prone to reproach himself but, without giving it much thought, he regards it as a sign of conscientious honesty with himself.

He may also be aware that he accepts accusations from others all too readily, and realizes only later that they may actually have been without foundation and that it comes easier to him to declare himself guilty than to accuse others. In fact his response to admitting guilt, or a fault when criticized, comes with such quick and automatic reaction that his reason has no time to interfere. But he is unaware of the fact that he is positively abusing himself, and still less of the extent to which he does it. His dreams are replete with symbols of self-contempt and self-condemnation. Typical for the latter are execution-dreams: he is condemned to death; he does not know why, but accepts it; nobody shows him any mercy or even concern. Or he has dreams or fantasies in which he is tortured. The fear of torture may appear in hypochondriac fears: a headache becomes a brain tumor; a sore throat, tuberculosis; a stomach upset, cancer.

As analysis proceeds, the intensity of his self-accusations and self-torture comes into clear focus. Any difficulty of his that comes up for discussion may be used to batter himself down. An emerging awareness of his hostility may make him feel like a potential murderer. Discovering how much he expects of others makes him a predatory exploiter. A realization of his disorganization with regard to time and money may arouse in him the fear of "deterioration." The very existence of anxiety may make him feel like somebody utterly unbalanced and on the verge of insanity. In case these responses are out in the open, the analysis at the beginning may then seem to aggravate the condition.

We may therefore get the impression at first that his self-hate or self-contempt is more intense, more vicious than in other kinds of neurosis. But as we get to know him better, and compare his situation with other clinical experiences, we discard this possibility and realize that he is merely more helpless about his self-hate. Most of the effective means to ward off self-hate which are available to the expansive type are not at his disposal. He does try, though, to abide by his special shoulds and taboos and, as in every neurosis, his reasoning and his imagination help to obscure and to embellish the picture.

But he cannot stave off self-accusations by self-righteousness, because by doing so he would violate his taboos on arrogance and conceit. Nor can he, effectively, hate or despise others for what he rejects in himself, because he must be "understanding" and forgiving. Accusing others, or any kind of hostility toward others, would in fact frighten him (rather than reassure him) because of his taboos on aggression. Also, as we shall see presently, he needs others so much that he must avoid friction for this very reason. Finally, because of all these factors, he simply is not a good fighter, and this applies not only to his relations to others but to his attacks on himself as well. In other words he is just as defenseless against his own self-accusations, his self-contempt, his self-torture, etc., as he is against attacks on the part of others. He takes it all lying down. He accepts the verdict of his inner tyranny—which in turn increases his already reduced feelings about himself.

Nevertheless he of course needs self-protection, and does develop defensive measures of his own kind. The terror with which he may respond to the assaults of his self-hate actually emerges only if his special defenses are not properly functioning. The very process of self-minimizing is not only a means of avoiding expansive attitudes and keeping within the confines set by his taboos but also a means of appeasing his self-hate. I can best describe this process in terms of the way in which the self-effacing type characteristically behaves toward people when he feels attacked. He tries to placate and take the edge off accusations by (for instance) an overeager admission of guilt: "You are quite right . . . I am no good anyhow . . . it is all my fault." He tries to elicit sympathetic reassurance by being apologetic and by expressing remorse and self-reproaches. He may also plead for mercy by emphasizing his helplessness. In the same appeasing way he takes the sting out of his own self-accusations. He exaggerates in his mind his feelings of guilt, his helplessness, his being so badly off in every way—in short, he emphasizes his suffering.

A different way of releasing his inner tension is through passive externalization. This shows in his feeling accused by others, suspected or neglected, kept down, treated with contempt, abused, exploited, or treated with outright cruelty. However, this passive externalization, while allaying anxiety, does not seem to be as effective a means of getting rid of self-accusations as does active externalization. Besides (like all externalization), it disturbs his relations to others—a disturbance to which, for many reasons, he is particularly sensitive.

All these defensive measures, however, still leave him in a precarious inner situation. He still needs a more powerful reassurance. Even at those times in which his self-hate keeps within moderate limits, his feeling that everything which he does by himself or for himself is meaningless—his self-minimizing, etc.—makes him profoundly insecure. So, following his old pattern, he reaches out for others to strengthen his inner position by giving him the feeling of being accepted, approved of, needed, wanted, liked, loved, appreciated. *His salvation lies in others.* Hence his need for people is not only greatly reinforced but often attains a frantic character. We begin to understand the appeal which love has for this type. I use "love" as a common denominator for all kinds of positive feelings, whether they be sympathy, tenderness, affection, gratitude, sexual love, or feeling needed and appreciated. We shall leave for a separate chapter how this appeal of love influences a person's love life in the stricter sense. Here we shall discuss how it operates in his human relations in general.

The expansive type needs people for the confirmation of his power and of his spurious values. He also needs them as a safety valve for his own self-hate. But, since he has easier recourse to his own resources and greater support from his pride, his needs for others are neither as impelling nor as comprehensive as they are for the self-effacing type. The nature and magnitude of these needs account for a basic characteristic in the latter's *expectations of others.* While the arrogant-vindictive type primarily expects evil unless he has proof to the contrary, while the truly detached type (about whom we shall speak later) expects neither good nor bad, the self-effacing type keeps expecting good. On the surface it looks as though he had an unshakable faith in the essential goodness of humanity. And it is true that he is more open, more sensitive to likable qualities in others. But the compulsiveness of his expectations makes it impossible for him to be discriminating. He cannot as a rule distinguish between genuine friendliness and its many counterfeits. He is too easily bribed by any show of warmth or interest. In addition, his inner dictates tell him that he *should* like everybody, that he *should* not be suspicious. Finally his fear of antagonism and possible fights makes him overlook, discard, minimize, or explain away such traits as lying, crookedness, exploiting, cruelty, treachery.

When confronted with the unmistakable evidence of such

trends, he is taken by surprise each time; but even so he refuses to believe in any *intent* to deceive, humiliate, or exploit. Although he often is, and still more often feels, abused, this does not change his basic expectations. Even though by bitter personal experience he may know that nothing good could possibly come to him from a particular group or person, he still persists in expecting it—consciously or unconsciously. Particularly when such blindness occurs in someone who is otherwise psychologically astute his friends or colleagues may be flabbergasted by it. But it simply indicates that the emotional needs are so great that they override evidence. The more he expects of people, the more he tends to idealize them. He has not, therefore, a real faith in mankind but a Pollyanna attitude which inevitably brings with it many disappointments and makes him more insecure with people.

Here is a brief survey of what he expects of others. In the first place, he must feel accepted by others. He needs such acceptance in whatever form it is available: attention, approval, gratitude, affection, sympathy, love, sex. To make it clear by comparison: just as in our civilization many people feel worth as much as the money they are "making," so the self-effacing type measures his value in the currency of love, using the word here as a comprehensive term for the various forms of acceptance. He is worth as much as he is liked, needed, wanted, or loved.

Furthermore, he needs human contact and company because he cannot stand being alone for any length of time. He easily feels lost, as if he were cut off from life. Painful as this feeling is, it can still be tolerable as long as his self-abuse keeps within limits. As soon, however, as self-accusations or self-contempt become acute his feeling lost may grow into a nameless terror, and it is exactly at this point that the need for others becomes frantic.

This need for company is all the greater since being alone means to him proof of being unwanted and unliked and is therefore a disgrace, to be kept secret. It is a disgrace to go alone to the movies or on a vacation and a disgrace to be alone over the week end when others are sociable. This is an illustration of the extent to which his self-confidence is dependent upon somebody's caring for him in some way. He also needs others to give meaning and zest to whatever he is doing. The self-effacing type needs someone for whom to sew, cook, or garden, a teacher for whom he can play the piano, patients or clients who rely on him.

Besides all this emotional support, however, he needs help— and plenty of it. In his own mind the help he needs stays within most reasonable limits, partly because most of his needs for help are unconscious and partly because he focuses on certain requests for help as though they were isolated and unique: help in getting him a job, in speaking to his landlord, going shopping with or for him, lending him money. Moreover, any wish for help of which he is aware, appears to him eminently reasonable because the need behind it is so great. But when in analysis we see the total picture, his need for help actually amounts to the expectation that everything will be done for him. Others should supply the initiative, do his work, take the responsibility, give meaning to his life, or take over his life so that he can live through them. When recognizing the whole scope of these needs and expectations, the power which the appeal of love has for the self-effacing type becomes perfectly clear. It is not only a means to allay anxiety; without love he and his life are without value and without meaning. *Love therefore is an intrinsic part of the self-effacing solution.* In terms of the type's personal feelings, love becomes as indispensable for him as oxygen is for breathing.

Naturally he carries these expectations also into the analytic relationship. In contrast to most expansive types, he is not at all ashamed to ask for help. On the contrary, he may dramatize his needs and his helplessness and plead for help. But of course he wants it his own way. He expects at bottom a cure through "love." He may be quite willing to put efforts into the analytic work but, as it turns out later, he is prompted by his hungry expectation that salvation and redemption must and can come only from without (here from the analyst)—through being accepted. He expects the analyst to remove his feelings of guilt by love, which may mean by sexual love in the case of an analyst of the opposite sex. More often it means in more general ways signs of friendship, special attention, or interest.

As always happens in neurosis, needs turn into claims, which means that he feels entitled to having all these goods come to him. The needs for love, affection, understanding, sympathy, or help turn into: "I am entitled to love, affection, understanding, sympathy. I am entitled to have things done for me. I am entitled not to the pursuit of happiness but to have happiness fall into my lap." It goes almost without saying that these claims —as claims—remain more unconscious than in the expansive type.

The relevant questions in this regard are: upon what does the self-effacing type base his claims and how does he assert them? The most conscious, and in a way realistic, basis is that of his endeavors to make himself agreeable and useful. Varying with his temperament, his neurotic structure, and the situation, he may be charming, compliant, considerate, sensitive to wishes of others, available, helpful, sacrificing, understanding. It is but natural that he overrates what, in this or that way, he does for another person. He is oblivious to the fact that the latter may not at all like this kind of attention or generosity; he is unaware that there are strings attached to his offers; he omits from his consideration all the unpleasant traits he has. And so it all appears to him as the pure gold of friendliness, for which he could reasonably expect returns.

Another basis for his claims is more detrimental for himself and more coercive of others. Because he is afraid to be alone, others should stay at home; because he cannot stand noise, everybody should tiptoe around the house. A premium is thus set on neurotic needs and suffering. Suffering is unconsciously put into the service of asserting claims, which not only checks the incentive to overcome it but also leads to inadvertent exaggerations of suffering. This does not mean that his suffering is merely "put on" for demonstrative purposes. It affects him in a much deeper way because he must primarily prove to himself, to his own satisfaction, that he is entitled to the fulfillment of his needs. He must feel that his suffering is so exceptional and so excessive that it entitles him to help. In other words this process makes a person actually feel his suffering more intensely than he would without its having acquired an unconscious strategic value.

A third basis, still more unconscious and more destructive, is his feeling abused and being entitled to having others make up for the injuries perpetrated on him. In dreams he may present himself as being ruined beyond repair and hence entitled to having all his needs fulfilled. In order to understand these vindictive elements we must survey the factors accounting for his feeling abused.

In a typically self-effacing person, feeling abused is an almost constant undercurrent in his whole attitude toward life. If we wanted to characterize him crudely and glibly in a few words, we would say that he is a person who craves affection and feels abused most of the time. To begin with, as I have mentioned, others often do take advantage of his defenselessness and his overeagerness to help or to sacrifice. On account of his feeling unworthy, and his inability to stand up for himself, he sometimes does not take conscious cognizance of such abuse. Also, due to his shrinking process and all it entails, he often does come out on the short end, without there having been any harmful intent on the part of others. Even if in actual fact he is in some regards more fortunate than others, his taboos do not allow him to recognize his advantages and he must present himself to himself (and hence experience himself) as being worse off than others.

Furthermore he feels abused when his many unconscious claims are not fulfilled—for instance, when others do not respond with gratitude to his compulsive efforts to please, to help, to make sacrifices for them. His typical response to frustration of claims is not so much righteous indignation as a self-pitying feeling of being unfairly treated.

Probably more poignant than any of these other sources is all the abuse he inflicts upon himself, through self-minimizing as well as through self-reproaches, self-contempt, and self-torture —all of which is externalized. The more intense the self-abuse, the less can good external conditions prevail against it. He often will tell heartbreaking tales of his woes, arouse sympathy and the wish to give him a better deal, only to find himself in the same predicament soon after. In actual fact he may not have been so unfairly treated as it seems to him; at any rate, behind the feeling is the reality of his self-abuse. The connection between a sudden rise in self-accusations and the subsequent feeling of being abused is not too difficult to observe. In analysis for instance, as soon as self-accusations are aroused by his seeing a difficulty of his own his thoughts may immediately take him back to incidents or periods of his life when he actually was badly treated—whether they occurred in his childhood, in previous medical treatment, or in former jobs. He may dramatize the wrong done to him and dwell on it monotonously, as he had done many a time before. The same pattern may occur in other human relations. If for instance he is dimly aware of having been inconsiderate, he may, with the speed of lightning, switch to feeling abused. In short, his terror of wrongdoing simply compels him to feel himself the victim, even when in actual fact he has been the one who failed others or who, through his implicit demands, has imposed upon them. Because feeling victimized thus becomes a protection against his self-hate, it is a strategical position, to be defended vigorously. The more vicious the self-accusations, the more frantically must he prove and exaggerate the wrong done to him—and the more deeply he experiences the "wrong." This need can be so cogent that it makes him inaccessible to help for the time being. For to accept help, or even to admit to himself that help is being offered, would cause the defensive position of his being altogether the victim to collapse. Conversely, it is profitable at any sudden rise in feeling abused to look for a possible increase of guilt-feelings. We can often observe in analysis that the wrong done to him shrinks to reasonable proportions, or indeed ceases to be a wrong, as soon as he recognizes his share in the particular situation and can look at it in a matter-of-fact way, i.e., without self-condemnation.

The passive externalization of self-hate may go beyond merely feeling abused. He may provoke others to treat him badly, and thus transfer the inner scene to the outside. In this way too he becomes the noble victim suffering under an ignoble and cruel world.

All these powerful sources combine to engender his feeling abused. But closer observation shows that he not only feels abused for this or that reason but that something in him welcomes this feeling, indeed may avidly seize upon it. This points to the fact that feeling abused also must have some important function. This function is to allow him an outlet for the suppressed expansive drives—and almost the only one he can tolerate—and at the same time cover them up. It allows him to feel secretly superior to the others (the crown of martyrdom); it allows him to put his hostile aggression against others on a legitimate basis; and it finally allows him to disguise his hostile aggression because, as we shall see presently, most of the hostility is suppressed, and expressed in suffering. Feeling abused is therefore the greatest stumbling block to the patient's seeing and experiencing the inner conflict for which his self-effacement was a solution. And, while analysis of each individual factor helps to diminish its tenacity, it cannot vanish until he comes face to face with this conflict.

As long as this feeling abused persists—and usually it does not remain static but increases as time goes on—it makes for an increasing vindictive resentment against others. The bulk of this vindictive hostility remains unconscious. It must be deeply suppressed because it endangers all the subjective values he lives by. It mars his idealized image of absolute goodness and magnanimity; it makes him feel unlovable and conflicts with all his expectations of others; it violates his inner dictates of being all understanding and all forgiving. Therefore, when he is resentful he not only turns against others but simultaneously against himself. Hence such resentment is a disruptive factor of the first order for this type.

Despite this pervasive suppression of resentment, reproaches will occasionally be expressed, in mitigated form. Only when he feels driven to despair will the locked gates break open and a flood of violent accusations rush out. Though these may express accurately what he feels deep down, he usually discards them on the grounds of having been too upset to say what he means. But his most characteristic way of expressing vindictive resentment is again through suffering. Rage can be absorbed in increased suffering from whatever psychosomatic symptoms he has, or from feeling prostrate or depressed. If in analysis such a patient's vindictiveness is aroused, he will not be outright angry but his condition will be impaired. He will come with increased complaints, and indicate that analysis seems to make him worse instead of better. The analyst may know what has hit the patient in the previous session and may try to bring it to the patient's awareness. But the patient is not interested in seeing a connection that might relieve his suffering. He simply re-emphasizes his complaints, as if he has to make sure that the analyst gets the full impact of how bad the depression was. Without knowing it, he is out to make the analyst feel guilty for having made him suffer. This is often an exact replica of what happens in the domestic scene. Suffering thus acquires another function: that of absorbing rage and making others feel guilty, which is the only effective way of getting back at them.

All of these factors lend a curious ambivalence to his attitude toward people: a surface prevalence of "naïve" optimistic trust and an undercurrent of just as indiscriminate suspiciousness and resentment.

The inner tension created by an increased vindictiveness can be enormous. And the puzzle often is *not* that he has this or that emotional upset but that he manages to keep a fair equilibrium. Whether he can do it, and for how long, depends partly upon the intensity of the inner tension and partly upon circumstances. With his helplessness and dependence upon others, the latter are more important for him than for other neurotic types. An environment is favorable for him that does not tax him beyond what, with his inhibitions, he can do, and that affords such a measure of satisfaction as, according to his structure, he needs and can allow himself. Provided his neurosis is not too severe, he can derive satisfaction from leading a life dedicated to others or to a cause; a life in which he can lose himself by being useful and helpful and where he feels needed, wanted, and liked. However, even under the very best inner and outer conditions, his life rests on a precarious foundation. It can be threatened by a change in the external situation. The people he takes care of may die or no longer need him. The cause for which he has worked may fail, or lose its significance for him. Such losses, which a healthy person can weather, may bring him to the verge of a "breakdown," with all his anxiety and feelings of futility coming into the foreground. The other danger threatens primarily from the inside. There are just too many factors in his unavowed hostility against self and others that may give rise to a greater inner tension than he can bear. Or, in other words, the chances of his feeling abused are too great to make any situation safe for him.

On the other hand, prevailing conditions may not contain even the partially favorable elements I have just described. If the inner tension is great and the environmental conditions difficult, he not only may become extremely miserable but his equilibrium may break down. Whatever the symptoms—panic, insomnia, anorexia (loss of appetite)—it comes about and is characterized by hostility breaking the dam and overflooding the system. All his piled-up, bitter accusations against others then come to the fore; his claims become openly vindictive and unreasoning; his self-hate becomes conscious and reaches formidable proportions. His condition is one of unmitigated despair. He may have severe panics and the danger of suicide is considerable. A very different picture from that of the too-soft person who is so anxious to please. And yet the beginning and the end stages are part and parcel of one kind of neurotic development. It would be a wrong conclusion to think that the *amount* of destructiveness appearing in the end stages has been under check all the time. Certainly, under the surface of sweet reasonableness, there has been more tension than met the eye. But only a considerable increase of frustration and hostility brings about the end stages.

Since some other aspects of the self-effacing solution will be discussed in the context of morbid dependency, I should like to conclude the general outline of this structure with a few comments on the problem of neurotic suffering. Every neurosis entails real suffering, usually more than a person is aware of. The self-effacing type suffers under the shackles that prevent his expansion, under his self-abuse, under his ambivalent attitude toward others. All of this is plain suffering; it is not in the service of some secret purpose; it is not put on to impress others in this or that way. But in addition his suffering takes over certain functions. I suggest calling the suffering resulting from this process *neurotic* or *functional suffering*. I have mentioned some of these functions. Suffering becomes a basis for his claims. It is not only a plea for attention, care, and sympathy but it entitles him to all these. It serves to maintain his solution and hence has an integrating function. Suffering also is his specific way of expressing vindictiveness. Frequent indeed are the examples where the psychic ailments of one of the marriage partners are used as a deadly weapon against the other, or where they are used to cramp the children by instilling in them feelings of guilt for an independent move.

How does he square with himself the infliction of so much misery on others—he who is anxious not to hurt anybody's feelings? He may be more or less dimly aware that he is a drag on his environment, but he does not squarely face it because his own suffering exonerates him. To put it briefly: *his suffering accuses others and excuses himself!* It excuses in his mind everything—his demands, his irritability, his dampening of the spirits of others. Suffering not only assuages his own self-accusation,[3] but also wards off the possible reproaches of others. And again his need for forgiveness turns into a claim. His suffering entitles him to "understanding." If others are critical, *they* are unfeeling. No matter what he does, it should arouse sympathy and the wish to help.

Suffering exonerates the self-effacing person in still another way. It provides him with an over-all alibi both for not actually making more of his life and for not achieving ambitious goals. Although, as we have seen, he anxiously shuns ambition and triumph, the need for achievement and triumph still operates. And his suffering allows him to save his face by maintaining in his mind—consciously or unconsciously—the possibility of supreme achievements, were it not for his being afflicted with mysterious ailments.

Lastly, neurotic suffering may entail a playing with the idea of going to pieces, or an unconscious determination to do so. The appeal of doing so naturally is greater in times of distress

---

[3] Alexander has described this phenomenon as the "need for punishment" and has illustrated it with many convincing examples. This meant a definite progress in the understanding of intrapsychic processes. The difference between Alexander's views and my own is this: the freeing from neurotic guilt-feelings by way of suffering is in my opinion not a process valid for all neuroses but specific for the self-effacing type. Also to pay in the currency of suffering does not make him feel free, as it were, to sin again. The dictates of his inner tyranny are so many and so rigid that he cannot help violating them again. *Cf.* Franz Alexander, *Psychoanalysis of the Total Personality*, Nervous and Mental Disease Publishing Co., New York, Washington, 1930.

and can then be conscious. More often in such periods only reactive fears reach consciousness, such as fears of mental, physical, or moral deterioration, of becoming unproductive, of becoming too old for this or that. These fears indicate that the more healthy part of the person wants to have a full life and reacts with apprehension to another part which is bent on going to pieces. This tendency may also work unconsciously. The person may not even be cognizant that his whole condition has been impaired—that, for instance, he is less able to do things, is more afraid of people, more despondent—until one day when he suddenly wakes up to the fact that he is in danger of going downhill, and that something in himself drives him down.

In times of distress the "going under" may have a powerful appeal for him. It appears as a way out of all his difficulties: giving up the hopeless struggle for love and the frantic attempts to fulfill contradictory shoulds, and freeing himself from the terror of self-accusations by accepting defeat. It is moreover a way which appeals to him through his very passivity. It is not as active as suicidal tendencies, which rarely occur at such times. He simply stops struggling and lets the self-destructive forces take their course.

Finally, going to pieces under the assault of an unfeeling world appears to him as the ultimate triumph. It may take the conspicuous form of "dying at the offender's doorstep." But more often it is not a demonstrative suffering that intends to put others to shame and to raise claims on these grounds. It goes deeper, and hence is more dangerous. It is a triumph primarily in the person's mind, and even this may be unconscious. When we uncover it in analysis we find a glorification of weakness and suffering supported by confused half-truths. Suffering per se appears as the proof of nobility. What else can a sensitive person in an ignoble world do but go to pieces! Should he fight and assert himself and hence stoop down to the same level of crude vulgarity? He can but forgive and perish with the crowning glory of martyrdom.

All these functions of neurotic suffering account for its tenacity and depth. And all of them stem from dire necessities of the whole structure, and can be understood only against this background. To put it in terms of therapy: he cannot dispense with them without radical change in his whole character structure.

For the understanding of the self-effacing solution it is indispensable to consider the totality of the picture: both the totality of the historical development and the totality of processes going on at any given time. When briefly surveying the theories on this subject, it seems that their inadequacies stem essentially from a one-sided focus on certain aspects. There may be, for instance, a one-sided focus on either intrapsychic or interpersonal factors. We cannot, however, understand the dynamics from either one of these aspects alone but only as a process in which interpersonal conflicts lead to a peculiar intrapsychic configuration, and this latter in turn depends on and modifies the old patterns of human relations. It makes them more compulsive and more destructive.

Moreover some theories, like those of Freud and Karl Menninger,[4] focus too much on the conspicuously morbid phenomena such as "masochistic" perversions, wallowing in guilt-feelings, or self-inflicted martyrdom. They leave out trends which are closer to the healthy. To be sure, the needs to win people, to be close to others, to live in peace are determined by weakness and fear and hence are indiscriminate, but they contain germs of healthy human attitudes. The humility of this type and his capacity to subordinate himself in himself (granted his spurious foundation) seem closer to the normal than for instance the flaunting arrogance of the aggressive-vindictive type. These qualities make the self-effacing person, as it were, more "human" than many other neurotics. I am not speaking here in his defense; the very trends just mentioned are the ones which start his alienation from himself and initiate the further pathologic development. I merely want to say that not understanding them as an intrinsic part of the whole solution inevitably leads to misinterpretations of the entire process.

Lastly, some theories focus on the neurotic suffering—which is indeed a central problem—but divorce it from the whole background. This inevitably leads to an undue stress on stra-

---

[4] Cf. Sigmund Freud, *Beyond the Pleasure Principle*, International Psychoanalytic Library, London, 1921. Karl A. Menninger, *Man Against Himself*, Harcourt, Brace, New York, 1938.

tegic devices. Thus Alfred Adler [5] saw suffering as a means to get attention, to shirk responsibility, and to attain a devious superiority. Theodore Reik [6] stresses demonstrative suffering as a means to get love and to express vindictiveness. Franz Alexander, as already mentioned, emphasizes the function which suffering has for removing guilt-feelings. All these theories rest on valid observations but nevertheless, when insufficiently embedded in the whole structure, bring into the picture an undesirable approximation of popular beliefs that the self-effacing type simply wants to suffer or is only happy when miserable.

To see the total picture is not only important for theoretical understanding but also for the analyst's attitude toward patients of this kind. Through their hidden demands and their special brand of neurotic dishonesty they may easily arouse resentment, but perhaps even more than the others they need a sympathetic understanding.

---

[5] Alfred Adler, *Understanding Human Nature*, Greenberg, 1927.
[6] Theodore Reik, *Masochism in Modern Man*, Farrar and Rinehart, 1941.

CHAPTER 10

MORBID DEPENDENCY

Among the three major solutions of the inner conflict within the pride system the self-effacing seems the least satisfactory one. Besides having the drawback entailed in every neurotic solution, it makes for a greater subjective feeling of unhappiness than the others. The genuine suffering of the self-effacing type may not be greater than in other kinds of neurosis, but subjectively he feels miserable more often and more intensely than others because of the many functions suffering has assumed for him.

Besides, his needs and expectations of others make for a too great dependency upon them. And, while every enforced dependency is painful, this one is particularly unfortunate because his relation to people cannot but be divided. Nevertheless love (still in its broad meaning) is the only thing that gives a positive content to his life. Love, in the specific sense of erotic love, plays so peculiar and significant a role in his life that its presentation warrants a separate chapter. Although this unavoidably makes for certain repetitions, it also gives us a better opportunity to bring into clearer relief certain salient factors of the whole structure.

Erotic love lures this type as the supreme fulfillment. Love must and does appear as the ticket to paradise, where all woe

ends: no more loneliness; no more feeling lost, guilty, and unworthy; no more responsibility for self; no more struggle with
a harsh world for which he feels hopelessly unequipped. Instead
love seems to promise protection, support, affection, encouragement, sympathy, understanding. It will give him a feeling of
worth. It will give meaning to his life. It will be salvation and
redemption. No wonder then that for him people often are
divided into the haves and have-nots, not in terms of money
and social status but of being (or not being) married or having
an equivalent relationship.

Thus far the significance of love lies primarily in all he expects from being loved. Because psychiatric writers who have
described the love of dependent persons have put a one-sided
emphasis on this aspect, they have called it parasitic, sponging,
or "oral-erotic." And this aspect may indeed be in the foreground. But for the typical self-effacing person (a person with
prevailing self-effacing trends) the appeal is as much in loving
as in being loved. To love, for him, means to lose, to submerge
himself in more or less ecstatic feelings, to merge with another
being, to become one heart and one flesh, and in this merger to
find a unity which he cannot find in himself. His longing for
love thus is fed by deep and powerful sources: the longing for
surrender and the longing for unity. And we cannot understand
the depth of his emotional involvement without considering
these sources. The search for unity is one of the strongest motivating forces in human beings and is even more important to
the neurotic, with his inner division. The longing to surrender
to something bigger than we are seems to be the essential element in most forms of religion. And although the self-effacing
surrender is a caricature of the healthy yearning, it nevertheless
has the same power. It appears not only in the craving for love
but also in many other ways.[1] It is one factor in his propensity
to lose himself in all kinds of feelings: in a "sea of tears"; in
ecstatic feelings about nature; in wallowing in guilt-feelings; in

---

[1] *Cf.* Karen Horney, *The Neurotic Personality of Our Time*, W. W. Norton,
1936, "The Problem of Masochism." In that book I suggested the longing for
self-extinction as the basic explanatory principle for what I then still called
masochistic phenomena. I would think now that this longing arises from the
background of the special self-effacing structure.

his yearning for oblivion in orgasm or in fading out in sleep; and often in his longing for death as the ultimate extinction of self.

Going still another step deeper: the appeal love has for him resides not only in his hopes for satisfaction, peace, and unity, but love also appears to him as the only way to actualize his idealized self. In loving, he can develop to the full the lovable attributes of his idealized self; in being loved he obtains the supreme confirmation of it.

Because love has for him a unique value, *lovableness* ranks first among all the factors determining his self-evaluation. I have already mentioned that the cultivation of lovable qualities started in this type with his early need for affection. It becomes all the more necessary the more crucial others become for his peace of mind; and all the more encompassing, the more expansive moves are suppressed. Lovable qualities are the only ones invested with a kind of subdued pride, the latter showing in his hypersensitivity to any criticism or questioning on this score. He feels deeply hurt if his generosity or his attentiveness to the needs of others is not appreciated or even, on the contrary, irritates them. Since these lovable qualities are the only factors he values in himself, he experiences any rejection of them as a total rejection of himself. Accordingly his fear of rejection is poignant. Rejection to him means not only losing all the hopes he had attached to somebody but also being left with a feeling of utter worthlessness.

In analysis we can study more closely how lovable attributes are enforced through a system of rigorous shoulds. He should not only be sympathetic but also attain the *absolute* in understanding. He should never feel personal hurts because everything of this sort should be wiped out by such understanding. To feel hurt, in addition to being painful, arouses self-condemnatory reproaches for being petty or selfish. Particularly he should not be vulnerable to the pangs of jealousy—a dictate entirely impossible of fulfillment for a person whose fear of rejection and desertion is bound to be aroused easily. All he can do at best is to insist upon a pretense of "broad-mindedness." Any friction that arises is his fault. He should have been more serene, more thoughtful, more forgiving. The extent to which he feels his shoulds as his own varies. Usually some are externalized to the partner. What he is aware of then is an anxiety to measure up to the latter's expectations. The two most relevant shoulds on this score are that he should be able to develop any love relationship into a state of absolute harmony and that he should be able to make the partner love him. When enmeshed in an untenable relation and having enough sense to know that it would be all for his own good to end it, his pride presents this solution as a disgraceful failure and demands that he should make the relation work. On the other hand, just because the lovable qualities—no matter how spurious—are invested with a secret pride, they also become a basis for his many hidden claims. They entitle him to exclusive devotion, and to the fulfillment of his many needs which we discussed in the last chapter. He feels entitled to be loved not only for his attentiveness, which may be real, but also for his very weakness and helplessness, for his very suffering and self-sacrificing.

Between these shoulds and claims conflicting currents can arise in which he may get inextricably caught. One day he is all abused innocence and may resolve to tell the partner off. But then he becomes frightened of his own courage, both in terms of demanding anything for himself and of accusing the other. He also becomes frightened at the prospect of losing him. And so the pendulum swings to the other extreme. His shoulds and self-reproaches get the upper hand. He should not resent anything, he should be unruffled, he should be more loving and understanding—and it all is his fault anyway. Similarly he wavers in his estimate of the partner, who sometimes seems strong and adorable, sometimes incredibly and inhumanly cruel. Thus everything is befogged and any decision out of the question.

Although the inner conditions in which he enters a love relationship are always precarious, they do not necessarily lead to disaster. He can reach a measure of happiness, provided he is not too destructive and provided he finds a partner who is either fairly healthy or, for neurotic reasons of his own, rather cherishes his weakness and dependency. Although such a partner may feel his clinging attitude burdensome at times, it may also make him feel strong and safe to be the protector and to arouse so much personal devotion—or what he conceives as such. Under these circumstances the neurotic solution might be called a successful one. The feeling of being cherished and sheltered brings out the very best qualities of the self-effacing person. Such a situation, however, will inevitably prevent him from outgrowing his neurotic difficulties.

How often such fortuitous circumstances occur is not in the analyst's domain to judge. What comes to his attention are the less fortunate relations, in which the partners torment each other and in which the dependent partner is in danger of destroying himself, slowly and painfully. In these instances we speak of a morbid dependency. Its occurrence is not restricted to sexual relations. Many of its characteristic features may operate in nonsexual friendships between parent and child, teacher and pupil, doctor and patient, leader and follower. But they are most pronounced in love relations, and having once grasped them therein one will easily recognize them in other relations when they may be clouded over by such rationalizations as loyalty or obligation.

Morbidly dependent relations are initiated by the unfortunate choice of a partner. To be more accurate, we should not speak of choice. The self-effacing person actually does not choose but instead is "spellbound" by certain types. He is naturally attracted by a person of the same or opposite sex who impresses him as stronger and superior. Leaving out of consideration here the healthy partner, he may easily fall in love with a detached person, provided the latter has some glamour through wealth, position, reputation, or particular gifts; with an outgoing narcissistic type possessing a buoyant self-assurance similar to his own; with an arrogant-vindictive type who dares to make open claims and is unconcerned about being haughty and offensive. Several reasons combine for his being easily infatuated with these personalities. He is inclined to overrate them because they all seem to possess attributes which he not only bitterly misses in himself but ones for the lack of which he despises himself. It may be a question of independence, of self-sufficiency, of an invincible assurance of superiority, a boldness in flaunting arrogance or aggressiveness. Only these strong, superior people—as he sees them—can fulfill all his needs and take him over. To follow the fantasies of one woman patient: only a man with strong arms can save her from a burning house, a shipwreck, or threatening burglars.

But what accounts specifically for being fascinated or spell-bound—i.e., for the compulsive element in such an infatuation —is the suppression of his expansive drives. As we have seen, he must go to any length to disavow them. Whatever hidden pride and drives for mastery he has, remain foreign to him—while, conversely, he experiences the subdued helpless part of his pride system as the very essence of himself. But on the other hand, because he suffers under the results of his shrinking process, the capacity to master life aggressively and arrogantly also appears to him to be most desirable. Unconsciously and even—when he feels free enough to express it—consciously, he thinks that if only he could be as proud and ruthless as the Spanish conquistadors he would be "free," with the world at his feet. But since this quality is out of reach for him, he is fascinated by it in others. He externalizes his own expansive drives and admires them in others. It is their pride and arrogance that touch him to the core. Not knowing that he can solve his conflict in himself only, he tries to solve it by love. To love a proud person, to merge with him, to live vicariously through him would allow him to participate in the mastery of life without having to own it to himself. If in the course of the relationship he discovers that the god has feet of clay, he may sometimes lose interest because he can no longer transfer his pride to him.

On the other hand a person with self-effacing trends does not appeal to him as a sexual partner. He may like him as a friend because he finds in him more sympathy, understanding, or devotion than in others. But when starting a more intimate relationship with him, he may feel even repelled. He sees in him, as in a mirror, his own weakness and despises him for it or at least is irritated by it. He is also afraid of the clinging-vine attitude of such a partner because the mere idea that he himself must be the stronger one terrifies him. These negative emotional responses then may render it impossible to value existing assets in such a partner.

Among the obviously proud people those of the arrogant-vindictive type as a rule exert the greatest fascination on the dependent person although, in terms of his real self-interest, he has stringent reasons to be afraid of them. The cause of the fascination lies in part in their pride in the most conspicuous way. But even more crucial is the fact that they are most likely to knock his own pride out from under him. The relationship may start indeed with some crude offense on the part of the arrogant person. Somerset Maugham in *Of Human Bondage* had described this in the first meeting between Philip and Mildred. Stefan Zweig has a similar instance in his *Amok*. In both cases the dependent person responds first with anger and an impulse to get back at the offender—in each case a woman—but almost simultaneously is so fascinated that he "falls" for her hopelessly and passionately and has thereafter but the one driving interest: to win her love. Thereby he ruins, or almost ruins, himself. Insulting behavior frequently precipitates a dependent relationship. It need not always be as dramatic as in *Of Human Bondage* or *Amok*. It may be much more subtle and insidious. But I wonder if it is ever entirely missing in such a relationship. It may consist of a mere lack of interest or an arrogant reserve, of paying attention to others, of joking or facetious remarks, of being unimpressed by whatever assets in the partner usually impress others—such as name, profession, knowledge, beauty. These are "insults" because they are felt as rejections, and—as I have mentioned—a rejection is an insult for anybody whose pride is largely invested in making everybody love him. The frequency of such occurrences throws light upon the appeal detached people have for him. Their very aloofness and unavailability constitute the insulting rejection.

Incidents such as these seem to lend weight to the notion that the self-effacing person merely craves for suffering and avidly seizes the prospect of it offered by the insults. Actually nothing has more blocked a real understanding of morbid dependency than this notion. It is all the more misleading since it contains a grain of truth. We know that suffering has manifold neurotic values for him and it is also true that insulting behavior attracts him magnetically. The error lies in establishing a too neat causal connection between these two facts by assuming that the magnetic attraction is determined by the prospect of suffering. The reason lies in two other factors, both of which we mentioned separately: the fascination that arrogance and aggressiveness in others exert on him, and his own need for surrender. We now can see that these two factors are more closely interlinked than we have hitherto realized. He craves to surrender himself body and soul, but can do so only if his pride is bent or broken. In other words the initial offense is not so much intriguing because it hurts as because it opens the possibility for self-riddance and self-surrender. To use a patient's words: "The person who shakes my pride from under me releases me from my arrogance and pride." Or: "If he can insult me, then I am just an ordinary human being"—and, one might add, "only then can I love." We may think here too of Bizet's Carmen, whose passion was inflamed only if she were not loved.

No doubt the abandoning of pride as a rigid condition for love-surrender is pathological, particularly (as we shall see presently) since the pronounced self-effacing type can love only if he feels, or is, degraded. But the phenomenon ceases to seem unique and mysterious if we remember that for the healthy person love and *true* humility go together. It also is not quite as widely different from what we have seen in the expansive type as we might at first be led to believe. The latter's fear of love is mainly determined by his unconscious realization that he would have to relinquish much of his neurotic pride for the sake of love. To put it succinctly: *neurotic pride is the enemy of love.* Here the difference between the expansive and the self-effacing type is that the former does not need love in any vital way but, on the contrary, shuns it as a danger; while for the latter love-surrender appears as a solution for everything, and hence as a vital necessity. The expansive type, too, can surrender only if his pride is broken, but then may become passionately enslaved. Stendhal has described this process in the proud Mathilde's passion for Julien in *The Red and the Black*. It shows that the arrogant person's fear of love is well founded —for him. But mostly he is too much on his guard to allow himself to fall in love.

Although we can study the characteristics of a morbid dependency in any relationship, they come into clearest relief in the sexual relationship between a self-effacing and an arrogant-vindictive type. The conflicts generated here are more intense, and can develop more fully, since for reasons residing in both partners the relationship is usually of longer duration. The narcissistic or detached partner more easily becomes tired of the implicit demands made upon him and is liable to quit,[2] while the sadistic partner is more prone to fasten himself onto his victim. For the dependent person, in turn, it is much more difficult to extricate himself from a relation with an arrogant-vindictive type. With his peculiar weakness, he is as unequipped for such an involvement as a ship built for navigation in still waters is for crossing a rough, stormy ocean. Her whole lack of sturdiness, every weak spot in her structure will then make itself felt and may mean ruin. Similarly a self-effacing person may have functioned fairly well in life, but when tossed into the conflicts involved in such a relationship every hidden neurotic factor in him will come into operation. I shall describe the process here primarily from the standpoint of the dependent person. For the sake of simplifying the presentation I shall assume that the self-effacing partner is a woman and the aggressive one a man. Actually this combination seems to be more frequent in our civilization although, as many instances show, self-effacement has nothing to do with femininity nor aggressive arrogance with masculinity. Both are exquisitely neurotic phenomena.

The first characteristic to strike us is such a woman's total absorption in the relationship. The partner becomes the sole center of her existence. Everything revolves around him. Her mood depends upon whether his attitude toward her is more positive or negative. She does not dare make any plans lest she might miss a call or an evening with him. Her thoughts are centered on understanding or helping him. Her endeavors are directed toward measuring up to what she feels he expects. She has but one fear—that of antagonizing and losing him. Conversely her other interests subside. Her work, unless connected

---

[2] *Cf.* Flaubert's *Madame Bovary*. Both her lovers become tired of her and break away. *Cf.* also Karen Horney, *Self-Analysis*, Claire's self-analysis.

with him, becomes comparatively meaningless. This may even be true of professional work otherwise dear to her heart, or productive work in which she has accomplished things. Naturally the latter suffers most.

Other human relations are neglected. She may neglect or leave her children, her home. Friendships serve more and more merely to fill the time when he is not available. Engagements are dropped at a moment's notice when he appears. The impairment of other relations often is fostered by the partner, because he in turn wants to make her more and more dependent upon him. Also she starts to look at her relatives or friends through his eyes. He scorns her trust in people and instills his own suspiciousness in her. So she loses roots and becomes more and more impoverished. In addition her self-interest, always at a low ebb, sinks. She may incur debts, risk her reputation, her health, her dignity. If she is in analysis, or used to analyzing herself, the interest in self-recognition gives way to a concern for understanding *his* motivations and helping *him*.

The trouble may set in, full fledged, right at the beginning. But sometimes things look fairly auspicious for a while. In certain neurotic ways the two seem to fit together. He needs to be the master; she needs to surrender. He is openly demanding, she complying. She can surrender only if her pride is broken, and for many reasons of his own he cannot fail to do so. But sooner or later clashes are bound to occur between two temperaments —or, more accurately, between two neurotic structures—which in all essentials are diametrically opposed. The main clashes occur on the issue of feelings, of "love." She insists upon love, affection, closeness. He is desperately afraid of positive feelings. Their display seems indecent to him. Her assurances of love seem like pure hypocrisy to him—and indeed, as we know, it is actually more a need to lose herself and merge with him that motivates her than personal love for him. He cannot keep from striking out against her feelings, and hence against her. This in turn makes her feel neglected or abused, arouses anxiety, and reinforces her clinging attitudes. And here another collision occurs. Although he does everything to make her dependent upon him, her clinging to him terrifies and repels him. He is afraid and contemptuous of any weakness in himself and despises it in her. This means another rejection for her, provoking more anxiety and more clinging. Her implicit demands are felt as coercion, and he has to hit out in order to retain his feelings of mastery. Her compulsive helpfulness offends his pride in self-sufficiency. Her insistence upon "understanding" him likewise hurts his pride. And actually, with all her often sincere attempts, she does not really understand him—hardly can do so. Besides in her "understanding" there is too much need to excuse and to forgive, for she feels all *her* attitudes as good and natural. He in turn senses her feeling morally superior and feels provoked to tear down the pretenses involved. There is but scant possibility for a good talk about these matters because at bottom they are both self-righteous. So she starts to see him as a brute and he her as a moral prig. The tearing down of her pretenses could be eminently helpful if it were done in a constructive way. But as it is mostly done in a sarcastic, derogatory way, it merely hurts her and makes her more insecure and more dependent.

It is an idle speculation to ask whether or not, with all these clashes, they might be helpful to each other. Certainly he could stand some softening and she some toughening. But mostly they are both too deeply entrenched in their particular neurotic needs and aversions. Vicious circles which bring out the worst in both keep operating, and can result only in mutual tormenting.

The frustrations and limitations to which she is exposed vary not so much in kind as in being more or less civilized, more or less intense. There is always some cat-and-mouse play of attracting and repulsing, binding and withdrawing. Satisfactory sexual relations may be followed by crude offenses; an enjoyable evening by forgetting a date; eliciting confidences by sarcastically using them against her. She may try to play the same game, but is too inhibited to do it well. But she is always a good instrument on which to play, since his attacks make her despondent and his seemingly positive moods throw her into fallacious hopes that from now on everything will be better. There are always plenty of things he feels entitled to do without allowing any questioning. His claims may concern financial support or gifts for himself and his friends or relatives; work to be done for him, like housework or typing; furthering his career; strict consideration of his needs. These latter may, for instance, concern time arrangements, undivided and uncritical interest in his pursuits, having or not having company, remaining unruffled when he is sulky or irritable, and so on and so forth.

Whatever he demands is his self-evident due. There is no appreciation forthcoming but much nagging irritability when his wishes are not fulfilled. He feels and declares in no uncertain terms that he is not at all demanding but that she is stingy, sloppy, inconsiderate, unappreciative—and that he has to put up with all sorts of abuse. On the other hand he is astute at spotting her claims, which he finds altogether neurotic. Her need for affection, time, or company is possessive, her wanting sex or good food, overindulgence. So when he frustrates her needs, which he must do for reasons of his own, it is in his mind no frustration at all. It is better to disregard her needs because she should be ashamed of having them. Actually his frustrating techniques are highly developed. They include dampening joy by sulkiness, making her feel unwelcome and unwanted, withdrawing physically or psychically. The most harmful and, for her, least tangible part is his pervasive attitude of disregard and contempt. Whatever actual regard he may have for her faculties or qualities is seldom expressed. On the other hand, as I have already said, he does despise her for her softness and for her caginess and indirectness. But in addition, because of his need for active externalization of his self-hate, he is faultfinding and derogatory. If she in turn dares to criticize him, he discards what she says in a highhanded manner or proves that she is vindictive.

We find the greatest variation in sexual matters. Sexual relations may stand out as the only satisfactory contact. Or, in case he is inhibited in enjoying sex, he may frustrate her in this regard too, which is felt all the more keenly since in view of his lack of tenderness sex may mean for her the only assurance of love. Or sex may be a means of degrading and humiliating her. He may make it clear that for him she is nothing but a sexual object. He may flaunt sexual relations with other women, intermingled with derogatory comments about her being less attractive or responsive than these others. Sexual intercourse may be degrading because of the absence of any tenderness or because he uses sadistic techniques.

Her attitudes toward such maltreatment are full of contradictions. As we shall see presently, it is not a static set of reactions but a fluctuating process leading her into more and more conflicts. To begin with, she is simply helpless, as she always has been toward aggressive people. She never could assert herself against them and fight back in any effective way. Complying has always been easier for her. And, being prone to feel guilty anyhow, she rather agrees with her many reproaches, particularly since they often contain a good grain of truth.

But her compliance now assumes greater proportions and also changes in quality. It remains an expression of her need to please and appease but in addition is determined now by her longing for total surrender. This, as we have seen, she can do only when most of her pride has been broken. Thus part of her secretly welcomes his behavior and most actively collaborates with him. He is obviously—though unconsciously—out to crush her pride; she secretly has a complimentary irresistible urge to immolate it. In sexual performances this urge may come into full awareness. With orgiastic lust she may prostrate herself, assume humiliating positions, be beaten, bitten, insulted. And sometimes these are the only conditions under which she can reach a full satisfaction. This urge for total surrender by means of self-degradation seems to account more fully than other explanations for the masochistic perversions.

Such frank expressions of a lust to degrade herself are evidence of the enormous power such a drive can assume. It may also show in fantasies—often connected with masturbation—of degrading sexual orgies, of being publicly exposed, raped, tied, beaten. Finally, this drive may be expressed in dreams of lying destitute in a gutter and being lifted up by the partner, of being treated by him like a prostitute, of groveling at his feet.

The drive toward self-degradation may be too disguised to come into clear relief. But for the experienced observer it shows in many other ways, such as her eagerness—or rather urgency—

to whitewash him and to take upon herself the blame for his misdemeanor; or in her abjectness in serving and deferring to him. She is not aware of it, because in her mind such deference registers as humility or love, or humility in loving, since as a rule the urge to prostrate herself—except in sexual matters— is most deeply suppressed. Yet the urge is there and enforces a compromise, which is to let the degradation occur without being aware that it happens. This explains why for a long time she may not even notice his offensive behavior although it is flagrantly obvious to others. Or, if she takes cognizance of it, she does not experience it emotionally and does not really mind it. Sometimes a friend may call it to her attention. But even though she may be convinced of its truth and of her friend's interest in her welfare, it may merely irritate her. In fact it must do so, because it touches too closely upon her conflict in this respect. Even more telling are her own attempts at a time when she tries to struggle out of the situation. Over and over again she may then recall all his insulting and humiliating attitudes, hoping that this will help her to take a stand against him. And only after long futile attempts of this kind will she realize, with surprise, that they simply do not carry any weight.

Her need for total surrender also makes it necessary to idealize the partner. Because she can find her unity only with somebody to whom she has delegated her pride, he should be the proud one and she the subdued. I have mentioned the initial fascination that his arrogance has for her. Although this conscious fascination may subside, her glorification of him persists in more subtle ways. She may see him more clearly in many details later on, but she does not get a sober total picture of him until she has actually made the break—and even then the glorification may linger on. She is meanwhile inclined to think, for instance, that notwithstanding his difficulties he is mostly right and knows better than anybody else. Both her need to idealize him and her need to surrender operate here hand in hand. She has extinguished her personal self to the extent of seeing him, others, and herself through his eyes—another factor that makes the breaking away so difficult.

So far all plays in with the partner. But there is a turning point, or rather a long-drawn-out turning process, as the stake she is gambling for fails to materialize. Her self-degradation is largely (although not altogether) after all a means to an end: that of finding inner unity through surrender of self and merging with the partner. In order for her to reach this fulfillment the partner has to accept her love-surrender and return her love. But on exactly this decisive point he fails her—as we know, he is bound to do so by dint of his own neurosis. Therefore, while she does not mind—or rather secretly welcomes—his arrogance, she fears and resents bitterly the rejections as well as the implicit and explicit frustrations in matters of love. There are involved here both her deep longing for salvation and that part of her pride which demands in its service that she should be able to make him love her and to make a go of the relation. Besides, like most people, she cannot easily relinquish a goal in which she has invested so heavily. And so she responds to his maltreatment with becoming anxious, despondent, or desperate, only to regain hope soon after, clinging—against evidence to the contrary—to the belief that one day he will love her.

At this very point conflicts set in, at first short lived and quickly surmounted but gradually deepening and becoming permanent. On the one hand she tries desperately to improve the relationship. To her this appears as a commendable way of putting efforts into cultivating it; to him as increased clinging. Both are right up to a point; but both also miss the essential issue, which is her fighting for what appears to her as the ultimate good. More than ever she stands on tiptoe to please, to measure up to his expectations, to see the fault in herself, to overlook or not to resent any crudeness, to understand, to smooth over. Not realizing that all these efforts are in the service of radically wrong goals, she evaluates these efforts as "improvements." Similarly she typically adheres to the usually fallacious belief that he "improves" too.

On the other hand she starts to hate him. At first this is repressed altogether because it would annihilate her hopes. Then it may become conscious in flashes. She now starts to resent his offensive treatment, again hesitating to admit it to herself. With this turn vindictive trends come to the fore. There are blowups in which her true resentment appears, but still without her knowing how true it is. She becomes more critical, is less willing to let herself be exploited. Characteristically most of this vindictiveness appears in indirect ways, in complaints, suffering, martyrdom, increased clinging. The vindictive elements also creep into her goal. They were always there in a latent form but now they spread like a cancerous growth. Though the longing to make him love her persists, it becomes more strongly a matter of a vindictive triumph.

This is unfortunate for her in every way. Although it remains unconscious, to be sharply divided in so crucial an issue makes for genuine unhappiness. Also, for the very reason that it is unconscious, this vindictiveness serves to tie her more closely to him because it supplies her with another strong incentive to work toward a "happy ending." And even when she succeeds and he does fall in love with her after all—which he may, if he is not too rigid and she is not too self-destructive— she does not reap the benefits. Her need for triumph is fulfilled and dwindles, her pride has its due but she is no longer interested. She may be grateful, appreciative for love given, but she feels it is now too late. Actually she cannot love with her pride satisfied.

If, however, her redoubled efforts do not essentially change the picture, she may turn more vehemently against herself and thereby come into a cross fire. Since the idea of surrender gradually loses its value, and since therefore she becomes aware of tolerating too much abuse, she feels exploited and hates herself for it. Also she begins to realize at last that her "love" is in actual fact a morbid dependency (whatever term she may use). This is a healthy recognition, but at first she reacts to it with self-contempt. In addition, condemning the vindictive trends in herself, she hates herself for having them. And finally she runs herself down mercilessly for failing to elicit his love. She is aware of some of this self-hate, but usually most of it is externalized in the passive way characteristic of the self-effacing type. This means that there is now a massive and pervasive feeling of being abused by him. This makes for a new split in her attitude toward him. The increased resentment stemming from this feeling of being abused drives her away. But also the very self-hate either is so frightening that it calls for reassuring affection or reinforces on a purely self-destructive basis her receptiveness to maltreatment. The partner then becomes the executor of her own self-destruction. She is driven to be tormented and humiliated because she hates and despises herself.

The self-observations of two patients, both about to extricate themselves from a dependent relationship, may illustrate the role of self-hate in this period. The first patient, a man, decided to go on a brief vacation alone in order to find out what his true feelings were toward the woman upon whom he was dependent. Attempts of this kind, although understandable, mostly prove futile—partly because compulsive factors befog the issue and partly because the individual is usually not really concerned with his own problems and their relation to the situation but only with "finding out," in a vacuum, whether or not he loves the other person.

In this case his very determination to go to the root of the trouble did bear fruit, although he could not of course find the answer to his question. Feelings did emerge; in fact, he got into a hurricane of feelings. First he became immersed in feeling that the woman was so inhumanly cruel that no punishment was drastic enough. Soon after, he felt just as intensely that he would give everything for a friendly move on her part. These extreme feelings alternated several times, and each of them felt so real that for the time being he forgot the opposite feeling. Only after he had gone through this process three times did he realize that his feelings were contradictory. Only then did he realize that none of these extremes represented his true feelings and only then did he see clearly that both were compulsive. This realization relieved him. Instead of being swept helplessly from one emotional experience into its opposite, he could now start to regard both as a problem to be understood. The following piece of analysis brought about the surprising realization that both feelings, at bottom, had less to do with the partner than with his own inner processes.

Two questions helped to clarify the emotional upheaval: Why did he have to exaggerate her offenses to the extent of making her an inhuman monster? Why did it take him so long to recognize the apparent contradiction in his mood-swings?

The first question led us to see the following sequences: increased self-hate (for several reasons), increased feeling of being abused by the woman, and responding to his externalized self-hate with vindictive hate toward her. After having seen this process the answer to the second question was easy. His feelings were contradictory only when taken at their face value as expressing love and hate for the woman. Actually he was frightened by the vindictiveness expressed in the idea of no punishment being drastic enough, and he tried to allay this anxiety by longing for the woman in order to reassure himself.

The other illustration concerns a woman patient who at the particular period wavered between feeling rather independent and feeling an almost irresistible urge to call up her partner. Once when she was about to reach for the telephone—knowing full well she only made things harder for herself by a renewed contact—she thought: "I wish somebody would tie me to a mast like Ulysses . . . like Ulysses? But he needed to be tied in order to resist the lure of Circe who turned men into swine! [3] So that is what drives me: a violent urge to degrade myself and to be humiliated by him." This felt right, and the spell was broken. Being able at this time to analyze herself, she then asked herself the pertinent question: what made this urge so strong just now? She then experienced considerable self-hate and self-contempt of which she had not been aware. Incidents of previous days emerged, ones which had caused her to turn against herself. After this she felt relieved and on more solid ground, for at this period she wanted to leave him and through this self-analysis she did get hold of one of the strings that still tied her to him. She started the next analytic session by saying: "We have to work more at my self-hate."

There is thus a crescendo of inner turmoil through all the factors mentioned: the dwindling hope for fulfillment, the redoubled efforts, the emerging of hate and vindictiveness with their repercussions and the violence against self. The inner situation becomes increasingly untenable. She is actually at the point where it becomes a proposition of sink or swim. Two moves set in now and it all depends on which wins. The one

---

[3] The patient in question confused the incident of the Sirens with those about Circe. This did not of course affect the validity of her discovery.

to go under—as we have discussed before—has for this type the appeal of a final solution of all conflicts. She may contemplate suicide, threaten it, attempt it, do it. She may fall ill and succumb to her illness. She may become morally sloppy and for instance plunge into meaningless affairs. She may hit out vindictively against her partner, usually injuring herself more than him. Or without knowing it she may simply lose her zest for living, become indolent, neglect her appearance, her work, and put on weight.

The other move is in the direction of health, and consists in efforts to get out of the situation. Sometimes it is the very realization of being actually in danger of going to pieces that gives her the necessary courage. Sometimes the two moves go on intermittently. The process of struggling out is eminently painful. Incentive and strength to do so come from both healthy and neurotic sources. There is an awakening constructive self-interest; there is also an increasing resentment against him, not only for actual alleged abuse but also for making her feel "cheated"; there is hurt pride over having played a losing game. On the other hand she is up against terrific odds. She has cut herself off from so many things and people and, being as torn as she is, is petrified at the idea of being thrown on her own. Also to break away would mean to declare herself defeated, and another kind of pride rebels against that. There are usually ups and downs—times when she feels she is able to leave him and others when she would rather suffer any indignity than get out. It is largely as it were a struggle between one pride and another with herself, terrified, in the middle. The outcome depends on many factors. Most of them are in herself, but many also are in her whole life situation—and, to be sure, the help of a friend or analyst may be of considerable importance.

Assuming that she does manage to struggle out of her involvement, the value of her action would depend upon these questions: did she, by hook or crook, get out of the one dependency only sooner or later to rush into another one? Or did she get so wary of her feelings that she tended to deaden all of them? She may then appear "normal" but actually be scarred for life. Or has she changed in a more radical way and come out a really stronger person? Any of these possibilities may be realized. Naturally an analysis offers the best chance to outgrow the neurotic difficulties which led her into distress and danger. But, provided she can mobilize sufficient constructive forces during her struggle and has matured through the real suffering involved, plain ordinary honesty with self and efforts to get on her own feet can go far toward attaining a measure of inner freedom.

Morbid dependency is one of the most complicated phenomena with which we have to deal. We cannot hope to understand it as long as we are unreconciled to the complexities of human psychology and insist upon a simple formula to explain it all. We cannot explain the total picture as manifold branches of sexual masochism. If it is present at all, it is an *outcome* of many other factors and not their root. Nor is it all the inverted sadism of a weak and hopeless person. Nor do we grasp its essentials when focusing on the parasitic or symbiotic aspects, or on the neurotic's drive to lose himself. Nor does self-destructiveness, with the urge to inflict suffering upon self, alone suffice as an explanatory principle. Nor, finally, can we regard the whole condition as being merely an externalization of pride and self-hate. When we regard one or another factor as *the* deep root of the whole phenomenon we cannot help getting a one-sided picture which fails to embrace all the peculiarities involved. Moreover all such explanations give too static a picture. Morbid dependency is not a static condition but a process in which all or most of these factors come into play—coming to the fore, receding in importance, one determining or reinforcing the other or conflicting with it.

And, finally, all the factors mentioned, though relevant to the total picture, are, as it were, too negative to account for the passionate character of the involvement. For a passion it is, whether it flares up or smolders. But there is no passion without the expectation of some vital fulfillment. And it makes no difference whether or not these expectations arise on neurotic premises. This factor, which in its turn cannot be isolated but may be grasped only in the framework of the whole self-effacing structure, is the drive for total surrender and the longing to find unity through merging with the partner.

RESIGNATION: THE APPEAL OF FREEDOM

THE THIRD major solution of the intrapsychic conflicts consists essentially in the neurotic's withdrawing from the inner battlefield and declaring himself uninterested. If he can muster and maintain an attitude of "don't care," he feels less bothered by his inner conflicts and can attain a semblance of inner peace. Since he can do this only by resigning from active living, "resignation" seems a proper name for this solution. It is in a way the most radical of all solutions and, perhaps for this very reason, most often produces conditions that allow for a fairly smooth functioning. And, since our sense of what is healthy is generally blunted, resigned people often pass for "normal."

Resignation may have a constructive meaning. We can think of many older people who have recognized the intrinsic futility of ambition and success, who have mellowed by expecting and demanding less, and who through renunciation of nonessentials have become wiser. In many forms of religion or philosophy renunciation of nonessentials is advocated as one of the conditions for greater spiritual growth and fulfillment: give up the expression of personal will, sexual desires, and cravings for worldly goods for the sake of being closer to God. Give up cravings for things transitory for the sake of life eternal. Give up personal strivings and satisfactions for the sake of attaining the spiritual power which exists potentially in human beings.

For the neurotic solution we are discussing here, however, resignation implies settling for a peace which is merely the absence of conflicts. In religious practice the pursuit of peace does not involve giving up struggle and striving but rather directing them toward higher goals. For the neurotic it means giving up struggle and striving and settling for less. His resignation therefore is a process of shrinking, of restricting, of curtailing life and growth.

As we shall see later on, the distinction between healthy and neurotic resignation is not as neat as I have just presented it. Even in the latter there is a positive value involved. But what meets the eye are certain negative qualities resulting from the process. This is clearer if we think back to the other two major solutions. In them we see a more turbulent picture, one of reaching out for something, going after something, becoming passionately engaged in some pursuit—no matter whether this concerns mastery or love. In them we see hope, anger, despair. Even the arrogant-vindictive type, although cold as a result of having stifled his emotions, still ardently wants—or is driven to want—success, power, triumph. By contrast the picture of resignation, when maintained consistently, is one of life at a constantly low ebb—of a life without pain or friction but also without zest.

No wonder then that the *basic characteristics* of neurotic resignation are distinguished by an aura of restriction, of something that is avoided, that is *not* wanted or *not* done. There is some resignation in every neurotic. What I shall describe here is a cross section of those for whom it has become the major solution.

The direct expression of the neurotic having removed himself from the inner battlefield is his being an *onlooker at himself and his life*. I have described this attitude as one of the general measures to relieve inner tension. Since detachment is a ubiquitous and prominent attitude of his, he is also an onlooker at others. He lives as if he were sitting in the orchestra and observing a drama acted on the stage, and a drama which is most of the time not too exciting at that. Though he is not necessarily a good observer, he may be most astute. Even in the very first consultation he may, with the help of some pertinent questions, develop a picture of himself replete with a wealth of candid observation. But he will usually add that all this knowledge has not changed anything. Of course it has not—for none of his findings has been an experience for him. Being an onlooker at himself means just that: not actively participating in living and unconsciously refusing to do so. In analysis he tries to maintain the same attitude. He may be immensely interested, yet that interest may stay for quite a while at the level of a fascinating entertainment—and nothing changes.

One thing, however, which he avoids even intellectually is the risk of seeing any of his conflicts. If he is taken by surprise and, as it were, stumbles into one, he may suffer from severe panic. But mostly he is too much on his guard to allow anything to touch him. As soon as he comes close to a conflict his interest in the whole subject will peter out. Or he may argue himself out of it, proving that the conflict is no conflict. When the analyst perceives his "avoidance" tactics and tells him, "Look here, this is *your* life that is at stake," the patient does not quite know what he is talking about. For him it is not his life but a life which he observes, and in which he has no active part.

A second characteristic, intimately connected with nonparticipation, is the *absence of any serious striving for achievement and the aversion to effort.* I put the two attitudes together because their combination is typical for the resigned person. Many neurotics set their hearts on achieving something and chafe under the inhibitions preventing them from attaining it. Not so the resigned person. He unconsciously rejects both achievement and effort. He minimizes or flatly denies his assets, and settles for less. Pointing out evidence to the contrary does not budge him. He may become rather annoyed. Does the analyst want to push him into some ambition? Does he want him to become president of the United States? If, finally, he cannot help realizing the existence of some gifts, he may become frightened.

Again he may compose beautiful music, paint pictures, write books—in his imagination. This is an alternative means of doing away with both aspiration and effort. He may actually have good and original ideas on some subject, but the writing of a paper would require initiative and the arduous work of thinking the ideas through and organizing them. So the paper remains unwritten. He may have a vague desire to write a novel or a play, but waits for the inspiration to come. Then the plot would be clear and everything would flow from his pen.

Also he is most ingenious at finding reasons for *not* doing things. How much good would a book be that had to be sweated out in hard labor! And are not too many uninspired books written anyhow? Would not the concentration on one pursuit curtail other interests and thus narrow his horizon? Does not going into politics, or into any competitive field, spoil the character?

This aversion to effort may extend to all activities. It then brings about a complete inertia, to which we shall return later. He may then procrastinate over doing such simple things as writing a letter, reading a book, shopping. Or he may do them against inner resistance, slowly, listlessly, ineffectively. The mere prospect of unavoidable larger activities, such as moving or handling accumulated tasks in his job, may make him tired before he begins.

Concomitantly there is an absence of *goal-direction and planning*, which may concern major and minor issues. What does he actually want to do with his life? The question has never occurred to him and is easily discarded, as if it were none of his concern. In this respect there is a remarkable contrast to the arrogant-vindictive type, with the latter's elaborate planning in long-range terms.

In analysis it appears that his goals are limited and again negative. Analysis he feels should rid him of disturbing symptoms, such as awkwardness with strangers, fear of blushing or of fainting in the street. Or perhaps analysis should remove one or another aspect of his inertia, such as his difficulty in reading.

He may also have a broader vision of a goal which, in character-istically vague terms, he may call "serenity." This, however, means for him simply the absence of all troubles, irritations, or upsets. And naturally whatever he hopes for should come easily, without pain or strain. The analyst should do the work. After all, is he not the expert? Analysis should be like going to a dentist who pulls a tooth, or to a doctor who gives an injection: he is willing to wait patiently for the analyst to present the clue that will solve everything. It would be better though if the patient didn't have to talk so much. The analyst should have some sort of X ray which would reveal the patient's thoughts. Or perhaps hypnosis would bring things out more quickly— that is, without any effort on the part of the patient. When a new problem crystallizes, his first response may be exasperation at the prospect of so much more work to be done. As indicated before, he may not mind observing things in himself. What he always minds is the effort of changing.

A step deeper and we come to the very essence of resigna-tion: the *restriction of wishes*. We have seen checks on wishes in other types. But then the lid was put on certain categories of wishes, such as those for human closeness or for triumph. We are also familiar with uncertainty about wishes, mainly result-ing from a person's wishes being determined by what he should wish. All of these trends operate here too. Here, too, one area is usually more affected than another. Here, too, spontaneous wishes are blurred by inner dictates. But over and beyond these the resigned person believes, consciously or unconsciously, that it is *better* not to wish or to expect anything. Sometimes this goes with a conscious pessimistic outlook on life, a sense of its being futile anyhow and of nothing being sufficiently desirable to make an effort for it. More often many things appear de-sirable in a vague, idle way but fail to arouse a concrete, alive wish. If a wish or interest has enough zest to penetrate through the "don't care" attitude, it fades out soon after and the smooth surface of "nothing matters" or "nothing should matter" is re-established. Such "wishlessness" may concern both professional and personal life—the wish for a different job or an advance-ment as well as for a marriage, a house, a car, or other posses-sions. The fulfillment of these wishes may loom primarily as a burden, and in fact would sabotage the one wish he does have—that of not being bothered. The retraction of wishes is closely interlinked with the three basic characteristics mentioned before. He can be an onlooker at his life only if he has no strong wishes of any kind. He can hardly have aspirations or purposeful goals if he has not the motive power of wishes. And, finally, no wish is strong enough to warrant effort. Hence the two outstanding neurotic claims are that life should be easy, painless, and effortless and that he should not be bothered.

He is particularly anxious not to get attached to anything to the extent of really needing it. Nothing should be so important for him that he could not do without it. It is all right to like a woman, a place in the country, or certain drinks, but one should not become dependent upon them. As soon as he becomes aware that a place, a person, or a group of people means so much to him that its loss would be painful he tends to retract his feelings. No other person should ever have the feeling of being necessary to him or take the relationship for granted. If he suspects the existence of either attitude he tends to withdraw.

The principle of nonparticipation, as it is expressed in his being an onlooker at life as well as in his retraction of wishes, also operates in his human relations. They are characterized by *detachment*, i.e., his emotional distance from others. He can enjoy distant or transitory relationships but he should not become emotionally involved. He should not become so attached to a person as to need his company, his help, or sexual relations with him. The detachment is all the easier to maintain since, in contrast to other neurotic types, he does not expect much, either good or bad—if anything—from others. Even in emergencies it may not occur to him to ask for help. On the other hand he may be quite willing to help others, provided again that it does not involve him emotionally. He does not want, or even expect, gratitude.[1]

The role of sex varies considerably. Sometimes sex is for him the only bridge to others. He may then have plenty of transient sexual relations, backing out of them sooner or later. They should not, as it were, degenerate into love. He may be entirely

---

[1] For more details on the nature of detachment see Karen Horney, *Our Inner Conflicts*, Chapter 5, Moving away from People.

aware of his need not to become involved with anybody. Or he may give satisfied curiosity as the reason for terminating a relationship. He will point out then that it is the curiosity for a new experience that drives him toward this or that woman, and that now that he has had this new experience she does not intrigue him any more. In these instances he may respond to women exactly as he does to a new landscape or to a new circle of people. Now that he knows them they no longer elicit his curiosity, and so he turns to something else. This is more than mere rationalization for his detachment. He has carried through his attitude of being an onlooker at life more consciously and more consistently than others, and this sometimes may give the deceptive appearance of a zest for living.

In some instances, on the other hand, he excludes the whole area of sex from his life—to the extent of stifling all wishes in this regard. He may then not even have erotic fantasies or, if he does, a few abortive fantasies may be all that his sex life consists of. His actual contacts with others will then stay on the level of distant friendly interest.

When he does have lasting relationships he must of course maintain his distance in them too. In this respect he is at the opposite pole from the self-effacing type, with the latter's need to merge with a partner. The way in which he maintains distance varies greatly. He may exclude sex as being too intimate for a permanent relationship, and instead satisfy his sexual needs with a stranger. Conversely he may more or less restrict a relationship to merely sexual contacts and not share other experiences with the partner.[2] In marriage he may be attentive to the partner but never talk intimately about himself. He may insist on having a good deal of time strictly to himself or on taking a trip alone. He may restrict a relationship to occasional week ends or trips.

I want to add here a comment, the significance of which we shall understand later. Being afraid of emotional involvement with others is not the same as an absence of positive feelings.

---

[2] Freud has observed this particular phenomenon: he thought it was a peculiarity in love life occurring in men only, and tried to explain it on the grounds of a divided attitude toward their mothers. Sigmund Freud. "Contributions to the Psychology of Love," *Collected Papers*, IV.

On the contrary, he would not have to be on his guard so vigilantly if he had put a general check on tender feelings. He may have his own deep feelings, but these should stay in his inner sanctum. They are his private affair and nobody else's business. In this respect he is different from the arrogant-vindictive type, who is also detached but has unconsciously trained himself not to have positive feelings. He is also different in that he does not want to be involved with others in friction or anger any more than in any other way, whereas the arrogant type is quick to anger and finds in battle his natural element.

Another characteristic of a resigned person is his *hypersensitivity to influence, pressure, coercion* or *ties* of any kind. This is a relevant factor too in his detachment. Even before he enters into a personal relationship or a group activity the fear of a lasting tie may be aroused. And the question as to how he can extricate himself may be present from the very beginning. Before marriage this fear may grow into a panic.

Exactly what he resents as coercion varies. It may be any contract, such as signing a lease or any long-term engagement. It may be any physical pressure, even collars, girdles, shoes. It may be an obstructed view. He may resent anything that others expect, or might possibly expect, from him—like Christmas presents, letters, or paying his bills at certain times. It may extend to institutions, traffic regulations, conventions, government interference. He does not fight all of this because he is no fighter; but he rebels inwardly and may consciously or unconsciously frustrate others in his own passive way by not responding or by forgetting.

His sensitivity to coercion is connected with his inertia and with the retraction of wishes. Since he does not want to budge, he may feel any expectation of his doing something as a coercion, even if it is obviously in his own interest. The connection with the retraction of wishes is more complex. He is afraid, and has reason to be so, that anybody with stronger wishes might easily impose upon him and push him into something by dint of his greater determination. But there is also externalization operating. Not experiencing his own wishes or preferences, he will easily feel that he yields to the wishes of another person when he actually follows his own preferences. To illustrate with a simple example from daily life: a person was invited to a party to be held on a night on which he had a date with his girl. However, this was not the way he experienced the situation at the time. He went to see the girl, feeling that he had "complied" with her wishes and resenting the "coercion" she had exerted. A very intelligent patient characterized the whole process with these words: "Nature abhors a vacuum. When your own wishes are silent, those of others rush in." We could add: either their existing wishes, their alleged wishes, or those he has externalized to them.

The sensitivity to coercion constitutes a real difficulty in analysis—the more difficult the more the patient is not only negative but negativistic. He may harbor an everlasting suspicion that the analyst wants to influence and mold him into a preconceived pattern. This suspicion is all the less accessible the more the patient's inertia prevents him from testing out any suggestion offered, as he is repeatedly asked to do. On the grounds of the analyst's exerting undue influence, he may refute any question, statement, or interpretation that implicitly or explicitly attacks some neurotic position of his. What renders progress in this respect still more difficult is the fact that he will not express his suspicion for a long time, because he dislikes friction. He may simply feel that this or that is the analyst's personal prejudice or hobby. Hence he need not bother with it, and discards it as negligible. The analyst may suggest for instance that the patient's relations with people would be worth examining. He is immediately on his guard while secretly thinking that the analyst wants to make him gregarious.

Lastly, an *aversion to change*, to anything new, goes with resignation. This too varies in intensity and form. The more prominent the inertia, the more he dreads the risk and the effort of any change. He would much rather put up with the *status quo*—whether this is a job, his living quarters, an employee, or a marriage partner—than change. Nor does it occur to him that he might be able to improve his situation. He might for instance rearrange his furniture, make more time for leisure, be more helpful to his wife in her difficulties. Suggestions of this sort are met with polite indifference. Two factors enter into this attitude besides his inertia. Since he does not expect much from any situation, his incentive to change it is small anyhow. And he is inclined to regard things as unalterable. People are just so: this is their constitution. Life is just so—it is fate. Although he does not complain about situations which would be unbearable for most people, his putting up with things often looks like the martyrdom of the self-effacing person. But the resemblance is only a superficial one: they spring from different sources.

The examples of the aversion to change which I have mentioned so far all concern external matters. This is not the reason, however, that I list it among the basic characteristics of resignation. The hesitation to change something in the environment is conspicuous in some instances but in other resigned people the opposite impression prevails—that of restlessness. But in all cases there is a marked aversion to *inner* changes. This applies in a way to all neuroses,[8] but the aversion is usually one to the tackling and changing of special factors—mostly those pertaining to the particular main solution. This is equally true for the resigned type but, because of the static concept of self rooted in the nature of his solution, he is averse to the very idea of change itself. The very essence of this solution is withdrawing from active living, from active wishing, striving, planning, from efforts and doing. His accepting others as unalterable is a reflection of his view of himself, no matter how much he may talk about evolution—or even intellectually appreciate the idea of it. Analysis, in his mind, should be a one-time revelation which, once received, settles things for good and all. It is at the beginning alien to him to realize that it is a process, in which we tackle a problem from ever-new angles, see ever-new connections, discover ever-new meanings until we get to the root of it and something can change from within.

The whole attitude of resignation may be conscious; in that case the person regards it as the better part of wisdom. Much more often, in my experience, a person is unaware of it but knows about some of the aspects mentioned here—although, as we shall see presently, he may think of them in other terms be-

[8] Karen Horney, *Self-Analysis*. Chapter 10, Dealing with Resistance, W. W. Norton, 1942.

cause he sees them in a different light. Most frequently he is aware only of his detachment and of his sensitivity to coercion. But, as always where neurotic needs are concerned, we can recognize the nature of the resigned individual's needs by observing *when* he reacts to frustration, when he becomes listless or fatigued, exasperated, panicky, or resentful.

For the analyst a knowledge of the basic characteristics is of great help in sizing up the whole picture quickly. When one or another of them strikes our attention we must look for the others; and we are reasonably sure to find them. As I have been careful to point out, they are not a series of unrelated peculiarities but a closely interknit structure. It is, at least in its basic composition, a picture of great consistency and unity, looking as if it had been painted in one hue.

We shall now try to arrive at an understanding of the dynamics of this picture, its meaning and its history. All we have pointed out as yet is that resignation represents a major solution of the intrapsychic conflicts by way of withdrawing from them. At first glance we get the impression that the resigned person primarily gives up his ambition. This is the aspect which he himself often emphasizes and tends to regard as a clue to the whole development. His history too sometimes seems to confirm this impression, in so far as he may have changed conspicuously in terms of ambition. In or around adolescence he often does things which show remarkable energies and gifts. He may be resourceful, surmount economic handicaps, and make a place for himself. He may be ambitious at school, first in his class, excel in debating or some progressive political movement. At least there often is a period in which he is comparatively alive and interested in many things, in which he rebels against the tradition in which he has grown up and thinks of accomplishing something in the future.

Subsequently there is often a period of distress: of anxiety, of depression, of despair about some failure or about some unfortunate life situation in which he has become involved through his very rebellious streak. After that the curve of his life seems to flatten out. People say that he got "adjusted" and settled down. They remark that he had his youthful flight toward the sun and came back down to earth. That, they say, is the "normal" course. But others, more thoughtful, are worried about him. For he also seems to have lost his zest for living, his interest in many things, and seems to have settled for much less than his gifts or opportunities warrant. What has happened to him? Certainly a person's wings can be clipped through a series of disasters or deprivations. But in the instances we have in mind circumstances were not sufficiently unfavorable to be entirely responsible. Hence some psychic distress must have been the determining factor. This answer, however, is not satisfactory either, because we can remember others who likewise experienced inner turmoil and emerged from it differently. Actually the change is not the result either of the existence of conflicts or of their magnitude but rather of the way in which he has made peace with himself. What has happened is that he got a taste of his inner conflicts and solved them by withdrawing. Why he tried to solve them this way, why he could do it this way only is a matter of his previous history, about which more later. First we need to have a clearer picture of the nature of the withdrawing.

Let us look first at the major inner conflict between expansive and self-effacing drives. In the two types discussed in the previous three chapters one of these drives is in the foreground and the other one is suppressed. But if resignation prevails, the typical picture we get in relation to this conflict is different. Neither expansive nor self-effacing trends seem to be suppressed. Provided we are familiar with their manifestations and implications, it is not difficult to observe them nor—up to a point—to bring them to awareness. In fact, if we insisted upon classifying all neuroses as either expansive or self-effacing, we would be at a loss to decide in which category to place the resigned type. We could only state that as a rule one or the other trend prevails, either in the sense of being closer to awareness or of being stronger. Individual differences within this whole group depend in part upon such a prevalence. Sometimes, however, there seems to be a fairly even balance.

Expansive trends may show in his having rather grandiose fantasies about the great things he could do in his imagination, or about his general attributes. Furthermore he often feels consciously superior to others, and may show this in his behavior by an exaggerated dignity. In his feelings about himself he may tend to be his proud self. The attributes, though, of which he is proud—in contrast to the expansive type—are in the service of resignation. He is proud of his detachment, his "stoicism," his self-sufficiency, his independence, his dislike of coercion, his being above competition. He may also be quite aware of his claims and able to assert them effectively. Their content, however, is different because they arise from the need to protect his ivory tower. He feels entitled to having others not intrude upon his privacy, to having them not expect anything of him nor bother him, to be exempt from having to make a living and from responsibilities. Lastly, expansive trends may show in some secondary developments evolving from the basic resignation, such as his cherishing prestige or being openly rebellious.

But these expansive trends no longer constitute an active force, because he has relinquished his ambition in the sense of *giving up any active pursuit of ambitious goals* and active strivings toward them. He is determined not to want them, and not even to try to attain them. Even if he is able to do some productive work, he may do it with a supreme disdain for, or in defiance of, what the world around him wants or appreciates. This is characteristic of the rebellious group. Nor does he want to do anything active or aggressive for the sake of revenge or vindictive triumph; he has abandoned the drive for actual mastery. Indeed, in a way consistent with his detachment, the idea of being a leader, of influencing or manipulating people, is rather distasteful to him.

On the other hand, if self-effacing trends are in the foreground, resigned people tend to have a low estimate of themselves. They may be timid and feel that they do not amount to much. They may also show certain attitudes which we would hardly recognize as self-effacing, if it were not for our knowledge of the full-fledged self-effacing solution. They are frequently keenly sensitive to the needs of other people, and may actually spend a good deal of their lives in helping others or serving a cause. They often are defenseless toward impositions and attacks and would rather put the blame on themselves than accuse others. They may be overanxious never to hurt others' feelings. They also tend to be compliant. This latter tendency, however, is not determined by a need for affection, as it is in the self-effacing type, but by the need to avoid friction. And there are undercurrents of fear, indicating that they are afraid of the potential force of self-effacing trends. They may for instance express an alarmed conviction that if it were not for their aloofness others would run all over them.

Similarly to what we have seen in regard to expansive trends, the self-effacing ones are more attitudes than active, powerful drives. The appeal of love, which gives these drives a passionate character, is lacking because the resigned type is determined not to want or expect anything of others and not to become emotionally involved with them.

We understand now the meaning of withdrawing from the inner conflict between the expansive and the self-effacing drives. When the active elements in both are eliminated they cease to be opposing forces; hence they no longer constitute a conflict. Comparing the three major attempts, a person hopes to reach integration by trying to *exclude* one of the conflicting forces; in the resigned solution he tries to *immobilize* both of them. And he can do so because he has given up an active pursuit of glory. He still must be his idealized self, which means that the pride system with its shoulds keeps operating, but he has given up the active drive for its actualization—i.e., to make it real in action.

A similar immobilizing tendency operates also with regard to his real self. He still wants to be himself but, with his checks on initiative, effort, alive wishes, and strivings, he also puts a check on his natural drive toward self-realization. Both in terms of his idealized and his real self he lays an emphasis on *being*, not on attaining or growing. But the fact that he still wants to be himself allows him to retain some spontaneity in his emotional life, and in this regard he may be less alienated from himself than any other neurotic type. He can have strong personal feelings for religion, art, nature—i.e., for something impersonal. And often, although he does not allow his feelings to involve him with other people, he can emotionally experience others and their peculiar needs. This retained capacity comes into clear relief when we compare him with the self-effacing type. The latter likewise does not stifle positive feelings, but on the contrary cultivates them. But they become dramatized and falsified, because they are all put to the service of love—that is, surrender. He wants to lose himself with his feelings, and ultimately to find a unity in merging with others. The resigned person wants to keep his feelings strictly in the privacy of his own heart. The very idea of merging is obnoxious to him. He wants to be "himself," although he has but a vague notion of what that means and in fact, without realizing it, is confused about it.

It is this very process of immobilization that gives resignation its negative or static character. But here we must raise an important question. This impression of a static condition, characterized by negative qualities, is constantly reinforced by new observations. Yet does it do justice to the whole phenomenon? After all, nobody can live by negation alone. Is there not something missing in our understanding of the meaning of resignation? Is not the resigned person out for something positive too? Peace at any price? Certainly, but that still has a negative quality. In the other two solutions there is a motivating force in addition to the need for integration—a powerful appeal of something positive that gives meaning to life: the appeal of mastery in the one case, that of love in the other. Is there not perhaps an equivalent appeal of some more positive aim in the resigned solution?

When questions like these arise during analytic work it is usually helpful to listen attentively to what the patient himself has to say about it. There is usually something he has told us which we have not taken seriously enough. Let us do the same thing here, and examine more closely how our type looks at himself. We have seen that, like anybody else, he rationalizes and embellishes his needs so that they all appear as superior attitudes. But in this regard we have to make a distinction. Sometimes he obviously makes a virtue out of a need, such as presenting his lack of striving in terms of being above competition or accounting for his inertia by his scorn of the sweat of hard work. And as the analysis proceeds, these glorifications usually drop out without much talk about them. But there are others which are not discarded as easily because they apparently have a real meaning for him. And these concern all that he says about independence and *freedom*. In fact most of the basic characteristics which we have regarded from the viewpoint of resignation also make sense when seen from the viewpoint of freedom. Any stronger attachment would curtail his freedom. So would needs. He would be dependent upon such needs and they would easily make him dependent upon others too. If he devoted his energies to one pursuit, he would not be free to do many other things in which he might be interested. Particularly, his sensitivity to coercion appears in a new light. He wants to be free and hence will not tolerate pressure.

Accordingly, when in analysis this subject comes up for discussion, the patient goes into a vigorous defense. Is it not natural for man to want freedom? Does not anybody become listless when he does things under pressure? Did not his aunt or his friend become colorless, or lifeless, because they always did what was expected of them? Does the analyst want to domesticate him, to force him into a pattern, so that he will be like one house in a row of settlement houses, each indistinguishable from the others? He hates regimentation. He never goes to the Zoo because he simply cannot stand seeing animals in a cage. He wants to do what he pleases when he pleases.

Let us look at some of his arguments, leaving others for later. We learn from them that freedom means to him doing what he likes. The analyst observes here an obvious flaw. Since the patient has done his best to freeze his wishes, he simply does not know what he wants. And as a result he often does nothing, or nothing that amounts to anything. This, however, does not disturb him because he seems to see freedom primarily in terms of no interference by others—whether people or institutions. Whatever makes this attitude so important, he means to defend it to the last ditch. Granted that his idea of freedom seems again to be a negative one—freedom *from* and not freedom *for*—it does have an appeal for him which (to this degree) is absent in the other solutions. The self-effacing person is rather afraid of freedom, because of his needs for attachment and dependence.

The expansive type, with his craving for mastery of this or that sort, tends to scorn this idea of freedom.

How can we account for this appeal of freedom? Which are the inner necessities from which it arises? What is its meaning? In order to arrive at some understanding we must go back to the early history of those people who later on solve their problems by resignation. There were often cramping influences against which the child could not rebel openly, either because they were too strong or too intangible. There may have been so tight a family atmosphere, so closed an emotional corporation that it did not leave room for his individual ways and threatened to crush him. On the other hand he may have received affection, but in a way that more repelled than warmed him. There may have been for instance a parent who was too ego-centric to have any understanding of the child's needs yet made great demands for the child to understand him or give him emotional support. Or he may have had a parent so erratic in his mood-swings that he gave effusive demonstrative affection at one time and at others could scold or beat him in a fit of temper without any reason that the child could understand. In short there was an environment which made explicit and implicit demands for him to fit in this way or that way and threatened to engulf him without sufficient regard for his individuality, not to speak of encouraging his personal growth.

So the child is torn for a longer or shorter time between futile attempts to get affection and interest and resenting the bonds put around him. He solves this early conflict by withdrawing from others. By putting an emotional distance between himself and others, he sets his conflict out of operation.[4] He no longer wants others' affection nor does he want to fight them. Hence he is no longer torn by contradictory feelings toward them and manages to get along with them on a fairly even keel. Moreover, by withdrawing into a world of his own, he saves his individuality from being altogether cramped and engulfed. *His early detachment thus not only serves his integration, but has a most significant positive meaning: the keeping intact of his inner life.* The freedom from bondage gives him

---

[4] *Cf.* Karen Horney, *Our Inner Conflicts,* Chapter 5, Moving away from People.

the possibility of inner independence. But he must do more than put a check on his feelings for or against others. He must also retract all those wishes and needs which would require others for their fulfillment: his natural needs for understanding, for sharing experiences, for affection, sympathy, protection. This, however, has far-reaching implications. It means that he must keep his joys, his pains, his sorrows, his fears to himself. He often makes, for instance, pathetic and desperate efforts to conquer his fears—of the dark, of dogs, etc.—without letting anybody know about them. He trains himself (automatically) not only not to show suffering but also not to feel it. He does not want sympathy or help, not only because he has reasons to suspect their genuineness but because even if they are temporarily given they have become alarm signals for threatening bondage. Over and beyond putting a lid on these needs, he feels it safer not to let anybody know that anything matters to him lest his wishes either be frustrated or used as a means to make him dependent. And so the general retraction of all wishes, so characteristic of the process of resignation, begins. He still knows that he would like a garment, a kitten, or some toy, but he does not say so. But gradually, just as with his fears, here too he comes to feel it safer not to have wishes at all. The fewer wishes he actually has, the safer he is in his retreat, the more difficult it will be for anybody to have a hold on him.

The resulting picture so far is not yet resignation, but it contains the germs from which it may develop. Even if the condition remained unchanged, it involves grave dangers for future growth. We cannot grow in a vacuum, without closeness to and friction with other human beings. But the condition can hardly remain static. Unless favorable circumstances change it for the better, the process grows by its own momentum, in vicious circles—as we have seen in other neurotic developments. We have already mentioned one of these circles. To maintain detachment, it is necessary for a person to put a check on wishes and strivings. The retraction of wishes, however, is double edged in its effect. It does make him more independent of others but it also weakens him. It saps his vitality and maims his sense of direction. He has less to set against the wishes and expectations of others. He must be doubly vigilant against any influence or interference. To use a good expression of Harry Stack Sullivan's, he must "elaborate his distance machinery."

The main reinforcements of the early development come from the intrapsychic processes. The very needs which drive others on the search for glory operate here too. His early detachment removes his conflicts with others, if he can carry it through consistently. But the reliability of his solution depends upon the retraction of wishes, and at an early age this process is fluctuating; it has not yet matured into a determined attitude. He still wants more things from life than is good for his peace of mind. When sufficiently tempted, he may for instance be drawn into a close relationship. Hence his conflicts are easily mobilized and he needs more integration. But the early development leaves him not only divided but also alienated from himself, lacking in self-confidence and feeling unequipped for actual life. He can deal with others only when at a safe emotional distance; thrown into closer contact, he is inhibited in addition to being handicapped by his recoil from fighting. Hence he too is driven to find an answer to all these needs, in self-idealization. He may try to realize ambitions in actuality, but for many reasons in himself tends to give up the pursuit in the face of difficulties. His idealized image, chiefly, is a glorification of the needs which have developed. It is a composite of self-sufficiency, independence, self-contained serenity, freedom from desires and passions, stoicism, and fairness. Fairness for him is less a glorification of vindictiveness (as is the "justice" of the aggressive type) than an idealization of noncommitment and of not infringing upon anybody's rights.

The shoulds corresponding to such an image bring him into a new danger. While originally he had to protect his inner self against the outside world, he now must protect it against this much more formidable inner tyranny. The outcome depends on the degree of inner aliveness he has safeguarded so far. If it is strong and he is, as it were, unconsciously determined to preserve it come hell or high water, he can still maintain some of it, although only at the price of enforcing the restrictions we discussed at the beginning—only at the cost of resigning from active living, of checking his drives toward self-realization.

There is no clinical evidence pointing to the inner dictates being more stringent here than in other types of neurosis. The difference lies rather in his chafing more under them because of his very need for freedom. He tries to cope with them in part by externalizing them. Because of his taboos on aggression, he can do so only in a passive way—which means that the expectations of others, or what he feels as such, acquire the character of commands to be obeyed without question. Moreover he is convinced that people would coldly turn against him if he did not comply with their expectations. In essence this means that he has not only externalized his shoulds but also his self-hate. Others would turn as sharply against him as he would himself for not measuring up to his shoulds. And because this anticipation of hostility is an externalization it cannot be remedied by experiences to the contrary. A patient for instance may have had a long experience with the analyst's patience and understanding and yet, under duress, may feel that the analyst would drop him at a moment's notice in case of open opposition.

Hence his original sensitivity to outside pressure is greatly reinforced. We understand now why he keeps experiencing external coercion, even though the latter environment may exert very little pressure. In addition the externalization of his shoulds, while relieving inner tension, brings a new conflict into his life. He should comply with the expectations of others; he should not hurt their feelings; he must appease their anticipated hostility—but he also should maintain his independence. This conflict is reflected in his ambivalent way of responding to others. In many variations it is a curious mixture of compliance and defiance. He may for instance politely comply with a request but forget about it or procrastinate in doing it. The forgetting may reach such disturbing proportions that he can keep a fair order in his life only by the help of a notebook in which he jots down appointments or jobs to be done. Or he may go through the motions of complying with the wishes of others but sabotage them in spirit, without in the least being aware of doing so. In analysis for instance he may comply with the obvious rules, such as being on time or saying what is on his mind, but assimilate so little of what is discussed that the work is rendered futile.

It is unavoidable that these conflicts make for a strain in his associations with others. He may at times feel this strain consciously. But, whether or not he is aware of it, it does reinforce his tendency to withdraw from others.

The passive resistance which he sets against the expectations of others also operates in regard to those shoulds which are not externalized. The mere feeling that he *should* do something is often sufficient to make him listless. This unconscious sit-down strike would not be so important if it were restricted to activities which he at bottom dislikes, such as participating in social gatherings, writing certain letters, or paying his bills, as the case may be. But the more radically he has eliminated personal wishes the more anything he does—good, bad, or indifferent— may register as something he *should* do: brushing his teeth, reading the newspaper, taking a walk, doing his work, eating his meals, or having sexual relations with a woman. Everything then meets with a silent resistance, resulting in a pervasive inertia. Activities therefore are restricted to a minimum or, more frequently, are performed under a strain. Hence he is unproductive, tires easily, or suffers from a chronic fatigue.

When in analysis this inner process becomes clear, two factors appear which tend to perpetuate it. As long as the patient has no recourse to his spontaneous energies he may fully realize that this way of living is wasteful and unsatisfactory but will see no possibility for change because—as he feels it—he would simply not do anything if it were not for his driving himself. The other factor resides in the important function his very inertia has assumed. His psychic paralysis may have turned in his mind into an unalterable affliction, and he uses it to stave off self-accusations and self-contempt.

The premium which is thus put on inactivity is also reinforced from another source. Just as his way of solving his conflicts was to immobilize them, so he also tries to set his shoulds out of operation. He does so by trying to avoid situations in which they would start harassing him. Here then is another reason that he avoids contacts with others as well as a serious pursuit of anything. He follows the unconscious motto that as long as he does not do anything he will not violate any shoulds and taboos. Sometimes he rationalizes these avoidances by thinking that any pursuits of his would impinge on the rights of others.

In these many ways the intrapsychic processes keep reinforcing the original solution of detachment and gradually create the entanglements which constitute the picture of resignation. This condition would be inaccessible to therapy—because of the minimal incentive to change—if it were not for the positive elements in the appeal of freedom. Patients in whom these prevail often have a more immediate understanding of the harmful character of the inner dictates than do others. If conditions are favorable, they may quickly recognize them for the yoke they actually are and may take an unequivocal stand against them.[5] Certainly such a conscious attitude does not in itself dispel them, but it is a considerable help in overcoming them gradually.

Looking back now at the total structure of resignation from the viewpoint of the preservation of integrity, certain observations fall in line and gain significance. To begin with, the integrity of truly detached people has always struck an alert observer. I for one have always been aware of it, but what I did not realize earlier was that it is an intrinsic and nuclear part of the structure. Detached, resigned people may be impractical, inert, inefficient, difficult to deal with because of their defiant wariness of influences and closer contact, but they possess—to a greater or lesser extent—an essential sincerity, an innocence in their innermost thoughts and feelings which are not to be bribed or corrupted by the lure of power, success, flattery, or "love."

Furthermore we recognize in the need to maintain inner integrity another determinant for the basic characteristics. We saw first that avoidances and restrictions were put to the service of integration. Then we saw them also being determined by a need for freedom, not yet knowing its meaning. Now we understand that they need freedom from involvement, influence, pressure, from the shackles of ambition and competition, for preserving their inner life unsoiled and untarnished.

We may feel puzzled that the patient does not talk about this

---

[5] *Cf.* "Finding the Real Self," *American Journal of Psychoanalysis*, vol. IX, 1949, *A Letter*, with a Foreword by Karen Horney.

crucial matter. Actually he has indicated in many indirect ways that he wants to remain "himself"; that he is afraid of "losing his individuality" through analysis; that analysis would make him like everybody else; that the analyst inadvertently might mold him according to his, the analyst's, pattern, etc. But the analyst often does not grasp the full implications of such utterances. The context in which they were made suggests the patient's wanting to remain either his actual neurotic self or his idealized grandiose self. And the patient meant indeed to defend his *status quo*. But his insistence on being himself also expresses an anxious concern about preserving the integrity of his real self, although he is not yet able to define it. Only through analytic work can he learn the old truth that he must lose himself (his neurotic glorified self) in order to find himself (his true self).

From this basic process three most different forms of living result. In a first group *persistent resignation*, resignation and all it entails, is carried through fairly consistently. In a second, the appeal of freedom turns the passive resistance into a more active rebellion: the *rebellious group*. In a third, deteriorating processes prevail and lead to *shallow living*.

Individual differences in the first group are related to the prevalence of expansive or self-effacing trends and to the degree of retiring from activities. In spite of a cultivated emotional distance from others, some are capable of doing things for their families, their friends, or for those with whom they come in contact through their work. And, perhaps because of being disinterested, they often are effective in the help they give. In contrast to both the expansive and the self-effacing types, they do not expect much in return. In contrast to the latter, it rather exasperates them if others mistake their willingness to help for personal affection, and want more of it in addition to the help given.

In spite of a restriction of activities, many such people are capable of doing their daily work. It is, though, usually felt as a strain because it is done against the inner odds of inertia. The inertia becomes more noticeable as soon as the work accumulates, requires initiative, or involves fighting for or against something. The motivations for doing routine work usually are mixed. Besides economic necessity and the traditional shoulds, there also is often a need to be useful to others despite being themselves resigned. Besides, daily work may also be a means of getting away from the feeling of futility they possess when left to their own resources. They often do not know what to do with their leisure time. Contacts with others are too much of a strain to be enjoyable. They like being by themselves, but they are unproductive. Even reading a book may meet with inner resistance. So they dream, think, listen to music, or enjoy nature if it is available without effort. They are mostly unaware of the lurking fear of futility but may automatically arrange their work in a way that leaves little free time by themselves.

Finally, the inertia and the accompanying aversion to regular work may prevail. If they have no financial means they may take occasional jobs or else sink down to a parasitic existence. Or, if moderate means are available, they rather restrict their needs to the utmost in order to feel free to do as they please. The things they do, however, often have the character of hobbies. Or they may succumb to a more or less complete inertia. This outcome is presented in a masterly fashion in Goncharov's unforgettable Oblomov, who resents even having to put on his shoes. His friend invites him on a trip to some other countries and makes all the preparations for him, down to the last detail. Oblomov sees himself in his imagination in Paris and in the Swiss mountains, and we are kept in suspense: will he or won't he go? Of course he backs down. The prospect of what seems to him a turbulent moving around and ever-new impressions is too much.

Even if not carried to such extremes, a pervasive inertia bears within it the danger of deterioration, as is shown in Oblomov's and his servant's later fate. (Here then would be a transition to the shallow living of the third group.) It is also dangerous because it may extend beyond a resistance against doing to one against thinking and feeling as well. Both thinking and feeling may then become purely reactive. Some train of thought may be set in motion by a conversation or by the analyst's comments, but since no energies are mobilized by it, it peters out. Some feeling, positive or negative, may be stimulated by a visit or a letter, but it likewise fades out soon after. A letter may evoke an impulse to answer it, but if not acted upon right away it may be forgotten. The inertia in thinking can be well observed in analysis and often is a great hindrance to work. Simple mental operations become difficult. Whatever is discussed during one hour may then be forgotten—not because of any specific "resistance" but because the patient lets the content lie in his brain like a foreign body. Sometimes he feels helpless and confused in analysis, as well as in reading or discussing somewhat difficult matters, because the strain of connecting data is too great. One patient expressed this aimless confusion in a dream, in which he found himself in various places all over the world. He had no intention of going to any of them; he did not know how he got there, or how he would go on from there.

The more the inertia spreads, the more the person's feelings are affected by it. He needs stronger stimuli to respond at all. A group of beautiful trees in a park no longer arouses any feelings; he requires a riotous sunset. Such an inertia of feelings entails a tragic element. As we have seen, the resigned type largely restricts his expansiveness in order to maintain intact the genuineness of his feelings. But if carried to extremes the process chokes off the very aliveness it was meant to preserve. Hence when his emotional life becomes paralyzed he suffers under the resulting deadness of his feelings more than other patients, and this may be the one thing which he does want to change. As the analysis proceeds he may at times have the experience of his feelings being more alive as soon as he is generally more active. Even so he hates to realize that his emotional deadness is but one expression of his pervasive inertia, and hence that it can change only as the latter is lessened.

If some activity is maintained and living conditions are fairly appropriate, this picture of persistent resignation may remain stationary. Many attributes of the resigned type combine to make it so: his check on strivings and expectations, his aversion to change and inner struggle, his capacity to put up with things. Against all of this, however, militates one disquieting element —the appeal freedom has for him. Actually the resigned person is a subdued rebel. So far in our study we have seen this quality expressed in a passive resistance against internal and external pressure. But it might turn at any time into an *active rebelliousness*. Whether it actually does, depends on the relative strength of expansive and self-effacing trends and on the degree of inner aliveness a person has managed to salvage. The stronger his expansive tendencies and the more alive he is, the more easily will he become discontented with the restrictions of his life. The discontentment with the external situation may prevail; then it is primarily a "rebellion *against*." Or, if his discontent with himself prevails, it is primarily a "rebellion *for*."

The environmental situation—home, work—may become so unsatisfactory that the person finally stops putting up with it any longer and in some form or other rebels openly. He may leave his home or his job and become militantly aggressive toward everybody with whom he associates as well as toward conventions and institutions. His attitude is one of "I don't give a damn what you expect of me or think of me." This may be expressed in more or less urbane ways—or in more or less offensive forms. It is a development of great interest from the social point of view. If such a rebellion is directed mainly outward, it is in itself not a constructive step and may drive a person further away from himself, although it releases his energies.

However, the rebellion may be more an inward process and be directed primarily against the inner tyranny. Then, within limits, it can have a liberating effect. In this latter case it is more often a gradual development than a turbulent rebellion, more of an evolution than a revolution. A person then suffers increasingly under his shackles. He realizes how hemmed in he is, how little to his liking his way of living is, how much he does merely to conform with rules, how little he actually cares for the people around him, for their standards of living or their moral standards. He becomes more and more bent on "being himself" which, as we said before, is a curious mixture of protest, conceit, and genuine elements. Energies are liberated and he can become productive in whatever way he is gifted. In his *The Moon and Sixpence* SomersetMaugham has described such a process in the character of the painter Strickland. And it seems that Gauguin, after whom Strickland is roughly patterned, as well as other artists went through such an evolution.

Naturally the value of what is created depends on existing gifts and skills. Needless to say, this is not the only way to become productive. It is *one* way in which creative faculties, stifled before, can become free for expression.

The liberation in these instances nevertheless is a limited one. People who have achieved it still bear many earmarks of resignation. They still must carefully guard their detachment. Their whole attitude toward the world is still defensive or militant. They still are largely indifferent toward their personal lives, except in matters pertaining to their productivity, which hence may have a hectic character. All of this points to their not having solved their conflicts but to having found a workable compromise solution.

This process can also occur under analysis. And since it brings about, after all, a tangible liberation, some analysts [6] regard it as a most desirable outcome. We must not forget, however, that it is a partial solution only. By working through the whole structure of resignation, not only may creative energies be freed but the person as a whole may find a better relation to himself and to others.

Theoretically the outcome of active rebellion demonstrates the crucial significance which the appeal of freedom has within the structure of resignation, and its connection with the preservation of an autonomous inner life. Conversely we shall see now that the more a person becomes alienated from himself—and in the degree to which he does—the more meaningless freedom becomes. Withdrawing from his inner conflicts, from active living, from an active interest in his own growth, the individual incurs the danger of moving away also from the depths of his feelings. The feeling of futility, already a problem in persistent resignation, then produces a dread of emptiness that calls for unceasing distractions. The check on strivings and goal-directed activity leads to a loss of direction, with a resultant drifting or floating with the stream. The insistence upon life being easy, without pain and friction, can become a corrupting

[6] *Cf.* Daniel Schneider, "The Motion of the Neurotic Pattern; Its Distortion of Creative Mastery and Sexual Power," paper read before the New York Academy of Medicine, 1943.

factor, particularly when he succumbs to the temptation of money, success, and prestige. Persistent resignation means a restricted life, but it is not hopeless; people still have something to live by. But when they lose sight of the depth and autonomy of their own lives, the negative attributes of resignation remain while the positive values fade out. Only then does it become hopeless. They move to the periphery of life. This characterizes that last group, that of *shallow living*.

A person thus moving away from himself in a centrifugal way loses the depth and intensity of his feelings. In his attitude toward people he becomes indiscriminate. Anyone can be a "very good friend," "such a nice fellow," or "such a beautiful girl." But out of sight, out of mind. He may lose interest in them at the slightest provocation without even going to the trouble of examining what is happening. Detachment deteriorates into unrelatedness.

Similarly his enjoyments become shallow. Sexual affairs, eating, drinking, gossip about people, plays, or politics form a large content of his life. He loses the sense for essentials. Interests become superficial. He no longer forms his own judgment or convictions; instead he takes over current opinions. He generally is overawed by what "people" think. With all that, he loses faith in himself, in others, in any values. He becomes cynical.

We can distinguish three forms of shallow living, each differing from the others merely in the emphasis upon certain aspects. In one, the emphasis is on *fun*, on having a good time. This may superficially look like a zest for living, in contrast to a basic characteristic of resignation—a not-wanting. But the motive force here is not a reaching out for enjoyment but the necessity to push down a gnawing feeling of futility by means of distracting pleasures. The following poem, entitled "Palm Springs," which I found in Harper's Magazine [7] characterizes such fun-seeking in the leisure class:

> Oh, give me a home
> Where the millionaires roam

---

[7] From the article "Palm Springs: Wind, Sand and Stars," by Cleveland Amory.

And the dear little glamour girls play.
Where never is heard
An intelligent word
And we round up the dollars all day.

It is, however, by no means restricted to the leisure class but goes far down the social scale to people with small incomes. It is after all merely a question of money whether "fun" is found in expensive night clubs and cocktail and theater parties or in getting together in homes for drinking, playing cards, and chatting. It may also be more localized through collecting stamps, becoming a gourmet, or going to the movies, all of which would be all right if they were not the only real content of life. It is not necessarily socialized, but may consist of reading mystery stories, listening to the radio, looking at television, or daydreaming. If fun is socialized, two things are strictly avoided: being alone for any length of time and having serious talk. The latter is regarded as rather bad manners. The cynicism is thinly covered up by "tolerance" or "broad-mindedness."

In the second group the emphasis is on *prestige* or *opportunistic success*. The check on strivings and efforts which is characteristic for resignation is here undiminished. The motivations are mixed. It is in part the wish for a life made easier by the possession of money. In part it is a need to give an artificial lift to self-esteem, which in this whole group of shallow living sinks to zero. This however, with the loss of inner autonomy, can be done only by lifting oneself up in the eyes of others. One writes a book because it might be a best seller; one marries for money; one joins a political party which is likely to offer advantages. In social life there is less emphasis on fun and more on the prestige of belonging to certain circles or going to certain places. The only moral code is to be smart, to get by and to not be caught. George Eliot has given us in *Romola* an excellent picture of such an opportunistic person in the figure of Tito. We see in him the evasion of conflicts, the insistence on an easy life, the noncommitment, and the gradual moral deterioration. The latter is not accidental but is bound to happen with the moral fiber becoming weaker and weaker.

The third form is the *"well-adapted"* automaton. Here the loss of authentic thinking and feeling leads to a general flattening out of the personality, ably described by Marquand in many of his characters. Such a person then fits in with the others and takes over their codes and conventions. He feels, thinks, does, believes in what is expected or considered right in his environment. The emotional deadness here is not greater, but more obvious, than in the other two groups.

Erich Fromm [8] has well described this overadaptation and has seen its social significance. If we include, as we must, the other two forms of shallow living, this significance is all the greater because of the frequency of such ways of living. Fromm saw correctly that the picture is different from the common run of neuroses. Here are people not obviously driven as the neurotic usually is, not obviously disturbed by conflicts. Also they often have no particular "symptoms" like anxiety and depression. The impression is in short that they do not suffer from disturbances but that they lack something. Fromm's conclusion is that these are conditions of defect rather than neuroses. He does not regard the defect as innate but as a result of being crushed by authority early in life. His speaking of defect and my speaking of shallow living may seem like mere difference in terminology. But, as so often, the difference in terminology results from significant differences as to the meaning of the phenomenon. Actually Fromm's contention raises two interesting questions: is shallow living a condition which has nothing to do with neurosis or is it the outcome of a neurotic process as I have presented it here? And: do people indulging in shallow living actually lack depth, moral fiber, and autonomy?

The questions are interrelated. Let us see what analytic observation has to say about them. Observations are available because people belonging to this group may come to be analyzed. If the process of shallow living is fully developed there is of course no incentive for therapy. But, when not far advanced, they may want it because they are disturbed either by psychosomatic disorders or by repeated failures, inhibitions in work, and an increasing feeling of futility. They may sense that they are going downhill and be disquieted about it. Our first impres-

---

[8] Erich Fromm, "The Individual and Social Origin of Neurosis," *American Sociological Review*, 1944.

sion in analysis is that already described from the point of view of general curiosity. They stay on the surface, seem to lack psychological curiosity, are ready with glib explanations, are interested only in external matters connected with money or prestige. All that makes us think that there is more than meets the eye in their history. As described before in terms of the general movement toward resignation, there were periods earlier, in or after adolescence, in which they had active strivings and went through some emotional distress. This would not only put the onset of the conditions later than Fromm assumes but point to its being an outcome of a neurosis which at some time was manifest.

As the analysis proceeds, a baffling discrepancy appears between their waking lives and their dreams. Their dreams unequivocally show emotional depth and turbulence. These dreams, and often they only, reveal a deeply buried sadness, self-hate and hate for others, self-pity, despair, anxiety. In other words there *is* a world of conflicts and passionate feelings under the smooth surface. We try to awaken their interest in their dreams, but they tend to discard them. They seem to live in two worlds, entirely disconnected. More and more we realize that here is not a given superficiality but that they are anxious to stay away from their own depth. They get a fleeting glimpse of it and close up tightly as if nothing had happened. A little later feelings may suddenly emerge in their waking life from the abandoned depth: some memory may make them cry, some nostalgia or some religious feeling may appear and vanish. These observations, confirmed by the later analytic work, contradict the concept of a defect and point to a determined flight from their inner personal life.

Considering shallow living as an unfortunate outcome of a neurotic process gives us a less pessimistic outlook, both for prophylaxis and therapy. The frequency of shallow living at the present time makes it highly desirable to recognize it as a disturbance and to prevent its development. Its prophylaxis coincides with preventive measures concerning neuroses in general. Much work is being done in this regard but much more is necessary and apparently can be done, particularly in schools.

For any therapeutic work with resigned patients the first requisite is to recognize the condition as a neurotic disturbance and not to discard it as either a constitutional or a cultural peculiarity. The latter concepts imply that it is unalterable or that it does not belong in the range of problems to be tackled by a psychiatrist. As yet it is less well known than other neurotic problems. It has probably aroused less interest for two reasons. Many disturbances occurring in this process, although they may cramp a person's life, are rather inconspicuous and therefore call less urgently for therapy. On the other hand, gross disturbances that may arise from this background have not been connected with the basic process. The only factor in it with which psychiatrists are thoroughly familiar is the detachment. But resignation is a much more encompassing process, presenting specific problems and specific difficulties in therapy. These can be tackled successfully only with a full knowledge of its dynamics and its meaning.

CHAPTER 12

NEUROTIC DISTURBANCES IN HUMAN RELATIONSHIPS

WHILE THE emphasis in this book has been on intrapsychic processes, we could not in our presentation separate them from the interpersonal ones. We could not do so because there is in fact a constant interaction between the two. Even at the beginning, when introducing the search for glory, we saw elements like the need to be superior to others, or to triumph over them, which directly concerned interpersonal relations. Neurotic claims, while growing from inner needs, are mainly directed toward others. We could not discuss neurotic pride without the effect its vulnerability has on human relations. We have seen that every single intrapsychic factor can be externalized, and how radically this process modifies our attitudes toward others. Finally we have discussed the more specific form human relations assume in each of the major solutions of the inner conflicts. In this chapter I want to return from the specific to the general and make a brief systematic survey of how in principle the pride system influences our relations to others.

To begin with, the pride system removes the neurotic from others by making him *egocentric*. To avoid misunderstandings: by egocentricity I do not mean selfishness or egotism in the sense of considering merely one's own advantage. The neurotic may be callously selfish or too unselfish—there is nothing in this regard that is characteristic for all neuroses. But he is always egocentric in the sense of being wrapped up in himself. This need not be apparent on the surface—he may be a lone wolf or live for and through others. Nevertheless he lives in any case by his private religion (his idealized image), abides by his own laws (his shoulds), within the barbed-wire fence of his own pride and with his own guards to protect him against dangers from within and without. As a result he not only becomes more isolated emotionally but it also becomes more difficult for him to see other people as individuals in their own right, different from himself. They are subordinated to his prime concern: himself.

The picture of others, thus far, is blurred but not yet distorted. But there are other factors operating in the pride system which even more drastically prevent him from seeing others as they are and make for positive *distortions* in his picture of them. We cannot do away with this problem by saying glibly that of course our concept of others is blurred to the same extent as is our concept of ourselves. Although this is roughly true it is nevertheless misleading, because it suggests a simple parallel between a distorted view of others and that of ourselves. We can obtain a more accurate and a more comprehensive picture of the distortions if we examine the factors in the pride system bringing them about.

In part the actual distortions come in because the neurotic sees others *in the light of the needs* engendered by the pride system. These needs may be directed toward others or affect his attitudes toward them indirectly. His need for admiration turns them into an admiring audience. His need for magic help endows them with mysterious magic faculties. His need to be right makes them faulty and fallible. His need for triumph divides them into followers and scheming adversaries. His need to hurt them with impunity makes them "neurotic." His need to minimize himself turns them into giants.

He sees others, finally, *in the light of his externalizations*. He does not experience his own self-idealization; instead he idealizes others. He does not experience his own tyranny, but others become tyrants. The most relevant externalizations are those of self-hate. If this is prevailingly an active trend, he tends to see others as contemptible and blameworthy. If anything goes wrong it is their fault. They should be perfect. They are not to be trusted. They should be changed and reformed. Since they are poor, erring mortals he must assume a godlike responsibility for them. In case passive externalizations prevail, others sit in judgment, ready to find fault with him, to condemn him. They keep him down, they abuse him, they coerce and intimidate him. They do not like him; they do not want him. He must appease them and measure up to their expectations.

Among all the factors which distort the neurotic's view of others, externalizations probably rank first in effectiveness. And they are the ones which are most difficult to recognize in himself. For, according to his own experience, others *are* as he sees them in the light of his externalizations and he merely responds to their being that way. What he does not feel is the fact that he responds to something which he himself has put into them.

Externalizations are the more difficult to recognize since they are often mixed up with his reactions to others on the grounds of his needs or the frustrations of those needs. It would be an untenable generalization, for instance, to say that all irritability against others is at bottom an externalization of our rage at ourselves. Only a careful analysis of a particular situation allows us to discern whether, and to what extent, a person is really furious at himself or actually angry at others for, say, a frustration of his claims. Finally, of course, his irritability may stem from both sources. When we analyze ourselves or others we must always pay *impartial* attention to both possibilities—i.e., we must not tend exclusively to the one or the other kind of explanation. Only then do we gradually see the ways and the extent to which they influence our relations to others.

But even if we realize that we carry something into our relations with others which does not belong there, such a realization does not keep the externalization from operating. We can relinquish them only to the extent that we "take them back" to ourselves and are able to experience the particular process in ourselves.

We can roughly distinguish three ways in which the picture

of others can be distorted by externalization. Distortions may result from endowing others with characteristics they do not have or have only to a negligible degree. The neurotic may see them as completely ideal persons, endowed with godlike perfection and power. He may see them as contemptible and guilty. He may turn them into giants or into dwarfs.

Externalizations may also make a person blind toward the existing assets or drawbacks of others. He may transfer to them his own (unrecognized) taboos on exploiting and lying, and hence may fail to see in them even flagrant intents at exploitation and deception. Or, having stifled his own positive feelings, he may be incapable of recognizing in others an existing friendliness or devotion. He would then be prone to regard them as hypocrites and be on his guard not to be taken in by such "maneuvers."

Finally his externalizations may make him clearsighted toward certain trends which others actually have. Thus one patient who in his mind had monopolized all the Christian virtues, and who was blind toward pronounced predatory trends in himself, was quick to spot hypocritical attitudes in others— especially pretenses of goodness and love. Another patient, with considerable unavowed propensities toward disloyalty and treachery, was alert to such tendencies in others. Such occurrences seem to contradict my assertion of the distorting power of externalization. Would it perhaps be more correct to say that externalization can do both—make a person particularly blind or particularly clearsighted? I do not believe so. The perspicacity he may gain in discerning certain attributes is marred by the personal significance they have for him. This makes them loom so large that the individual having them almost disappears as an individual and turns into a symbol for the particular externalized trend or trends. Hence the perspective on the total personality is so one sided that it is decidedly distorted. Naturally these last kinds of externalization are most difficult to recognize as such because the patient himself can always take refuge in the "fact" that after all his observations are correct.

All the factors mentioned—the neurotic's needs, his reactions to others, and his externalizations—make it difficult for others to deal with him, at least in any close relationship. The neurotic himself does not see it this way. Since in his eyes his needs, or the claims resulting from them, are all legitimate, if at all conscious; since his reactions to others likewise are warranted; since his externalizations are merely a response to given attitudes in the others, he usually is aware of no such difficulty —feels indeed that he is easy to live with. While most understandable, this is nevertheless an illusion.

As far as their own difficulties permit it, others often try hard to live in peace with the most obviously neurotic member of the family. And here again his externalizations are the greatest impediment to such efforts. Since externalizations, by their very nature, have little if anything to do with the actual behavior of the others, they are helpless against them. They may try for instance to come to terms with a militantly righteous person by not contradicting or criticizing him, by taking care of his clothes or his meals exactly as he desires, etc. But their very endeavors may arouse his self-accusations and he may start to hate the others in order to ward off his own guilt-feelings (to wit, Mr. Hicks in *The Iceman Cometh*).

As a result of all these distortions, the *insecurity* which the neurotic feels with regard to others is considerably reinforced. Although in his mind he may be convinced that he is an astute observer of others, that he knows them, that indeed his estimate of others is always right, all of this can at best be only partially true. *Observation and critical intelligence are no substitute for that inner certainty with reference to others which is possessed by a person who is realistically aware of himself as himself and others as themselves, and who is not swayed in his estimate of them by all kinds of compulsive needs.* Even with a pervasive uncertainty about others, a neurotic person may be able to give a fairly accurate description of their behavior and even of some neurotic mechanisms if he is trained in intelligent observation of other people. But the existing insecurity is bound to show in his actual dealings with them, if he is subject to the insecurity caused by all these distortions. It appears then that the picture he has arrived at by dint of observations and conclusions, and the estimate based upon them, has no staying power. There are too many subjective factors which come into play and which may change his attitude rapidly. He may easily turn against somebody whom he has held in high regard, or lose interest in him, and somebody else may as suddenly rise in his estimation.

Among the many ways in which such inner uncertainty manifests itself two seem to be present fairly regularly and to be rather independent of the particular neurotic structure. The individual does not know where he stands with regard to another person and where the latter stands with regard to him. He may call him a friend, but the word has lost its deep meaning. Any argument, any rumor, any misinterpretation he puts on something the friend is saying, doing, or omitting may arouse not only temporary doubts but shake the very foundation of the relationship.

The second rather ubiquitous uncertainty about others is an uncertainty of confidence or trust. It shows not only in trusting too much or too little but also in not knowing with his heart in what regard another person is trustworthy and where his limits lie. If this uncertainty becomes more intensive he has no feeling for either the decent or the mean things another person is capable of doing, or utterly incapable of doing, even though he may have been closely associated with him for years.

In his fundamental uncertainty about others he will as a rule tend to expect the worst—consciously or unconsciously—because the pride system also *increases his fear of people*. His uncertainty is closely interwoven with his fears because, even though others do in fact represent a greater threat to him, his fears would not skyrocket as easily as they do if it were not that his picture of others is distorted anyway. Our fear of others is, generally speaking, dependent both upon their power to hurt us and upon our own helplessness. And both of these factors are hugely reinforced by the pride system. No matter how blustering self-assurance may be on the surface, intrinsically the system does weaken a person. It does so primarily by the alienation from self, but also by the self-contempt and the inner conflicts it entails, which make him divided against himself. The reason lies in his increased vulnerability. And he becomes vulnerable on many scores. It takes so little to hurt his pride or to elicit his guilt-feelings or his self-contempt. His claims are of such a nature that they are bound to be frustrated. His equilibrium is so precarious that it can be easily disturbed. Finally his externalizations and his own hostility against others, aroused by the externalization as well as by many other factors, make others more formidable than they actually are. All these fears account for his main attitude toward others being a defensive one, no matter whether it takes more aggressive or more appeasing forms.

When surveying all the factors mentioned hitherto we are struck by the similarity with the constituents of the basic anxiety which, to repeat, is one of feeling isolated and helpless toward a world potentially hostile. And this indeed is in principle the influence of the pride system on human relationships: *it reinforces the basic anxiety.* What in adult neurotics we identify as basic anxiety is not basic anxiety in its original form but rather modified by the accretions acquired through the years from the intrapsychic processes. It has become a composite attitude toward others which is determined by more complex factors than those involved at first. Just as, because of his basic anxiety, the child had to find ways to cope with others, so the adult neurotic must in his turn find such ways. And he finds them in the major solutions which we have described. Although these again bear similarities to the earlier solutions of moving toward, against, or away from people—and in part follow from them—actually the new solutions of self-effacement, expansiveness, and resignation are different in their structure from the old ones. While they also determine the form of human relationships, they are principally solutions for the intrapsychic conflicts.

To complete the picture: while the pride system reinforces the basic anxiety, at the same time it lends to other people an overimportance through the needs it generates. Others become overimportant, or indeed indispensable, for the neurotic in the following ways: he needs them for a direct confirmation of the fictitious values he has arrogated to himself (admiration, approval, love). His neurotic guilt-feelings and his self-contempt make for a stringent need for his vindication. But the very self-hate that engendered these needs renders it close to impossible to find this vindication in his own eyes. He can find it only through others. He must prove to them that he has whatever special values have become important for him. He must show them how good he is, how fortunate, how successful, how capable, how intelligent, how powerful, and what he can do for or to them.

Furthermore, whether for his active pursuit of glory or for his vindication, he needs and does derive a great deal of his incentive for his activities from others. This is most pronounced in the self-effacing type, who can hardly do anything on his own and in his own behalf. But how active and energetic would a more aggressive type be if it were not for the incentive to impress, to fight, or to defeat others? Even the rebellious type still needs others against whom to rebel, in order to free his energies.

Last but not least the neurotic needs others to protect him against his own self-hate. As a matter of fact, the confirmation he gets from others for his idealized image, as well as the possibilities of vindicating himself, also fortify him against his self-hate. Besides, in many obvious and subtle ways he needs others to allay the anxiety arising from an onrush of self-hate or self-contempt. And, most relevant, if it were not for the others he could not avail himself of his most powerful means of self-protection: his externalizations.

Thus it happens that the pride system brings a fundamental incongruity into his human relations: he feels remote from other people, is most uncertain with regard to them, is afraid of them, hostile to them, and yet needs them in ways vital to him.

All the factors disturbing human relationships in general also unavoidably operate in a love relationship as soon as it becomes one of more than short duration. This statement is self-evident from our point of view but needs to be said nevertheless, because many people have the fallacious notion that any love relationship is good if only the partners have satisfaction in sexual relations. Actually sexual relations may help to ease tensions temporarily, or even to perpetuate a relationship if it is based essentially on neurotic foundations, but they do not make it any healthier. To discuss therefore the neurotic difficulties which may arise in a marriage or in an equivalent relationship would not add anything to the principles presented thus far. But the intrapsychic processes also have a particular influence on the *meaning and the functions which love and sex assume for the neurotic.* And I want to conclude this chapter by presenting some general viewpoints on the nature of this influence.

The meaning and significance which *love* has for the neurotic person varies too much with his kind of solution to allow for generalizations. But one disturbing factor is regularly present: his deeply ingrained feeling of being unlovable. I am not referring here to his not feeling loved by this or that particular person but to his belief, which may amount to an unconscious conviction, that nobody does or ever could love him. Oh, he may believe that others love him for his looks, his voice, for his help, or for the sexual satisfaction he gives them. But they do not love him for himself, because he simply is unlovable. If evidence seems to contradict such a belief, he tends to discard it on various grounds. Perhaps that particular person is lonely, or needs somebody to lean on, or is charitably inclined anyway, etc.

But instead of tackling this problem concretely—if he is aware of it—he deals with it in two vague ways, not noticing that the two are contradictory. He tends on the one hand to hold on to the illusion, even if he does not particularly care for love, that sometime, somewhere he will meet the "right" person who will love him. On the other hand he assumes the same attitude he has toward self-confidence: he regards lovableness as an attribute which is independent of existing likable qualities. And because he disconnects it from personal qualities he does not see any possibility of its changing with his future development. He tends therefore to assume a fatalistic attitude and to regard his unlovableness as a mysterious but unalterable fact.

The self-effacing type becomes most easily aware of his disbelief in being lovable and, as we have seen, is the one who tries hardest to cultivate in himself likable qualities, or at least the appearance thereof. But even he, with his absorbing interest in love, does not spontaneously go to the root of the question: what exactly is it that gives him the conviction of unlovableness?

It springs from three main sources. One of them is the impairment of the neurotic's own capacity to love. This capacity is bound to be impaired because of all the factors we discussed in this chapter: his being too wrapped up in himself, his being too vulnerable, too afraid of people, etc. This connection between feeling lovable and being ourselves able to love, although fairly often recognized intellectually, has a deep, vital meaning to very few of us. Yet in fact, if our capacity to love is well developed, we are not bothered about the question of whether or not we are lovable. Nor is it then of crucial importance whether or not we are actually loved by others.

The second source of the neurotic's feeling of being unlovable is his self-hate and its externalization. As long as he is unacceptable to himself—indeed hateworthy or contemptible —he cannot possibly believe that anybody else could love him.

These two sources, both strong and omnipresent in neurosis, account for the feeling of unlovableness not being easily removed in therapy. We can see its existence in a patient and can examine its consequences for his love life. But it can diminish only to the extent that these sources become less potent.

A third source contributes less directly but is important to mention for other reasons. It lies in the neurotic's expecting more of love than it can at best give (the "perfect love"), or expecting something different from what it can give (it cannot, for instance, relieve him of his self-hate). And since no love he does get can fulfill his expectations, he tends to feel that he is not "really" loved.

The particular kind of expectations of love varies. Generally speaking it is the fulfillment of many neurotic needs, often in themselves contradictory, or—in the case of the self-effacing type—of all his neurotic needs. And this fact of love being put into the service of neurotic needs makes it not only desirable but badly needed. Thus we find in love life the same incongruity that exists with regard to human relations in general: an increased need and a decreased capacity for it.

It is probably as little accurate to make a too neat distinction between love and sex as it is to link them up too closely (Freud). Since, however, in neuroses sexual excitement or desires more often than not are separate from a feeling of love, I want to make a few special comments on the role which *sexuality* plays in them. Sexuality retains in neuroses the functions it naturally has as a means of physical satisfaction and of intimate human contact. Also sexual well-functioning adds in many ways to the feeling of self-confidence. But in neuroses all these functions are enlarged and take on a different coloring. Sexual activities become not only a release of sexual tensions but also of manifold nonsexual psychic tensions. They can be a vehicle to drain self-contempt (in masochistic activities) or a means to act out self-torment by sexual degrading or tormenting of others (sadistic practices). They form one of the most frequent ways of allaying anxiety. The individuals themselves are unaware of such connections. They may not even be aware of being under a particular tension, or of having anxiety, but merely experience a rising sexual excitement or desire. But in analysis we can observe these connections accurately. A patient may for instance come closer to experiencing his self-hate, and suddenly there emerge plans or fantasies of sleeping with some girl. Or he may talk about some weakness in himself which he profoundly despises, and have sadistic fantasies of torturing somebody weaker than he is.

Also the natural sexual functions of establishing an intimate human contact frequently assume greater proportions. This is a well-known fact about detached people for whom sexuality may be the only bridge to others, but it is not restricted to being an obvious substitute for human closeness. It shows also in the haste with which people may rush into sexual relations, without giving themselves a chance to find out whether they have anything in common or a chance to develop a liking and understanding. It is possible of course that an emotional relatedness may evolve later on. But more often than not it does not do so because usually the initial rush itself is a sign of their being too inhibited to develop a good human relationship.

Lastly the normal relation between sexuality and self-confidence shifts to one between sexuality and pride. Sexual functioning, being attractive or desirable, the choice of a partner, the quantity or variety of sexual experiences—all become a matter of pride more than of wishes and enjoyment. The more the personal factor in love relations recedes and the purely sexual ones ascend, the more does the unconscious concern about lovableness shift to a conscious concern about attractiveness.[1]

These increased functions which sexuality assumes in neuroses do not necessarily lead to more extensive sexual activities than in the comparatively healthy person. They may do so, but they may also be responsible for greater inhibitions. A comparison with the healthy individual is difficult anyway because of the great variations, even within the range of the "normal," in sexual excitability, in intensity and frequency of sexual desires, or in forms of sexual expressions. There is however one significant difference. In a way similar to that which we discussed with regard to imagination [2] sexuality is put in the service of neurotic needs. For this reason it often assumes an *undue* importance, in the sense of an importance stemming from nonsexual sources. Furthermore, for the same reason, sexual functions can be easily disturbed. There are fears, there is a whole host of inhibitions, there is the intricate problem of homosexuality, and there are perversions. Finally, because sexual activities (including masturbation and fantasies) and their particular forms are determined—or at least partly determined— by neurotic needs or taboos, they are often compulsive in nature. All of these factors may result in the neurotic patient's having sexual relations not because he wants them but because he should please his partner; because he must have a sign of being wanted or loved; because he must allay some anxiety; because he must prove his mastery and potency, etc. Sexual relations, in other words, are less determined by his real wishes and feelings than by the drive to satisfy some compulsive needs. Even without any intention to degrade the partner, the latter ceases to be an individual and becomes a sexual "object" (Freud).[3]

How in detail the neurotic deals with these problems varies within such a wide range that I cannot even try here to outline

---

[1] *Cf.* discussion of self-contempt in Chapter 5.

[2] See Chapter 1.

[3] Approaching the subject from the viewpoint of sex-morality, the English philosopher John Macmurray in his *Reason and Emotion*, Faber and Faber Ltd., London, 1935, makes emotional sincerity the criterion for the value of sexual relations.

the possibilities. *The special difficulties existing toward love and sex are after all only one expression of his total neurotic disturbances.* The variations in addition are so manifold because in kind they depend not only upon the individual's neurotic character structure but also on the particular partners he has had or still has.

This may seem like a superfluous qualification because we have learned through our analytic knowledge that there is more often than formerly was assumed an unconscious choice of partners. The validity of this concept can indeed be shown over and over again. But we have tended to go to the other extreme and assume that every partner is of the individual's choosing; and this generalization is not valid. It needs qualifications in two directions. We must first raise the question as to who does the "choosing." Properly speaking, the word "choice" presupposes a capacity to choose and a capacity to know the partner who is chosen. Both capacities are curtailed in the neurotic. He is able to choose only to the extent to which his picture of others is not distorted by the many factors we have discussed. In this strict sense there is no choice worth the name, or at least very little of it. What is meant by the term "choice of a partner" is the person's feeling attracted on the ground of his outstanding neurotic needs: his pride, his needs to dominate or to exploit, his need to surrender, etc.

But even in this qualified sense the neurotic has not much chance to "choose" a partner. He may marry because it is the thing to do; and he may be so remote from himself and so detached from others that he marries a person whom he just happens to know a little better than others or who happens to want to marry him. His estimate of himself may be so low, because of his self-contempt, that he simply cannot approach those persons of the other sex who—if only for neurotic reasons—would appeal to him. Adding to these psychological restrictions the factual ones of his often knowing very few available partners, we realize how much is left to incidental circumstances.

Instead of trying to do justice to the endless variations of erotic and sexual experiences resulting from these manifold factors involved, I shall merely indicate certain general tendencies operating in the neurotic's attitudes toward love and sex. *He may tend to exclude love* from his life. He may minimize or deny its significance or even its existence. Love then does not appear to him as desirable but is rather to be avoided or to be despised as a self-deceptive weakness.

Such a tendency to exclude love operates in a quiet but determined fashion in the resigned, detached type. Individual differences within this group mostly concern his attitude toward sexuality. He may have removed the actual possibility not only of love, but also of sex, so far from his personal life that he lives as if they did not exist or had no meaning for him personally. Toward the sexual experiences of others he feels neither envy nor disapproval, but may have considerable understanding for them if they are in some trouble.

Others may have had a few sexual relations in their younger years. But these did not penetrate through the armor of their detachment, were not too meaningful, and faded out without leaving a desire for further experiences.

For another detached person sexual experiences are important and enjoyable. He may have had them with many different people but always—consciously or unconsciously—was on his guard not to form any attachment. The nature of such transient sexual contacts depends on many factors. Among others the prevalence of expansive or self-effacing trends is relevant. The lower his estimate of himself, the more will these contacts be restricted to persons beneath his own social or cultural level, as for instance to prostitutes.

Again, others may happen to get married and may even be able to maintain a decent though distant relationship, provided the partner is likewise detached. If such a person marries somebody with whom he has not much in common, he may characteristically put up with the situation and try to abide by his duties as a husband and father. Only if the partner is too aggressive, violent, or sadistic to allow the detached person to withdraw inwardly may the latter either try to get out of the relationship or go to pieces under it.

The arrogant-vindictive type excludes love in a more militant and destructive way. His general attitude toward love usually is a derogating, debunking one. With respect to his sexual life there seem to be two principal possibilities. Either his sexual life is strikingly poor—he may merely have occasional sexual contacts for the main purpose of releasing physical or psychic tensions—or sexual relations may be important to him, provided he can give free range to his sadistic impulses. In this case he may either engage in sadistic sexual activities (which may be most exciting to him and give him satisfaction) or he may be stilted and overcontrolled in his sexual relations but treat his partner in a general sadistic fashion.

Another general tendency with regard to love and sex is also in the direction of excluding love—and sometimes also sex—from the actual life but giving it a *prominent place in his imagination*. Love then becomes a feeling so exalted and so celestial that any realistic fulfillment seems by comparison shallow and indeed despicable. E. T. A. Hoffmann, who has masterly described this aspect in the *Tales of Hoffmann*, calls love "that longing for infinity which weds us to Heaven." It is a delusion planted in our soul "through the cunning of man's hereditary enemy . . . that through love, through the pleasure of the flesh, there could be achieved on earth that which exists in our hearts as a heavenly promise only." Love therefore can be realized in fantasy only. Don Juan, in his interpretation, is destructive to women because "every betrayal of a loved bride, every joy destroyed by a fierce blow struck at the lover . . . represents an exalted triumph over that hostile monster and raises the seducer forever above our narrow life, above nature, above the Creator."

A third and last possibility to be mentioned here is an *overemphasis placed on love and sex in actual life*. Love and sex then constitute the main value of life and are glorified accordingly. We can distinguish here roughly between the conquering and the surrendering love. The latter evolves logically from the self-effacing solution and was described in that context. The former occurs in the narcissistic type, if for particular reasons his drive for mastery has focused upon love. His pride then is invested in being the ideal lover and in being irresistible. Women who are easily available do not appeal to him. He must prove his mastery by conquering those who, for whatever reasons, are difficult to attain. The conquest may consist in the consummation of the sexual act or he may aim at complete emotional surrender. When these aims are achieved his interest recedes.

I am not sure that this brief presentation, condensed as it is into a few pages, conveys the extent and the intensity of the influence which intrapsychic processes have on human relations. When we realize its full impact we must modify certain expectations, commonly harbored, as to the beneficial effect which better human relations can exercise on neurosis—or, in a broader sense, on a person's development. The expectations consist of the anticipation that a change of human environment, marriage, sexual affairs, or participation in any kind of group activity (in the community, in religious, professional groups, etc.) will help a person to outgrow his neurotic difficulties. In analytic therapy this expectation is expressed in the belief that the principal curative factor lies in the possibility of the patient's establishing a good relationship with the analyst, i.e., one in which the factors that were injurious in childhood are absent.[4] This belief follows from the premise held by certain analysts that neurosis primarily is and remains a disturbance in human relations, and hence can be remedied by the experience of a good human relationship. The other expectations mentioned are not based on so precise a premise but rather on the realization—in itself correct—that human relations are a crucial factor in all our lives.

All these expectations are justified with regard to the child and adolescent. Even though he may show definite signs of grandiose notions about himself, of claims for special privileges, of feeling easily abused, etc., he may be sufficiently flexible to respond to a favorable human environment. It may make him less apprehensive, less hostile, more trusting, and may still reverse the course of vicious circles driving him deeper into the

---

[4] Janet M. Rioch, "The Transference Phenomenon in Psychoanalytic Therapy, *Psychiatry*, 1943.

"What is curative in the process is that the patient discovers that part of himself which had to be repressed at the time of the original experience. He can only do this in an interpersonal relationship with the analyst which is suitable to such a rediscovery. . . . The reality gradually becomes 'undistorted,' the self re-found, in the personal relationship between the analyst and the patient."

neurosis. We must of course add the qualification of "more or less," depending upon the extent of the disturbance in the individual and on the duration, quality, and intensity of the good human influence.

Such a beneficial effect upon the person's inner growth may also take place in adults, provided the pride system and its consequences are not too deeply ingrained or—to state it positively —provided the idea of self-realization (in whatever individual terms) still has some meaning and vitality. We have seen often, for instance, that one marriage partner may take strides ahead in his development when the other partner is being analyzed and is changing for the better. In such cases several factors operate. Usually the analyzed partner will talk about the insights he has gained and the other one may pick up some valuable information for himself. Seeing with his own eyes that change in fact is possible, he will be encouraged to do something in his own behalf. And, seeing the possibility of a better relationship, he will have an incentive to outgrow his own troubles. A similar change may occur also without analysis playing any part, when a neurotic comes into close and prolonged contact with relatively healthy persons. Here again multiple factors may stimulate his growth: a reorientation in his sets of values; a feeling of belonging and of being acceptable; the possibility of externalizations being lessened and thereby of his being confronted with his own difficulties; a possibility of accepting and benefiting from serious and constructive criticism, etc.

But these possibilities are much more limited than is usually assumed. Granted that an analyst's experience is restricted through his seeing primarily instances where such hopes did not materialize, I would venture to say on theoretical grounds that the chances are too limited to warrant in any way the blind faith placed in them. We see over and over again that a person set in his particular solution of his inner conflicts enters a relationship with his rigid set of claims and shoulds, with his particular righteousness and vulnerability, with his self-hate and his externalizations, with his needs for mastery, surrender, or freedom. Hence, instead of a relationship being a medium in which both can enjoy each other and grow with each other, it becomes a means of satisfying his own neurotic needs. The effect which such a relationship has on the neurotic is primarily one of decreasing or increasing inner tensions, according to a satisfaction or a frustration of his needs. An expansive type for instance may both feel better and function better when he is in command of a situation or is surrounded by admiring disciples. The self-effacing type may blossom when he is less isolated and feels needed and wanted. Anybody who knows neurotic suffering certainly will appreciate the subjective value of such improvements. But they are not necessarily a sign of the person's inner growth. More often than not they merely indicate that a suitable human environment may allow him to feel comparatively at ease even though his neurosis has not changed at all.

The same viewpoints apply to expectations (of a more impersonal kind) based on changes in institutions, economic conditions, forms of political regimes. Certainly a totalitarian regime can successfully prevent individual growth and by its very nature must aim at stunting it. And no doubt only that political regime which gives as many individuals as possible the freedom to strive toward their self-realization is worth striving for. But even the best changes in the external situation do not in themselves bring about individual growth. They cannot do more than supply it with a better environment in which to grow.

The error involved in all these expectations does not lie in overrating the importance of human relations but in underrating the power of intrapsychic factors. Although human relations are of signal importance, they do not have the power to uproot a firmly planted pride system in a person who keeps his real self out of communication. In this crucial matter the pride system again proves to be the enemy of our growth.

Self-realization does not exclusively, or even primarily, aim at developing one's special gifts. The center of the process is the evolution of one's potentialities as a human being; hence it involves—in a central place—the development of one's capacities for good human relations.

CHAPTER 13

NEUROTIC DISTURBANCES IN WORK[1]

Disturbances in our work life may arise from many sources. They may result from external conditions, such as economic or political pressures, lack of quiet, solitude, or time, or the difficulties—to take a more specific frequent example of our modern times—facing a writer who must learn to express himself in a new language. Difficulties may spring also from cultural conditions, such as that pressure of public opinion on a man which may drive him to increase his earning capacities well beyond his actual needs—as exemplified by our urban businessmen. On the other hand such an attitude makes no sense to the Mexican Indian.

In this chapter I shall not discuss external difficulties, however, but neurotic disturbances as they are carried into work. To limit the subject still further: many neurotic impairments of work are linked up with our attitudes toward other people, superiors, subordinates, and equals. And although we cannot in fact separate these neatly from the difficulties concerning work itself, we shall omit them here as much as possible and focus on

---

[1] A few paragraphs of this chapter are taken from a paper on the same subject published in the *American Journal of Psychoanalysis*, 1948, under the title "Inhibitions in Work."

the influence of intrapsychic factors upon the process of work and the individual's attitude toward it. Lastly, neurotic disturbances are comparatively unimportant in any kind of routine work. They increase to the extent that the work requires personal initiative, vision, responsibility, self-reliance, ingenuity. I shall therefore restrict my comments to those kinds of work for which we have to tap our personal resources—to creative work in the broadest sense of the word. What is said in illustrations taken from artistic work or scientific writing applies just as well to the work of a teacher, a housewife and mother, a businessman, a lawyer, a doctor, a union organizer.

The range of neurotic disturbances in work is great. As we shall see presently, not all of these disturbances are consciously felt; many show instead in the quality of the work produced or in the lack of production. Others are expressed in various kinds of psychic distress connected with work, such as inordinate strain, fatigue, exhaustion; fears, panic, irritability or conscious suffering under inhibitions. There are only a few general and rather obvious factors which all kinds of neuroses have in common on this score. Difficulties *beyond* those inherent in the particular piece of work are never missing, even though they may not be apparent.

Self-confidence, probably the most crucial prerequisite for creative work, is always on a shaky basis, no matter how self-assured or realistic a person's attitude seems to be.

There is rarely an adequate appraisal of what is entailed in a particular job but rather an underrating or overrating of given difficulties. Nor is there as a rule an adequate estimate of the value of the work done.

The conditions under which work may be done are mostly too rigid. They are more peculiar in kind and more rigid in degree than the working habits which people usually develop.

The inner relatedness to the work itself is tenuous because of the neurotic's egocentricity. Questions as to how he made out or how he should perform are of greater concern to him than the work itself.

The joy or satisfaction that can be found in congenial work is usually impaired because the work is too compulsive, too laden with conflicts and fears, or too devaluated subjectively.

But as soon as we leave such generalities, and consider in detail how disturbances in work manifest themselves, we are struck much more by differences in different kinds of neurosis than by similarities. I have already mentioned differences in the awareness of existing difficulties, and in suffering under them. But the special conditions under which work can be done, or cannot be done, also vary. So does the capacity for making consistent effort, for taking risks, for planning, for accepting help, for delegating work to others, etc. These differences are determined mainly by the major solutions a person has found for his intrapsychic conflicts. We shall discuss each group separately.

The *expansive types*, regardless of their special characteristics, tend to overrate their capacities or their special gifts. Also they tend to regard the particular work they are doing as uniquely significant, and to overrate its quality. Others, not sharing their overevaluation of their activities, seem to them either incapable of understanding them (they have thrown pearls before swine) or too jealous to give them due credit. Any criticism, no matter how seriously or conscientiously given, is *eo ipso* felt as a hostile attack. And, because of their necessity to choke off any doubts about themselves, they tend not to examine the valadity of the criticism but to focus primarily upon warding it off in this way or that. For the same reason their need for recognition of their work, in whatever form, is boundless. They tend to feel entitled to such recognition and to be indignant if it is not forthcoming.

Concomitantly their capacity to give credit to others is extremely limited, at least within their field and age group. They may frankly admire Plato or Beethoven but may find it difficult to appreciate any contemporary philosopher or composer; the more so, the more he seems a threat to their own unique significance. They may be hypersensitive to having anybody's achievement praised in their presence.

Finally the appeal of mastery, characteristic of this group, entails the implicit belief that there is simply no obstacle which they cannot overcome through their will power or superior faculties. I gather it must have been an expansive type who first designed the motto to be found in some American offices: "The difficult we do right away, the impossible a little later." At any rate he would be the one to take it literally. The need for proving his mastery often makes him resourceful and gives him the incentive to have a try at tasks which others might be wary of tackling. It entails, however, the danger of underrating the difficulties involved. There simply is no business deal he could not bring about quickly; no illness he could not diagnose at first sight; no paper or lecture he could not deliver on short notice; no trouble with his car that he could not fix better than any mechanic.

All these factors together—the overrating of his capacities and of the quality of his work, the underrating of others and of given difficulties, and his relative imperviousness to criticism—account for his often being oblivious of existing disturbances with regard to work. These disturbances vary according to a prevalence of narcissistic, perfectionistic, or arrogant-vindictive trends.

The *narcissistic type,* being most likely to be swayed by his imagination, shows all the above criteria in a flagrant manner. Assuming approximately equal gifts, he is the most productive among the expansive types. But he may run up against various difficulties. One of them is the scattering of interests and energies in many directions. There is the woman for instance who has to be the perfect hostess, housewife, mother; who also has to be the best-dressed woman, to be active on committees, to have her hand in politics; and who must also be a great writer. Or there is the businessman who, besides having his hands in too many enterprises, pursues extensive political and social activities. When in the long run such a person becomes aware that he never gets around to doing certain things he usually ascribes it to the multitude of his gifts. With an ill-concealed arrogance he may express his envy of those less fortunate fellow beings who are endowed with just one gift. Actually the diversity of faculties may be real, but it is not the source of his troubles. The background is an insistent refusal to recognize that there are any limits to what he can accomplish. Hence a temporary resolution to restrict his activities usually has no lasting effect.

Against all evidence to the contrary he soon bounces back to his conviction that others may not be able to do so many things; but he can—and can do them all to perfection. To restrict his activities would to him smack of defeat and contemptible weakness. The prospect of being a human being like others, with limitations like others, is degrading and hence intolerable.

Other narcissistic persons may scatter their energies not by too many simultaneous activities but by successively starting and dropping one pursuit after the other. In gifted youngsters this still may look simply as though they needed time and experimenting in order to find out where their greatest interest lies. And only a closer examination of their whole personality can show whether so simple an explanation is valid. They may for instance develop a passionate interest in the stage, try out at dramatics, show promising beginnings—and give it up in a short time. Thereafter they may pursue the same course with the writing of poetry or with farming. Then they may take to nursing or the study of medicine, with the same steep curve from enthusiasm to loss of interest.

But the identical process may occur also in adults. They may make outlines for a big book, set an organization going, have vast business projects planned, work at an invention—but time and time again their interest peters out before anything is accomplished. Their imagination has painted a glowing picture of quick and glamorous achievement. But they withdraw interest at the very first real difficulty with which they are confronted. Their pride, however, does not permit them to admit that they are shirking difficulties. Therefore the loss of interest is a face-saving device.

Two factors contribute to the hectic swings which are characteristic of the narcissistic type in general: his aversion to attending to details in work and to consistent efforts. The former attitude may already be conspicuous in neurotic schoolchildren. They may for instance have quite imaginative ideas for a composition but put in a determined unconscious resistance to neat writing or correct spelling. The same sloppiness may mar the quality of work in adults. They may feel it behooves them to have brilliant ideas or projects but that the "detail work" should be done by the ordinary run of people. Hence they have no difficulty in delegating work to others, if this can be done. And, provided they have employees or co-workers who can carry their ideas into action, it may turn out well. If they have to do the work themselves—such as writing a paper, designing a dress, drawing up a legal document—they may regard the job as finished to their own supreme satisfaction before the real *work* of thinking through the ideas and checking, rechecking, and organizing them has even started. The same thing may happen with the patient in analysis. And here we see another determinant besides the general grandioseness: their fear of looking at themselves in concrete detail.

Their incapacity for making consistent efforts stems from the same roots. Their special brand of pride resides in "effortless superiority." It is the glory of the dramatic, of the unusual that captivates their imagination while the humble tasks of daily living are resented as humiliating. Conversely they can make sporadic efforts, be energetic and circumspect in an emergency, swing a big party, in a sudden onrush of energy write letters which have accumulated for months, etc. Such sporadic efforts feed their pride but consistent efforts insult it. Every Tom, Dick, and Harry can get somewhere with plodding work! Moreover, as long as no efforts are made there is always the reservation that they would have accomplished something great if they had put in real efforts. The most hidden aversion to consistent effort lies in the threat to the illusion of unlimited powers. Let us assume that somebody wants to cultivate a garden. Whether he wants it or not, he will soon become aware that the garden does not turn into a blossoming paradise overnight. It will progress exactly to the extent that he has put in work on it. He will have the same sobering experience when consistently working at reports or papers, when doing publicity work or teaching. There is a factual limit to time and energies and to what can be achieved within these limits. As long as the narcissistic type holds on to his illusions of unlimited energies and unlimited achievements he must by necessity be wary of exposing himself to such disillusioning experiences. Or, when he does, he must chafe under them as under an undignified yoke. Such resentment will in turn make him tired and exhausted.

Summarizing, we could say that the narcissistic type, despite good qualifications, often is disappointing in the quality of the work he actually produces because, in accordance with his neurotic structure, he simply does not know how to work. The difficulties of the *perfectionistic type* are in some ways opposite. He works methodically and attends rather too meticulously to details. But he is so cramped by what he should do and how he should do it that there is no room left for originality and spontaneity. He is therefore slow and unproductive. Because of his exacting demands on himself he is easily overworked and exhausted (as is well known of the perfectionistic housewife) and lets others suffer as a result. Also, since he is as exacting on others as he is on himself, his influence on others is often cramping, especially if he is in an executive position.

The *arrogant-vindictive type* too has his own assets and liabilities. Among all neurotics he is the most prodigious worker. If it were not so inappropriate to speak of passion with regard to an emotionally cold person, we could say that he has a passion for work. Because of his relentless ambition and the comparative emptiness of his life outside his work, every hour not spent on work is deemed lost. This does not mean that he enjoys work—he is mostly incapable of enjoying anything—but neither does work tire him. In fact he seems indefatigable, like a well oiled machine. Nevertheless, with all his resourcefulness, efficiency, and his often keen, critical intelligence, the work he produces is likely to be sterile. I am not thinking here of the deteriorated variety of this type, who has become opportunistic and is merely interested in the external result of his work— success, prestige, triumph—no matter whether he produces soap, portraits, or scientific papers. But even if he is interested in the work itself, in addition to his own glory, he will often stay at the fringes of his field and not go into the heart of the matter. As a teacher or social worker he will for instance be interested in methods of teaching or social work rather than in children or clients. He may write critical reviews rather than contribute something of his own. He may be anxious to cover completely all possible questions that may arise so that he has the final say in the matter without, however, having added anything of his own. In short his concern seems to be *to master the particular subject matter rather than to enrich it.*

Because his arrogance does not allow him to give credit to others, and because of his own lack of productivity, he may easily, without being aware of it, appropriate the ideas of others. But even these turn, in his hands, into something mechanical and lifeless.

In contrast to most neurotics he has the capacity for careful and minute planning and may have a fairly clear vision of future developments (in his own mind, his predictions are always correct). He may therefore be a good organizer. There are however several factors detracting from this capacity. He has difficulties in delegating work. Because of his arrogant contempt for people he is convinced that he is the only one who can do things properly. Also, in organizing he tends to employ dictatorial methods: to be intimidating and exploiting rather than stimulating; to kill incentive and joy rather than to kindle it.

Because of his long-range planning he can stand temporary setbacks comparatively well. In serious test situations, however, he may become panicky. When one lives almost exclusively in the categories of triumph or defeat a possible defeat is of course frightening. But since he should be above fear he gets violently angry at himself for being afraid. Besides, in such situations (i.e., an examination) he also gets violently angry at those who presume to sit in judgment over him. All these emotions are usually suppressed, and the results of the inner upheaval may be such psychosomatic symptoms as headaches, intestinal cramps, palpitations of the heart, etc.

The difficulties which the *self-effacing type* has with regard to work are almost point for point opposite to those of the expansive types. He tends to set his aims too low and to underrate his gifts as well as the importance and the value of his work. He is plagued by doubts and self-berating criticisms. Far from believing that he can do the impossible, he tends to be easily overwhelmed by a feeling of "I can't." The quality of his work does not necessarily suffer, but he himself always does.

The self-effacing types may feel fairly at ease and in fact work well as long as they work for others: as a housewife or housekeeper, as a secretary, as a social worker or teacher, as a nurse, as a pupil (for an admired teacher). In this case either one of two frequently observed peculiarities may point to an existing disturbance. There may be marked differences between their working alone and their working with others. An anthropological fieldworker, for instance, can be most resourceful in making contact with the natives but utterly lost when it comes to formulating his findings; the social worker may be competent with clients or as a supervisor but get panicky over making a report or an evaluation; an art student may paint fairly well with his teacher present but forget all he has learned when alone. Secondly, these types may stay at a level of work which is actually beneath their given faculties. And it may never occur to them that they may have hidden a talent in the earth.

Yet for various reasons they may start to do something on their own. They may advance to a position which requires writing or public speaking; their own (unavowed) ambition may push them forward toward more independent activities; or, last but not least, the most healthy and most irresistible reason of all may pertain: their existing gifts may finally urge them toward adequate expression. And it is at this point, when they try to reach beyond the narrow confines set by the "shrinking process" in their structure, that the real troubles start.

On the one hand their demands for perfection are just as high as those of the expansive types. But, while the latter easily basks in the smug satisfaction of excellency attained, the self-effacing types with their unceasing self-berating trends are always alert to flaws in their work. Even after a good performance (perhaps in giving a party or delivering a lecture) they still will emphasize the fact that they forgot this or that, that they did not emphasize clearly what they meant to say, that they were too subdued or too offensive, etc. They thus are pushed into an almost hopeless battle in which they struggle for perfection while at the same time they beat themselves down. In addition the demands for excelling are reinforced from a peculiar source. Their taboos on ambition and pride make them feel "guilty" if they reach out for personal achievements, and only the ultimate attainment is a redemption for this guilt. ("If you are not the perfect musician, you had better scrub floors.")

On the other hand they turn self-destructive if they trespass against these very taboos, or at least if they become aware of doing so. It is the same process I have described with regard to competitive games: as soon as this type becomes aware of winning he cannot play any more. He thus is constantly between the devil and the deep sea, between having to reach the peak and having to keep himself down.

The dilemma is most conspicuous when the conflict between expansive and self-effacing drives is close to the surface. A painter for instance, struck by the beauty of a certain object, visualizes a glorious composition. He starts to paint. The first statement on the canvas looks superb. He feels elated. But then, whether this beginning is too good (for what he could stand) or whether it has not yet reached the perfection of his first vision, he turns against himself. He tries to improve the statement. It turns out worse. At this point he gets frantic. He keeps "improving" but the colors become duller and deader. And in no time the picture is destroyed; he gives up in utter despair. After a while he starts another picture, only to go through the same agonizing process.

Similarly a writer may write fluently for a while, until he becomes aware that things have proceeded very well indeed. At this point—without of course knowing that his very satisfaction was the point of danger—he becomes faultfinding. Perhaps he really has run up against a difficulty as to how his main character should act in a particular situation; perhaps, however, the difficulty merely appeared great because he was already hampered by a destructive self-contempt. At any rate he becomes listless, cannot get himself to work for some days, and in a fit of rage tears the last pages to shreds. He may have a nightmare in which he is caught in a room with a maniac who is out to kill him—a pure-and-simple expression of murderous rage against himself.[2]

In these two instances, which could easily be multiplied, we see two distinct moves: a forward creative mood and a self-destructive one. Turning now to the persons in whom expansive drives are suppressed and self-effacing ones prevail, clear forward moves become extremely rare and the self-destructive

---

[2] When in the paper on "Inhibitions in Work" I cited these two examples I mentioned only the response to not having attained the expected excellency.

ones are less violent and dramatic. The conflicts are more hidden, the whole inner process going on during work is more chronic and more intricate—which makes it more difficult to disentangle the factors involved. Although in these cases the disturbances in work may be the outstanding complaint, they may not be directly accessible to understanding. Their nature may only gradually become clearer, after the whole structure has loosened up.

What the person himself notices while doing creative work is his lack of concentration. He easily loses his trend of thought or his mind goes blank; his thoughts wander off to all kinds of daily occurrences. He becomes fidgety, restless, doodles, plays solitaire, makes some phone calls which could just as well wait, files his fingernails, catches flies. He gets disgusted with himself, makes heroic efforts to work, but in a short time is so deadly fatigued that he has to give up.

Without being aware of it, he is up against two kinds of chronic handicaps: his self-minimizing and his inefficiency in tackling the subject matter. His self-minimizing largely results, as we know, from his need to keep himself down in order not to trespass against the taboo on anything "presumptuous." It is a subtle undermining, berating, doubting, which saps the energies without his being aware of what he is doing to himself. (One patient visualized himself with two ugly vicious dwarfs hunched one on each shoulder and incessantly making nagging, derogatory comments.) He may forget what he has read, observed, thought, or even what he himself has previously written on the subject. He may forget what he was going to write. All the materials out of which to build a paper are there, and they may reappear after much fumbling work, but they may not be available at the moment he needs them. Similarly, when called upon to speak in a discussion, he may start with a crushing feeling of having nothing to say and only gradually will it turn out that he has many pertinent comments to contribute.

His need to keep himself down, in other words, prevents him from tapping his resources. As a result he works with the oppressive feeling of impotence and insignificance. While for the expansive type everything he does assumes a general importance, even though its objective importance may be negligible, the self-effacing type is rather apologetic about his work even though it may have a greater objective importance. Characteristically he will merely say that he "has to" work. In his case this is not an expression of being supersensitive to coercion, as it would be in the resigned type. But he would feel too presumptuous, too ambitious if he admitted that he wished to achieve something. He cannot even *feel* that he wants to do a good job—not only because in fact he is driven by his exacting demands for perfection but also because to own up to such an intention seems to him like an arrogant and reckless challenging of fate.

His inefficiency in tackling the subject matter is caused mainly by his taboos on all that implies assertion, aggression, mastery. As a rule, when speaking of his taboos on aggression, we think of his being not demanding, not manipulating, not dominating toward other people. But the same attitudes also prevail toward inanimate objects or mental problems. Just as he may feel helpless with a flat tire, or with a zipper that is stuck, so he feels helpless toward his own ideas. His difficulty is not in being unproductive. Good original ideas may emerge, but he is inhibited in taking hold of them, tackling them, grappling with them, wrestling with them, checking them, shaping them, organizing them. We are not usually aware of these mental operations as being assertive, aggressive moves, although the language indicates it; and we may realize this fact only when they are inhibited by a pervasive check on aggression. The self-effacing type may not lack the courage to express an opinion whenever, in the first place, he gets far enough to have one. The inhibition usually sets in at an earlier point—in his not daring to realize that he has arrived at a conclusion, or has an opinion, of his own.

These handicaps in themselves make for slow, wasteful, inefficient work or for not accomplishing anything at all. We might remember in this context Emerson's saying that we do not accomplish because we minimize ourselves. But the torment involved—and also the possibility of achieving something, for that matter—occurs because the person is at the same time driven by his need for ultimate perfection. Not only should the quality of the work produced satisfy his exacting demands; his work methods also should be perfect. A music student, for instance, is asked if she works systematically. She becomes embarrassed and answers with an "I don't know." For her, to work systematically means to sit fixed before the piano for eight hours, working intently all the time, hardly taking time off for lunch. Since she cannot give this ultimate of concentrated, sustained attention, she turns against herself and calls herself a dilettante who will never get anywhere. Actually she studies hard at a piece of music, studies the reading, the movements of the right and the left hand—in other words she might well have been entirely satisfied with the seriousness of her work. Having in mind exorbitant shoulds like these, we can easily imagine the amount of self-contempt produced by the self-effacing person's usually ineffectual ways of working. Lastly, to complete the picture of his difficulties: even if he works well, or has accomplished something worth while, he *should not* be aware of it. His left hand, as it were, must not know what his right hand is doing.

He is particularly helpless when initiating some kind of creative work—for instance, beginning the writing of a paper. His aversion to mastering a subject prevents him from planning thoroughly in advance. Hence, instead of first making an outline or fully organizing the material in his mind, he simply starts to write. Actually this may be a feasible way for other sorts of people. The expansive type for instance may be able to do so without hesitation, and his first draft may impress him as so wonderful that he fails to do any further work on it. But the self-effacing type is utterly incapable of simply jotting down a first draft with all the unavoidable imperfections in formulation of thought, style, and organization. He becomes keenly aware of any awkwardness, lack of clarity or continuity, etc. His criticisms may be pertinent in content but the unconscious self-contempt they evoke is so disturbing that he cannot continue. He may tell himself: "Now, for heaven's sake, put it down; you can always work it over later on"—but it is of no avail. He may make a fresh start, write a sentence or two, put down some loose thoughts on the subject. Only then, after much waste of work and time, may he finally ask himself: "Now what actually do you want to write?" Only then will he make a rough outline, then a second with more details, a third, a fourth, etc. Each time the subdued anxiety stemming from his conflicts subsides a little. But when it comes to giving the paper its final shape, ready for delivery or print, the anxiety may again increase, because now it should be flawless.

During this painful process acute anxiety may be aroused for two opposite reasons: he becomes disturbed when things become more difficult and he becomes disturbed when they go too well. Running up against a knotty problem, he may respond with a reaction of shock, become faint and nauseated—or he may feel paralyzed. When on the other hand he becomes aware of proceeding well he may start to sabotage his work more drastically than usual. Let me illustrate so self-destructive a repercussion from the case of a patient whose inhibitions had started to diminish. While about to finish a paper he noticed that some paragraphs at which he had worked had a familiar ring, and he suddenly realized that he must have written them already. Looking over his desk he found indeed a perfectly good draft of the paragraphs, which he had written only the previous day. He had spent almost two hours in formulating ideas which he had already formulated without realizing it. Startled by this "forgetting" and thinking about the reasons for it, he remembered that he had written these passages fairly fluently, that he had taken it for a hopeful sign of now overcoming his inhibitions and of being able to finish the particular paper in a short time. Although these thoughts had a solid foundation in reality, they were more than he could take and he reacted therefore with self-sabotage.

When we realize the terrific odds against which this type works, several peculiarities in his relation to work become clearer. One of them is his being apprehensive or even panicky before starting a piece of work that is difficult for him—a piece of work that, in view of the conflicts involved, presents him with an unrealizable task. One patient for instance regularly got colds before having to give a lecture or attend a conference; another felt sick before first performances on the stage; still another was completely exhausted before doing her Christmas shopping.

Also we come to understand why he can usually work only in installments. The inner tension under which he works is so great and tends so to increase while he works that he cannot stand it for a long time. This applies not only to mental work but may occur in any other work he does on his own. He may put one drawer in order and leave the others for a later date. He may do a little weeding or digging in the garden and then stop. He writes for half an hour, or an hour, but has to interrupt it. The same person, however, may be able to work consistently when he does it for or with others.

Finally we understand why he is so easily distracted from his work. He often accuses himself of not having any real interest in his work, which is understandable enough because he often behaves like a resentful schoolboy working under duress. Actually his interest may be entirely genuine and serious, but the process of work is even more exasperating than he realizes. I mentioned already the minor distractions, such as making a phone call or writing a letter. Moreover, in accordance with his need to please others and to win their affection, he is too easily available for any request which his family or his friends may make. The result sometimes is that, for reasons entirely different from the narcissistic type, he too may scatter his energies in too many directions. And there is lastly, particularly in younger years, the compelling appeal that love and sex have for him. While a love relation does not usually make him happy either, it promises the fulfillment of all his needs. No wonder, then, that he often plunges into a love affair when his difficulties in work become unbearable. Sometimes he goes through a repetitious cycle. He works for a while and may even accomplish something; then gets absorbed in a love relation, sometimes of the dependent type; work recedes or becomes impossible; he struggles out of the love relation, starts again to work—and so forth.

To summarize: any creative work which the self-effacing type does on his own is done against often insurmountable odds. He works not only under fairly permanent handicaps but also— more often than not—under the stress of anxiety. The degree of suffering linked up with such a creative process of course varies. But there are usually only brief intervals in which it is absent. He may enjoy the time when he first conceives of a project and, as it were, plays around with the ideas involved in it, without yet being caught in the pushes and pulls of contradictory inner dictates. He also may have a short-lived glow of satisfaction when the particular work is close to completion. Later on, however, he tends to lose not only the satisfaction of having done it but even the feeling that he was the one who did it, regardless of external success or acclaim. It is humiliating for him to think of it, or look at it, because he does not give himself credit for having accomplished it in spite of the inner difficulties. For him, to remember the very existence of these difficulties is plain humiliation.

Naturally, with all these harassing difficulties, the danger of not accomplishing anything is great. He may not dare to start doing something on his own in the first place. He may give up in the course of work. The quality of the work itself may suffer from the handicaps under which it was produced. But the chances are that, with sufficient gifts and stamina, he may turn out something substantially good because, notwithstanding his often staggering inefficiency, he has put in a great deal of consistent work.

The shackles hampering the work of the *resigned* type are distinctly different in nature from those of the expansive and the self-effacing types. The individual belonging to the group of persistent resignation may also settle for less than his faculties warrant, and in this way resemble the self-effacing type. But the latter does it because he feels safer in a work situation in which he can lean on somebody, feel liked and needed, in addition to abiding by his taboos on pride and aggression. The resigned person settles for less because to do so is part and parcel of his general resigning from active living. The conditions under which he can work productively are also diametrically opposite to those of the self-effacing person. Because of his detachment he can work better alone. And his sensitivity to coercion makes it difficult for him to work for a boss or in an organization with definite rules and regulations. He may, however, "adjust" himself to such a situation. Because of the check he has put on wishes and aspirations, and also because of his aversion to change, he may put up with conditions which are not congenial to him. And, because of his lack of competitiveness and his anxious avoidance of friction, he may be able to get along with most people although in his feelings he keeps strictly apart. But he is neither happy nor productive.

By preference he would be a free-lance worker, if work he must; although here too he feels easily coerced by the expectations of others. A deadline for instance for a publication or the delivery of a design or a dress may be welcome to the self-effacing type because the external pressure relieves his inner pressure. Without a deadline he may feel impelled to improve his product ad infinitum. The deadline makes it permissible to be less exacting and also makes it possible to put his own wish to achieve something, or get something done, on the basis of working for somebody else who expects it. For the resigned type the deadline is coercion which he plainly resents and which may arouse so much unconscious opposition that it makes him listless and inert.

His attitude on this score is but one illustration of his general sensitivity to coercion. This applies to anything that is suggested to him, that is expected, required, or requested of him, or to any necessity confronting him—such as having to put in work if he wants to accomplish something.

Probably the greatest handicap is his inertia, the meaning and manifestations of which we have discussed.[8] The more pervasive it is, the more he tends to do things only in his imagination. The ineffectualness in work resulting from inertia is different from that of the self-effacing type, not only in its determinants but also in its manifestations. The self-effacing person, driven hither and thither by contradictory shoulds, displays a fluttering activity like a bird caught in a cage. The resigned type instead appears listless, without initiative, slow in physical or mental action. He may procrastinate or may have to jot down in a notebook everything he has to do in order not to forget it. But again, in full contrast to the self-effacing type, this picture may be reversed as soon as he does things on his own.

---

[8] *Cf.* Chapter 11, Resignation.

A doctor for instance was able to attend to his duties in a hospital only with the help of a notebook. He had to make a note of every patient to be examined, every conference to be attended, every letter or report to be written, every medicine to be prescribed. But in his free time he was most active in reading books that interested him, in playing the piano, and in doing some writing on philosophical subjects. He did all of this with an alive interest and could enjoy it. Here in the privacy of his room, so he felt, he could be himself. And he had indeed preserved a good deal of the integrity of his real self, yet characteristically had been able to do so only by keeping it out of touch with the world around him. He did the same with his activities in his free time. He did not expect to become an accomplished pianist nor did he plan to publish his writings.

The more such a type comes to rebel against conforming to expectations, the more he tends to cut down any work which is done with or for people or which puts him on a regular schedule. He rather restricts his living standards to a minimum in order to do what he pleases. Such an evolution may give him the possibility of constructive work, provided his real self is sufficiently alive to grow under the condition of greater freedom. He may then find the possibility for creative expression. This would depend however on existing gifts. Not everybody, breaking up his family ties and going to the South Seas, becomes a Gauguin. Without such favorable inner conditions, the danger is that he will merely become a rugged individualist who takes a certain delight in doing the unexpected or in living in a way that is different from the common run of people.

In the group of *shallow living* work presents no problem. It partakes of the deteriorating processes which go on generally. Both the striving toward self-realization and the drive to actualize his idealized self are not only checked but abandoned. Hence work becomes meaningless, because he neither has an incentive to develop his given potentials nor one to pursue exalted goals. Work may become a necessary evil, interrupting the "good time in which one has fun." It may be done because it is expected, without any personal participation. It may sink to a mere means of procuring money or prestige.

Freud saw the frequency of neurotic disturbances in work and recognized their importance by making the capacity to work one of his aims in therapy. But he considered this capacity separately from motivations, aims, attitudes toward work; from conditions under which it can be done and from the quality of the work produced. He recognized therefore only obvious interferences in the process of work. It is one of the general conclusions evolving from the discussion presented here that this way of looking at difficulties in work is far too formalistic. We can grasp the wide range of existing disturbances only when we consider all the factors mentioned. This is but another way of saying that peculiarities and disturbances in work are, and cannot but be, an expression of the total personality.

Still another factor comes into clear relief when we consider in detail all the factors involved in work. We realize that it is not valid to think of neurotic disturbances in work in a general way—i.e., of disturbances occurring in neurosis per se. As I mentioned at the beginning, there are but a few general statements which with caution, reservations, and qualifications can be made for all neuroses. We can have an accurate picture of particular disturbances only when discerning the kinds of difficulty that arise on the basis of different neurotic structures. Each neurotic structure produces its peculiar assets and difficulties in work. This relation is so definite that when we know a particular structure we can—almost!—predict the nature of probable disturbances. And, since in therapy we do not deal with "the" neurotic but with a particular neurotic individual, such an exactness helps us not only to spot the particular difficulties more quickly but also to understand them more thoroughly.

It is difficult to convey the amount of suffering engendered by many neurotic disturbances in work. However, disturbances in work do not always entail conscious suffering; many people are not even aware of having any difficulties in their work. What these disturbances invariably do entail is a waste of good human energies: a waste of energies in the process of work; a waste in not daring to do the work that is commensurate with existing abilities; a waste in not tapping existing resources; and a waste in the impairment of the quality of work produced. For the individual this means that he cannot fulfill himself in an essential area of his life. Multiplying such individual losses by the thousands, disturbances in work become a loss to mankind.

While not disputing the fact of such losses, many people are nevertheless disquieted by the relation between art and neurosis or, more precisely, by that between the creative ability of an artist and his neurosis. "Granted," they will say, "that neurosis makes for suffering in general, and for hardships in work in particular—is it not, however, the indispensable condition for artistic creativity? Are not most artists neurotic? Would it not, conversely, curtail or even destroy his creativity if an artist were analyzed?" We can arrive at least at some clarification if we take these questions apart and examine the elements involved.

To begin with, there is little if any doubt that the existing gifts themselves are independent of neurosis. Recent educational ventures have shown that most people can paint when properly encouraged, but even so not everybody can become a Rembrandt or a Renoir. This does not mean that a gift, if sufficiently great, will always express itself. As these same experiments demonstrate, there is no doubt that neurosis has a considerable share in preventing their expression. The less self-conscious, the less intimidated, the less a person tries to comply with expectations of others, the less his need to be right or perfect, the better he can express whatever gifts he has. Analytic experiences show in still greater detail the neurotic factors which can be a hindrance to creative work.

Thus far the concern about artistic creativity entails either unclear thinking or an underrating of the weight and power of existing gifts, i.e., of the faculties of artistic expression in a particular medium. However, here a second question sets in: granted that the gifts themselves are independent of neurosis, is not the artist's faculty to work creatively tied up to certain neurotic conditions? The path to an answer lies in discerning more clearly exactly which neurotic conditions may be favorable to artistic work. Prevailing self-effacing trends are distinctly unfavorable. And in fact people having these trends are not among those harboring any concern on this score. They know too well—in their blood and bones—that their neurosis clips their wings, that it prevents them from daring to express themselves. Only people with prevailing expansive drives and those belonging to the rebellious group of the resigned type are afraid of losing their faculty for creative work through analysis.

Of what are they really afraid? Putting it into my terminology, they feel that, even though the need for mastery may be neurotic, it is the driving force that gives them the courage and ebulliency to do creative work and that enables them to overcome all the difficulties involved in it. Or they feel that they can create only when rigorously shaking off any bonds tying them to others and refusing to be bothered by others' expectations. Their (unconscious!) fear is that budging an inch from the feeling of godlike mastery would flood them with self-doubts and plunge them into self-contempt. Or in the case of rebellion they feel that, in addition to succumbing to self-doubts, they would become conforming automatons and in this way lose their creative power.

These fears are understandable because the other extremes of which they are afraid are present in them—in the sense of being an actual possibility. Nevertheless the fears are based on false reasoning. We see such oscillating between the extremes in many patients at a time when they are still so caught in neurotic conflicts that they can think only in terms of "either-or" and cannot yet visualize a real resolution of their conflicts. Provided analysis proceeds properly and benefits them, they will have to see and experience self-contempt or the tendency to comply, but will certainly not stay with such attitudes for good. They will overcome the compulsive components of both extremes.

At this point a further argument is raised, which is more thoughtful and more relevant than the others: assuming analysis can resolve neurotic conflicts and make a person happier, would it not also remove so much inner tension that he would simply be content with *being* and would lose the inner urge to create? This argument may have two meanings, neither of which can be discarded lightly. It contains the general contention that an artist needs inner tension or even distress in order to elicit his urge to create. I do not know whether this is generally true—but, even if it is, must all distress necessarily stem from neurotic conflicts? It would seem to me that there is enough distress in life even without them. This is particularly true for an artist, with his greater-than-average sensitivity to beauty and harmony but also to discords and suffering, and with his greater capacity for emotional experiences.

The argument moreover contains the specific contention that neurotic conflicts may constitute a productive force. The reason for taking this contention seriously lies in our experience with dreams. We know that in dreams our unconscious imagination can create solutions for an inner conflict that is disquieting us for the time being. And the images used in dreams are so condensed, so pertinent, so concisely express the essentials that in these regards they resemble artistic creations. Therefore why should not a gifted artist, who commands the forms of expression in his medium and can put in the necessary work, create a poem, a painting, or a piece of music in an equivalent way? Personally I am inclined to believe in such a possibility.

Yet we must qualify such an assumption by the following considerations. In dreams a person can arrive at different kinds of solution. They may be constructive or neurotic ones, with a great range of possibilities in between. This fact cannot be irrelevant for the value of an artistic creation either. We could say that, even if an artist presents only his particular neurotic solution well, he may still find a powerful resonance because there will be many others tending toward the same solution. But I wonder if the general validity of, for instance, what the paintings of Dali or the novels of Sartre have to say is not thereby—despite superb artistic facility and astute psychological understanding—diminished? To avoid misunderstandings: I do not mean that a play or a novel should not present neurotic problems. On the contrary, at a time when most people suffer from them artistic presentation can help many to wake up to their existence and significance and to clarify them in their minds. Nor do I of course mean that plays or novels dealing with psychological problems should have a happy ending. *Death of a Salesman* for instance has no happy ending. *But it does not leave us confused.* It is, in addition to being an indictment of a society and a way of living, a clear statement of what may logically happen to a person going off in his imagination (in the sense of a narcissistic solution) instead of ever squaring himself with his problems. A work of art leaves us confused if we do not sense where the author stands, or if he presents or advocates a neurotic solution as *the* only one.

Perhaps in the consideration just presented there lies an answer to another problem involved. Since neurotic conflicts or their neurotic solutions may paralyze or impair artistic creativity, we could certainly not say without qualifications that they are inducive to it at the same time. Probably by far the majority of such conflicts and solutions has an untoward effect on the artist's work. But where should we draw the line between those conflicts which still may provide a constructive impetus to create and those which stifle or curtail his faculties, or which impair the value of the product of his work? Is the line determined by a mere quantitative factor? We could certainly not say that the more conflicts the artist has the better it is for his work. Is it good for him to have some but not good to have too many? But then where is the line between "some" and "too many"?

Apparently, when thinking in terms of quantity, we are left hovering in the air. The considerations about constructive and neurotic solutions, and what is implied in them, point in another direction. Whatever the nature of the artist's conflicts, he must not be lost in them. Something in him must be sufficiently constructive to inspire him with a wish to struggle out of them and to take a stand toward them. This however is identical with saying that his real self must be sufficiently alive to operate, notwithstanding his conflicts.

It follows from these considerations that the frequently expressed conviction of the value of neurosis for artistic creativity is unfounded. The only tangible possibility that remains is that the artist's neurotic conflicts may contribute to an incentive for his doing creative work. Also his conflicts and his search for a way out of them may be the subject of his work. Just as a painter may for instance express his personal experience of a mountain scene, he may express his personal experience of his inner struggle. But he can create only to the extent to which his real self is alive, giving him the capacity for deep personal experiences and the spontaneous desire as well as the ability to express them. These very faculties however are jeopardized in neurosis through alienation from self.

And here we come to see the flaw in the contention that neurotic conflicts are an indispensable moving force for the artist. They may at best mobilize a temporary incentive, but the creative urge itself and the creative power can stem only from his desire for self-realization and the energies in its service. To the extent to which these energies are shifted from the simple and direct *experiencing* of life to having to *prove* something—that he is something he is not—his creative abilities are bound to be impaired. Conversely an artist may retrieve his productivity when in analysis his desire for (his drive toward) self-realization is liberated. And if the power of this drive had been recognized, the whole argument of the value of neurosis for the artist would never have arisen in the first place. *An artist then creates not because of his neurosis but in spite of it.* "The spontaneity of art . . . is *personal creativeness*, is self-expression." [4]

---

[4] John Macmurray, *Reason and Emotion*, Faber and Faber, Ltd., London, 1935.

CHAPTER 14

THE ROAD OF PSYCHO-ANALYTIC THERAPY

ALTHOUGH neurosis may produce acute disturbances or may at times remain fairly static, it implies in its nature neither the one condition nor the other. It is a *process* that grows by its own momentum, that with a ruthless logic of its own envelops more and more areas of personality. It is a process that breeds conflicts and a need for their solution. But, since the solutions the individual finds are only artificial ones, new conflicts arise which again call for new solutions—which may allow him to function in a fairly smooth way. It is a process which drives him farther and farther away from his real self and which thus endangers his personal growth.

We must be clear about the seriousness of the involvement in order to guard against false optimism, envisioning quick and easy cures. In fact the word "cure" is appropriate only as long as we think of a relief of symptoms, like a phobia or an insomnia, and this as we know can be effected in many ways. But we cannot "cure" the wrong course which the development of a person has taken. We can only assist him in gradually outgrowing his difficulties so that his development may assume a more constructive course. We cannot discuss here the many ways in which the aims of psychoanalytic therapy have been defined.

Naturally for any analyst the aims evolve from what, according to his convictions, he considers the essentials of neurosis. As long for instance as we believed that a disturbance in human relations was the crucial factor in neurosis, we aimed in therapy to help patients to establish good relations with others. Having seen the nature and the importance of intrapsychic processes, we are now inclined to formulate the aim in a more inclusive way. We want to help the patient to find himself, and with that the possibility of working toward his self-realization. His capacity for good human relations is an essential part of his self-realization, but it also includes his faculty for creative work and that of assuming responsibility for himself. The analyst must keep in mind the aim of his work from the very first session to the last, because the aim determines the work to be done and the spirit in which it is done.

In order to arrive at a rough estimate of the difficulties of the therapeutic process we must consider what it involves for the patient. Briefly, he must overcome all those needs, drives, or attitudes which obstruct his growth: only when he begins to relinquish his illusions about himself and his illusory goals has he a chance to find his real potentialities and to develop them. Only to the extent to which he gives up his false pride can he become less hostile to himself and evolve a solid self-confidence. Only as his shoulds lose their coercive power can he discover his real feelings, wishes, beliefs, and ideals. Only when he faces his existing conflicts has he the chance for a real integration—and so forth.

But while this is undeniably true, and clear to the analyst, it is not what the patient feels. He is convinced that his way of life—his solution—is right, and that in this way alone can he find peace and fulfillment. He feels that his pride gives him inner fortitude and worth, that without his shoulds his life would be chaotic, etc. It is easy for the objective outsider to say that all these values are spurious ones. But as long as the patient feels that they are the only ones he has he must cling to them.

Moreover the patient must hold on to his subjective values because not to do so would endanger his whole psychic existence. The solutions he has found for his inner conflicts, briefly characterized by the words "mastery," "love" or "freedom," not only appear to him as right, wise, and desirable ways but as the only safe ones. They give him a feeling of unity; coming face to face with his conflicts entails for him the terrifying prospect of being split apart. His pride not only gives him a feeling of worth or significance but also safeguards him against the equally terrifying danger of being delivered over to his self-hate and self-contempt.

The particular means by which a patient in analysis wards off the realization of conflicts or of self-hate are those which, in accordance with his whole structure, are available to him. The expansive type steers clear of the realization of having any fears, of feeling helpless, of a need for affection, care, help, or sympathy. The self-effacing type most anxiously averts his eyes from his pride or his being out for his own advantage. The resigned type may present an imperturbable front of polite un-interestedness and inertia in order to prevent his conflicts from being mobilized. In all patients the avoidance of conflicts has a double structure: they do not let conflicting trends come to the surface and they do not let any insight into them sink in. Some will try to escape the comprehension of conflicts by intel-lectualizing or by compartmentalizing. In others the defense is even more diffuse and shows in an unconscious resistance to-ward thinking anything through clearly or in holding onto an unconscious cynicism (in the sense of a denial of values). Both the muddled thinking and the cynical attitudes in these cases so befog the issue of conflicts that they are indeed unable to see them.

The central issue in the patient's endeavors to ward off an experience of self-hate or self-contempt is to avoid any realiza-tion of unfulfilled shoulds. In analysis he must therefore fight off any real insight into those shortcomings which according to his inner dictates are unpardonable sins. Therefore any sugges-tion of these shortcomings is felt by him as an unfair accusation and puts him on the defensive. And whether in his defense he becomes militant or appeasing, the effect is the same: it pre-vents him from a sober examination of the truth.

All these stringent needs of the patient to protect his sub-jective values and to ward off dangers—or the subjective feeling of anxiety and terror—account for the impairment of his ability to co-operate with an analyst despite good conscious intentions. They account for the necessity of his being on the defensive.

His defensive attitude so far aims at maintaining the *status quo*.[1] And for most periods of the analytic work this is its outstanding characteristic. For instance in the beginning phase of work with a resigned type the patient's need to preserve intact every bit of his detachment, of his "freedom," of his policy of not-wanting or not-fighting entirely determines his attitudes toward analysis. But in the expansive and the self-effacing types there is, particularly at the beginning, still another force obstructing analytic progress. Just as in their lives they are out for the positive goals of attaining the absolute mastery, triumph, or love, they are out for attaining these very goals in and through analysis. Analysis should remove all impediments to their having an undiluted triumph or a never-failing, magic will power, an irresistible attractiveness, an unruffled saintliness, etc. Hence here it is not simply a question of the patient's being on the defensive but of patient and analyst pulling actively in opposite directions. Although both may talk in terms of evolution, growth, development, they mean entirely different things. The analyst has in mind the growth of the real self; the patient can think only of perfecting his idealized self.

All these obstructive forces operate already in the patient's motivations for seeking analytic help. People want to be analyzed because of some disturbance like a phobia, a depression, a headache, an inhibition in work, sexual difficulties, repeated failures of some kind or other. They come because they cannot cope with some distressing life situation like the infidelity of the marriage partner or his leaving home. They may also come because in some vague way they feel stuck in their general development. All these disturbances would seem to be sufficient reasons for considering analysis and would not seem to require further examination. But for reasons to be mentioned presently we had better ask: *who* is disturbed? The person himself—with his real wishes for happiness and growth—or his pride?

Certainly we cannot make too neat a distinction, but we must

---

[1] This was the definition of "resistance" that I propounded in *Self-Analysis,* Chapter 10, Dealing With Resistances, W. W. Norton, 1939.

be cognizant that pride plays an overwhelming part in making some existing distress intolerable. A street phobia, for instance, may be unbearable for a person because it hurts his pride in mastering every situation. Being deserted by a husband becomes a catastrophe if it frustrates a neurotic claim for a fair deal. ("I have been such a good wife and hence am entitled to his lasting devotion.") The very sexual difficulty which does not disquiet one person is unbearable to him who must be the utmost of "normality." Being stuck in one's development may be so distressing because the claims for effortless superiority do not seem to be working out. The role of pride also shows in the fact that a person may seek help for a minor disturbance which hurts his pride—like blushing, fear of public speaking, the trembling of his hands—while much more handicapping disturbances are passed over lightly and in fact play but a vague part in his resolution to be analyzed.

On the other hand pride may prevent people from going to an analyst—people who need help and could be helped. Their pride in self-sufficiency and "independence" may render it humiliating to consider the prospect of any help. To do so would be an unpermissible "indulgence"; they should be able to cope with their disturbance by themselves. Or their pride in self-mastery may even prohibit an admission of having any neurotic troubles. They may at best come for a consultation to discuss the neurosis of some friend or relative. And the analyst must in these instances be alert to the possibility that this is the only way for them to talk indirectly about their own difficulties. Pride may thus prevent a realistic appraisal of their difficulties and the attaining of help. Of course it is not necessarily a special pride that prohibits their considering analysis. They may be inhibited by any factor stemming from one of the solutions of the inner conflicts. Their resignation for instance may be so great that they would rather reconcile themselves to their disturbances ("I am made this way"). Or their self-effacement may prohibit them from "selfishly" doing something for themselves.

The obstructive forces also operate in what the patient secretly expects of analysis—which I mentioned when discussing the general difficulties of analytic work. To repeat, he expects in part that analysis should remove some disturbing factors without changing anything in his neurotic structure; in part that it should actualize the infinite powers of his idealized self. Furthermore these expectations concern not only the goal of analysis but also the way in which it should be attained. There is rarely, if ever, a sober appreciation of the work to be done. Several factors are involved here. It is of course difficult for anybody to appraise the work who knows analysis only from reading or from occasional attempts to analyze others or himself. But, just as in any other new work, the patient would in time learn what is entailed if his pride did not interfere. The expansive type underrates his difficulties and overrates his capacity to overcome them. With his master mind, or his omnipotent will power, he should be able to straighten them out in no time. The resigned type, paralyzed by his lack of initiative and his inertia, instead expects the analyst to supply miraculous clues while he waits patiently, an interested bystander. The more the self-effacing elements prevail in a patient the more will he expect the analyst to wave a magic wand simply because of his suffering and his pleading for help. All these beliefs and hopes are of course hidden beneath a layer of rational expectations.

The retarding effect of such expectations is fairly obvious. No matter whether the patient expects the analyst's or his own magic powers to bring about the desired results, his own incentive to muster the energies necessary for the work is impaired and analysis becomes a rather mysterious process. Needless to say, rationalized explanations are ineffective because they do not remotely touch the inner necessities determining the shoulds and claims behind them. As long as these tendencies operate, the appeal of short therapies is enormous. Patients overlook the fact that publications about these therapies refer merely to symptomatic changes and they are fascinated by what they mistake for an easy leap into health and perfection.

The forms in which these obstructive forces show during the analytic work vary infinitely. Although a knowledge of them is important for the analyst for the sake of quick recognition, I shall mention only a few of them. And I shall not discuss them at any length, for we are not interested here in analytic technique but in the essentials of the therapeutic process.

The patient may become argumentative, sarcastic, assaultive; he may take shelter behind a façade of polite compliance; he may be evasive, drop the subject, forget about it; he may talk about it with sterile intelligence as if it did not concern himself; he may respond with spells of self-hate or self-contempt, thus cautioning the analyst not to proceed any further—and so on. All these difficulties may appear in the direct work on the patient's problem or in his relationship with the analyst. Compared with other human relationships, the analytic one is in one regard easier for the patient. The analyst's responses to him come comparatively less into play because he is concentrating on understanding the patient's problems. In other regards it is more difficult, because the patient's conflicts and anxieties are stirred up. Nevertheless it is a *human* relationship, and all the difficulties the patient has with regard to other people operate here too. To mention only a few outstanding ones: his compulsive need for mastery, love, or freedom largely determines the tenor of the relationship and makes him hypersensitive to guidance, rejection, or coercion. Because his pride is bound to be hurt in the process, he tends easily to feel humiliated. Because of his expectations and claims, he often feels frustrated and abused. The mobilization of his self-accusations and his self-contempt makes him feel accused and despised. Or, when under the impact of a self-destructive rage, he will quickly become vituperative and abusive toward the analyst.

Lastly, patients regularly overrate the analyst's significance. He is for them not simply a human being who by dint of his training and his self-knowledge may help them. No matter how sophisticated they are, they secretly do regard him as a medicine man endowed with superhuman faculties for good and evil. Both their fears and their expectations combine to produce this attitude. The analyst has the power to hurt them, to crush their pride, to arouse their self-contempt—but also to effect a magic cure! He is in short the magician who has the power to plunge them into hell or to lift them into heaven.

We can appraise the significance of these defenses from several viewpoints. When working with a patient we are impressed with the retarding effect they have on the analytic process. They make it difficult—and sometimes impossible— for the patient to examine himself, to understand himself, and to change. On the other hand—as Freud has recognized, speaking of "resistance"—they are also road signs directing our inquiries. To the extent that we gradually understand the subjective values the patient needs to protect or to enhance, and the danger he is fending off, we learn something about the significant forces operating in him.

Moreover, while the defenses make for manifold perplexities in therapy and—naïvely speaking—the analyst sometimes wishes that there were fewer of them, they also render the procedure much less precarious than it would be without them. The analyst strives to avoid premature interpretations, but since he has no godlike omniscience he cannot prevent the fact that at times more disquieting factors are stirred up in a patient than he is able to cope with. The analyst may make a comment which he considers harmless but the patient will interpret it in an alarmed way. Or, even without such comments, the patient through his own associations or dreams may open up vistas which are frightening without as yet being instructive. Hence, no matter how obstructive in effect the defenses are, they also entail positive factors in so far as they are an expression of intuitive self-protective processes, necessary because of the precarious inner condition created by the pride system.

Any anxiety that does arise during analytic therapy is usually alarming to the patient because he tends to regard it as a sign of impairment. But more often than not this is not so. Its significance can be evaluated only in the context in which it appears. It may mean that the patient has come closer to facing his conflicts or his self-hate than he could stand at the given time. In that case his customary ways of allaying anxiety usually will help him to cope with it. The avenue that seemed to open up closes again; he fails to benefit from the experience. On the other hand an emergent anxiety also may have an eminently positive meaning. For it may indicate that the patient now feels strong enough to take the risk of facing his problems more squarely.

The road of analytic therapy is an old one, advocated time and again throughout human history. In the terms of Socrates and the Hindu philosophy, among others, it is the *road to re-orientation through self-knowledge*. What is new and specific about it is the method of gaining self-knowledge, which we owe to the genius of Freud. The analyst helps the patient to become aware of all the forces operating in him, the obstructive and the constructive ones; he helps him to combat the former and to mobilize the latter. Though the undermining of the obstructive forces goes on simultaneously with the eliciting of the constructive ones, we shall discuss them separately.

When giving a series of lectures [2] on the subjects presented in this book I was asked after the ninth lecture when I was finally going to talk about therapy. My answer was that everything I had said pertained to therapy. All information about possible psychic involvements gives everyone a chance to find out about his own troubles. When similarly we ask here what must the patient become aware of in order to uproot his pride system and all its entails we can simply say that he must become aware of every single aspect of what we have discussed in this book: his search for glory, his claims, his shoulds, his pride, his self-hate, his alienation from self, his conflicts, his particular solution— and the effect of all these factors have on his human relations and his capacity for creative work.

Moreover the patient must not become aware only of these individual factors but also of their connections and interactions. Most relevant on this score is his recognizing that self-hate is pride's inseparable companion and that he cannot have one without the other. Every single factor must be seen in the context of the whole structure. He must realize for instance that his shoulds are determined by his kinds of pride, that their non-fulfillment elicits his self-accusations, and that these in turn account for the need to protect himself from their onslaughts.

Becoming aware of all these factors does not mean having information about them, but having a knowledge of them. As Macmurray says:

---

[2] At the New School for Social Research, in 1947 and 1948.

"This concentration on the object, this indifference to the persons concerned, which is characteristic of the 'information' attitude, is often called objectivity. It is really only impersonality. . . . Information is always information about something, not knowledge of it. Science cannot teach you to know your dog; it can only tell you about dogs in general. You can only get to know your dog by nursing him through distemper, teaching him how to behave about the house and playing ball with him. Of course you can *use* the information that science gives you about dogs in general to get to know your dog better, but that is another matter. Science is concerned with generalities, with more or less universal characteristics of things in general, not with anything in particular. And anything real is always something in particular. In some queer way things depend for the knowledge of them upon our personal interest in them." [8]

But such a knowledge of self implies two things. It is of no help for the patient to have a general idea of his having quite a lot of false pride, or of his being hypersensitive to criticism and failures, or of his tendency to reproach himself, or of his having conflicts. What counts is his becoming aware of the *specific* ways in which these factors operate within him and how in *concrete detail* they manifest themselves in his *particular* life, past and present. It may seem self-evident that it does not help anybody to know, for instance, about shoulds in general or even about the general fact of their operating in himself, and that instead he must recognize their particular content, the particular factors in him making them necessary, and the particular effects they have on his particular life. But the emphasis on the specific and the particular is necessary because for many reasons (his alienation from self, his need to camouflage unconscious pretenses) the patient tends to be either ambiguous or impersonal.

Furthermore his knowledge of himself must not remain an intellectual knowledge, though it may start this way, but must become an *emotional experience*. Both of these factors are closely interwoven because nobody can experience, for instance,

---

[8] John Macmurray, *Reason and Emotion*, Faber and Faber, Ltd., London, 1935, p. 151 ff.

pride in general: he can only experience his particular pride in something definite.[4]

Why then is it important that the patient not only think about the forces in himself but feel them? Because the mere intellectual realization is in the strict sense of the word no "realization" [5] at all: it does not become real to him; it does not become his personal property; it does not take roots in him. What in particular he sees with his intellect may be correct; yet, like a mirror that does not absorb a ray of light but can only reflect it, he may apply such "insights" to others, not to himself. Or his pride in intellect may take over with the speed of lightning in several ways: he becomes proud of having made a discovery which other people shun and shirk; he starts to manipulate the particular problem, to turn and twist it so that in no time his vindictiveness, or his feeling abused, for instance, has become an entirely rational response. Or finally the power of his intellect alone may seem to him sufficient to dispel the problem: seeing *is* solving.

Moreover only when experiencing the full impact in its irrationality of a hitherto unconscious or semiconscious feeling or drive do we gradually come to know the intensity and the compulsiveness of unconscious forces operating within ourselves. It is not enough for a patient to admit the probability that his despair over unrequited love is in reality a feeling of being humiliated because his pride in irresistibility, or in possessing the partner body and soul, is hurt. He must *feel* the humiliation and, later on, the hold which his pride has on him.

---

[4] In the history of psychoanalysis intellectual knowledge at first seemed to be the curative agent. At that time it meant the emergence of childhood memories. The overrating of intellectual mastery also showed at that time in the expectation that the mere recognition of the irrationality of some trend would suffice to set things right. Then the pendulum swung to the other extreme: the emotional experiencing of a factor became all important and has since been stressed in various ways. As a matter of fact this shift in emphasis seems to be characteristic of the progress of most analysts. Each one seems to need to rediscover for himself the importance of emotional experience. *Cf.* Otto Rank and Sandor Ferenczi, *The Development of Psychoanalysis*, Nervous and Mental Disease Publ. No. 40, Washington, 1925. Theodore Reik, *Surprise and the Psychoanalyst*, Kegan Paul, London, 1936. J. G. Auerbach, "Change of Values through Psychotherapy," *Personality*, vol. I, 1950.

[5] According to *Webster*, "realization is the act or process of becoming real."

It is not enough to know vaguely that hi₅ anger or self-reproach is probably greater than warranted by the occasion. He must *feel* the full impact of his rage or the very depths of his self-condemnation: only then does the force of some unconscious process (and its irrationality) stare him in the face. Only then may he have an incentive to find out more and more about himself.

It is also important to feel feelings in their proper context and to try to experience those feelings or drives which as yet are merely seen, not felt. To come back for instance to the example of the woman who was afraid of a dog when she had not been able to climb to the mountain top—the fear itself was felt in its full intensity. What helped her over this particular fear was the realization that it resulted from self-contempt. Although the latter was barely experienced, her discovery meant all the same that the fear was felt in its proper context. But other kinds of fear kept occurring as long as she did not feel the depth of her self-contempt. And the experience of self-contempt in turn helped only when she felt it in the context of her irrational demands on herself for mastering every difficulty.

The emotional experiencing of some hitherto unconscious feeling or drive may occur suddenly and then impress us as a revelation. More often it occurs gradually, in the process of seriously working at a problem. A patient may become cognizant first, for instance, of an existing irritability containing vindictive elements. He may spot a connection between this condition and hurt pride. But at some point he must experience the whole intensity of his feeling hurt and the emotional impact of the vindictiveness. Again he may first spot feeling more indignant or abused than the occasion warrants. He may recognize that these feelings were his responses to being disappointed in some expectation. He takes cognizance of the analyst's suggestion that they may be unreasonable but he himself considers them entirely legitimate. Gradually he will spot expectations which strike even him as unreasonable. Later on he realizes that they are not harmless wishes but rather rigid claims. He will discover in time their scope and their fantastic nature. Then he will experience how utterly crushed or how furiously indignant he is when they are frustrated. At last their inherent power dawns on him. But all of this is still a far cry from feeling that he would rather die than give them up.

A last illustration: he may know that he regards it as most desirable to "get by" or that sometimes he likes to fool or cheat others. As his awareness on this score widens, he may realize how envious he is of others who "get by" with something better than he does or how furious he is when he is the one who is fooled or cheated. He will increasingly recognize how proud he actually is of his capacity to cheat or bluff. And at some point he must also feel in his very bones that it actually is an absorbing passion.

What, however, if the patient simply does not feel certain emotions, urges, longings—or whatever? We cannot after all induce feelings artificially. It is of some help, however, if both patient and analyst are convinced of the *desirability* of letting feelings emerge—whatever they may concern—and letting them emerge in their given intensity. This will alert both of them to the differences between mere brainwork and emotional participation. Besides it will arouse their interest in analyzing the factors interfering with emotional experiences. These may vary in extent, intensity, and kind. It is important for the analyst to ascertain whether they prevent the experiencing of all feelings or only of particular ones. Outstanding among them is the patient's inability or scant ability to experience anything with *suspended judgment*. It dawned upon one patient who believed himself the ultimate of considerateness that he could be unpleasantly domineering. Then he rushed in with a value judgment, that this attitude was wrong and that he must stop it.

Such responses look like taking a square stand against a neurotic trend and wanting to change it. Actually in such instances patients are caught between the wheels of their pride and their fear of self-condemnation, and therefore try to erase the particular trends hastily before they have had time to realize and experience them in their intensity. Another patient, who had a taboo on accepting or taking advantage of others, discovered that buried under his overmodesty was a need to look out for his own advantage; that in fact he was furious if he did not get something out of a situation, that he got sick every time he was with people who in some ways important for him were better off than he. Then again, with the swiftness of lightning, he jumped to the conclusion that he was utterly obnoxious—and thereby nipped in the bud a possible experience and a subsequent understanding of suppressed aggressive trends. The door also was closed to a realization of an existing conflict between a compulsive "unselfishness" and an equally greedy acquisitiveness.

People who have thought about themselves and perceived quite a few inner problems and conflicts often say: "I know so much (or even all) about myself, and it has helped me to get myself under better control; but at bottom I still feel just as insecure or miserable." Usually in such instances it turns out that their insights were both too one sided and too superficial; i.e., it was not an awareness in the deep and comprehensive sense just presented. But assuming that a person has really experienced some important forces operating in himself and has seen their effects on his life, how and to what an extent do these insights in themselves help to liberate him? They may of course at times upset him and at others relieve him, but what do they actually change in a personality? Offhand, this question may seem too general to allow for a satisfactory answer. But I suspect that we all tend to overrate their therapeutic effect. And, since we want to make clear exactly what the therapeutic agents are, let us examine the changes which are brought about by such realizations—their possibilities and their limitations.

Nobody can acquire knowledge of his pride system and his solutions without some reorientation going on within him. He begins to realize that certain ideas he has had about himself were fantastic. He begins to doubt whether his demands upon himself are not perhaps impossible of attainment for any human being, whether his claims on others, besides resting on shaky foundations, are not simply unrealizable.

He begins to see that he was inordinately proud of certain attributes which he does not possess—or at least not to the extent he believed—that for instance his independence, of which he was so proud, is rather a sensitivity to coercion than a real inner freedom; that in fact he is not so immaculately

honest as he saw himself because he is shot through with unconscious pretenses; that with all his pride in mastery he is
not even master in his own house; that a good deal of his love
for people (which made him so wonderful) results from a compulsive need to be liked or admired.

Finally he begins to question the validity of his set of values
and of his goals. Perhaps his self-reproaches are not simply a
sign of his moral sensitivity? Perhaps his cynicism is not an
indication of his being above common prejudice but merely
an expedient escape from squaring himself with his beliefs?
Perhaps it is not sheer worldly wisdom to regard everybody else
as a crook? Perhaps he loses a great deal through his detachment? Perhaps mastery or love is not the ultimate answer to
everything?

All such changes can be described as a gradual work of reality-
testing and value-testing. Through these steps the pride system
is increasingly undermined. They are all necessary conditions
for the reorientation which is the aim of therapy. But so far
they are all *disillusioning processes*. And they alone could not
and would not have a thorough and lasting liberating effect (if
any) if constructive moves did not set in simultaneously.

When in the early history of psychoanalysis psychiatrists began to consider analysis as a possible form of psychotherapy,
some advocated the point of view that a synthesis would have
to follow the analysis. They granted, as it were, the necessity to
tear something down. But, after this was done, the therapist
must give his patient something positive by which he could live,
in which he could believe, or for which he could work. While
such suggestions probably arose out of a misunderstanding of
analysis and contained many fallacies, they were nevertheless
prompted by good intuitive feelings. Actually these suggestions
are more pertinent for the analytic thinking of our school than
for that of Freud, because he did not see the curative process as
we see it: as concerning something obstructive to be relinquished in order to give something constructive the possibility
to grow. The main fallacy in the old suggestions was in the role
they ascribed to the therapist. Instead of trusting the patient's

own constructive forces they felt that the therapist should in a rather artificial way, like a *deus ex machina*, provide for a more positive way of living.

We have come back to the ancient medical wisdom that curative forces are inherent in the mind as they are in the body, and that in cases of disorders of body or mind the physician merely gives a helping hand to remove the harmful and to support the healing forces. *The therapeutic value of the disillusioning process lies in the possibility that, with the weakening of the obstructive forces, the constructive forces of the real self have a chance to grow.*

The task of the analyst in supporting this process is rather different from that in analyzing the pride system. The latter work requires, besides a training in technical skills, an extensive knowledge of possible unconscious complexities and personal ingenuity in discovering, understanding, connecting. To help the patient to find himself the analyst also needs a knowledge, to be gained by experience, of the ways in which—through dreams and other channels—the real self may emerge. Such knowledge is desirable because these ways are not at all obvious. He must also know when and how to enlist the patient's conscious participation in this process. But more important than any of these factors is that of the analyst himself being a constructive person and having a clear vision of his ultimate goal as that of helping the patient to find himself.

There are healing forces operating in the patient from the very beginning. But at the onset of analysis they are usually deficient in vigor and must be mobilized before they can provide any real help in combating the pride system. Hence at the beginning the analyst must simply work with the good will or positive interest in analysis that is available. For whatever reasons the patient is interested in getting rid of certain disturbances. Usually (again for whatever reasons) he does want to improve this or that: his marriage, his relation with his children, his sexual functions, his reading, his capacity for mental concentration, his social ease, his earning capacity, etc. He may have an intellectual curiosity about analysis or even about himself; he may want to impress the analyst with the originality of his mind or the swiftness with which he gains insight; he may want to please, or be the perfect patient. Also the patient may initially be willing or even eager to co-operate in the analytic work because of his expectations of his or the analyst's power to bring about a magic cure. He may for instance realize the mere fact of his being overcompliant or overgrateful for any attention paid him—and he is "cured" of it right away. These kinds of incentive would not carry him through upsetting periods of analytic work, but they are sufficient for the initial phase, which mostly is not too difficult anyway. In the meantime he learns a few things about himself and develops an interest on more solid grounds. It is as necessary for the analyst to make use of these motivations as it is to be clear about their nature—and to decide upon the proper time to make these unreliable incentives themselves an object of analysis.

It would appear most desirable to start mobilizing the real self early in the analytic work. But whether such attempts are feasible and meaningful depends, as does everything, on the patient's interest. As long as his energies are bent on consolidating his self-idealization, and consequently on keeping down his real self, these attempts are liable to be ineffective. However our experience on this score is brief and there may be many more roads accessible then we now envision. The greatest help at the beginning, as well as later on, comes from the patient's dreams. I cannot develop here our theory of dreams. It must suffice to mention briefly our basic tenets: that in dreams we are closer to the reality of ourselves; that they represent attempts to solve our conflicts, either in a neurotic or in a healthy way; that in them constructive forces can be at work, even at a time when they are hardly visible otherwise.

From dreams with constructive elements the patient can catch a glimpse, even in the initial phase of analysis, of a world operating within him which is peculiarly his own and which is more true to his feelings than the world of his illusions. There are dreams in which the patient expresses in symbolic form the sympathy he feels for himself because of what he is doing to himself. There are dreams which reveal a deep well of sadness, of nostalgia, of longing; dreams in which he is struggling to come alive; dreams in which he realizes that he is imprisoned and wants to get out; dreams in which he tenderly cultivates a growing plant or in which he discovers a room in his house of which he did not know before. The analyst will of course help him to understand the meaning of what is expressed in symbolic language. But in addition he may emphasize the significance of the patient's expressing in his dreams feelings or longings which he does not dare to feel in waking life. And he may raise the question of whether, for instance, the feeling of sadness is not more truly what the patient does feel about himself than the optimism he displays consciously.

In time other approaches are possible. The patient himself may start to wonder about how little he knows about his feelings, his wishes, or his beliefs. The analyst will then encourage such puzzled feelings. In whatever way he does it the much-misused word "natural" seems appropriate. For it is indeed natural for man—it is in his nature—to feel his feelings, to know his wishes or beliefs. And there is reason to wonder when these natural capacities do not function. And if the wonder is not volunteered the analyst may initiate such questioning at the proper time.

All of this may seem very little. But not only does the general truth that wondering is the beginning of wisdom obtain here; it is, to be more specific, important that the patient become aware of his remoteness from himself instead of being oblivious to it. The effect is to be compared with the moment when a youngster who has grown up under a dictatorship learns of a democratic way of living. The message may penetrate immediately or it may be received with skepticism because democracies have been discredited. Nevertheless it may gradually dawn on him that he is missing out on something desirable.

For a while such occasional comments may be all that is necessary. Only when the patient has become interested in the question "Who am I?" will the analyst more actively try to bring to his awareness how little he does know or care about his real feelings, wishes, or beliefs. As an illustration: a patient is frightened when he sees even a minor conflict in himself. He is afraid of being split apart and of going insane. The problem has been tackled from several angles, such as his feeling safe only when everything is under the control of reason or his fear that any minor conflict will weaken him for his fight against the outside world, which he perceives as hostile. By focusing on the real self, the analyst can point out that a conflict may either be frightening because of its magnitude or because there is as yet too little of the patient's real self operating for him to cope with even a minor conflict.

Or let us say that a patient cannot decide between two women. As the analysis proceeds it becomes increasingly clear that he has the greatest difficulty in committing himself in any situation, no matter whether it concerns women or ideas, jobs or living quarters. Again the analyst can approach the problem from various angles. At first, as long as the general difficulty is not apparent, he has to find out what is involved in the particular decision. As the pervasiveness of the indecision comes into relief he may uncover the patient's pride in managing to have everything—to have his cake and eat it too—and hence his feeling that the necessity for a choice is a disgraceful comedown. From the standpoint of the real self, on the other hand, he would suggest that the patient cannot commit himself because he is too remote from himself to know his preferences and his directions.

Again a patient complains about his compliance. Day in and day out he promises or does things he does not care for simply because others want or expect them. Here too, according to the context at the given time, the problem may be tackled from many vantage points: his having to avoid friction, his placing no value on his own time, his pride in being able to do every thing. However the analyst can simply raise the question: "Has it never occurred to you to consult yourself about what you want or deem right?" Besides mobilizing the real self in such indirect ways, the analyst will not lose an opportunity to encourage explicitly any sign the patient gives of greater independence in his thinking or feeling, of assuming responsibility for himself, of being more interested in the truth about himself, of catching on by himself to his pretenses, his shoulds, his externalizations. This would include the encouraging of every attempt at self-analysis in between analytic sessions. Moreover the analyst will show, or underline, the specific influence such steps have upon the patient's human relations: his being less afraid of others, less dependent upon them, and hence being better able to have friendly or sympathetic feelings for them.

Sometimes the patient needs hardly any encouragement because he feels freer and more alive anyway. Sometimes he tends to minimize the importance of the steps taken. The tendency to make light of them must be analyzed because it may indicate a fear concerning the emergence of the real self. In addition the analyst will raise the question as to what made it possible at this point to be more spontaneous, to make a decision, or to be active in his own behalf. For this question may open up an understanding of the factors relevant to the patient's courage to be himself.

As the patient comes to have a little firm ground on which to stand he becomes more capable of *grappling with his conflicts*. This does not mean that the conflicts only now become visible. The analyst has seen them long before, and even the patient has perceived signs of them. The same is true as for any other neurotic problem: the process of becoming aware of it, with all the steps it entails, is a gradual one and the work at it goes on throughout analysis. But without a diminution of the alienation from self the patient cannot possibly experience such conflicts as *his* and wrestle with them. As we have seen, many factors contribute to make the realization of conflicts a disruptive experience. But among them the alienation from self is outstanding. The simplest way of understanding this connection is to visualize a conflict in terms of interpersonal relations. Let us assume that a person is intimately associated with two people—father and mother, or two women—who try to pull him in opposite directions. The less he knows his own feelings and beliefs the more easily will he be swayed back and forth, and he may go to pieces in the process. And, vice versa, the more firmly he is rooted in himself the less wear and tear will he suffer from such opposite pulls.

The ways in which patients gradually become aware of their conflicts vary greatly. They may be or become aware of divided feelings with regard to particular situations—such as ambivalent feelings toward a parent or a marriage partner—or of contradictory attitudes with regard to sexual activities, or to schools of thought. A patient may for instance become aware of both hating his mother and being devoted to her. It looks as if he were aware of a conflict, even though merely with regard to one particular person. But actually this is the way he visualizes it: on the one hand he feels sorry for his mother because, being the martyr type, she is always unhappy; on the other hand he is furious at her on account of her stifling demands for exclusive devotion. Both would be most understandable reactions for the kind of person he is. Next, what he has conceived as love or sympathy becomes clearer. He should be the ideal son and should be able to make her happy and contented. Since this is impossible he feels "guilty" and makes up with redoubled attention. This should (as next appears) is not restricted to this one situation; there is no situation in life where he should not be the *absolute* of perfection. Then the other component of his conflict emerges. He is also quite a detached person, harboring claims to have nobody bother him or expect things of him and hating everybody who does so. *The progress here is from attributing his contradictory feelings to the external situation* (the character of the mother), to *realizing his own conflict* in the particular relationship, *finally to recognizing a major conflict within himself* which, because it is within him, operates in all spheres of his life.

Other patients may at first have mere flashes of sighting contradictions of their main philosophy of life. A self-effacing type for instance may suddenly realize that there is in him quite a lot of contempt for people or that he rebels against having to be "nice" to others. Or he may have a fleeting recognition of having extravagant claims for special privileges. While at first these have not struck him even as contradictions, to say nothing of conflicts, he gradually realizes that they are indeed contradictory to his overmodesty and to his liking everybody. Then he may have transient experiences of a conflict, such as a blinding rage at himself for being a "sucker" when the returns of "love" for his compulsive helpfulness fail to come. He is completely stunned—and the experience submerges. Next his taboo on pride and advantages may come into clear relief, so rigid and so irrational that he starts to wonder about it. As his pride in goodness and saintliness is undermined he may begin to recognize his envy of others; to see some calculating greediness for self-gain, or the way he grudges giving. In part the process going on in him can be described as a growing familiarity with the existence of contradictory trends within himself. This alone accounts to some extent for the way in which the shock of seeing them is gradually mitigated. More important dynamically is his growing so much stronger through all the analytic work that he can gradually face these trends without being basically shaken—and hence is able to work at them.

Again, other patients may become cognizant of a conflict within themselves so vague in its contours, so unsettled in its meaning that at first it remains incomprehensible. They may speak of a conflict between reason and emotion or of one between love and work. It is inaccessible in this form because love is not incompatible with work, nor is reason with emotion. The analyst cannot tackle it directly in any way. He merely takes cognizance of the fact that some conflict must be operating in these spheres. He keeps it in mind and tries to understand gradually what is involved for the particular patient. Again patients may not at first feel it as a personal conflict but may relate it to existing situations. Women for instance may put the conflict between love and work on the basis of cultural conditions. They may point out that it is in fact difficult for a woman to combine a career with being a wife and a mother. Gradually it may come home to them that they have a personal conflict on this score and that it is more relevant than existing external difficulties. To make a long story short: in their love life they may tend toward a morbid dependency while in their career they may show all the earmarks of neurotic ambition and a need for triumph. These latter trends are usually suppressed but sufficiently alive to allow them a measure of productivity —or at least of success. In theoretical terms they have tried to relegate their self-effacing trends to their love life and their expansive drives to their work. In actual fact so neat a division is not feasible. And it will become apparent in analysis that, roughly, a drive for mastery also operates in their love relations, as do self-abnegating trends in their careers—with the result that they have become increasingly unhappy.

Patients may also frankly present what appears to the analyst as blatant contradictions in their ways of life or in their sets of values. They may first show an aspect of themselves that is all sweetness and light, overcompliance, even abjectness. Then a drive for power and prestige may come to the fore, showing for instance in a craving for social prestige or for conquering women, with distinct undercurrents of sadism and callousness. At times they may express a belief that they cannot sustain a grudge and at others—*without being disquieted by the contradiction*—have rather savage spells of vindictive rage. Or on the one hand they may want to attain through analysis a capacity for revenge that is undisturbed by any emotions and on the other the saintly detachment of a hermit. But they simply have no understanding whatever that these attitudes, drives, or beliefs constitute conflicts. They are instead proud of being capable of a wider range of feelings or beliefs than people following the "narrow path of virtue." The compartmentalization is carried to extremes. But the analyst cannot tackle it directly because the need to maintain this fragmentation requires an unusual amount of dulling of the sense of truth and of value, of discarding the evidence of reality, of shunning any responsibility for self. Here too the meaning and the power of expansive and self-effacing drives will gradually come into clearer relief. But this alone is of no avail unless much work is done at their evasiveness and their unconscious dishonesty. This usually entails work at their extensive and tenacious externalizations, at their fulfilling their shoulds in imagination only, and at their ingenuity in finding and believing in flimsy excuses as a protection against their self-accusations. ("I have tried so hard, I am sick, I am harassed by so many troubles, I don't know, I am helpless, it is already much better," etc.) All these measures allow them a kind of inner peace but also tend to weaken their moral fiber as life goes on, and thus to make them more incapable of facing their self-hate and their conflicts. These problems require long-drawn-out work, but thereby the patients may gradually gain sufficient solidity to dare to experience and to grapple with their conflicts.

To summarize: conflicts, because of their disrupting nature, are blurred at the beginning of analytic work. Provided they are seen at all, it may be only in relation to specific situations— or they may be visualized in too vague, general forms. They may emerge in flashes, too short lived to acquire new meaning. They may be compartmentalized. Changes on this score take place in these directions: they come closer home as conflicts and as *their* particular conflicts; and they come down to essentials: instead of seeing only remote manifestations patients start to see exactly what is conflicting in them.

While this work is hard and upsetting, it is also liberating. Instead of a rigid solution there are now conflicts accessible to analytical work. The particular main solution, the value of which has been in process of deflation all along, finally collapses. Furthermore unfamiliar or little-developed aspects of the personality have been uncovered and given an opportunity to develop. To be sure, what emerge first are still more neurotic drives. But this is useful, for the self-effacing person must first see his self-seeking egocentricity before he has a chance for healthy assertiveness; he must first experience his neurotic pride before he can approximate a real self-respect. Conversely the expansive type must first experience his abjectness and his need for people before he can develop genuine humility and tender feelings.

With all this work well under way, the patient now can tackle more directly the most comprehensive conflict of all— that between his pride system and his real self, between his drive to perfect his idealized self and his desire to develop his given potentials as a human being. A gradual line-up of forces occurs, the central inner conflict comes into focus, and it is the foremost task of the analyst in the ensuing time to see to it that it stays in sharp focus because the patient himself is liable to lose sight of it. With this line-up of forces a most profitable but also most turbulent period of analysis sets in, varying in degree and duration. The turbulence is a direct expression of the violence of the inner battle. Its intensity is commensurate with the basic importance of the issue at stake. It is at bottom this question: does the patient want to keep whatever is left of the grandeur and glamor of his illusions, his claims, and his false pride or can he accept himself as a human being with all the general limitations this implies, and with his special difficulties but also with the possibility of his growth? There is, I gather, no more fundamental crossroad situation in our life than this one.

This period is characterized by ups and downs, often in rapid succession. At times the patient is on the forward move, which may show in a great variety of ways. His feelings are more alive; he can be more spontaneous, more direct; he can think of constructive things to do; he feels more friendly or sympathetic to others. He becomes more alert to the many aspects of his alienation and catches on to them on his own. He may for instance quickly recognize when he is not "in" a situation or when, instead of facing something in himself, he is blaming others. He may realize how little he has actually done on his own behalf. He may remember incidents in the past when he has been dishonest or cruel with a more somber judgment and with regret, but without crushing guilt-feelings. He begins to see something good in himself, to become aware of certain existing assets. He may give himself due credit for the tenacity of his strivings.

This more realistic appraisal of himself may also appear in dreams. In one of these a patient appeared in the symbol of summer cottages, which were delapidated because they had not been lived in for a long time but which were nevertheless of good material. Another dream indicated attempts to get out of assuming responsibility for self, but in the end a forthright recognition of it: the patient saw himself as an adolescent boy who, just for fun, folded up another boy in a suitcase. He did not mean to hurt him nor did he feel any hostility toward him, but he simply forgot him and the boy died. The dreamer tried to make a halfhearted escape, but then an official talked to him and showed him in a very human way the plain facts and consequences.

These constructive periods are followed by *repercussions* in which the essential element is a renewed onrush of self-hate and self-contempt. These self-destructive feelings may be experienced as such or they may be externalized through becoming vindictive—feeling abused or having sadistic or masochistic fantasies. Or the patient may but vaguely recognize his self-hate but sharply feel the anxiety with which he responds to the self-destructive impulses. Or finally not even the anxiety appears as such, but his customary defenses against it—such as drinking, sexual activities, a compulsive need for company, or being grandiose or arrogant—become active again.

All these upsets follow real changes for the better, but in order to evaluate them accurately we must consider the solidity of the improvement and the factors precipitating the "relapses."

There is the possibility that the patient will overrate the progress that he has made. He forgets, as it were, that Rome was not built in a day. He goes on what I jokingly call a "binge of health." Now that he can do many things he could not do before he should be—and is, in his imagination—the perfectly adjusted specimen, the perfectly healthy specimen. While on the one hand more ready to be himself, he also seizes his very improvement as the last chance to actualize his idealized self in the shining glory of perfect health. And the appeal of this goal is still sufficiently powerful to throw him out of gear—temporarily. A mild elation carries him for a while over still-existing difficulties and makes him all the more certain of now being over all his troubles. But with his general awareness of himself being much greater than before, this condition cannot possibly last. He is bound to recognize that, notwithstanding his actually dealing better with many situations, plenty of old difficulties still persist. And, just because he has believed himself to be on the peak, he strikes out against himself all the harder.

Other patients seem to be sober and cautious in admitting, to themselves and to the analyst, that they have progressed. They rather tend to minimize their improvements, often in a very subtle way. Nevertheless a similar "relapse" may set in when they run up against a problem in themselves or an external situation with which they cannot cope. Here the same process is going on as in the first group, but without the glorifying work of imagination. Both sorts are not yet ready to accept themselves with difficulties and limitations or without unusual assets. Their reluctance may be externalized (I would be ready to accept myself but people loathe me if I am not perfect. They only like me when I am the utmost in generosity, productivity, etc.).

The factor precipitating an acute impairment so far is a difficulty with which the patient cannot yet cope. In a last kind of repercussion the precipitating factor is not a difficulty not yet outgrown but, on the contrary, a definite move forward in a constructive direction. This is not necessarily a spectacular action. The patient may simply feel sympathetic toward himself and experience himself for the first time as being neither particularly wonderful nor despicable but as the struggling and often harassed human being which he really is. It has dawned upon him that "this self-loathing is an artificial product of pride" or that he need not necessarily be a unique hero or genius in order to have any self-respect. A similar change of attitude may also occur in dreams. One patient dreamed of a thoroughbred race horse which now limped and looked bedraggled. But he thought: "I can love him this way too." But after such experiences the patient may become despondent, be unable to work, and feel generally discouraged. It turns out that his pride has rebelled and gotten the upper hand. He has been suffering from an acute spell of self-contempt and resented it as despicable "to set his aims so low" and to indulge in "self-pity."

Often such repercussions occur after a patient has made a well-considered decision and done something constructive in his own behalf. For one patient for instance it meant a step ahead that he was able to refuse a request on his time without feeling irritated or guilty, because he considered the work he was doing more important. Another patient could end a love relationship because she arrived at a square recognition that the relationship had been based mainly on neurotic needs operating in herself and her lover, that it had lost meaning for her and held no promise for the future. She carried out this decision in a firm way and with as little hurt to her partner as possible. In both instances the patients first felt good about their ability to handle the particular situations but soon afterward became panicky; they were scared of their independence, scared of becoming unlikable and "aggressive," called themselves down for being "selfish brutes" and were—for a while—all for retrieving shelter within the safe confines of a self-abnegating overmodesty.

A last illustration requires fuller treatment since it involves a further positive step than these others. The example worked with a considerably older brother in a concern which they had taken over together from their father and had developed successfully. The brother was capable, righteous, dominating, and had many typically arrogant-vindictive trends. My patient had always stood in his shadow, was intimidated by him, adored him blindly and, without knowing it, went out of his way to appease him. During analysis the reverse side of his conflict came to the fore. He became critical of the brother, openly competitive and at times quite belligerent. The brother responded in kind; one reaction reinforced the other and soon they were hardly on speaking terms. The atmosphere in the office became tense; co-workers and employees took sides with one or the other. My patient was glad at first that he could at last "assert" himself against the brother, but he recognized gradually that he was also vindictively out to get him off his high horse. After some months of productive analytic work at his own conflicts, he finally got a broader perspective of the whole situation and could realize that bigger issues were at stake than personal fights and grudges. He saw not only his share in the general tension—but what was considerably more—was ready to assume an active responsibility. He decided to have a talk with the brother, knowing full well that it would not be easy. And in the ensuing talk he was neither intimidated nor vindictive but held his own. Thereby he opened the possibility of a future co-operation on a healthier basis than before.

He knew he had done well and was glad about it. But that very same afternoon he became panicky and felt so nauseated and faint that he had to go home and lie down. He was not exactly suicidal but thoughts flashed through his mind that he could understand why people committed suicide. He tried to understand this condition, re-examined his motives for having the talk and his behavior during it, but could not find anything objectionable. He was entirely bewildered. Nevertheless he was able to sleep and felt much calmer the next morning. Yet he woke up remembering all kinds of insults he had suffered from his brother, with a renewed resentment against him. When we analyzed the upset we saw that he had been hit in two ways.

The spirit in which he had requested the talk with his brother and in which he had carried it through was diametrically opposite to all the (unconscious) values by which he had lived hitherto. From the viewpoint of his expansive drives he *should have been vindictive* and attained a vindictive triumph. On this score he had hurled at himself vituperative accusations for being an appeaser and taking things lying down. On the other hand, from the viewpoint of his remaining self-effacing trends, he *should have been meek* and self-subordinating. So on this score he attacked himself with ridicule: "Little brother wanting to be superior to big brother!" If now in actual fact he had been either arrogant or appeasing, he also might have been upset afterward, though in a lesser degree, and it would not have been in the least puzzling; because any person just struggling out of such a conflict will for a long time to come be very sensitive to residuals of either vindictive or self-effacing trends—i.e., to respond with self-reproaches if they make themselves felt.

The point here, to make it unmistakably clear, is that these self-accusations operated *without* his having been vindictive or appeasing. But he had taken a decisive and positive step away from both tendencies; he had not only acted realistically and constructively but had also gained a real sense of himself and the "context" of his life. That is, he had come to see and *feel* his responsibilities in this difficult situation, not as a burden or pressure but as an integral part of the pattern of his individual life. There he was and there the situation was—and he dealt with it honestly. He had accepted his place in the world and the responsibility that goes with that acceptance.

He had then already acquired sufficient strength to take an actual step toward self-realization, but he had not even begun to square himself with the conflict between the real self and the pride system, which such a step must inevitably stir up. It was the severity of this conflict into which he was suddenly plunged that accounted for the intense repercussion of the previous day.

When in the grip of a repercussion the patient naturally does not know what is going on. He feels simply that he is getting worse. He may feel desperate. Perhaps his improvements were illusory? Perhaps he is too far gone to be helped? He may have fleeting impulses to quit analysis—thoughts which he may never have had before, even in upsetting times. He feels bewildered, disappointed, discouraged.

Actually these are in all instances constructive signs of the patient's grappling with the decision between self-idealization and self-realization. And perhaps nothing else shows so clearly that these two drives are incompatible as the inner struggle going on during the repercussions and the spirit of the constructive moves precipitating them. They do not occur because he sees himself more realistically but because he is willing to accept himself with limitations; not because he can make a decision and do something in his own behalf but because he is willing to heed his real interests and assume responsibility for himself; not because he can assert himself in a matter-of-fact way but because he is willing to assume his place in the world. To put it briefly: *they are growing pains.*

But they yield their full benefits only when the patient becomes aware of the significance of his constructive moves. It is hence all the more important that the analyst does not get bewildered by the seeming relapses but recognizes the swings of the pendulum for what they are and helps the patient to see them. Since the repercussions often set in with predictable regularity, it seems advisable after they have occurred a few times to forewarn the patient when he is on the upward move. This may not forestall the coming repercussions, but the patient may not be quite so helpless before them if he too realizes the predictability of the forces operating at a given time. It helps him to become more objective toward them. It is more relevant than at any other time for the analyst to be an unambiguous ally of the endangered self. If his vision and his stand are clear, then he can give patients the support they so badly need in these trying times. The support consists mostly not of general assurances but of conveying to the patient the fact that he is engaged in a final battle and in showing him the odds against which, and the aims for which, he is fighting.

Each time the meaning of a repercussion is understood by the patient he comes out of it stronger than before. The repercussions gradually become shorter and less intense. Conversely the good periods become more definitely constructive. The prospect of his changing and growing becomes a tangible possibility, within his reach.

But whatever work is still to be done—and there will always be plenty—the time has come close at hand when the patient can try to do it on his own. Just as vicious circles were at work to entangle him more and more deeply in his neurosis, now there are circles working in the reverse direction. If for instance the patient lessens his standards of absolute perfection, his self-accusations also decrease. Hence he can afford to be more truthful about himself. He can examine himself without becoming frightened. This in turn renders him less dependent upon the analyst and gives him confidence in his own resources. At the same time his need to externalize his self-accusations decreases too. So he feels less threatened by others, or less hostile toward them, and can begin to have friendly feelings for them.

Besides, the patient's courage and confidence in his ability to take charge of his own development gradually increase. In our discussions of the repercussions we focused upon the terror that results from the inner conflicts. This terror diminishes as the patient becomes clear about the direction he wants to take in his life. And his sense of direction alone gives him a greater feeling of unity and strength. Yet there is still another fear attached to his forward moves, one which we have not yet fully appreciated. This is a realistic fear of not being able to cope with life without his neurotic props. The neurotic is after all a magician living by his magic powers. Any step toward self-realization means relinquishing these powers and living by his existing resources. But as he realizes that he can in fact live without such illusions, and even live better without them, he gains faith in himself.

Moreover any move toward being himself gives him a sense of fulfillment which is different from anything he has known before. And while such an experience is at first short lived, it may in time recur more and more often and for periods of longer duration. Even at first it gives him a greater conviction of being on the right path than anything else he may think or the analyst can say. For it shows him the possibility of feeling in accord with himself and with life. It is probably the greatest incentive for him to work at his own growth, toward a greater self-realization.

The therapeutic process is so fraught with difficulties of manifold kinds that the patient may not attain the stage described. When carried through successfully it will of course bring about observable improvements in his relation to himself, to others, to his work. These improvements, however, are not the criteria for terminating regular analytic work. For they are but the tangible expressions of a deeper change. And only the analyst and the patient himself are aware of this one: a beginning change of values, of direction, of goals. The fictitious values of the patient's neurotic pride and of the phantoms of mastery, surrender, and freedom have lost much of their fascination and he is more strongly bent on realizing his given potentials. He still has ahead of him much work at hidden kinds of pride, of claims, of pretenses, of externalizations, etc. But, being more firmly grounded in himself, he can recognize them for what they are: a hindrance to his growth. Hence he is willing to discover them and to overcome them in time. And this willingness is now not (or, at least, is less) the frantic impatience to remove imperfections by magic. Having begun to accept himself as he is, with his difficulties, he also accepts the work at himself as an integral part of the process of living.

Putting the work to be done in positive terms, it concerns all that is involved in self-realization. With regard to himself it means striving toward a clearer and deeper experiencing of his feelings, wishes, and beliefs; toward a greater ability to tap his resources and to use them for constructive ends; toward a clearer perception of his direction in life, with the assumption of responsibility for himself and his decisions. With regard to others it means his striving toward relating himself to others with his genuine feelings; toward respecting them as individuals in their own right and with their own peculiarities; toward developing a spirit of mutuality (instead of using them as a means to an end). With regard to work it means that the work itself will become more important to him than the satisfaction of his pride or vanity and that he will aim at realizing and developing his special gifts and at becoming more productive.

While evolving in these ways, he also will sooner or later take a step that goes beyond his merely personal interests. Outgrowing his neurotic egocentricity, he will become more aware of the broader issues involved in his particular life and in the world at large. From having been in his own mind the uniquely significant exception he will gradually experience himself as part of a bigger whole. And he will be willing and able to assume his share of responsibility in it and contribute to it constructively in whatever way he is best able. This may concern— as in the example of the young businessman—the awareness of general issues in the group with which he is working. It may concern his place in the family, in the community, or in a political situation. This step is important not only because it widens his personal horizon but because the finding or accepting of his place in the world gives him the inner certainty which comes from the feeling of belonging through active participation.

CHAPTER 15

THEORETICAL CONSIDER-
ATIONS

THE THEORY of neurosis presented in this book has evolved gradually from the concepts discussed in earlier publications. We have discussed in the previous chapter the implications which this evolution has for therapy. It remains to take stock of the theoretical changes that have occurred in my thinking with regard to individual concepts as well as the whole perspective on neurosis.

Together with many others [1] who had discarded Freud's theory of instincts, I first saw the core of neurosis in human relations. Generally, I pointed out, these were brought about by cultural conditions; specifically, through environmental factors which obstructed the child's unhampered psychic growth. Instead of developing a basic confidence in self and others the child developed basic anxiety, which I defined as a feeling of being isolated and helpless toward a world potentially hostile. In order to keep this basic anxiety at a minimum the spontaneous moves toward, against, and away from others became compulsive. While the spontaneous moves were compatible, each with the others, the compulsive ones collided. The conflicts

---

[1] Like Erich Fromm, Adolph Meyer, James S. Plant, H. S. Sullivan.

generated in this way, which I called basic conflicts, were therefore the result of conflicting needs and conflicting attitudes with regard to other people. And the first attempts at solution were largely attempts at integration, through giving full rein to some of these needs and attitudes and suppressing others.

This is a somewhat streamlined summary because the intrapsychic processes are too closely interwoven with those going on in interpersonal relations for me to have left them out altogether. They were touched upon at various points. To mention but a few: I could not discuss the neurotic's need for affection, or any equivalent need pertaining to others, without considering the qualities and attitudes which he must cultivate within himself in the service of such a need. Again, among the "neurotic trends" I enumerated in *Self-Analysis* there were some which had an intrapsychic meaning, such as a compulsive need for control through will power or reason or a compulsive need for perfection. For that matter, in the discussion of Claire's analysis of her morbid dependency (also in *Self-Analysis*) I dealt in condensed form with many intrapsychic factors presented in the same context in the present book. Nevertheless the focus was decidedly on the interpersonal factors. To me neurosis was still essentially a disturbance in human relationships.

The first explicit step beyond this definition was the contention that conflicts with regard to others could be solved by self-idealization. When, in *Our Inner Conflicts,* I propounded the concept of the idealized image I did not yet know its full significance. I saw it at that time simply as another attempt to solve inner conflicts. And its very integrating function accounted for the tenacity with which people adhered to it.

But in subsequent years the concept of the idealized image became the central issue from which new insights evolved. It actually was the gateway to the whole area of intrapsychic processes presented in this book. Having grown up scientifically with Freud's concepts, I was aware of the existence of this area. But because Freud's interpretations of it made sense to me only in spots it had remained strange territory.

I now saw gradually that the neurotic's idealized image did not merely constitute a false belief in his value and significance; it was rather like the creation of a Frankenstein monster which in time usurped his best energies. It eventually usurped his drive to grow, to realize his given potentialities. And this meant that he was no longer interested in realistically tackling or outgrowing his difficulties, and in fulfilling his potentials, but was bent on actualizing his idealized self. It entails not only the compulsive drive for worldly glory through success, power, and triumph but also the tyrannical inner system by which he tries to mold himself into a godlike being; it entails neurotic claims and the development of neurotic pride.

With these elaborations of the original concept of the idealized image another problem emerged. While focusing on the attitude toward self, I realized that people hated and despised themselves with the same intensity and the same irrationality with which they idealized themselves. These two opposite extremes remained separate in my mind for a while. But finally I saw that they were not only closely interrelated but were in fact two aspects of one process. This then was, in its original draft, the main thesis of this book: *the godlike being is bound to hate his actual being*. With the recognition of this process as an entity, both extremes become more accessible to therapy. The definition of neurosis too had changed. *Neurosis now became a disturbance in one's relation to self and to others.*

Although this thesis remains to some extent the main contention, in recent years it has grown in two directions. The question of the real self, always puzzling to me as to so many others, pushed itself into the foreground of my thought and I came to see the whole inner psychic process, beginning with self-idealization, as a growing alienation from self. More important, I realized that in the last analysis self-hate was directed against the real self. The conflict between the pride system and the real self I called the central inner conflict. This made for an enlargement of the concept of neurotic conflict. I had defined it as a conflict between two incompatible compulsive drives. While retaining this concept, I began to see that it was not the only kind of neurotic conflict. The central inner conflict is one between the constructive forces of the real self and the obstructive forces of the pride system, between healthy growth and the drive to prove in actuality the perfection of the idealized self. Therapy therefore became a help toward self-realization. Through the clinical work of our whole group the general validity of the intrapsychic processes described above became more and more clearly established in our minds.

The body of knowledge also grew as we worked from general to more specific questions. My interest shifted to the variations in different "kinds" of neurosis or of neurotic personalities. At first these appeared as differences in awareness or in accessibility of one or another aspect of the inner processes. Gradually, however, I realized that they resulted from various pseudosolutions of the intrapsychic conflicts. These solutions offered a new—tentative—basis for establishing types of neurotic personalities.

When one arrives at certain theoretical formulations, a wish arises to compare them with those of others working in the same field. How had they seen these problems? For the simple but inexorable reason that time and energies are too limited to do both productive work *and* conscientious reading, I must restrict myself here to pointing out certain similarities to, and differences from, comparable concepts of Freud's. Even so limited a task meets with great difficulties. In comparing individual concepts it is hardly possible to do justice to the subtlety of the thinking by which Freud arrived at certain theories. Moreover, from a philosophic point of view, it is not permissible to tear isolated concepts out of context and then compare them. Hence it is not useful to go into detail, although in the interpretation of details the differences are particularly startling.

When I review the factors involved in the search for glory I have the same experience as before when embarking on a voyage into relatively new areas: I am struck with admiration for Freud's power of observation. It is all the more impressive since he did pioneer work in scientifically unexplored territory and did it against the odds of cramping theoretical premises. There are only a few (although relevant) aspects of it, which he either did not see at all or did not consider important. One of these concerns what I have described as neurotic claims.[2] Freud saw

---

[2] Harald Schultz-Hencke was the first to recognize their significance in neuroses. According to Schultz-Hencke, a person develops unconscious claims because of his fears and his helplessness. The claims in their turn contribute greatly to pervasive inhibitions. Harald Schultz-Hencke, *Schicksal und Neurose,* Gustav Fischer, Jena, 1931.

of course the fact that many neurotic patients were liable to ex-pect an unreasonable amount from others. He also saw that these expectations could be urgent. But, regarding them as an expression of oral libido, he did not realize that they could as-sume the specific character of "claims," i.e., of demands to the fulfillment of which one feels entitled.[8] Nor did he conse-quently realize the key role they play in neurosis. Also, in spite of using the term "pride" in this or that context, Freud was not cognizant of the specific properties and implications of neurotic pride. But Freud did observe belief in magical powers and fan-tasies of omnipotence; infatuation with oneself or with one's "ego ideal"—self-aggrandizement, glorification of inhibitions, etc.; compulsive competitiveness and ambition; the need for power, perfection, admiration, recognition.

These manifold factors which Freud observed remained for him diverse and unrelated phenomena. He failed to see that they were expressions of one powerful current. He did not in other words see the unity in the diversity.

Three main reasons combined to prevent Freud from recog-nizing the impact of the drive for glory and its significance for the neurotic process. To begin with, he was not cognizant of the power of cultural conditions to mold human character—a lack of knowledge which he shared with most European scholars of his time.[4] The implication which interests us in this context is, in simple terms, that Freud mistook the craving for prestige and success, which he saw all around him, for a universal human propensity. Hence for instance a compulsive drive for suprem-acy, dominance, or triumph could not and did not strike him as a problem worth examining, except when such ambition did not fit into the given pattern of what was considered "normal." Freud considered it problematic only when it reached obviously disturbing proportions or when, occurring in women, it did not concur with the given code of "femininity."

Another reason resides in Freud's tendency to explain neu-

---

[8] The only place where Freud remotely saw something resembling claims was in the context of the so-called secondary gains from illness, which in itself is a most dubious concept.

[4] Cf. Karen Horney, *New Ways in Psychoanalysis*, Chapter 10, Culture and Neurosis, W. W. Norton, 1939.

rotic drives as libidinal phenomena. Thus self-glorification was an expression of a libidinal infatuation with self. (A person overrates himself as he may overrate another "love-object." An ambitious woman "really" suffers from "penis-envy." A need for admiration is a need for "narcissistic supplies," etc.) As a result the inquiry in theory and therapy was directed toward particulars of the love life past and present (i.e., libidinal relation to self and others) and not toward the specific qualities, functions, and effects of self-glorification, ambition, etc.

The third reason lies in Freud's evolutionistic-mechanistic thinking. "It implies that present manifestations not only are conditioned by the past, but contain nothing but the past; nothing really new is created in the process of development: what we see today is only the old in a changed form." [5] It is, according to William James, "really nothing more than the results of the redistribution of the original and unchanged materials." On the grounds of this philosophical premise, excessive competitiveness is satisfactorily explained if it is seen as the result of an unresolved Oedipus complex, or of sibling-rivalry. Fantasies of omnipotence are regarded as a fixation on, or a retrogression to, the infantile level of "primary narcissism," etc. It is consistent with this viewpoint that only those interpretations are and can be considered "deep" and satisfactory which established a connection with infantile experiences of a libidinal kind.

From my viewpoint the therapeutic effects of interpretations of this kind are limited, if not positively obstructive to important insights. Let us assume for instance that a patient has become aware that he tends too easily to feel humiliated by the analyst; he also realizes that in approaching women he is in constant dread of humiliation. He does not feel as virile or as attractive as other men. He may remember scenes when he was humiliated by his father, perhaps in connection with sexual activities. On the grounds of many detailed dates like these from the present and the past, and of dreams, interpretations are given along these lines: that for the patient the analyst, as well as other authoritative figures, represents the father; that in feeling humiliated, or in his fear thereof, the patient still responds

---

[5] Quoted from Karen Horney, *New Ways in Psychoanalysis*, Chapter 2, Some General Premises of Freud's Thinking.

according to the infantile pattern of an unresolved Oedipus complex.

As a result of this work the patient may feel relieved and the feelings of humiliation may be lessened. In part he has in fact benefited from this piece of analysis. He has learned a few things about himself and has realized that his feeling humiliated is irrational. But without his pride being tackled the change cannot possibly be a thorough one. On the contrary it is likely that the surface improvement is largely due to the fact that his pride will not tolerate his being irrational and particularly his being "infantile." The likelihood is that he merely has developed a new set of shoulds. He *should not* be infantile and *should* be mature. He should not feel humiliated because it is infantile to do so; so he does no longer feel humiliated. In this way a seeming progress can in reality be an obstruction to the patient's growth. His feeling of being humiliated is driven underground, and the possibility of his squaring himself with it is considerably lessened. Therapy has thus made use of the patient's pride instead of working against it.

Because of all the theoretical reasons mentioned, Freud could not possibly see the impact of the search for glory. Those factors in the expansive drives which he did observe were not what they seemed to be but were "really" derivatives of infantile libidinal drives. His way of thinking prevented him from appreciating expansive drives as forces carrying their own weight and having their own consequences.

This statement becomes clearer when we compare Freud with Adler. It was Adler's great contribution to realize the importance for neuroses of drives for power and superiority. Adler, however, was too preoccupied with devices of how to gain power and how to assert superiority to realize the depths of distress entailed for the individual, and hence stayed too much on the surface of the problems involved.

We are struck offhand by much greater similarities between my concept of self-hate and Freud's postulation of a self-destructive instinct, the death instinct. At least here we find the same appreciation of the intensity and significance of self-destructive drives. Also certain details are viewed similarly, such as the self-destructive character of inner taboos, of self-accusations and resultant guilt-feelings. Nevertheless in this area too there are significant differences. The instinctual character of self-destructive drives, as assumed by Freud, gives them the stamp of finality. When conceived as instinctual they do not arise out of definite psychic conditions and cannot be overcome with changes in these conditions. Their existence and operation then constitute an attribute of human nature. Man has therefore at bottom only the choice of suffering and destroying himself or of making others suffer and destroying them. These drives can be mitigated and controlled but ultimately are unalterable. Moreover, when with Freud we assume an instinctual drive toward self-annihilation, self-destruction, or death, we must consider self-hate, with its many implications, as simply one expression of that drive. The idea of a person hating or despising himself for being as he is, is actually alien to Freud's thinking.

Of course, Freud—as well as others sharing his basic premises —observed the occurrence of self-hate, although he was far from recognizing its manifold hidden forms and effects. As he interprets it, what seems to be self-hate is "really" the expression of something else. It may be an unconscious hate for somebody else. And it can happen indeed that a depressed patient accuses himself for offenses committed by another person whom he unconsciously hates because of feeling frustrated in his need for "narcissistic supplies." Although this is not a regular occurrence, it became the main clinical basis for Freud's theory of depressions.[6] Briefly, the depressed consciously hates and accuses himself but in fact *unconsciously* hates and accuses an introjected enemy. ("Hostility toward the frustrating object has turned into hostility toward one's own ego."[7]) Or what *seems* to be self-hate is *"really"* the punitive process of the superego, the latter being an internalized authority. Here again self-hate turns into an interpersonal phenomenon: hate for somebody else or fear of his hate. Or, lastly, self-hate is seen as the sadism of the superego, resulting from a regression to an anal-sadistic

---

[6] *Cf.* Sigmund Freud, *Mourning and Melancholia*, Coll. Papers, IV.

[7] Quoted from Otto Fenichel, *The Psychoanalytic Theory of Neurosis*, W. W. Norton, 1948.

phase of infantile libido. Self-hate is thus not only accounted for in ways entirely different from mine but the nature of the phenomenon itself is altogether different.[8]

Many analysts, otherwise thinking strictly along Freud's lines, have rejected the death instinct for what I consider valid reasons.[9] But if one discards the instinctual nature of self-destructiveness, it is difficult within the framework of Freudian theory to account for it at all. And I wonder whether a feeling of the insufficiency of other explanations in this regard was not one of the reasons for Freud's propounding a self-destructive instinct.

Another distinct similarity exists between the demands and taboos ascribed to the superego and what I have described as the tyranny of the should. But as soon as we consider their meaning we come to a parting of the ways. To begin with, for Freud the superego is a normal phenomenon representing conscience and morality; it is neurotic if particularly cruel and sadistic. For me the equivalent shoulds and taboos of whatever kind and degree are altogether a neurotic force, counterfeiting morality and conscience. According to Freud the superego is partly a derivative of the Oedipus complex, partly a derivative of instinctual forces (destructive and sadistic). According to my views, the inner dictates are an expression of the individual's unconscious drive to make himself over into something he is not (a godlike, perfect being), and he hates himself for not being able to do so. Among the many implications entailed in these differences I mention but one. Seeing the shoulds and taboos as corollaries of a special kind of pride allows for a much more accurate understanding of why the same thing is violently demanded in one character structure and forbidden in another. The same possibility for greater exactness applies also to the various attitudes an individual may have toward the superego demands—or inner dictates—some of which are mentioned in Freudian literature: [10] attitudes of appeasement, subordination, bribery, rebellion. These are either generalized as pertaining to all neuroses (Alex-

---

[8] Cf. Chapter 5, Self-Hate and Self-Contempt.

[9] To mention only one: Otto Fenichel, The Psychoanalytic Theory of Neurosis, W. W. Norton, 1945.

[10] Cf. Otto Fenichel; see also Franz Alexander, Psychoanalysis of the Total Personality, Nervous and Mental Disease Publishing Co., New York and Washington, 1930.

ander) or are merely related to certain sympathetic pictures such as depression or compulsion neurosis. On the other hand, in the framework of my theory of neurosis their quality is strictly determined by the whole particular character structure. It follows from these differences that the therapeutic aim on this score is different. Freud can aim merely at reducing the severity of the superego while I aim at the individual's being able to dispense with his inner dictates altogether and to assume the direction of his life in accordance with his true wishes and beliefs. This latter possibility does not exist in Freud's thinking.

Summarizing this far, we can say that in the two approaches certain individual phenomena are observed and described in a similar way. But the interpretations of their dynamics and meaning are entirely different. If we now leave the individual aspects and consider the whole complex of their interrelations as it is presented in this book, we see that the possibilities for comparison are exhausted.

The most significant interrelation is that between the search for unlimited perfection and powers, and self-hate. The realization that they are inseparable is an ancient one. To my mind it is best symbolized by the stories of the devil's pact, the essentials of which seem always to be alike. There is a human being in psychic or spiritual distress.[11] There is a temptation, presented in some symbol of an evil principle: the devil, the sorcerer, witches, the serpent (in the story of Adam and Eve), the antique dealer (in Balzac's *The Magic Skin*), the cynical Lord Henry Wotton (in Oscar Wilde's *The Picture of Dorian Gray*). Then there are the promises of not only a miraculous riddance of the distress but of the possession of infinite powers. And it is a testimony of true greatness when one person can resist the temptation, as the story of Christ's temptation shows. Finally

---

[11] Sometimes this distress may be symbolized by external misfortunes, as it is in Stephen Vincent Benét's *The Devil and Daniel Webster*. Sometimes it is merely indicated, as it is in the biblical story of Christ's temptation. Sometimes no distress seems to be present but, as in the old *Faustbuch* and Christopher Marlowe's *Dr. Faustus*, a person is carried away by his craving for the glory of magical powers. At any rate we know that only a psychically disturbed person will develop such a craving. In Hans Christian Andersen's "Snow Queen" it is the devil who creates the disturbance in the first place by mischievously breaking a mirror and letting its splinters invade human hearts.

there is the price to pay, which (presented in various forms) is the loss of the soul (Adam and Eve lose the innocence of their feelings), its surrender to the forces of evil. "All these will I give thee if thou wilt fall down and worship me," says Satan to Christ. The price may be psychic torment in this life (as in *The Magic Skin*) or the torment of hell. In *The Devil and Daniel Webster* we have the beautifully realized symbol of the shriveled souls collected by the devil.

The same theme, variously symbolized but with the interpretation of its significance constant, has appeared again and again in folklore, in mythology, and in theology—whatever the basic dualism of good and evil has been entertained. Hence it has long inhabited the popular consciousness. And the time may be ripe for psychiatry too to recognize its psychological wisdom. Certainly the parallel with the neurotic process described in this book is striking: an individual in psychic distress arrogates to himself infinite powers, losing his soul and suffering the torments of hell in his self-hate.

To come back from this lengthy metaphorical statement of the problem to Freud: Freud has not seen it, and we can understand more clearly why he could not see it, when we remember that he did not recognize the search for glory as the compound of inextricably linked drives which I have described and therefore could not realize its power either. He saw the hell of self-destructiveness clearly enough; but, regarding it as the expression of an autonomous drive, he saw it out of context.

Seen from another perspective, the neurotic process presented in this book is a problem of the self. It is a process of abandoning the real self for an idealized one; of trying to actualize this pseudoself instead of our given human potentials; of a destructive warfare between the two selves; of allaying this warfare the best, or at any rate the only, way we can; and finally, through having our constructive forces mobilized by life or by therapy, of finding our real selves. In this sense the problem could hardly have any meaning for Freud. In his concept of the "ego" he depicts the "self" of a neurotic person who is alienated from his spontaneous energies, from his authentic wishes, who does not make any decisions of his own and assume responsibility for them, who merely sees to it that he does not collide too badly with his environment ("reality-testing"). If this neurotic self is mistaken for its healthy alive counterpart, the whole complex problem of the real self as seen by Kierkegaard or William James cannot arise.

Finally we can look at the process from the perspective of moral or spiritual values. From this standpoint it has all the elements of a true human tragedy. However great man's possibilities for becoming destructive, the history of mankind also shows an alive and untiring striving toward greater knowledge about himself and the world around him, toward deeper religious experiences, toward developing greater spiritual powers and greater moral courage, toward greater achievements in all fields, and toward better ways of living. And his very best energies go into these strivings. By dint of his intellect and the power of his imagination, man can visualize things not yet existing. He reaches beyond what he is or can do at any given time. He has limitations, but his limits are not fast and final. Usually he lags behind what he wants to achieve within or outside himself. This in itself is not a tragic situation. But the inner psychic process which is the neurotic equivalent to healthy, human striving *is* tragic. Man under the pressure of inner distress reaches out for the ultimate and the infinite which—though his limits are not fixed—it is not given to him to reach; and in this very process he destroys himself, shifting his very best drive for self-realization to the actualization of his idealized image and thereby wasting the potentialities he actually possesses.

Freud had a pessimistic outlook on human nature and, on the grounds of his premises, was bound to have it. As he saw it, man is doomed to dissatisfaction whichever way he turns. He cannot live out satisfactorily his primitive instinctual drives without wrecking himself and civilization. He cannot be happy alone or with others. He has but the alternative of suffering himself or making others suffer. It is all to Freud's credit that, seeing things this way, he did not compromise with a glib solution. Actually within the framework of his thinking there is no escape from one of these two alternative evils. At best there may be a less unfavorable distribution of forces, better control, and "sublimation."

Freud was pessimistic but he did not see the human tragedy

in neurosis. We see tragic waste in human experience only if there are constructive, creative strivings and these are wrecked by obstructive or destructive forces. And not only did Freud not have any clear vision of constructive forces in man; he had to deny their authentic character. For in his system of thought there were only destructive and libidinal forces, their derivatives and their combinations. Creativity and love (*eros*) for him were sublimated forms of libidinal drives. In most general terms, what we regard as a healthy striving toward self-realization for Freud was—and could be—only an expression of narcissistic libido.

Albert Schweitzer uses the terms "optimistic" and "pessimistic" in the sense of "world and life affirmation" and "world and life negation." Freud's philosophy, in this deep sense, is a pessimistic one. Ours, with all its cognizance of the tragic element in neurosis, is an optimistic one.

REFERENCE READINGS

CHAPTER 1

Kurt Goldstein, *Human Nature*. Harvard University Press, 1940.

S. Radhakrishnan, *Eastern Religions and Western Thought*. London, Oxford University Press, 1939.

Muriel Ivimey, "Basic Anxiety." *American Journal of Psychoanalysis*, 1946.

A. H. Maslow, "The Expressive Component of Behaviour." *Psychological Review*, 1949.

Harold Kelman, "The Process of Symbolization." A lecture reviewed in *American Journal of Psychoanalysis*, 1949.

CHAPTER 5

A. Myerson, "Anhedonia." Monograph Series, *Neurotic and Mental Diseases*, Vol. 52, 1930.

Erich Fromm, *Man for Himself*. Rinehart, 1947.

Muriel Ivimey, "Neurotic Guilt and Healthy Moral Judgment." *American Journal of Psychoanalysis*, 1949.

Elizabeth Kilpatrick, "A Psychoanalytic Understanding of Suicide." *American Journal of Psychoanalysis*, 1946.

CHAPTER 7

Gertrud Lederer-Eckardt, "Gymnastic and Personality." *American Journal of Psychoanalysis*, 1947.

CHAPTER 8

Harold Kelman, "The Traumatic Syndrome." *American Journal of Psychoanalysis*, 1946.

Muriel Ivimey, "Compulsive Assaultiveness." *American Journal of Psychoanalysis*, 1947.

CHAPTER 9

Harold D. Lasswell, *Democracy Through Public Opinion*. Menasha, Wisconsin, George Banta Publishing Co.

CHAPTER 10

Harry M. Tiebout, "The Act of Surrender in the Therapeutic Process." *Quarterly Journal of Studies on Alcohol,* 1949.

CHAPTER 11

Harold Kelman, *The Psychoanalytic Process: A Manual.*
Marie Rasey, *Something to Go By.* Montrose Press, 1948.

CHAPTER 13

Alexander R. Martin, "On Making Real Efforts." Paper presented before the Association for the Advancement of Psychoanalysis, 1943.

CHAPTER 14

Krishnamurti, *Oak Grove Talks.* Ojai, California, Krishnamurti Writings, Inc., 1945.
Paul Bjerre, *Das Träumen als ein Heilungsweg der Seele.* Zurich, Rascher, 1926.
Harold Kelman, "A New Approach to the Interpretation of Dreams." *American Journal of Psychoanalysis,* 1947.
Frederick A. Weiss, "Constructive Forces in Dreams." *American Journal of Psychoanalysis,* 1949.

INDEX

ACTUAL OR EMPIRICAL SELF, 158; alienation from, 156, 157; definition of, 111; self-hate of, 113

Adler, Alfred, comparison with Freud, 28, 372; concept of expansive type, 192; of neurotic suffering, 238; of search for glory, 28; contribution to theory of neurosis, 372; *Understanding Human Nature*, 238

Aggrandizement of self (*see* Self-aggrandizement)

Aggressive impulses and fear, 206

Aggressive–vindictive type (*see* Arrogant–vindictive type)

Alcoholic tendencies and loss of identity, 188; as means to allay anxiety, 189; and vindictive rage, 199

Alexander, Franz, concept of neurotic suffering of, 238; *The Psychoanalysis of the Total Personality*, 117, 235, 374

Alienation from actual self, definition of, 156 ff.

Alienation from real self, 13, 21, 157

Alienation from Self (Chap. 6), 21, 123, 155 ff.; and appeal of freedom, 285; and avoidance of responsibility, 168 ff.; and compulsive needs, 159; definition of, 155, 160; denial of "shoulds," 123; and devil's pact, 155; forms of, 156; general symptoms for, 151; and idealized image, 13, 22, 368; and inability to assume responsibility, 160, 171; lack of inner direction, of, 167; and need for feeling of identity, 21; as measure to relieve tension, 177, 182; and neurotic claims, 159; and neurotic development, 187; and neurotic pseudo-solutions, 159; and pride-system, 162, 173, 296; and process of externalization, 160; reasons for, 177; reinforcing of, 21, 177; responsible forces for, 159; and self-destructive tendencies, 149; and self-effacement, 237; and self-hate, 115, 160; and suicidal tendencies, 149; and tyranny of the "should," 159

Ambitious drives, 26; taboos on, 317

American Journal of Psychoanalysis, 83, 118, 197, 201, 280, 309

Amnesia, 155, 161

Analytical therapy (*see* Psychoanalytic therapy)

Andersen, Hans Christian, *Snow Queen*, 375

Anorexia, 234

Anxiety (*see also* Basic anxieties), allaying of, through alcoholic tendencies, 189; emerging of, during analytic process, 340; and externalization, 225; and inhibitions in work, 321, 322; in morbid dependency, 245; reactions of, 100; in resigned type, 224; and sexual relations, 307; and "shoulds," 74

Appeal of Freedom (Chap. 11), 259 ff. (*see also* Neurotic resignation)

Appeal of Love (Chap. 9), 214 ff. (*see also* Self-effacing solution)

Appeal of Mastery (Chap. 8), 187 ff., 212 (*see also* Expansive solutions of major conflicts)

Appel, Kenneth, and Strecker, Edward A., *Discovering Ourselves*, 179

Arrogant–vindictive type, 193; and disturbances at work, 312, 315; and emotions, 212; and externalization, forms of, 208; and intrapsychic factors, 209; and motivating forces, 197; and role of pride and self-hate, 208, 209; and sadistic attitudes, 204, 305; and sacrifice of real self, 204; and search for glory, 193, 197; and self-effacing trends, 207; and sexual relations, 304; and suicidal tendencies, 204

Association for the Advancement of Psychoanalysis, 38, 87

Auerbach, J. G., "Change of Values through Psychotherapy," 343

Automatic control-system, 181; lessening of, and panic reactions, 182; physical expressions of, 182

Avoidance tactics and neurotic resignation, 261, 279

BALZAC, HONORÉ DE, *The Magic Skin*, 375

Barrie, James M., *Tommy and Grizel*, 195

Basic anxieties, allaying of, 18; in childhood, 18, 19, 297, 366; constituents of, 297; and intrapsychic processes, 297; reinforcement of, through pride-system, 297

Basic confidence in childhood, definition of, 86, 87

Basic conflict, 18 ff., 177; aspect of, 23; in childhood, 19; definition of, 367; idealization of particular solution of, 22; solution of, in self-effacing type, 223

Benét, Stephen Vincent, *The Devil and Daniel Webster*, 375, 376

Bloch-Michel, Jean, *The Witness*, 119, 120

Brontë, Emily Jane, *Wuthering Heights*, 198

Buck, Pearl, *Pavilion of Women*, 72, 83

CENTRAL INNER CONFLICTS, definition of, 112, 368; emerging of, 190; and pride-system, 190; and psychoanalytic therapy, 356; and real self, 112

Childhood, 17; attempts at solving neurotic conflicts in, 19, 20; and basic anxiety, 18, 19, 297, 366; and basic confidence, 86; and basic conflict, 19; and compliant trends, 20; daydreaming in, 40; and early detachment, 275; hardening process in, 210; influences in, and neurotic resignation, 275; and need for triumph, 203; neurotic development in, 27, 87, 202; and retrospective "shoulds," 68; self-effacing solution in, 221, 222

Compartmentalization of conflicts, 185, 190; as measure to relieve tension, 179; and psychoanalytic therapy, 335, 355, 356

Competitive culture and compulsive drive for success, 26

Compliance and lack of directive powers, 168; in resigned type, 272

Comprehensive neurotic solution, definition of, 23

Compulsion and spontaneity, 38

Compulsiveness, meaning of, 24; of neurotic claims, 210; in search for glory, 209; and vindictiveness, 209

Compulsive drives in neurosis, definition of, 29; and genuine striving, 39; recognition of, through reactions to frustration, 31

Compulsive needs and alienation from self, 159; and alleviation of self-contempt, 136, 137; and self-idealization, 24; for success in competitive culture, 26

Creative ability, in dreams, 330; and neurosis, 328 ff.; and self-realization, 332

DAYDREAMING, 29, 71; and alienation from self, 167; in childhood, 40; and role of imagination in search for glory, 233

Death-instinct and self-hate, comparison with Freud's concepts, 56, 117, 372

Depersonalization, 160 (*see also* Alienation from self)

Detached type, definition of, 226, 243

Detachment, 159; in childhood, 275, 277; deterioration of, in shallow living, 286; and exclusion of love, 304; and fear of injuries to pride, 107; and integration, 275; and integrity, 280; and intrapsychic processes, 277, 280; maintaining of, 264, 276, 285; nature of, 264; in neurotic resignation, 261, 264, 271, 280, 285, 324; and role of sexuality, 301, 302, 304; and search for glory, 35, 39

Devil's pact, as symbol for interrelation between search for glory and self-hate, 154, 375; and abandoning of self, 155; and neurotic pride, 87; and neurotic process, 87; and search for glory, 39; and self-idealization, 87

Dollard, John, 56

Dostoevski, Feodor, *Crime and Punishment*, 119

Dreams, 31; 111, 120; as attempts to solve inner conflicts, 349; and creative ability, 330; as expression of feeling abused, 230; and feelings of identity, 188; and impoverishment of feelings, 164; and self-destructiveness, 152, 153; of self-effacing type, 230; of shallow living type, 289; significance of, in psychoanalytic therapy, 340, 348,

349, 359, 361 ff.; as symbols of self-contempt, 133, 224

EGOCENTRICITY, DEFINITION OF, 291; role of, in neurotic disturbances at work, 310; of neurotic claims, 48; and pride-system, 292

Eliot, George, *Romola*, 287

Empirical or actual self, definition of, 157

Expansive drives, and ambition, 26; externalization of, 193; suppression of, in self-effacing type, 220

Expansive solutions of major conflicts (Chap. 8), 103, 187 ff.; aim of, 212; and emotional atmosphere, 212; and identification of glorified self, 192

Expansive trends, compulsive character of, 192; and neurotic resignation, 191, 271, 283

Expansive types, Adler's concepts of, 192; attitudes of, in analysis, 212; characteristics of, 192, 214; and denial of failures, 193; Freud's concept of, 192; and neurotic disturbances at work, 195, 311; and self-effacing trends, 192, 207; and self-glorification, 192; and self-hate, 195; and "shoulds," 76, 195; subdivisions of, 193

Externalization, of alienation from self, 160; of condemnatory, punitive trends toward self, 196, 208; definition of, 179; distinction between active and passive, 116, 121, 179; and distortion of pictures of others, 199, 295; and hostility, 207; of inner experiences, 178, 225; of fear, 220; as protection against self-hate, 121, 130, 208; of neurotic resignation, 266; recognition of, 293, 355; of sadistic impulses, 146; of self-accusations, 129, 224, 225, 230, 231, 363; of self-contempt, 135, 136; of self-effacing solution, 214, 220; of self-frustrating impulses, 145, 208; of self-idealization, 292; of self-hate, 116, 220, 231, 293, 300; of "shoulds," 78, 81, 123; of taboos, 294

FEAR, AND AGGRESSIVE IMPULSES, 206; externalization of, 220; of injury to pride, 101, 108, 296; of rejection, 241;

of ridicule, 220; of "shoulds," 72, 278; of torture, 148; of triumph, 217

Fenichel, Otto, *The Psychoanalytic Theory of Neurosis*, 273, 374

Ferenczi, Sandor, and Rank, Otto, *The Development of Psychoanalysis*, 343

"Finding the Real Self," *American Journal of Psychoanalysis*, 83, 280

Flaubert, Gustave, *Madame Bovary*, 33, 247

Freud, Sigmund, 14, 341, 347, 367; *Beyond the Pleasure Principle*, 237; *Contributions to Psychology of Love*, 265; *The Ego and the Id*, 201; *Mourning and Melancholia*, 373; *On Narcissism*, 194, 378; comparison with Adler, 28, 372; premises of his thinking, 369 ff.

Freud's theories, 29; of death-instinct, 56, 117, 372; of depressions and concept of self-hate, 373; of instincts, 56, 366; of "Ego" and comparison with real self, 178, 367; of expansive type, 192; of love and sex, 301, 302; of resistance, 340; and recognition of importance of work-disturbances, 327; and search for glory, 369, 371, 372; and neurotic resignation, 265; of "oral-libido" and comparison with neurotic claims, 369; of Oedipus complex 371, 372, 374; and self-effacing solution, 237; of "super-ego" and comparison with "shoulds," 78, 374

Freudian literature, concept of narcissism in, 194

Fromm, Erich, 131, 288, 289, 366; *Man for Himself*, 129; "The Individual and Social Origin of Neurosis," *Am. Soc. Rev.*, 288

Frustrating techniques, 250

Frustration of neurotic claims, reactions to, 31, 57, 230; in search for glory, 31; in self-effacing type, 230

Functional suffering (*see* Neurotic suffering)

GENERAL MEASURES to Relieve Tension (Chap. 7), 176 ff. (*see also* Measures to relieve tension)

Glorification of self (*see* Self-glorification)

Glueck, Bernard, "The God Man or Jehovah Complex," *Med. J.,* 194

Goldstein, Dr. Kurt, *Human Nature,* 38

Goncharov, Ivan, *Oblomov,* 282

Growth, definition of, 17, 18

Guilt feelings, 235, 237, 240; and feeling abused, 231; and neurotic suffering, 225, 235; and self-hate, 116

HITLER, ADOLF, 27, 117

Hoffmann, E. T. A., *Tales of Hoffmann,* 305

Homosexuality, as reaction to fear of injury to pride, 108

Horney, Karen, *The Neurotic Personality of Our Time,* 111, 221, 240; *New Ways in Psychoanalysis,* 194, 370, 371; *Our Inner Conflicts,* 18, 23, 38, 151, 177, 179, 199, 221, 264, 367; "The Problem of the Negative Therapeutic Reaction," *Psa. Quar.,* 201; *Self-analysis,* 222, 247, 268, 367

Hostility, and externalizations, 297; and fear, 206; and frustration, 56; and neurotic pride, 99; and psychosomatic symptoms, 56; taboos of, 83

Hugo, Victor, *Les Miserables,* 67

IBSEN, HENRIK, *Hedda Gabler,* 51, 150, 185, 193; *John Gabriel Borkman,* 30, 195; *Peer Gynt,* 90, 91, 94, 185, 193

Idealized image, 18, 22, 25; actualization of, in neurosis, 36, 123, 377; and alienation from self, 13, 22, 368; concept of, 367; and idealized self, 23; and imagination, 23, 184; and feelings of identity, 23; and neurotic pride, 90; in resigned type, 277; and self-realization, 109, 377; and the "shoulds," 72

Idealized self, 158 (*see also* Self-idealization), and abandoning of real self, 23, 24, 34, 376; actualization of, 24, 38, 64, 66, 111, 123, 368, 377; and mastery of life, 215; and morbid dependency, 241; and need for perfection, 25; and neurotic claims, 62, 368; and search for glory, 38; and self-hate, 112; and theory of neurosis, 367

Identity, feelings of — in dreams, 188; through idealized image, 23

Imagination, and daydreams, 33; and idealized image, 23; and differences between healthy, neurotic, and psychotic personalities, 32, 34; in narcissistic type, 312; in neurosis, 32; and neurotic pride, 91; and role of love and sex, 305; and search for glory, 31, 32, 35, 36; and self-idealization, 31, 184

Inertia, 165; definition of, 60; of feelings, 283; and neurotic claims, 60; and neurotic disturbances in work, 325; and neurotic resignation, 262, 267, 279, 282, 325, 338; and psychoanalytic therapy, 267, 283, 338; and sensitivity to coercion in resigned type, 266, 279

Inhibitions, and claims of deference, 41; of sexual functioning, 302

Inhibitions in work (*see also* Neurotic disturbances in work), 71, 320; in narcissistic type, 195, 312; as motive to seek analytic help, 336

Insomnia, 233, 234

Integrating forces, 167

Integration, 334; attempts at, 159, 367; and early detachment, 275; need for, in childhood, 20; lack of, 172; and real self, 171

Intrapsychic conflicts, as basis for neurotic types, 190, 191; and pseudosolutions, 369; and neurotic resignation, 259, 269; solutions of, 187, 297, 311

Intrapsychic factors, in analysis, 209; and disturbances in work, 310; externalization of, 291; power of, 308; pride in, and intellectual powers, 204; in self-effacing solution, 237; in vindictiveness, 204, 210

Intrapsychic processes, 235, 334; and alienation from self, 366; and basic anxiety, 297; and early detachment, 277; and interpersonal processes, 291; and love relations, 299, 305; and theory of neurosis, 367

Ivimey, Muriel, 112; "The Negative Therapeutic Reaction," *Am. J. Psa.,* 201

JACKSON, CHARLES, *The Lost Weekend,* 152

James, William, 371, 377; *The Principles of Psychology,* 156, 157; *The Varieties of Religious Experience,* 191

KAFKA, FRANZ, *The Trial*, 129

Kelman, Harold, "The Traumatic Syndrome," *Am. J. Psa.*, 197

Kierkegaard, Sören, 377; *Sickness unto Death*, 35, 158

LOVABLENESS, as basis for hidden claims, 242; disbelief in, 299, 300; enforcement of, through "shoulds," 241, 242; and morbid dependency, 241; need for, 241

Love and sex, meaning of, for neurotic person, 299 ff. (*see also* Sexuality in neurosis); expectations of, 300; exclusion of, in arrogant–vindictive type, 305, in detached type, 304; Freud's concepts of, 300 ff.; and imagination, 305; and impairment of capacity for, 300; in morbid dependency, 239; in narcissistic type, 305; and neurotic pride, 108, 247; overemphasis on, 305; in service of neurotic needs, 300

MACMURRAY, JOHN, *Reason and Emotion*, 332, 342

Marquand, J. P., 77, 288

Marlowe, Christopher, *Dr. Faustus*, 375

Masochism, the problem of, 240; in morbid dependency, 258

Masochistic activity, as means to drain self-contempt, 301; and self-degradation, 301

Masochistic perversions, 237

Masturbation, 96, 302; fantasies, 147; reactions of shame to, 96

Maugham, Somerset, *Christmas Holiday*, 203; *Of Human Bondage*, 245; *The Moon and Sixpence*, 284

Measures to Relieve Tension (Chap. 7), 172, 176 ff.; and alienation from self, 182; and analytic process, 357, 359, 361 ff.; and automatic control, 181 ff.; and belief in supremacy of mind, 182; and compartmentalization, 179; and elimination of real self, 181; and neurotic resignation, 261; and passive externalization, 178, 179, 225; and pride-system, 178; in self-effacing type, 182; and self frustration, 812

Melville, Herman, *Moby Dick*, 198

Menninger, Karl A., *Man Against Himself*, 117, 237

Meyer, Adolph, 366

Miller, Arthur, *The Death of a Salesman*, 195, 330

Morality of evolution, definition of, 11 ff.; goal of, 12; problems involved in, 13; and self-realization, 13

Morbid Dependency (Chap. 10), 239 ff.; and abandoning of pride, 246; and actualization of idealized self, 24; and anxiety, 249; and appeal of arrogant–vindictive type, 245; characteristics of, 243, 247; and choice of partners, 243, 244; and externalization of expansive drives, 244; and pride, 258; and self-hate, 254, 255, 258; and fear of rejection, 241; and pride-system, 244, 257; recognition of, 254; role of love in, 239 ff., 244; and search for inner unity, 258; self-analysis of, 222, 256; and self-contempt, 254; and self-degradation, 251, 253; and self-destructiveness, 258; and self-effacing solution, 221, 234, 243, 245; and sexual relations, 250, 258; and shrinking process, 244; and "shoulds," 119, 241; and suffering, 245, 258; and suicidal tendencies, 257; understanding of, 258

Morgenstern, Christian, 76; *Auf vielen Wegen*, 113

Myerson, A., *Anhedonia*, 379

NARCISSISM, in Freudian literature, 193; and self aggrandizement, 192; and self-idealization, 194

Narcissistic type, 193; and emotions, 219, and expe ding of self hate, 195; and imagination, 312; and neurotic disturbances in work, 195, 312 ff.; and self-effacing trends, 197; and tyranny of the "should," 197

Negative therapeutic reactions, 201

Neurosis, characteristics of, 166; and creative abilities, 328 ff.; definition of, 368; and disregard of evidence, 37, 40; and imagination, 32; new theory of, 366 ff.

Neurotic ambition, 24, 166; and competitive culture, 26; in search for glory, 25

Neurotic Claims (Chap. 2), 40 ff.; and actualization of idealized self, 62, 368; and alienation from self, 159;

Neurotic Claims (*continued*)
   assertion of, 55, 92, 229; awareness
   of, 51; common characteristics of, 47,
   49; concealment of, 52; as differentiated from needs, 42; egocentricity of,
   48; effects of, 57; and Freud's concepts of oral–libido, 369; and human
   relations, 43, 46; implications of, 47;
   for immunity and impunity, 205,
   206; and illusions about self, 41; and
   inertia, 60; irrationality of, 46; justification of, 53, 55; of narcissistic type,
   197; and neurotic needs, 121, 229;
   over-all function of, 63; and overemphasis on justice, 54, 55; as protection against self-hate, 208; and reactions to frustrations, 55, 56; relinquishing of, 57; and resignation,
   264; for special considerations, 21,
   121; and suffering, 234; and theory of
   neurosis, 368, 370; and vindictiveness, 51

Neurotic conflicts, attempts at solving,
   20, 172; in childhood, 19; and central inner conflicts, 113; through
   compartmentalization, 185, 190; and
   disturbances in work, 318; as incentive for creative work, 331; and lack
   of spontaneous integration, 172

Neurotic development, 13; and alienation from self, 187; in childhood, 27,
   202; and self-confidence, 86

Neurotic Disturbances in Human Relationships (Chap. 12), 18, 291 ff.; and
   analytic relationship, 306; efforts at
   control of, 71; externalization of, 293,
   298 ff.; and feelings of insecurity, 295,
   296; and influence of intrapsychic
   factors, 299, 306; and pride system,
   291, 296, 297, 298; and role of love
   and sex, 299 ff.; in self-effacing type,
   298; and self-realization, 307; in shallow living, 288

Neurotic Disturbances in Work (Chap.
   13), 309 ff.; and arising of anxiety,
   321; in arrogant–vindictive type, 312,
   315; and aversion to effort, 314; and
   egocentricity, 310; in expansive type,
   195, 311; expressions of, 310; Freud's
   concepts of, 327; incapacity for effort
   in, 314; and inertia, 325; and intrapsychic conflicts, 311; and intrapsy-

chic factors, 310; in narcissistic type,
   312 ff.; and neurotic conflicts, 318;
   and panic reactions, 310; in perfectionistic type, 312, 315; and psychosomatic symptoms, 316; in resigned
   type, 288, 325 ff.; in self-effacing type,
   316 ff.; and self-minimizing, 319; suffering involved in, 310, 327; and taboos, 318

Neurotic drives, and healthy strivings,
   37, 38

Neurotic guilt feelings (*see* Guilt feelings)

Neurotic needs, compulsiveness of, 24;
   differentiated from claims, 42; transformed into claims, 121, 198; and
   imagination, 32; for perfection and
   actualization of idealized self, 25; and
   pride system, 292; for restoration of
   pride, 210; and role of love and sex,
   300, 302; for vindictive triumph, 24,
   27, 103, 197, 210

Neurotic Pride (Chap. 4.) (*see also* Pride
   system), 86 ff.; in asserting claims, 92;
   and checking on wishes, 109; in contrast to healthy pride, 88; and demands of superiority, 134; and detachment, 107; exclusion of, in self-
   effacing solution, 223; and externalization of morbid dependency, 258;
   and fear, 100, 107; in "honesty," 206,
   207; in idealized image, 90; in intellectual powers, 204; in imagination,
   91, 93; and invulnerability, 95, 205,
   210, 211; and irrational hostility, 99;
   and love and sex, 108, 247; manifestations of, 223; in prestige, 89; and reactions of fear, 101; to hurt, 95, 96 ff.,
   105, 257; and refusal of responsibility, 106; restoration of, 103, 104 ff.,
   210; and search for glory, 109; and
   self-confidence, 87; and self-contempt, 102, 137; and self-hate, 109,
   110; and self-idealization, 110; and
   sexual relations, 301; and "shoulds,"
   92, 118; in supremacy of mind, 92; as
   system to avoid hurt, 107 ff.; and vindictive triumph, 209; vulnerability
   of, 95, 103, 106, 136, 205, 210

Neurotic process, definition of, 13; and
   devil's pact, 377

Neurotic pseudo-solutions, 159

Neurotic resignation (Chap. 11), 191, 295 ff.; and appeal of freedom, 259 ff., 274, 280, 285; and aversion to change, 45, 263, 267; and aversion to effort, 261, 262; and attitudes toward others, 278; and avoidance tactics, 261, 279; characteristics of, 260, 263, 268, 273, 280, 286; and childhood influences, 275; compared with constructive resignation, 259; and conflict between expansive and self-effacing drives, 270; and detachment, 261, 264, 271, 280, 285, 324; and discontentment, 283; and expansive trends, 191, 271, 283; externalization of, 266, 278; Freud's observations on, 265; and inertia, 262, 267, 279, 281, 283, 325; and intrapsychic conflicts, 259, 269; as measure to relieve tension, 261; and neurotic claims, 264; and neurotic solutions, 191, 270; and restriction of activities, 281, 285; and restriction of wishes, 263, 276; and self-effacing trends, 271, 273; and self-realization, 272; and sensitivity to coercion, 266, 324; and sex, 264; and "shoulds," 77, 263, 277 ff., 282; as shrinking process, 259, 260; and taboos on aggression, 278; total structure of, 285

Neurotic resigned types: persistent type, 281, 283, 280; rebellious type, 281; shallow living type, 281 ff., 286, 289; and appeal of freedom, 283, 285; and disturbances in work, 288, 322 ff.; and idealized image, 277; and psychoanalytic therapy, 288 ff., 337

Neurotic solutions, definition of, 186, 194; of expansive type, 191; of self-effacing type, 191, 271; and self-idealization, 23, 29, 194

Neurotic or functional suffering, in analysis, 338; as basis for neurotic claims, 229, 234; and disturbances in work, 310, 327; as expression of vindictiveness, 230, 233; functions of, 234 ff.; and morbid dependency, 245; various theories of, 237, 238

Neurotic suspiciousness, 56

Neurotic trends, 29

Neurotic types, criteria of, 195; and intrapsychic conflicts, 191

Nietzsche, Friedrich, 59, 211

O'NEILL, EUGENE, The Iceman Cometh, 295

Orwell, George, Nineteen Eighty-four, 34, 109, 118, 152

PANIC REACTIONS, 100, 143, 182; and disturbances at work, 310; and frustration of search for glory, 31; and lessening of automatic control, 182; in self-effacing type, 234; and self-destructiveness, 153

Perfectionistic type, characteristics of, 196; and disturbances in work, 312, 315; and emotions, 212; and neurotic claims, 197; and self-condemnation, 196; and "shoulds," 197

Phobias, 31, 72, 143, 333; in dreams, 31; as motivations to seek analytic help, 336, 337

Plant, James S., 336

Plato, Philebus, 30

Pride system, absorbing of energies in, 166; and alienation from self, 162, 173, 296; autonomy of, 123, 178; and basic anxiety, 297; as censor of emotions, 163, 164; and central inner conflict, 190; and conflicts within, 112, 187, 296; and conflicts with real self, 112, 113, 187, 209; definition of, 111; and egocentricity, 291, 292; and fear of people, 296; and genuine feelings, 162; and influence on human relations, 291, 296 ff.; as measure to relieve tension, 178; and morbid dependency, 244; and neurotic needs, 292; in psychoanalytic therapy, 174, 340, 347, 353; and responsibility for self, 174; and self-realization, 166; and suffering, 163; in vindictive type, 209

Psychic fragmentation, 45, 191; function of, 179, 180

Psychoanalytic therapy (Chap. 14), 333 ff.; aims of, 333 ff.; and alienation from self, 352; and arising of anxiety, 340; and central inner conflict, 356; and compartmentalization, 335, 355, 356; defensive attitudes of patients in, 336, 339, 340; difference of expectations of, in different types, 357, 358; and disbelief in lovableness, 300; and dreams, 348, 349, 359, 361 ff.; and encouraging of self-analysis, 351; and

Psychoanalytic therapy (*continued*)
externalizations, 355; and Freud's
concept of resistance, 340; implications for, 148; and inertia, 267, 282;
mobilizing of healing forces in, 306,
348, 356; and motivations for seeking
help, 333, 336; and need of emotional
experiencing, 342, 344, 356; and neurotic resignation, 279; and neurotic
suffering, 298; and obstructing forces,
336 ff., 348; and pride system, 170,
336, 340, 347, 353; and real self, 348,
349, 332, 351, 357, 359; and recognition of conflicts, 352; and reorientation, 346; and resigned types, 288 ff.,
337; and responsibility for self, 361;
and self-realization as ultimate goal,
364, 368; and sensitivity to coercion,
267; and shallow living type, 288; and
understanding of repercussions, 357,
359, 361 ff.

Psychosomatic symptoms, and inhibitions at work, 316; and hurt pride,
102; and self-destructive drives, 115;
in shallow living type, 288; and suppressed hostility, 56

RANK, OTTO, and Ferenczi, Sandor, *The
Development of Psychoanalysis*, 343

Rasey, Marie, "Psychoanalysis and Education," 87

Real self, 17; abandoning of, 23, 24, 34,
157, 171; alienation from, 11, 21, 257,
271; and central inner conflicts, 112;
definition of, 158, 173; development
of, 17; elimination of, 181; Freud's
concepts of, 173; and idealized self,
155; and pride system, 112; and
pseudo-self, 175; and self-hate, 112,
368; and theory of neurosis, 368; and
vindictiveness, 204

Reik, Theodore, *Masochism in Modern
Man*, 238; *Surprise and the Psychoanalyst*, 343

Resignation (*see* Neurotic resignation)

Responsibility for self, and alienation
from self, 168, 171; avoiding of, 171;
recognition of, 361; refusal of, 106;
and undermining of pride system,
173, 174

Rioch, Janet M., "The Transference
Phenomenon in Psychoanalytic Therapy," *Psychiatry*, 306

Road of Psychoanalytic Therapy (Chap.
14), 333 ff.

SADISM, and Freud's definition of superego, 374; inverted, 258

Sadistic attitudes, in arrogant–vindictive type, 204, 305

Sadistic fantasies, and impulses, 146, 147

Sadistic trends, comparison with vindictiveness, 190, 199; and externalization of self-torture, 146, 301

Sarton, May, "Now I Become Myself,"
172

Sartre, Jean-Paul, 330; *The Age of Reason*, 164

Scheler, Max, *Das Resentiment im Aufbau der Moralen*, 211

Schneider, Daniel, "The Motion of the
Neurotic Pattern," 255

Schultz-Henke, Harald, *Einfuehrung
zur Psychoanalyse*, 41; *Schicksal und
Neurose*, 369

Search for Glory (Chap. 1), 17 ff., 176;
and actualization of idealized self,
38; Adler's concept of, 28; compulsiveness of, 29; comparison with devil's pact, 39; concept of, 375; elements
of, 224 ff.; Freud's concept of, 309,
371; and frustration, 31; and idealized
self, 22, 24, 38; and imagination, 31,
32, 34 ff.; and neurotic ambition, 25;
and vindictive triumph, 26ff., 103, 197

Search for unity, 240; in morbid dependency, 258

Self-accusations, 114, 123 ff.; difference
between neurotic and healthy, 131;
in expansive type, 192; externalizations of, 129, 225, 230, 231, 263; forms
of, 125 ff.; and frustration of self-
respect, 141; mobilization of, 339; and
self-effacement, 223, 224; self-protective measures against, 130; and self-
righteousness, 116

Self-actualization, 64; and tyranny of
the "should," 65 ff.

Self-aggrandizement, 22, 192

Self-analysis, encouraging of, during
psychoanalytic treatment, 351; examples of, 79, 144, 222, 255, 256; in
self-effacing type, 218; and "shoulds,"
79, 102

Self-condemnation, 127, 128

Self-confidence, 133; and basic confidence, 86; need for, 20, 21, 86; and neurotic pride, 86; and sexuality, 301

Self-contempt (Chap. 5), 110 ff., 192, 302; alleviation of, 136, 137; and dreams, 133, 224; consequences of, 133 ff.; expressions of, 197 ff.; externalizations of, 135, 136; and frustration of self-respect, 141; and morbid dependency, 254; and self-destructive drives, 152; and self-disparaging, 139; in self-effacing type, 220; and self-glorification, 187; and self-hate (Chap. 5), 81, 110 ff., 132, 374; and sexual relations, 301; and vulnerability in human relations, 136

Self-degradation, in morbid dependency, 251, 253; in sexual activities, 301

Self-destructiveness, and alienation from self, 149; in dreams, 152, 153; Freud's concepts of, 373; in morbid dependency, 258; in organic illness, 149; and psychosomatic symptoms, 150; and psychic values, 151; reactions to, 153; and self-contempt, 152; in self-effacing type, 317; and self-hate, 148; and "shoulds," 118, 120

Self-effacement, and alienation from self, 237; and expansive types, 192, 207; in narcissistic type, 197; and self-accusations, 228

Self-effacing Solution (Chap. 9), 59, 191, 214 ff.; and appeal of love (Chap. 9), 214 ff., 227 ff.; in childhood, 221, 222; externalization of, 215; and intrapsychic factors, 236; and morbid dependency, 221, 234, 248, 245; and pride, 223; theories of, 237

Self-effacing type, attitudes of, toward analyst, 231, 233; toward life, 230, 233; toward self, 215; characteristics of, 215; childhood conditions of, 221, 222, 231; defensive measures of, 225; and disturbances in work, 316 ff.; and emphasis on feelings, 222; and expectations of analytic relationship, 226; and expectations of others, 226, 227; and externalizations, 216; and fear of ridicule, 220; and fear of triumph, 217; and feeling abused, 231, 233; and frustration-reactions, 230; and love, 227 ff.; and measures to relieve tensions, 182; and morbid dependency, 221, 234; and neurotic claims, 229; and self-contempt, 220; and self-hate, 116, 235; and self-idealization, 222; and self-minimizing process, 217, 218, 225, 230; and "shoulds," 77, 220, 224, 225; and shrinking process, 219, 223, 317; and suffering, 225, 229, 232 ff.; and suppression of expansive attitudes, 216, 220, 223, 232; and suppression of resentment, 232; and taboos, 218, 219, 224, 230, 317, 319, 320

Self-frustration, and healthy discipline, 140; externalization of, 145, 208; as measure to relieve tension, 182; realization of, 115; and self-hate, 140; and "shoulds," 139; and taboo on aspirations, 144

Self-glorification, and expansive type, 192; and imagination, 32; and self-contempt, 187; and self-hate, 114; and self-idealization, 22

Self-hate (Chap. 5), 110 ff., 132, 374; and actual self, 113; and alienation from self, 115, 116; and devil's pact, 154; in dreams, 133; effects of, 117; in expansive type, 195; experiencing of, 115; expressions of, 117; and externalizations of, 78, 116, 231, 209; Freud's concepts of, 117, 372, 373; frustrating character of, 141; functions of, 115; and idealized self, 118; in morbid dependency, 255; and neurotic pride, 109, 110, 116; power of, 114; protection against, 208, 231; and real self, 114, 118; results of, 116; and self-accusations, 115, 123, 128; and self-contempt (Chap. 5), 81, 110 ff., 132, 374; and self-destructive impulses, 148, 149; in self-effacing type, 116, 234; and self-frustration, 140; and self-glorification, 114; and self-righteousness, 208; and self-torture, 145, 146; in sexual relations, 147; and "shoulds," 85, 118, 120, 123; and suicidal tendencies, 114; and vindictiveness, 207, 208

Self-idealization, 22 ff.; actualization of, 38; as comprehensive neurotic solution, 23, 29, 176, 194; and compulsive needs, 24; definition of, 23, and dev-

Self-idealization (continued)
il's pact, 87; externalization of, 292;
and imagination, 31, 184; and narcissism, 194; and neurotic pride, 87,
110; in resigned type, 277; and search
for glory, 22, 24; and self-effacing
type, 222; and self-realization, 362
Self-knowledge, definition of, 13; and
psychoanalytic therapy, 341; and
spontaneous growth, 14
Self-minimizing, 117; and disturbances
in work, 319; in self-effacing type,
217, 218, 225, 226, 230
Self-realization, aims of, 308; and creative ability, 332; and human relations, 307; and idealized image, 109,
377; and morality of evolution, 13,
14; in neurosis, 39; and pride system,
166; and psychoanalytic therapy, 348,
364; and resignations, 372; striving
for, 13, 17, 38
Self-righteousness, 98; and self-accusations, 116; and self-hate, 208
Self-torture, externalizations of, 147,
230; and self-hate, 145, 146
Sexuality in neurosis, 301 ff.; in arrogant–vindictive type, 304; and detachment, 301, 302; disturbance of,
302; Freud's concept of, 302; functioning of, 301, 302; and morbid dependency, 250, 258; and neurotic
pride, 301; and self-contempt, 301;
taboos on, 302
Shallow living (see also Neurotic resigned types), frequency of, 289
Shaw, Bernard, Pygmalion, 25, 64
"Shoulds," tyranny of (Chap. 3), 64 ff.;
and anxiety, 74; attitudes toward,
75, 76; characteristics of, 65, 74,
118; coerciveness of, 73, 75; destructiveness of, 118 ff.; and emotions, 83; and effects on personality,
81; in expansive type, 76, 195; experiencing of, 76; externalizations of,
72, 78, 81, 123; and Freud's concept
of superego, 73; as frustration of
freedom of choice, 141; functions of,
172; and genuine ideals, 72, 73; and
idealized image, 72, 123; intensity of,
84; measuring up to, 70, 122; and
morbid dependency, 119; operation

of, 66 ff.; and perfection, 73; and perfectionistic type, 197; and pride, 92,
118; rebellion against, 77; recognition
of, in self-analysis, 79, 102; in resigned type, 77, 263, 277, 278; in ret-
rospect, 68, 69; and self-actualization,
64 ff.; and self-destructiveness, 118,
120; and self-effacing type, 77; and
self-hate, 85, 118, 120, 123; and spontaneity, 81; traditional, 282; and taboos, 65, 76
Shrinking process, and morbid dependency, 244; and resignation, 259, 260;
and self-effacing type, 219, 223, 317
Simenon, Georges, The Man Who
Watched the Train Go By, 27
Solution of inner conflicts (see Neurotic solutions)
Stage-fright, 100, 101, 140
Stendhal (Marie Henri Beyle), The
Red and the Black, 118, 198, 199, 203,
305, 347
Stevenson, Robert Louis, Dr. Jekyll
and Mr. Hyde, 22, 189, 190
Strecker, Edward A., and Appel, Kenneth, Discovering Ourselves, 179
Suicidal tendencies, 236, 257; and alienation from self, 149; in arrogant–
vindictive type, 204; and morbid de-
pendency, 257; in self-effacing type,
234; and self-hate, 114
Sullivan, Harry Stack, 277, 366

Taboos, 345; on ambition, 317; on aggression, 219, 278, 320; on aspiration,
144; on enjoyment, 141; on exploiting, 294; externalization of, 294; and
Freud's concept of superego, 374; on
hostility, 83; and neurotic disturbances in work, 318; on pride, 353; of
self-effacing type, 224, 230, 317, 318,
319, 320; on sexuality, 302; and
"shoulds," 65, 76; on vindictiveness,
83; on wishes, 84
Theory of neurosis (Chap. 15), 366 ff.;
definition of, 366; and Freud's concepts, 369 ff.; and idealized self, 367;
and intrapsychic processes, 367 ff.;
and neurotic claims, 368, 370; and
real self, 368; and search for glory,
375

Therapy in psychoanalysis (*see* Psycho-analytic therapy)

Traumatic neurosis, 51, 197

Tyranny of the "should" (*see* "Shoulds")

VINDICTIVENESS, in analytic relation-ship, 201, 212; compulsiveness of, 209; expressions of, 198 ff.; intrapsychic factors in, 204, 210; and "justice," 55; and human relations, 198; and neu-rotic suffering, 230, 233; and real self, 204; and sadistic trends, 189, 199; and self-destructive tendencies, 198; and self-hate and self-contempt, 207, 208; sources of, 202; subjective value of, 204

Vindictive triumph, need for, 24, 27, 103, 197, 210; and neurotic pride and self-hate, 209; and search for glory, 26, 27, 197

Vindictive type, and emotions, 212; and genuine affection, 203; and pride system, 209

WILDE, OSCAR, *De Profundis*, 163; *The Picture of Dorian Gray*, 109, 114, 275

ZUZUKI, D. T., *Essays on Zen Buddhism*, 183

Zweig, Stefan, *Amok*, 245; *Balzac*, 245